W9-DBO-071

THE ANATOMY OF A PERSONAL INJURY LAWSUIT

2d
EDITION

A HANDBOOK OF BASIC TRIAL ADVOCACY

The Association of Trial Lawyers of America
Education Fund

CONTRIBUTORS TO THE FIRST EDITION

Robert M. Dudnik
EDITOR-in-CHIEF

James Leonard
C. Glennon Rau
ASSISTANT EDITORS

John E. Norton
CHAIRMAN

Thomas T. Anderson
Wade J. Dahood
Robert M. Dudnik
Francis H. Hare, Jr.
Lex Hawkins
James E. Hullverson
J. D. Lee

James J. Leonard, Jr.
Stanley E. Preiser
C. Glennon Rau
Paul D. Rheingold
Lawrence J. Smith
Shannon Stafford
Ward Wagner, Jr.

Published By

The Association of Trial Lawyers of America

Education Fund

1050 31st Street, N.W.
Washington, D.C. 20007

Francis J. Bolduc
Executive Director

James E. Rooks, Jr.
Director of Education

©1981 by The Association of Trial Lawyers of America

All rights reserved,
First Edition published 1968.

Tom Van Belkum

THE ANATOMY OF A PERSONAL INJURY LAWSUIT 2d EDITION

A handbook of basic trial advocacy

John E. Norton
EDITOR-in-CHIEF

Francis H. Hare, Jr.
Edward M. Ricci
Mary Frances Edwards
ASSOCIATE EDITORS

Lawrence J. Smith
COMMITTEE CHAIRMAN

AUTHORS

Scott Baldwin
  Marshall, Texas
Sidney Bernstein
  New York, New York
Michael F. Colley
  Columbus, Ohio
James A. George
  Baton Rouge, Louisiana
Francis H. Hare, Jr.
  Birmingham, Alabama
James E. Hullverson
  St. Louis, Missouri
J.D. Lee
  Madisonville, Tennessee

James J. Leonard, Jr.
  Phoenix, Arizona
John E. Norton
  Belleville, Illinois
Stanley E. Preiser
  Charleston, West Virginia
Paul D. Rheingold
  New York, New York
Edward M. Ricci
  West Palm Beach, Florida
Lawrence J. Smith
  New Orleans, Louisiana
Ward Wagner, Jr.
  West Palm Beach, Florida

International Standard Book Number: 0-941916-00-6

Library of Congress Catalog Card Number: 81-70743

The Association of Trial Lawyers of America
Education Fund
1050 31st St., N.W.
Washington, DC 20007

©1981 by the Association of Trial Lawyers of America Education
Fund. All rights reserved.
1st edition © 1968.

Printed in the United States of America

ACKNOWLEDGEMENTS

The editors and authors would like to thank the following people for their assistance in the preparation of this book: Charles F. Brega, Charles W. Smith, Sr., and Harvey F. Wachsman, M.D., ATLA members; and Kristine L. Meyer, James E. Rooks, Jr., Keith A. Searls, Donna A. Thomas, and Jonathan T. Zackey, ATLA staff.

All the medical illustrations in Chapter 3 were reproduced from the *Medical Atlas for Attorneys* by permission of the Bancroft-Whitney Co., San Francisco, California, and Lawyers Co-operative Publishing Co., Rochester, New York. William Meyer of Medical Research & Illustrations, Ltd., New Orleans, Louisiana, prepared the illustrations of medical examinations in Chapter 4 specifically for this book.

Table of Contents

Anatomy of a Personal Injury Lawsuit

Selected Bibliographies

Forms

Illustrations

Chapter 1

INITIAL INTERVIEW, INVESTIGATION, AND PREPARATION

INTRODUCTION

The plaintiff in a personal injury claim does not know in advance that he is going to be the victim of an injurious incident. Often, the occurrence of the incident is his first occasion ever to contact an attorney. From the moment of his initial contact, plaintiff's counsel's primary objective is to assist the client in obtaining a fair and successful determination of his legal rights.

However, the plaintiff's attorney's relationship with his client has an important secondary consequence. At each stage of the case, from the initial interview through settlement or verdict (and, if necessary, appeal), the attorney and client are building a rapport and earning mutual respect which may have implications reaching far beyond the case at hand. A satisfied client is of material assistance in building a successful trial practice.

The client comes to the lawyer seeking advice and assistance. The client will sense any lack of interest the attorney has in his problems. Even if the client's problems are small, the attorney's poor attitude will adversely affect their relationship from the outset. The attorney should strive to develop a close, personal rapport with the prospective client. He should not talk down to the client, and he should be patient in answering all of his questions. Counsel must impress the client from the beginning with the importance of his being completely honest and can-

1

did at all times. Even if the matter discussed with the prospective client does not require counsel's services, the attorney's time will not be wasted if he interviews properly. The client will leave the office thinking of him as "my lawyer," may consult him in the future, and may recommend him to friends.

THE INITIAL INTERVIEW

Many lawyers use some type of form as an aid in conducting the initial interview and organizing the information gathered from the client. Most interrogate the client and record his answers following the format of the form. Some prefer to have the client fill out an information form prior to the interview. (See Form No. 1, p. 1.)

As the attorney conducts the interview, questioning the client on the essential facts and circumstances of the case, he must be careful not to repress or intimidate the client. Rather, he should encourage the client to speak candidly.

Frequently, lawyers, especially the more inexperienced ones, fail to test (literally to cross-examine) their own client at the time of the initial interview when they first obtain the facts. Perhaps out of fear of appearing skeptical about the client's story or out of naiveté, the lawyer may take on face value the accuracy of the reported incident. If the lawyer first learns the truth when damaging facts come out at his client's deposition or at trial, the result could be the defendant's victory.

Of course, there are many reasons for a client not to give his lawyer a completely accurate account of the events. The client may feel that the lawyer will not take the case if he confesses everything: how much he had to drink before the accident, that she has a past drug conviction. However, more frequently, the client unconsciously wants to present his behavior in the best light.

Whatever the client's motive, the lawyer does his client and himself a disservice if he does not probe the story. The lawyer can do this subtly so that the client does not become defensive or resentful. An effective technique is to say, "You know, the lawyers for the defendant are going to ask you _____; how would you answer that question?" or "What do you suppose the other driver will say about where your car ~ just before the accident?" The client should be reassured that only wyer knows everything about the case will he be able to represent him. The client is often concealing something. Although this is undesirable, the lawyer can live with it if he knows about it.

The client's ultimate sense of satisfaction both with a legal system and his attorney is influenced to a great extent by the underlying motive that led him to hire a lawyer. If the client mistrusts the American system of justice or is inspired solely by an intense, personal desire for revenge, it may be impossible for the lawyer to bring about results that will satisfy him. Experienced lawyers, like psychiatrists, learn to "listen with their third ear." This is an important skill for the lawyer to develop in acquiring insight into the client's basic motivation. Does the person want something which the law cannot obtain for him? Will he follow the advice of counsel? It is important to understand the client's motives not only to decide whether to accept the case but also to present the client's testimony at trial in such a way that the jury identifies with the client and his objectives.

If the attorney employs an investigator, it is preferable for him to be present at the initial interview. In any event, counsel should advise his client that his investigator will be in touch with him and he should cooperate fully. Occasionally, a client may tell the investigator things he is not inclined to tell the attorney.

In some instances, the injured client comes to the lawyer with rather fixed ideas about the value of his case, but with little knowledge of the law as it relates to his case. Although the attorney should not attempt to give the client an extensive legal education, he should give most clients a brief explanation of the basic legal principles relating to their case. Such an explanation may enable the client to lend additional assistance to his attorney.

During the initial interview, there are two methods which the attorney can follow to obtain the plaintiff's version of how the incident occurred. Some attorneys take detailed notes; others prefer to record only the basic facts and to have an investigator take the client to the scene of the incident at a later time to obtain a detailed explanation.

Complex Litigation

In more complex litigation, different methods may be used. For example, the significant distinguishing characteristics of a products liability case or the professional negligence or malpractice case are not so much the principles of law that apply, but the factual complexity and technical idiosyncrasies that typify such litigation. An analysis of these issues begins with the client interview. Therefore, the conduct of the client interview in complex litigation is important not only for all of the many reasons that exist in other tort cases, but because it provides the initial basis for the ultimate resolution of the complex factual issues that are inherent in virtually every products or professional negligence case.

Although the ultimate need for factual detail is greater in complex litigation, it is ironic that in many instances the attorney will not—at the time of the initial interview—be able to anticipate fully the areas in which he will need information.

Products Liability

The attorney simply cannot foresee the significance of small details that may later be paramount to a critical issue in the case.

For example, whether the left rear window was rolled down prior to impact or was broken out in the crash may ultimately prove to be of pivotal importance in a rear-end gas tank case but not even suggest itself initially as a topic for inquiry. Therefore, in covering the three topics suggested below, the lawyer should explain to the client during his first interview that the conference will probably have to be repeated a number of times. In fact, in many products cases it may be preferable to defer any exhaustive examination of the client until after counsel has conducted a preliminary investigation. The first interview should result in only a general statement about the incident and the manner in which it occurred. The reasons for this procedure are simple and practical. In the typical products liability case the incident usually involves causative factors of a technical nature of which the plaintiff himself is not fully cognizant. He can accurately recollect what took place only after he has acquired a truthful and factual understanding of the engineering principles and events involved in the occurrence of the incident. The attorney cannot even ask the right questions until he has investigated, interrogated the witnesses, and acquired a thorough technical knowledge of the product involved.

With this understanding, the following are three areas the attorney should cover in the initial interview of a client with a products claim:

A. A complete history of the product, including its prior use and condition from the date of purchase to the present date.

B. A full and chronological description of what happened in and immediately following the incident; the correct sequence of events is important.

C. A complete description of the client's injuries and damages.

Professional Negligence Cases

In professional negligence cases, as in product cases, counsel may not be able to foresee the later significance of many small details until he has acquired the necessary technical facts with which to begin his inquiry. In such cases, counsel should advise his client during the initial interview that it may have to be repeated several times. Since, in contrast to products liability cases, the client in a professional negligence case frequently has personal knowledge of what the defendant did to cause his injury, it is recommended that the client be exhaustively examined at the time of the initial interview. Counsel is well advised to record the client interview. The facts will then be submitted to a professional expert for review.

With this understanding, the following are areas of inquiry that should be covered in an initial interview involving a claim of medical negligence:

A. A complete medical history.

B. All symptoms before, during, and after the alleged malpractice.

C. A complete list of every symptom that was related to the doctor (or other health care provider) by the client or his family. This list should be in chronological order stating the name and identity of each person present when the information was provided.

D. A chronological list of all tests and examinations that were performed by the doctor or other health care provider.

E. A complete and chronological summary of every statement made by the doctor or other health care provider. This summary should identify each person present on each occasion.

F. A summary of what the client believes that the doctor or health care provider did or failed to do that resulted in injury.

G. A complete description of the injuries and damages.

Typical Tort Cases

Below is a list and discussion of a number of the topics that should be covered with the client in the initial interview of virtually all personal injury cases:

A. Date and location of the incident. It is essential to determine the exact date of the occurrence of the incident. This may reveal a potential problem with the statute of limitations. If the applicable statute already bars the case, counsel must immediately and clearly advise his client that his case is proscribed. Counsel should record this advice and the date of the interview in writing. If the date of the running of the statute of limitations is dangerously near, counsel should make a note of that fact to himself and in the file to take appropriate action (e.g., file suit or decline employment) as far in advance of the ultimate date as the circumstances permit.

Counsel should also identify the exact location of the occurrence of the incident. This may have important implications on the questions of jurisdiction and of venue.

B. Identity of plaintiffs. Counsel should obtain a complete biography on each of the potential plaintiffs. If minors are involved, this biography should include the name and address of the parents and/or guardian. If the claim involves a wrongful death, each of the statutory heirs should be identified.

C. Identity of defendants. Counsel should ask the client to provide any information he posseses that might be of assistance in identifying potential defendants, including the existence and nature of any agency relationship. If one of the defendants is a minor, local rules may require the appointment of a guardian. If one of the defendants is deceased, counsel may have to take steps to have a personal representative appointed and to file a claim against the deceased defendant's estate.

D. Investigative Agencies. Counsel should ask the client whether there was a policeman at the scene of the incident and if so whether from the state or city police or from the sheriff's department. Injuries incurred in the course of employment are frequently investigated by a workmen's compensation carrier, an employer's safety committee, a union safety committee, and, occasionally, by a state or federal Occupational Safety and Health Administration. Occasionally, other state and federal agencies participate in the investigation of individual incidents; if so, the client is likely to be aware of this.

E. Identification of Witnesses. The attorney should try to obtain the names, addresses, and telephone numbers of all persons who might have knowledge or information about any issue in the case. He should explain to the client that there are two types of potential witnesses: persons who have knowledge of the facts and circumstances relating to the occurrence of the incident and persons whose knowledge will relate to either the existence or effect of the client's injuries. The second type of witness may be used at trial to give a before-and-after picture of the plaintiff, showing how the injury has affected the plaintiff's life.

F. Statements. It is important to determine if the plaintiff has given any kind of statement to anyone, including his own or defendant's insurance company or his own employer, or has testified in any kind of investigative hearing. A client may think that he has not given a "statement" if he has not *signed* a written document; counsel needs to inquire into this carefully. It is imperative for counsel to take immediate steps to request and obtain any statement his client may have given, whether oral or written and whether signed or unsigned. Similarly, the attorney should instruct his client to be careful not to discuss the facts of the case with anyone other than the members of his family and not to give anyone a statement regarding the facts of the incident or his injury without the express permission of his lawyer.

Counsel should ask the client to describe as accurately as possible all conversations in which he participated or which he overheard at the scene of the incident. Particular attention should be paid to any comments made by the potential defendants because they may be admissible at trial as admissions.

G. Tangible Evidence and/or Photographs. Careful inquiry should be made into the client's knowledge of the identity and existence of any physical object that played any role in the occurrence of the incident, such as the offending product in a products liability case, the client's shoes in a "slip and fall" case, or the tools and equipment in a construction accident case.

Counsel should ascertain if any photographs were taken that might prove to be relevant to any issue, whether relating to liability or damages. Often, a newspaper or independent photographer may have taken photographs which could be invaluable. In an automobile case, if vehicles involved have been neither photographed nor repaired, counsel should note this fact and at a later time have his investigator take the necessary photographs.

H. Defendant's Insurance Carrier. Counsel should seek to identify the defendant's insurance company. It should be notified as soon as possible of the occurrence of the incident and requested to address inquiries about the claim to counsel's office. If a representative of the defendant's carrier has already been in touch with the plaintiff, counsel should record in detail the content of these communications. If the client has received an offer of settlement this fact and the amount of the offer must be confirmed in writing by the defendant's carrier.

I. Plaintiff's Insurance and Other Benefits. Counsel must take great care to identify any insurance policy that might provide the plaintiff with protection or benefits. The attorney should specifically request that the plaintiff provide a copy of any such insurance policy for inspection. Information concerning the plaintiff's insurance coverage is valuable for a number of reasons. The plaintiff's liability carrier must be notified of the occurrence of the incident in case other persons injured in the incident elect to institute proceedings against the client. In any event, the plaintiff's insurance company may have investigated the case, obtained photographs or have witnesses' statements which it will make available. The client may have uninsured motorists coverage which would protect him if the defendant responsible for his injuries were not covered by insurance at the time of the collision. In some states, insurance coverage is provided which will protect the client in the event that the person responsible for the injuries was *under-insured*. The client may wish to have his own insurance company pay the cost of repairing his property if his policy affords this type of coverage. In most incidents, counsel should direct his client to permit his own insurance company(s) to pay his medical expenses. The attorney should be aware that there may be more than one policy that provides benefits or coverage for the payment of medical expenses. (Counsel should first seek to exhaust the coverage for which there is no subrogation.) Similarly, the attorney should determine whether the client has other forms of insurance which will provide additional benefits like disability income and wage loss protection. There may be several other categories of benefits to which the client is entitled, such as a variety of social security benefits, workmen's compensation, and others which may be explored.

J. Injuries and Damages. The client should be asked to delineate all injuries suffered as a result of the incident. To insure a detailed description of all the injuries, pain, and discomfort experienced, counsel should suggest that the client start with his head and describe his problems down to his toes. He should also ask the client for a complete list of all the doctors and hospitals that treated him. The client must describe in detail all previous injuries, accidents, and claims. Counsel should ask whether the client ever sustained an injury at work, in the armed forces, in sports, in a fall, or in an auto accident. Many clients are hesitant to provide this information; clients should be warned that many unsatisfactory verdicts result from plaintiff's own counsel not being fully informed at the outset of prior injuries and claims. Point out to the client that the insurance industry has an index bureau which contains a record of every claim made against a party covered by insurance. The client should be assured that a prior injury or claim does not necessarily jeopardize his present case. Indeed, his attorney may be able to use such information to advantage; for instance, the plaintiff's doctor may be of the opinion that the present incident aggravated the previous condition. If there has been a prior injury, counsel should obtain the date and names of the doctors and hospitals that treated the client on that occasion.

If the client asks how much money he can expect, he should be told that it is far too early to make such an estimate. The attorney should never mention a specific monetary figure to the client during the initial interview or promise any particular return. If the client makes it clear, however, that he expects five or ten times more than a normally reasonable settlement, counsel should dispel his misconceptions. Counsel should also explain to the client that each case is different and warn him not to listen to advice about the value of his case from others.

He should point out that value is a function of liability, injury, and defendant's financial responsibility, as well as other factors. The attorney should make the client aware of the strong points of his case, but he should also point out the weak points just as candidly. The client should be aware that the wheels of justice move slowly and that he cannot expect immediate results.

The attorney should take a few minutes to acquaint the client, at least generally, with the work he must do and the procedures he will follow after the interview. He should tell the client that any offer of settlement will be made to his attorney either by the opposing counsel or the defendant's insurance carrier. The client should be advised that any and all such offers will be communicated to him along with the attorney's advice and recommendation. The client should also be advised that an accurate evaluation of his claim may itself take a great deal of investigation and analysis but that as soon as the attorney is able to suggest a range of figures representative of anticipated results, he will present them to the client for his consideration and that, in any event, the final settlement decision will be the client's.

Before concluding the initial interview, counsel should be able to decide whether or not the case has sufficient merit to justify further investigation. If, at the conclusion of the interview, counsel decides not to take the case—for whatever reason (lack of merit, conflict of interest, etc.)—counsel must clearly and expressly decline the client's offer of employment and record this fact in writing.

POST INTERVIEW PRACTICE

Some firms employ a procedure which may be described as a "thirty day review system." If the attorney is not able to determine the advisability of actually accepting employment at the time of the initial interview, he must inform his "client" of that fact and advise him that further investigation will be conducted before employment is accepted. The file may then be placed in a special color coded folder different from regular file folders. This file is then reviewed by the lawer and other office personnel to determine whether or not the case has sufficient merit to justify acceptance and further investigation. If, after further investigation, the attorney makes the decision not to accept employment, the client is then advised of that decision in writing by certified or registered mail. This letter should be sent to the client as soon as the circumstances permit the attorney to make the decision. This letter should advise the client of the existence and the effect of the applicable statute of limitations.

Important considerations relevant to the decision of whether or not to accept employment include (1) the probability of success, (2) the potential value of the claim, and (3) the anticipated costs of preparation, specifically including the fees of experts, which in complex litigation may be considerable.

Plaintiff's counsel should not accept employment in a case which he never expects to try. From the standpoints of both the attorney and the client, counsel should develop a reputation of accepting employment only in meritorious litigation. Counsel should not take a case of doubtful liability solely because he hopes to settle it.

Employment Agreement

If counsel decides to accept the offer of employment, he should have the client execute an employment agreement. This agreement should make adequate provisions for both fees and costs. Contingent fees are both appropriate and customary in personal injury cases. The agreed upon percentage should conform to local bar standards and state statutes in those jurisdictions which have enacted applicable legislation. The items and activity that will probably be necessary for an adequate investigation and preparation that are likely to result in expenses should be discussed with the client. Typically, such items and activities would include photographs, depositions, medical reports, and fees of investigators and experts. The American Bar Association Code of Professional Responsibility, promulgated by the ABA, and The American Lawyer's Code of Conduct, written by the Commission on Professional Responsibility of the Roscoe Pound-American Trial Lawyers Foundation, permit the attorney to advance these expenses on behalf of his client with the understanding that they will be borne by the client.[1] It is essential that the client understand this at the outset to prevent a possible misunderstanding at the time of distribution. Counsel should also explain that the client's personal medical bills are the client's personal obligation. Some states require that a copy of the contract be given to the client. (See Form No. 2.)

[1]CPR EC5-8 and ALCC Rule 5.6(c).

If at the conclusion of the initial interview, counsel cannot determine whether or not to accept employment, it is advisable to have the potential client sign a special authorization permitting counsel to investigate the claim but spelling out clearly that no "attorney client" relationship exists. (See Form No. 3.)

The client must also sign medical authorizations permitting the doctors and hospitals that treated the plaintiff to release the relevant records to counsel. The medical release form may include a paragraph expressly authorizing counsel to deduct and pay the amount of any unpaid medical bills from the funds that are recovered. Some attorneys prefer to leave the payment of the client's personal medical bills up to the client and his doctor(s)/hospital(s); this need not be a part of the authorization. If the client wants the attorney to handle this matter, express authorization to this effect should be executed. Furthermore, experience teaches that settlement distribution should not be made until all the doctors involved have been contacted and their bills paid. In some jurisdictions, doctors and hospitals have a legal lien against the plaintiff's claim which serves to protect unpaid medical bills. (See Form No. 4.)

It may be wise to affirm that counsel shares the concern of the client's family and physician in desiring the client's rapid return to good health. A client who develops an obsessive concern for his injury or his case is not likely to be satisfied with any result counsel obtains. In any event, the sooner a client returns to the way of living he enjoyed before the incident, the sooner he is likely to be happy, secure, and satisfied. Therefore, the injured client should be encouraged to take part in as many of his former activities as possible. For example, suggest that he return to work as soon as medically possible.

Instruction Sheet

At the close of the initial interview, counsel may wish to give the client an instruction sheet outlining some of the things that are likely to occur in the handling of his case. This instruction sheet may be given to the prospective client *before* he sees the attorney so it may help to reinforce some of the ideas discussed during the initial interview. Although the instruction sheet is self-explanatory, it should be emphasized that the plaintiff is not to talk to anyone except a representative of his lawyer's office. (See Form No. 5.) The instruction sheet may be followed by a pamphlet to be mailed to the client within two weeks of the initial interview. Such a device encourages the client to take an active part in his case. The information recorded by the client will provide the attorney with a graphic picture of how the injuries have affected the client's life. (See Form No. 6.)

The client's departure signals the time to begin processing the new file. Typically, four things should be done immediately:

1. Request for the report from the appropriate investigative agency.

2. Request for the hospital records and physicians' reports.

3. Notification to the defendant or his insurance carrier.

4. Notification to the plaintiff's insurance carrier.

Request for Hospital Records and Physicians' Reports

Some counsel send a letter simply advising the physician that their office is representing the client, but that the doctor need not send a written report unless and until requested to do so by the attorney at some future date. (See Form No. 7.) There are cases in which it may be preferable to secure the doctor's testimony by deposition rather than through a written report. (See Form No. 8 for a request for a written medical report.)

If the appropriate authorization has been executed, the request for medical letters may state that the health provider's unpaid bills will be protected in the event a recovery is ultimately effected. Before requesting the hospital records, the attorney must decide whether to order the complete records or merely some portion thereof. Even though the complete record is expensive, it generally gives a complete medical history and is helpful in informing doctors retained as experts. Nurses' notes also serve as good indicia of the patient's pain and suffering. (See Form No. 9.) If a death resulted from the accident, the death certificate or report of the coroner's inquest should be ordered.

Letter to the Defendant

A letter of notification should be addressed to the defendant, informing him that legal action is being contemplated and instructing that he so advise his insurance carrier. If counsel knows the defendant's insurance company, he should send a copy of this letter of notification to it. Prompt notification may be imperative where the defendant is a government unit or is deceased. Counsel should carefully check the law of his jurisdiction to determine in what circumstances formal notice and presentation of claim must be made and whether or not the state law requires written notification in order to set up an attorney's lien.

Counsel should be aware that if the case involves a claim of breach of warranty, some jurisdictions still require that the defendant be notified as a condition precedent to the filing of an action for breach of warranty. Likewise, the laws of some states require that in the event of the death of the potential defendant a claim be filed against his estate prior to the institution of a lawsuit against his estate. It should be emphasized that such a letter of notification should *never* be sent to an individual defendant, his insurance carrier, or any other prospective defendant until an attempt has been made to obtain his statement. The reason for this is that insurance companies customarily advise the policyholders not to give statements to anyone if they are informed of pending litigation involving their insured.

Request for Investigative Reports

As previously mentioned, counsel should immediately request the full and final report of any investigation conducted by any municipal, state or federal agency, including, where appropriate, the results of any action taken against the defendant or his employer as a result of that investigation.

Notification to the Plaintiff's Insurance Carrier

Such a notification might be in the form of a proof of loss in the event that the plaintiff's insurance policy requires such action. Some policies and some types of coverage require the claimant to provide notice as soon as possible after the occurrence of the incident.

INVESTIGATION

A lawsuit is no better or worse than the evidence developed. Though methods of presentation may vary, facts control a lawsuit. The first and most important thing the plaintiff's attorney can do is to learn every fact, whether favorable or unfavorable. The principles of investigation are the same for the professional investigator of the attorney.

Some firms regularly employ non-lawyer investigators. A trained professional investigator may be of enormous value in preparing a personal injury case, if only for the reason that they devote their full resources to the preparation of the factual and technical aspects of the case, thereby freeing the attorney to concentrate on legal matters and the implementation of overall strategy.

It is common knowledge among experienced lawyers that the case may be won or lost in the investigation. It is therefore essential that the investigator be both well trained in the art of conducting an investigation and carefully briefed in the specific objectives of his investigation of a particular case. Ordinarily, the attorney should not delegate the entire responsibility for the factual preparation of the case to an investigator. In any event, the activities of the non-lawyer investigator should be reviewed periodically in detail. In some cases, a non-lawyer investigator may actually be more effective in getting witnesses to open up and discuss the relevant facts. In those instances where the attorney personally conducts the investigation, he, of course, has the advantage of an intimate and firsthand knowledge of the witnesses. Counsel may wish to encourage his investigators to join the National Association of Legal Investigators (N.A.L.I.).

Every investigation ought to be approached with one key question in mind: "How could this accident have been prevented?" This approach will be effective in an automobile case, a "fall-down" case, or a products liability case. For the investigator to probe effectively, he must have some familiarity with principles of tort law, and the trial lawyer should work closely with the investigator—both before and after the initial investigation—to determine whether or not liability can be proved. Together, the attorney and investigator should periodically go over each file in the office to determine what investigation has been completed and what needs to be done.

When asked to recount the occurrence of a fortuitous and traumatic event, the typical layperson will describe as *fact* what is actually a personal and inaccurate estimate. Typically, the client's estimate of time, distance, and speed will not accurately reflect the physical facts.

Counsel must accurately identify the physical facts existing at the scene and apply known physical laws to them before he requires his client to commit himself to a statement describing the occurrence of the incident.

Soon after the initial client interview, the investigator may wish to meet the client at the scene of the incident to take a comprehensive statement of how the it occurred. At the scene, the investigator should diagram the area in the presence of the client; the diagram need not be made to scale, but it should contain accurate measurements. The investigator should locate the point of impact, if possible, and measure from that point to some known reference point on the scene diagram. This should be a reference point easy to locate, such as a telephone pole or the corner of a building. The client should point out where he was when he first saw the other vehicle, the location on the roadway where he first applied his brakes, and other important points of reference. Having located the point of impact, the point at which the brakes were first applied and other important points, the investigator should measure the distances involved. He should also measure the width of the pavement of the roadway where the incident occurred, noting any topographical features which are unusual. Ultimately, the value of the diagram will depend on the ingenuity of the person making it. At the time of deposition or trial, the client can refer to the diagram to refresh his memory of the scene and the pertinent facts relating to the incident. The time spent by the investigator and the client at the scene of the incident helps to prepare the investigator for subsequent investigation in the case.

Obtaining Photographs

The investigation should include as complete a photographic history of the incident as possible; photos should be taken as soon as feasible. When taking photos of the scene, the photographer should use his imagination and show various key features from more than one angle. He should take photographs which show the view available to both the plaintiff and the defendant. (Aerial photographs can be very valuable in certain cases, but their expense often outweighs their value.) The investigator should always be on the lookout for photographs taken by freelance or newspaper photographers. If the case warrants the effort, he may wish to go through newspaper archives in the area and check to see if any pictures appeared. Photographs should be taken of all the vehicles involved in the collision. If photographs were not taken at the scene of the collision, the investigator should attempt to locate the vehicles and photograph them from all possible angles. Often, the condition of the inside of the vehicle in which the plaintiff was riding dramatically portrays the force of impact at the time of collision. Photos should be taken as soon as possible because conditions will change and automobiles will be repaired.

In more complex litigation such as products liability cases, photographs are equally important. Everything about the product should be photographed, including warning labels, serial numbers, names of manufacturers, guards, or lack of guards, and other such materials that may be relevant to the case. It is extremely important, if possible, to obtain and preserve custody of the product. If the product is in existence but under some unco-operative third party's control, counsel should consider what method is used in his state to impound the product legally. Injunctive relief may be available to secure control of the product and place it in the custody of the court to prevent its alteration without the express approval of the court.

Experts

Both counsel and his investigator need the consultation of an expert early in the development of the case in order to acquire the necessary technical background. The acquisition of at least a basic knowledge of the technical aspects of the case may be necessary to determine whether or not the case is meritorious.

This threshold decision should be made early in the development of the case because of the tremendous cost and expense of these types of cases. It is better to withdraw from a case early rather than to expend a lot of time and money and then withdraw later. Considered solely from the client's standpoint, the attorney must make an early estimate of the value of the claim and compare that with the expenses that will necessarily be incurred to determine whether the client would be well advised to proceed. Such an analysis may reveal that the prospects of the client's obtaining a positive recovery do not justify a decision to proceed. The necessity of making such an analysis must be carefully explained to the client.

In a products liability case, counsel should retain a competent expert to inspect the product thoroughly and perform nondestructive testing if appropriate. Destructive testing should only be done by agreement of all parties or with court approval.

Products Liability

A discussion of the methods and approach to the investigation of a products case is beyond the scope of this chapter. What follows is a very brief outline of the major topics that should be covered:

A. Get the product and/or a similar one if possible.

B. Photograph both the product and the scene of the incident.

C. Hire and consult with an expert in the field as soon as possible.

D. Search the technical and trade literature for information relative to both the product and the industry involved.

E. Carefully trace the path of the product from the date it left the original manufacturer's control until the occurrence of the incident and then forward to the present time. Was there any prior abuse to, or alteration of, the product?

F. Identify all potential witnesses and interview them as soon as possible.

G. Identify all potential defendants.

The attorney should attempt to answer the following major questions in his investigation:

A. What actually occurred in the incident that resulted in the client's injury?

B. What could the manufacturer have done to avoid the occurrence of the incident?

C. What claims or representations has the manufacturer made about the quality or performance of his product?

D. Have other similar incidents occurred?

E. What do other manufacturers do in the design, construction, or instructions for maintenance of similar products?

F. What does the technical and trade literature say should be done in the design, construction, or instructions for maintenance of similar products?

G. Has the defendant altered or modified the product or the instructions for its maintenance and use?

H. Was the condition of the product changed at all after it left the defendant and before the incident?

I. Are there any applicable governmental standards or regulations?

Counsel should always remember that in dealing with products liability, medical malpractice, or other complex litigation that he risks a potential malpractice case if he attempts to handle to conclusion the preparation of a claim that exceeds his experience without the assistance of a specialist.

Medical Malpractice

The very bases of liability in professional negligence cases, such as medical or attorney malpractice, are both factually and technically complex. By necessity, therefore, the scope of a basic investigation is much more extensive than in the typical automobile collision.

In a medical malpractice case the investigator should immediately photograph and copy all records from the hospital or health care provider. He should also attempt to photograph or copy any physician records. After a complete and comprehensive record has been made of the client's version of the facts, all of this material should be reviewed by a competent physician in the specialty involved to advise whether or not to proceed with the case from a technical standpoint.

This screening process is extremely important and should be done early in the case. The most important thing that a lawyer can learn is how to turn down one of these cases. As in product cases, the attorney must estimate the potential value of his client's loss and compare that to the costs of the experts and of preparation to analyze whether or not it is economically feasible to proceed with the expense of such a case.

Attorney Malpractice

In an attorney malpractice case the investigator should copy all records from the courthouse or from any legal proceedings that may be involved. He should attempt to obtain a complete copy of the office records of the attorney, all depositions, and every other document or paper involving the potential case. In addition, the investigator should conduct a careful investigation of the important witnesses as well as record a complete and comprehensive statement from the client as to his version of the facts. In other words, the investigator and the lawyer will have to prepare a complete case so that these facts can be submitted, along with all of the records, for review by a competent attorney in the specialty involved to advise whether or not to proceed with the suit from a technical standpoint. As in the instance of medical malpractice cases, a screening process is extremely important and should be done as early as possible. As in products and malpractice cases, a "cost-value" economic analysis of the case should be made carefully before proceeding. In each instance, if the case is rejected, the client should be notified in writing by a letter which sets forth the reasons for the decision. It is advisable to send the letter by certified or registered mail.

Automobile Collisions

In a case involving an automobile collision, the attorney should obtain copies of repair estimates on the vehicles involved. He should pay special attention to whether the frame or bumper of the plaintiff's car was damaged; such damage indicates more than a minor impact. Finally, investigators should obtain information concerning the weight of the vehicle involved in the collision because at trial an engineering expert can utilize this information in connection with the law of kinetic energy to prove to the jury the amount of force exerted upon the body of the plaintiff.

Witness Contact

Witnesses should also be interviewed as soon as possible to record their observations. When the attorney (or the investigator) confronts a witness, there are certain things he can do which may help to win the lawsuit. Initially, the investigator should make clear that all he is interested in is the truth. Explain that our adversary system cannot function without the co-operation of sound thinking citizens who are willing to "become involved." If witnesses will consent to returning to the scene of the incident, the investigator should interview them there. With the help of the scene diagram, the investigator should ask these witnesses to go through the sequence of events as they remember them. The place where each person was when he saw the incident should be marked on the scene diagram. If a witness is unwilling to go to the scene of the incident, the investigator should talk to him at his home or any other place convenient to the witness. Photographs should be used to orient the witness to the scene of the incident properly. These photos should be marked at the points to which the witness refers, such as where he was located, where he first saw the cars, etc. In this way, the photographs become a permanent record of the witness's observations.

No matter where the witness is interviewed, his observations should, if possible, be recorded. Counsel may choose to have the interview recorded by a court reporter, or he may wish to take a written or a recorded statement. Although the use of a court reporter raises the cost of investigation, it may be justified because of the authoritative nature of such a statement. That is, the court reporter is a disinterested third party who is available as a witness at trial to testify to the accuracy of the statement if it is questioned by the witness. Some witnesses, however, do not feel comfortable when a third party, such as a court reporter, is present. When no court reporter is used, the investigator should take down in longhand all the comments made by the witness. When the interview concludes the investigator should ask the witness to read the longhand narrative and make any necessary corrections. If the witness will sign the statement, he should be encouraged to sign each page and initial all changes he has made. The modern day investigator should be equipped with recording devices to tape defendant's or witness' statements either in person or on the telephone. After he records the statement (with the defendant's or witness's permission), it should be typed and two copies sent by mail or taken to the witness. The witness should be requested to read his statement and then asked to sign it after he has made corrections. He should also be permitted to keep a copy of his statement so that he can refer to it if anyone else attempts to take his statement. On those occasions when the witness (or potential defendant) will permit an interview but will not allow his remarks to be recorded and will not sign a handwritten statement, the investigator should summarize his notes of the interview and this transcript may be mailed to the witness with a cover letter stating that the enclosed is a memo of the conversation with a request that the witness check it for accuracy and sign it and return in a self-addressed envelope if it does conform to his recollection and knowledge of the event. Again, an extra copy of this summary should be furnished to the potential defendant or witness.

In addition to getting a full account of what happened, the investigator should be certain that in all of these statements he records the correct names, addresses, and maiden names, including the addresses and telephone numbers of neighbors, relatives, and employers so that several months or even years later the witnesses can be found. If the defendant or witness is unwilling to give a detailed statement, it is helpful to get a "negative statement." That is an admission by the person: "I don't remember," "I have no idea of how fast he was going," "I didn't see anything," or "I didn't hear the horn." Negative admissions may subsequently be used if the witness suddenly starts to remember these things at the trial.

It is not unethical to attempt to obtain a statement from the defendant *before* he is represented by counsel. Therefore, an attempt should be made to obtain such a statement prior to filing the lawsuit. Once suit is filed, the defendant will be represented by counsel. Then it would be unethical to approach him for a statement. The attorney should instruct the investigator that, if the defendant is represented by counsel, he may not take a statement from him without having the defendant's attorney present.

The police officers who investigated the occurrence should be contacted. (Investigators would be wise to develop an amicable relationship with law enforcement officers in their area.) Policemen are more likely to cooperate if the investigator arranges to meet with them while they are on duty. Frequently, the officer will agree to meet the investigator at the scene of the incident; encourage this approach. The police officer should be requested to bring along original notes made at the scene of the incident because they may contain information not recorded in the official report. When a traffic signal is involved in the case, the time sequence of the signal at the hour of the incident should be checked with the local authorities.

Photographs of an injured client, if they show his disability and indicate discomfort and pain, can be very valuable at the time of trial. Such photographs, showing injuries, should be taken either at the hospital or in the home of the injured party—never at the lawyer's office. If photographs are taken at the hospital or at some other location, the investigator should be sure to include in the photograph any special type of equipment being used by the plaintiff. It is also imperative that the investigator or photographer note the dates and times that he has taken each of these photographs as it may become important at the trial when such photographs were taken. Photographs are particularly valuable to show scars, extensive bruising, extensive swelling, and lacerations. They are also indicated when the client is forced to wear a device such as a cervical collar or to employ some form of traction. Many times orthopedic surgeons, plastic surgeons, and other physicians take pictures in the ordinary course of their medical treatment; these pictures are often accessible to the lawyer.

Form No. 1

INITIAL INTERVIEW RECORD

Plaintiff(s)

Date of Incident   Statute of Limitations

Place of Incident

NOTES TO ATTORNEY

1. Jurisdiction Question?

2. Venue Question?

3. State or Federal Court?

4. Open Up Estate?

5. File Claim?
   a. City, County
   b. FTCA
   c. Defendant's Estate?

6. "Notice" Requirement?

7. Loss of Services?

8. Subrogation?

9. Associate Attorney?

Form No. 1 page 1

THE INCIDENT

Date: _____

Time: _____

Day of Week: _____

Place: _____

Diagram:

Note: Statute of Limitations?
      Jurisdictional Question?
      Venue Question?

Facts:

Agency Relationship:

CLIENT

_____   _____

Name   Date of Birth

_____

Address

Form No. 1 Page 2

Residence Phone

Business Phone   (Ext.)

Social Security Number

Other Identifying Number

                                             Married/Divorced
Name of Spouse/Parent   Circle One

Address of Spouse/Parent

Note: Loss of Services?
       Do You Need to Open Estate?
       Appoint Guardian?

DEFENDANT(S)

Name

Address

Employer   Employer's Address

Residence Phone   Business Phone   (Ext.)

1. Foreign Corporation.

   a. _____
      Where Organized

Form No. 1 Page 3

b. _____
Agent For Process

c. _____
Principal Place of Business

d. _____
Doing Business in _____

2. Domestic Corporation.

a. _____
County Organized

b. _____
County Doing Business

Note: Identify Parent and Subsidiary Companies, Affiliates, Divisions, etc.

3. Partnership.

a. _____
Name Under Which Partnership Does Business

b. _____

_____

_____

Individual Partners

4. Minor.

a. _____
Date of Birth

b. _____

Name and

_____

Address of Parents or Guardian

5. Estate.

a. _____

Court in Which Pending

b. _____

Style of Estate

c. _____

Name and

_____

Address of Representative of Estate

Note: Do You Need to File "Claim"?
Do You Need to Give "Notice"?
Special Service of Process Problems?

WITNESSES

_____

Name

_____

Address

_____   _____

Residence Phone   Business Phone

_____

Notes: Where Witness?   What Seen/Known?

Form No. 1 Page 5

Friendly/Hesitant?　　　Male/Female?　　　White/Minority?

Old/Young?

Name

Address

Residence Phone　　　　　Business Phone

Notes: Where Witness?　　　　　What Seen/Known?

Friendly/Hesitant?　　　Male/Female?　　　White/Minority?

Old/Young?

Name

Address

Residence Phone　　　　　Business Phone

Notes: Where Witness?　　　　　What Seen/Known?

Form No. 1 Page 6

Friendly/Hesitant?   Male/Female?   White/Minority?

Old/Young?

Note: Ask Them to Request Copy of Statement?
      If Vital, Take Deposition

SPECIFIC QUESTIONS

1. List every entity that might have investigated the incident. (E.g., Highway Patrol; Sheriff; Local Police; Federal or State Agency; Union; Workman's Comp Carrier; Plaintiff's Employer; Plaintiff's Insurance Company; Defendant's Insurance Company; Friend; etc.)

a. _____

b. _____

c. _____

REQUEST COPY!

2. Any criminal or other type charges or hearing result?

a. _____

b. _____

REQUEST COPY!

3. Any and all photographs (scene, vehicles, plaintiff, product, etc.).

Form No. 1 Page 7

REQUEST COPY!

4. Where is automobile or product?

OBTAIN! EXAMINE! PHOTOGRAPH!

5. Has client(s) given a statement? If so, who, when, what?

REQUEST COPY! ADVISE NOT TO GIVE STATEMENT!

6. Has witness(s) given a statement? If so, who, when, what?

REQUEST COPY!

INJURIES

1. Describe Fully: _____

_____

_____

_____

Form No. 1 Page 8

RIGHT

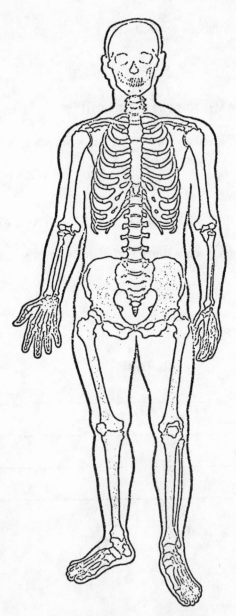

Form No. 1 Page 9

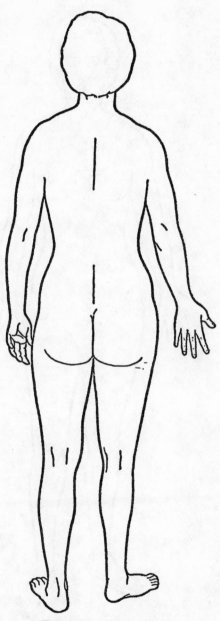

Form No. 1 Page 10

RIGHT

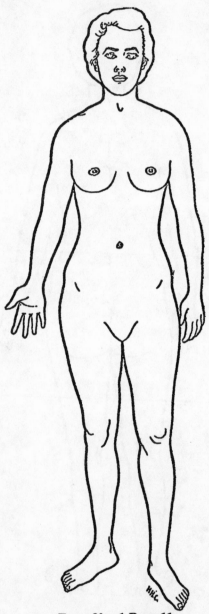

Form No. 1 Page 11

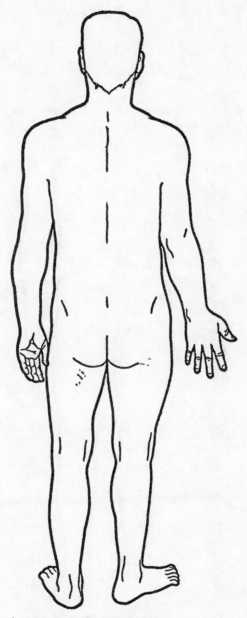

Form No. 1 Page 12

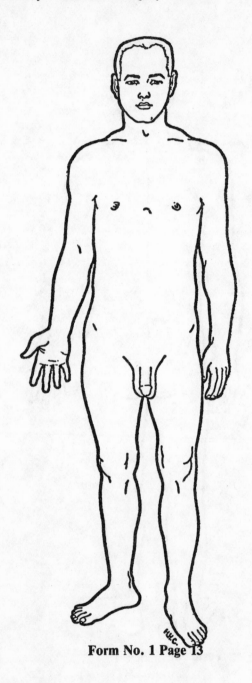

Form No. 1 Page 13

2. Doctor(s).

Name	Address	Still Under Care
_____	_____	_____
_____	_____	_____
_____	_____	_____
_____	_____	_____

3. Hospital(s).

Name	Address	Dates
_____	_____	_____
_____	_____	_____
_____	_____	_____
_____	_____	_____

SPECIALS

1. Doctor Bills.

Name	Amt. of Bill	To Date	Amt. Unpaid
_____	_____	_____	_____
_____	_____	_____	_____
_____	_____	_____	_____
_____	_____	_____	_____

2. Hospital Bills.

Name	Amt. of Bill	To Date	Amt. Unpaid
_____	_____	_____	_____
_____	_____	_____	_____
_____	_____	_____	_____
_____	_____	_____	_____

3. Medicine.

4. Medical Appliances/Devices/Prosthesis.

5. Nursing Service.

Name	Amt. of Bill	Dates	Amt. Unpaid
_____	_____	_____	_____
_____	_____	_____	_____
_____	_____	_____	_____
_____	_____	_____	_____

6. Damage to Property.

Describe	Date Purchase	Cost	Value Now
_____	_____	_____	_____

Form No. 1 Page 15

6. Damage to Property. (Cont.)

Describe	Date Purchase	Cost	Value Now
_____	_____	____	_____
_____	_____	____	_____
_____	_____	____	_____

7. Earning Capacity (wages, other income, lost profits, etc. - list dates off work, note whether paid or not and by whom).

Note: Verify wages.
      Get copies of tax returns.

8. Other Expenses.

Note: Subrogation Claims?
      Do you need authorization to withhold unpaid bills?

PRIOR INJURIES/DISABILITIES

1. Describe Nature.

2. Date Occurred and Facts.

Form No. 1 Page 16

3. Doctor(s).

    a.

    b.

    c.

4. Hospital(s).

    a.

    b.

    c.

5. Status at Time of Present Incident.

Note: Do You Need Records of Prior Injuries?

PRIOR CLAIMS/SUITS

1. Date of Each.

2. Nature or Basis.

3. Against Whom.

Form No. 1 Page 17

4. Suit Filed.
   If so, where? Attorney?

5. Result of Claim.

POLICE RECORD

1. Date: _____

2. Place:_____

3. Charge: _____

4. Result: _____

_____

Note: Get copy of Police Record?
      Get copy of Former Pleadings?

BIOGRAPHY OF CLIENT

A. NAME

_____
                                           Date of Birth

B. NEAREST RELATIVE

_____

Name

_____

Address   Relationship

C. DEPENDENTS

Name   Address   Date of Birth   Relationship

_____   _____   _____   _____

_____   _____   _____   _____

_____   _____   _____   _____

_____   _____   _____   _____

D. PRESENT EMPLOYMENT

1. Name: _____

2. Address: _____

3. Type of Work: _____

4. Job Title: _____

5. Wages/Income: _____

6. Time Lost From Work: _____

_____

_____

Form No. 1 Page 19

7. Who Can Confirm? _____

_____

8. Foreman/Fellow Employee (Lay Witness)_____

_____

_____

E. PRIOR WORK RECORD

1. _____
   Name

   _____
   Address

   _____   _____
   Type of Work   Dates of Employment

   _____   _____
   Wages   Why Left?

2. _____
   Name

   _____
   Address

   _____   _____
   Type of Work   Dates of Employment

   _____   _____
   Wages   Why Left?

Form No. 1 Page 20

3. _____
   Name

   _____
   Address

   _____   _____
   Type of Work   Dates of Employment

   _____   _____
   Wages   Why Left?

F. EDUCATIONAL BACKGROUND

_____

_____

G. MARITAL BACKGROUND

_____

_____

H. INCOME FOR LAST 4 YEARS

1. _____

2. _____

3. _____

4. _____

Note: Get Copies of Tax Returns?
      Verify Wages or Lost Income?
      Need Copy of Divorce/Custody Decree?

Form No. 1 Page 21

INSURANCE INFORMATION

A. Plaintiff

1. Name and Address of Company

   a. _____   _____

   b. _____   _____

   c. _____   _____

   d. _____   _____

   e. _____   _____

2. Type of Coverage and Limits

   a. _____   _____

   b. _____   _____

   c. _____   _____

   d. _____   _____

   e. _____   _____

3. Name, Address, Telephone Number and Employer of Adjuster(s).

Notes: 1. Has Carrier Been Notified?
        2. Do You Need to File "Proof of Loss?"
        3. What Benefits Can/Should Plaintiff Claim?

Form No. 1 Page 22

4. What Must You/Plaintiff Do to Claim These Benefits?
5. Has Carrier Acted in Good Faith?
6. Un-Insured Motorist?
7. Subrogation Claim?
8. Get Copies of Their Records/Investigation?

B. Defendant(s)

1. Name and Address of Company

a. _____   _____

b. _____   _____

c. _____   _____

d. _____   _____

e. _____   _____

f. _____   _____

2. Limits of Coverage

a. _____

b. _____

c. _____

d. _____

e. _____

f. _____

Form No. 1 Page 23

3. Name, Address, Telephone Number and Employer of Adjuster(s).

Notes: 1. Has Carrier Been Notified? How, When, and by Whom?
2. Do You Need to Send "Excess Liability" Notice?
3. Verify Any Offer Defendant Has Made to Plaintiff!!!
4. Can You Sue Insurance Company Directly?
5. If They Have Plaintiff's Statement—Get Copy!
6. Make Defendant Produce Policy?
7. Do You Have a Coverage Question?

FORM 2

EMPLOYMENT AGREEMENT

_____, 19_____

I/We hereby retain and employ _____

as my attorney(s) to represent me in my claim for damages against

_____ or any others who may

be liable on account of _____

on or about the _____ day of _____, 19 _____.

I/We agree to pay said attorneys' fees as follows (initial one):

_____   ☐ Contingency:

_____ of whatever may be
recovered from said claim whether by suit, settlement, or in any other manner;*

_____   ☐ Hourly:

$_____ per hour for all legal services
rendered in this matter.

I/We agree that associate counsel may be employed at the discretion
and expense of my attorney(s), and that any attorney so employed
may be designated to appear on my behalf or undertake my representation in this matter.

I/We further agree that in addition to the above attorneys' fees, all
court costs, subpoena costs, photos, depositions, court reporter costs,
reports, witness statements, and all other out-of-pocket expenses
directly incurred in investigating or litigating this claim shall be paid

Form No. 2 Page 1

by the undersigned, and that said expenses and attorneys' fees may be deducted from the proceeds of any recovery.

I/We have received a copy of this contract.

_____

Client

_____

Client

The above employment is hereby accepted on the terms stated, and if on a percentage contingent fee basis, we agree to make no charge for services unless recovery is had in this matter. In addition, we agree to make no settlement without the written consent of the claimant.

By _____

Attorney

*NOTE: Agreed upon percentage may be governed by statute or case law or local rule. The agreed upon percentage may vary according to the case and the circumstances.

_____ Copy of contract given to client.

Form No. 2 Page 2

FORM 3

AUTHORITY TO INVESTIGATE

I/We have discussed a potential claim with (Name of Attorney/ Firm) arising out of the following incident:

_____

Type Incident

_____

Date   Place

I/We have not employed (Name of Attorney/Firm) to file suit or to represent us as our legal attorneys.

I/We do authorize (Name of Attorney/Firm) to conduct an investigation of this incident with the understanding that the results of such investigation remain the property of (Name of Attorney/Firm).

Check One:
☐ I/We agree to pay the expenses incurredc in the conduct of this investigation.
☐ (Name of Attorney/Firm) agrees to pay the expenses involved in the conduct of this investigation.

I/We have no further responsibility or obligation to (Name of Attorney/Firm).

Form No. 3 Page 1

(Name of Attorney/Firm) has no further responsibility or obligation to me/us.

SIGNED this _____ day of _____, 19 _____.

For the Firm:

_____   Claimant(s):

1. _____

Address _____

_____

Phone: _____
          Home   Work

2. _____

Address _____

_____

Phone: _____
          Home   Work

Form No. 3 Page 2

FORM 4

MEDICAL AUTHORIZATION
and
PATIENT'S REQUEST FOR CONFIDENTIAL
TREATMENT OF MEDICAL INFORMATION

TO: FROM:

You are hereby authorized and directed to permit the examination of, and the copying or reproduction in any manner, whether, mechanical, photographic, or otherwise, by my attorney or such other person as he may authorize, all or any portions desired by him of the following:

a. Hospital records, X-rays, X-ray readings and reports, laboratory records and reports, all tests of any type, character and reports thereof, statement of charges, and any and all of my records pertaining to hospitalization, history, condition, treatment, diagnosis, prognosis, etiology or expense;

b. Medical records, including patient's record cards, X-rays, X-ray readings and reports, laboratory records and reports, all tests of any type and character and reports thereof, statements of charges, and any and all of my records pertaining to medical care, history, condition, treatment, diagnosis, prognosis, etiology or expense.

You are further authorized and directed to furnish oral and written reports to my attorney, or his delegate, as requested by him for any of the foregoing matters.

By reason of the fact that such information that you have acquired as my physician or surgeon is confidential to me, you are also requested to treat such information as confidential and requested not to furnish any of such information in any form to anyone, without written authorization from me. I hereby revoke any previously dated medical authorization.

Form No. 4 Page 1

I also authorize my attorneys or their delegate to photograph my person while I am present in any hospital.

I further authorize the sending of medical and hospital bills to my attorney, and in the event of recovery by trial or settlement to allow my attorney to withhold an amount sufficient to cover these bills and to make payment directly to you and to deduct the same from any recovery which may be due me. I agree that a photostatic copy of the authorization shall be considered as effective and as valid as the original.

_____
Patient

Subscribed and sworn to me this ____ day of _____, 19 ____

_____
Notary Public

Form No. 4 Page 2

FORM 5

(Name of Attorney/Firm)
(Address of Attorney/Firm)
(Telephone Number of Attorney/Firm)

Your File No. _____

TO OUR CLIENT:

We know that your case is important to you—we want you to know that it is important to us and that we are going to do the best we can to represent your interests.

This pamphlet is written for two reasons:

FIRST, To give you some idea of what to expect in the future and

SECOND, To offer some suggestions as to how you can help us prepare your case.

We hope this pamphlet answers some of your questions. It is not written to discourage you from calling us about other questions you may have—please feel free to call us anytime you feel the need to do so.

WHEN WILL THE CASE BE FILED?

It is entirely possible that we have already filed the case. If you would like to confirm that, you need only call the secretary of the attorney handling your file.

We may wait until we have completed a preliminary investigation of the matter before we file the case in court.

In the event that our investigation leads us to the conclusion that we cannot by legal action truly assist you, we will, of course, contact you immediately.

Form No. 5 Page 1

WHAT HAPPENS AFTER SUIT IS FILED?

Activities will take place in two areas after suit is filed.

First, we will continue our own investigation and research of your case. Frequently, we do this with the assistance of professional investigators and research assistants depending on the requirements of the case. Often, this investigation and research takes weeks and even months and may not require that we contact you personally.

The second area of activity is called "discovery." Various statutes and Court Rules permit both sides of a lawsuit to file certain papers in court requesting the other side to furnish information about the case. When either side files such a paper in court, the other side must respond within a fairly short time—usually 30 days. There are various types of discovery devices that the law allows:

1. *Interrogatories.* This is a series of written questions which one side asks the other. They must be answered in writing and under oath.

2. *Request for Production.* Each side may request the other to produce documents or things that might relate to the case.

3. *Depositions.* This is a procedure where the lawyer for one side orally asks questions to a witness. The witness is under oath and answers orally and a court reporter makes a transcript of the proceedings.

We almost certainly will use one or more of these discovery devices. The other side is likely to do so also. If and when they do, we will need your help in filing our response in court in time. If and when the other side files one of these papers, we will write you immediately and give you specific instructions about what to do. We will also ask you to call and make an appointment to come in to the office before we have to file our response to the court.

Form No. 5 Page 2

WHEN WILL THE CASE BE TRIED?

At the present time, cases are generally set in about _____ months after they are filed. You can figure from the filing date of your case the approximate time when your case will be set for trial.

THE PRINTED DOCKET.

All the cases that are set down to be tried in any calendar month appear in a printed docket which is given to the lawyers about thirty days in advance. For instance, about the 1st of January, we get a printed docket in which appear all the cases that are set for trial in February.

Furthermore, cases are tentatively set for trial in a particular week. All the cases the Court hopes to try are set at the first of a particular week. They are then assigned to a specific Judge for trial one at a time during the week as the Trial Judges become available. However, if a case is not reached for trial during the week when it is set, it is continued to another printed docket because it is unreached and is usually set again several months later.

The cases are set in numerical order with perhaps forty cases set on Monday and a like number set on Tuesday and Wednesday, and the presiding judge sends them out to the Trial Judges in numerical order as they are reached.

If your case is set on a certain morning at 9:00 o'clock but is behind a number of other cases, it may not be reached until later that day or later that week.

WHEN ARE YOU NOTIFIED OF THE TRIAL?

As soon as we receive the printed docket, we notify you that your case is set for trial which gives you about a month's notice in advance.

WHEN WILL YOU HEAR FROM US AFTER TODAY?

Other than having to get together to respond to the other side's use

Form No. 5 Page 3

of the discovery devices we discussed above, several months may go by during which it is not necessary for us to contact you in order to do what we must do to prepare your case.

If we find that we need additional information from you about your case, we will write you. If you secure information in addition to what you have already given us—such as the names of other witnesses or developments in your physical condition resulting from your injury or anything else—please communicate it to us in order that we may serve you to the fullest extent of our ability.

IF YOU MOVE OR CHANGE YOUR ADDRESS, PLEASE INFORM US, AS IT IS NECESSARY THAT WE BE ABLE TO REACH YOU AT ALL TIMES.

SUPPOSE YOU DO NOT HEAR FROM US FOR SEVERAL MONTHS?

It may well occur that months will pass without our having any necessity or occasion to get in touch with you. In that case, do not get the impression that your case is not receiving our interest and attention. In many other states, it takes four or five years for a case to be set for trial. In _____ it takes about _____ for a case to be set and in spite of everything everybody can do, a case is sometimes postponed, and all we can do is to see that we remain prepared so that the delay will not operate to your disadvantage.

One difference between the work of doctors and that of lawyers is this very thing. A doctor is working on your body and you are present when he is rendering his services and can see what he is doing. The work that a lawyer does for you is done in his office or in preliminary stages at the courthouse or other preparatory work when you are absent. For that reason, and because everyone justifiably feels that their case is important, we send you this pamphlet for your information.

SETTLEMENT.

After a case is turned over to a lawyer, it is possible a compromise

Form No. 5 Page 4

settlement can be made. We legally cannot make a settlement, and have no wish to make a settlement, unless it meets with your approval and consent. If you are not satisfied with the settlement offer, you have a right to let the jury decide your case. By the same token, there is no way in which we can make the defendant settle the case. The defendant has a right to a trial if the defendant sees fit not to settle. It is well to have that in mind, because haste and eagerness in a settlement are likely to cheapen the value of your case in the eyes of the defendant.

The intelligent evaluation and settlement of a case calls for legal services of just a high degree of skill as the trial of a lawsuit and often takes as much time if done properly.

THE TRIAL.

If the case has to be tried, do not consider it an ordeal or any reason to be afraid or embarrassed. Your neighbors in this county or district will sit on the jury. If you testify, you will only be asked to tell what you know in a simple straightforward manner. Almost everybody who goes through a trial is agreeably and pleasantly surprised that there was nothing bad about it.

WHAT HAPPENS AFTER THE TRIAL?

If you win your case, the defendant can either pay the verdict or he can make a motion for a new trial and if that is overruled, he can appeal. If you lose, you have the same two remedies. We naturally expect to win your case. We would not have accepted employment to bring your case if we did not think that you had a good case and that you were entitled to win.

MOTION FOR NEW TRIAL.

A motion for a new trial gives the Trial Judge the same chance that an appeal gives to the Supreme Court. The right to grant the losing side a new trial if it is shown that the first trial was not a fair trial, or that legal mistakes were made by the Trial Judge which make it right to grant the loser a new trial.

Many people think that an appeal entitles the loser to a second trial automatically. This is not true.

In many years of largely representing the plaintiff, we have found that this is the information which people usually want to have.

If you have any other questions, please let us hear from you.

PLEASE READ THE FOLLOWING INSTRUCTIONS CAREFULLY

1. TALK TO NO ONE—Please do not talk to anyone outside of your family about your case, unless one of the lawyers or investigators from our office is present. You should always require identification so that you are sure who you are talking to. DO NOT talk to your own insurance company; railroad claim agent; company representative; or any type of agent, attorney or investigator without first notifying our office so we can have these statements taken with one of our lawyers or investigators present. If you have already given a statement of *any kind*—call us *NOW!*

2. YOUR DOCTOR—You should return to each of your doctors as often as they feel it is necessary. You should always report each of your symptoms to them. You should not minimize your ailments to your doctors. A doctor must know these things in order to treat you properly. If you plan to see any additional doctors, please advise us before you see them and tell us their names and addresses.

3. RECORDS—Please Keep Accurate and Detailed Records of the following:

   a. Lost time and wages or income of any sort;
   b. Hospital, doctor, drug and other medical bills;
   c. Other losses directly resulting from your injury;

Form No. 5 Page 6

d. Notes or a diary reflecting the effect of your injury on your daily life; you need only make entries once every week;

e. Any insurance policy that might afford you coverage or protection.

All your bills should be paid by check or you should obtain and keep receipts. The keeping of these records will be very helpful when, a year later, you will be asked by the defense to recall your pain, difficulties, and expenses.

4. REPAIRS—Do not have your automobile, boat, airplane, farm implement, piece of machinery, household item, or other object that was involved in yhour accident repaired until we have had time to examine it; have it photographed; have it examined by an expert or impounded as we feel necessary in order to preserve the evidence as needed for your case. If your case involves a product or instrument not in your control, please try to see that it is not repaired or disposed of until we have photographed it and had it examined by an expert, if necessary.

5. OFFENSES, FINES OR DISCIPLINARY ACTION—Do not appear or give statements before: a traffic court; a coroner's inquest; a Federal Aviation Agency investigating board; a railroad investigating agency; a union investigating agency; a maritime investigating agency; or any other type of disciplinary board, panel or other proceedings without first notifying this office in order that we might have one of the attorneys from this office be with you and represent you at such a hearing. The reason for this is to be sure that you do not prejudice yourself in the action in which we represent you.

6. WITNESSES—IMMEDIATELY furnish us with the correct names, addresses and telephone numbers of any and all witnesses you may learn of. This includes people that know about how your injury has affected you (such as friends, family, neighbors, fellow workers or employees).

Form No. 5 Page 7

If you have any reason to think that a witness may be leaving the area permanently, please call us so we can take their deposition if necessary.

7. EVIDENCE—Please get and give to us or tell us about any photographs pertaining to your case which you or any of your friends have taken. If you are required to be in the hospital and are receiving any type of treatment like traction or physical therapy, please notify our office so that we can have you photographed by our investigator or one of the members of your family. If your injury requires a cast, a brace, traction, or other appliance, save it for evidence in trial. You should notify us that you are keeping these items, and when the case is set for hearing, you should bring these items with you. Please contact your own insurance carrier or company for a copy of all their photographs and investigation in your case.

Please talk to us about *any evidence* that you have or know there whereabouts of that may help us! Save any physical evidence and discuss it with your lawyer or investigator.

8. HOSPITAL AND DOCTOR BILLS—Have your own insurance carrier pay as many hospital and doctor bills as possible. You should also have your hospitalization insurance, such as Blue Cross and Blue Shield, pay as much on your bills as possible. Doctors and hospitals are more co-operative when their bills are paid. You should not expect them to wait until your case is tried or settled to receive payment. You should therefore pay any balance as soon as possible. If any bill remains unpaid, please call us. We will try to get your creditors to hold off until the case is concluded. If you do not call us until they have hired a lawyer or started collection procedure, it may be too late for us to help.

Form No. 5 Page 8

9. YOUR ADDRESS— Be sure to keep us advised of any change in your address or telephone number.

We appreciate the privilege of representing you in your case.

(Name of Attorney/Firm)

By: _____

FORM 6

"MY DAY"

1. *PURPOSE OF "MY DAY"*—We have talked to you about "My Day" when you were in the office. We would like each of you to start making notes separately and not to discuss your final notes with each other. As you go along, you may want to discuss things with each other but things may come up which might embarrass the other party, so we would prefer that you do your final writing of "My Day" in private and then mail it to this office. *It will be kept strictly confidential.*

2. *HOW THESE INJURIES HAVE AFFECTED YOUR LIFE*— We call it "My Day" because we want you to take a normal day, from the time you get up until the time you go to bed, and explain in detail how this occurrence has changed your life. For example, the way you put on your clothes, the way you get in and out of bed, the way you take a bath, etc. By your life, we mean your working life, your playtime, your hobbies, your life as a husband or as a wife, etc. This includes your disposition, your personality, your nervousness, etc. We need to know how it has affected the marital relations between you and your spouse. (The law calls this loss of consortium.)

3. *YOUR PAIN AND SUFFERING*—We want a description of your pain, both at the scene of the occurrence and at all times thereafter. We want to know whether or not it is a shooting pain, throbbing pain, etc. We want your words and not anyone else's. We are interested in your pain during the hospital treatment and your pain and discomfort since the injury. It may be helpful to keep a diary on these matters and also on your "My Day" material regarding how it has affected your life.

4. *START AT YOUR HEAD TO REMEMBER YOUR COM-PLAINTS AND INJURIES*—A good rule to follow in order to remember all of your problems is to start at your head and, in detail, go down through all parts of your body moving from your

Form No. 6 Page 1

head, neck, shoulders, etc., and explain in detail any problems that you have with each part of the body. Also give details with regard to your medication and what it has been for, if you know. For example, medication in the hospital for pain or afterwards for nervousness, etc.

5. *DON'T USE THE WORDS "I CAN'T"*—Please do not use the words "I can't," because can't means physical impossibility. For example, you can't use your left hand, because you haven't got one. But other than this definition of "can't" I think you should stay away from it. Don't say "I can't do it," "I never do it." We would prefer you would use such words as "I am not able to do it as well" or some other words meaning the same thing. You should always work towards the idea that "I am trying and I will continue to try and do more things." Everyone will admire you more if you try. In regard to your activities such as your housework, your yardwork, your work at the office or factory, you should detail things you are able to do and what things you are not able to do as well as before. If your injury seriously hampers your activities, then you should also show how many things you are able to do now.

6. *"MY DAY" WITNESSES*—We would like for you to contact your friends and neighbors, persons at work, etc., and on a separate sheet of paper for each witness give us his name, address and telephone number. Have them describe, or you describe in detail, on a separate sheet of paper what each witness knows about how this injury has changed your life. For example, your neighbor could tell about how you are not able to work as much around the house, or your friends could tell how you don't bowl now, or you don't do some other type of hobby. It is better if these witnesses are not your relatives. It is all right if they are your friends, because they would be more likely to have observed you. Again, please paint word pictures and give details and descriptions of specific instances. *It is impossible to be too detailed.*

7. *LOSS OF WAGES OR LOSS OF POTENTIAL INCOME*—One of the major things in your case may be the loss of income or

Form No. 6 Page 2

potential income. We will need a copy of your union contract showing wage rates, copies of your W-2 forms, and your income tax returns for at least the last five years. Please obtain from your employer the exact days you missed from work because of this accident and the amount of money you would have made if you would have been working these days. If this injury has prevented you from being advanced in your employment or has prevented you from obtaining employment, please give us the names, addresses, and telephone numbers of witnesses who may prove this for you. We would also like to know in detail what services you have been prevented from performing around the house, such as supervision of the children, and all the other services performed either by a husband or a wife.

8. *KEEP A COPY OF YOUR ANSWERS*—Please keep a copy of the answers that you give us in working up your material on "My Day" because this will be helpful to you for the trial, depositions (your sworn statement), and for the answering of interrogatories (answers to questions). If you cannot type, make yourself a copy by using a ball point pen and carbon paper.

9. *QUESTIONS OR HELP IN ANSWERING YOUR "MY DAY"*—If you need help in writing your "My Day," please call this office for an appointment. *Do not come in without an appointment.*

10. *START MAKING NOTES*—The best way to write your "My Day" is to just start, right now, making notes. Then after a few weeks, prepare the copy for us and the copy for yourself. As time goes on prepare additional information and send it in to the office.

11. *USE YOUR IMAGINATION*—*You* know your own life better than we do. Use your imagination and go into all aspects of your life. Explain to us, in the greatest detail possible, how this occurrence has affected your life. Paint a word picture so that we can sell your most important product—*YOU.*

FORM 7

LETTER TO DOCTOR

Client:_____

Address: _____

Date of Accident: _____

Dear Sir:

This is to advise you that we represent the above named patient for an action for personal injuries growing out of an accident on the date indicated.

We will encourage our client to pay your bill personally or by insurance if possible, but in any event we will protect your bill out of any amounts received in trial or settlement. Please mark our name on your records so that you know that we are in the case. It will, therefore, be unnecessary for you to send this matter to any collection agency for collection in the event the client is unable to pay the bill and you have to wait for termination of the litigation.

We are NOT at this time requesting any medical reports from you and please do not send us any unless they are specifically requested in writing.

Please note that the attached medical authorization revokes all prior medical authorizations that have been given by the above patient.

We wish to co-operate with you in every way and if you wish to discuss the medical matters of this case with us at any time, it would be most welcome.

Form No. 7 Page 1

In order to protect your bill, we will need to receive a copy of all your charges relating to this case. Please do not show any amounts paid by insurance or otherwise because we cannot use it in court. **Your bill should include your total charges for services without showing the source of payment.**

Cordially,

Enclosure

FORM 8

REQUEST FOR MEDICAL RECORDS FROM DOCTOR

Client:_____

Address: _____

Date of Accident: _____

Dear Doctor:

Our office represents the above named client for injuries received on the date indicated.

In order to properly handle this matter, we would appreciate receiving from you a detailed medical report setting forth the following:

(a) Patient's history of injury.
(b) Subjective and objective complaints.
(c) Results of your examination.
(d) Interpretation of X-rays or other tests. (Please enclose a copy of the report.)
(e) Treatment rendered the patient.
(f) Diagnosis and prognosis. (Including need for future treatment.)
(g) Copy of reports from other doctors or hospitals.

Also, please send us duplicate copies of your bill for services rendered and keep us advised of future billing or future developments. Please bill us separately for your medical report, and we will pay you promptly. Please bear in mind that this is an expense and must be borne by your patient out of any settlement. **On your bill for medical services please do not show any amounts paid by insurance as we cannot use these in court. Your bill should include your total charges for services without showing the source of payment.**

Form No. 8 Page 1

Enclosed please find Medical Authorization which authorizes us to receive this information. Thank you for your co-operation.

Cordially,

Enclosure

FORM 9

REQUEST FOR HOSPITAL RECORDS

Client:_____

Address: _____

Date of Accident: _____

Gentlemen:

Our office represents the above named client for injuries received on the date indicated.

Please forward to us the items checked below:

☐ Complete photocopies of all hospital records including X-ray reports; summary of charges; operational log, if any; emergency log; medical photographs, if any; all doctors' orders, nurses' notes, etc.; tissue committee report, if any; employees' day sheet showing names of nurses; physical therapy records; all outpatient records.

☐ Copies of all X-ray reports.

☐ Summary or abstract of hospital record.

Also, please send us duplicate copies of your bill for services rendered, and please keep us advised of future billing or future developments. Please bill us separately for your report or photocopy charges. **On your bill for hospital services, please do not show any amounts paid by insurance as we cannot use these in court. Your bill should include your total charges for services without showing the source of payment.**

Form No. 9 Page 1

Enclosed please find Medical Authorization which authorizes us to receive this information. May we thank you for your co-operation.

Cordially,

Enclosure
CC: Patient Accounts

ANNOTATIONS

Treatises

Frumer, et al., Personal Injury—Actions, Defenses, Damages.
Kelner, Successful Litigation Techniques.

Am Jur Trials—Articles

Interviewing the client, 1 AJT 1-92.
Investigating the civil case; general principles, 1 AJT 357-480.
Investigating particular civil actions, 2 AJT 1-170.
Locating and interviewing witnesses, 2 AJT 229-292.

Am Jur Trials—References

Preparation of motorboat accident litigation, 7 AJT 1-120.
Preparation of separate maintenance proceedings, 7 AJT 121-212.
Preparation of contact sports injury cases, 7 AJT 213-278.
Preparation of Miller Act litigation, 7 AJT 279-376.
Preparation of elevator accident cases, 7 AJT 377-476.
Preparation of airline passenger death cases, 8 AJT 173-358.
Preparation of Federal Tort Claims Act proceedings, 8 AJT 635-722.
Preparation of railroad trespasser accident litigation, 9 AJT 245-292.
Preparation of child-pedestrian accident cases, 9 AJT 427-512.
Preparation of exploding bottle litigation, 10 AJT 381 et seq.
Preparation of divider line automobile accident cases, 10 AJT 493 et seq.
Preparation of paternity cases, 10 AJT 653 et seq.
Preparation of uninsured motorist claims, 11 AJT 73 et seq.
Preparation of a blasting damage case, 11 AJT 357 et seq.
Preparation under the Federal Employers' Liability Act, 11 AJT 397 et seq.
Preparation of wrongful death actions, 12 AJT 317 et seq.
Preparation of dram shop litigation, 12 AJT 729 et seq.
Preparation of glass door accident cases, 14 AJT 101 et seq.
Preparation of actions against attorneys for professional negligence, 14 AJT 265 et seq.

Preparation of liquefied petroleum (LP) gas fires and explosion cases, 14 AJT 343 et seq.

Preparation of skiing accident litigation, 15 AJT 147-372

Preparation of attractive nuisance cases, 16 AJT 1-98.

Preparation of drug products liability and malpractice cases, 17 AJT 1-222.

Preparation of hospital emergency room accident cases, 18 AJT 103-340.

Preparation of unwitnessed automobile accident cases, 18 AJT 443-493.

Preparation of medical malpractice—cosmetic surgery cases, 18 AJT 595-753.

Preparation of railroad crossing accident litigation, 23 AJT 1-94.

Am Jur Proof of Facts

Damages, 3 POF 491-770.

Checklist, elements of damages

—personal injury action, 25 POF2d XI.

—survival action, 25 POF2d XIII.

—wrongful death action, 25 POF2d XII.

Maps, Diagrams, and Models, 7 POF 601-616.

Photographs as Evidence, 9 POF 147-223.

Refreshing Recollection, 10 POF 251-280.

Am Jur 2d

Impairment of earning ability: loss of time, and decreased earning capacity, Am Jur, Damages §§ 89-101.

Maps, diagrams, drawings, and models, Am Jur, Evidence §§ 802-805.

Real or demonstrative evidence, Am Jur, Automobiles and Highway Traffic §§ 974-980.

ALR Annotations

Admissibility, in civil motor vehicle accident case, of evidence that driver was or was not involved in previous accidents, 20 ALR2d 1210.

Refreshing recollection of witness by use of memorandum or other writings, 82 ALR2d 473.

Hospital records as evidence of facts as to cause of injury, 44 ALR2d 556.

Admissibility of aerial photographs 57ALR2d 1351.

Admissibility, under Rule 803(8)(c) of Federal Rules of Evidence, of "factual findings resulting from investigation made pursuant to authority granted by law," 47 ALR Fed. 321.

Other Aids

Handling Accident Cases, by Albert Averbach, vol 1, chs 2-4.

Cyclopedia of Trial Practice, by Sidney C. Schweitzer, vol 1, §§ 2, 3, 8-22, 28-30.

Chapter 2

ANALYSIS OF THE CASE

INTRODUCTION

After gathering the facts, plaintiff's counsel must then determine the following:

(a) Whether the facts support an actionable case;

(b) Whether basic procedural requirements can be satisfied; and

(c) What counsel may anticipate in the way of a defense(s).

These matters are considered in this chapter in a general fashion rather than in the context of any particular case and from an elementary perspective rather than in great detail. The reader may find it useful to consult this chapter from time to time as a "checklist."

Counsel for plaintiff should make a *prompt* and *thorough* analysis of both the substantive and procedural law applicable to the case he is considering filing. It could be a mistake to postpone this analysis until *after* the complaint has been drafted and served and issue has been joined. Many potential substantive and procedural pitfalls may be avoided by adopting the correct approach in the beginning. Without early analysis, counsel may first learn that he does not have a case after he has invested substantial time and effort in handling the file.[1] Even more tragically,

---

[1] As discussed in chapter one, should counsel's investigation and analysis reveal that the case is not meritorious, the client should be so advised as soon as possible.

he may learn of some procedural or jurisdictional flaw too late to correct it. Early analysis of the case will always be in the best interests of the client, the attorney, and the courts.

This chapter highlights in outline form the main points of substantive and procedural law which typically apply to personal injury actions. Obviously, a complete summary of the law in each state is beyond the scope of this chapter. Nonetheless, it is hoped that the attorney who is consulted concerning a tort case will find the outlines contained in this chapter of value. Such a review may stimulate him to think of additional remedies appropriate to the particular facts, remind him of basic procedural requirements which he must meet, or alert him to a potential defense which he might otherwise have overlooked.

The materials in this chapter are grouped into three parts. The first lists typical theories of liability applicable in tort cases. This section is in turn divided under ten basic headings. Special attention is given to statutes which give rise to tort cases or otherwise affect them. The second part approaches the question of liability by considering the basic fact situations plaintiff's counsel may encounter (for instance, motor vehicle accidents, products liability, premises injuries, etc.). The third part concerns the fundamental procedural requirements for initiating an action. The fourth lists a number of the commonly asserted defenses to tort actions.

ANALYSIS BY THEORIES OF LIABILITY

The grounds of legal recovery which may support a claim for personal injuries include at least the following ten categories:

A. Negligence (simple or gross).

   The usual elements of a negligence case are

   1. A duty owed by the defendant;

   2. A breach of that duty by defendant's act or omission, creating an unreasonable risk of harm (that is, a deviation from the reasonable standard of care); and

   3. Injury or damage to the plaintiff as a consequence of the defendant's breach.

In negligence cases against professionals, the legal standard of care may be determined by reference to the activities of like practitioners.

The legal definition of the causal relationship which must be shown to exist between the defendant's breach of his duty and the plaintiff's damages varies tremendously from state to state.

Counsel should be aware of the possibility of a derivative action; e.g., secondary injury to person related to plaintiff, such as spouse's action for consortium, parent's action for medical expenses for injured child. In identifying the potential defendants in a negligence action, counsel should consider the doctrine of *respondeat superior* (liability for acts of servants), negligent entrustment, and the doctrine of imputed negligence.

In determining the proof requirements of a negligence action, counsel should consider the application of the doctrine of *res ipsa loquitur,* sometimes used as a substitute for proof of fault.

The defendant's duty may arise from

1. The relationship between the parties;
2. A contract;
3. An undertaking on the defendant's part; or,
4. An applicable statute, regulation or ordinance. (See paragraph J.)

B. Wilful or Wanton Misconduct.

This may be an essential basis for actions under Guest Statutes and for claims for punitive damages.

C. Nuisance.
1. Public.
2. Private.

D. Breach of Warranty (U.S.C. and/or Common Law).
1. Express.

    2. Implied.

       a. Merchantability.

       b. Particular purpose.

       c. Habitability.

E . Strict Liability.

    1. Products liability.

       a. Strict tort, privity-free liability.

       b. Action for breach of express or implied warranty.

    2. Ultrahazardous or abnormal activities

    E.g., water, fire, electricity, gas, pesticides, blasting, nuclear explosions. The defendant's duty regarding such activities may be non-delegable.

    3. Animals.

    4. Admiralty.

    5. Statutory duty.

F. Defamation.

    1. Libel.

    2. Slander.

G. Fraud, Deceit, and Misrepresentation.

    1. Intentional.

    2. Negligent.

    3. Innocent. (E.g., *Restatement (Second), Torts* §402 B)

H. Other Intentional Acts.

    1. Assault and battery.

    2. False arrest and imprisonment.

    3. Malicious prosecution.

    4. Abuse of process.

    5. Alienation of affections, criminal conversation, and breach of promise (where not banned).

    6. Invasion of the right of privacy.

7. Intentional or reckless infliction of mental suffering.

8. Trespassing.

9. Outrage: Prima Facie Tort; Bad Faith.

I. Breach of Contract.

   1. Direct beneficiary.

   2. Third party beneficiary.

The existence and requirements of a contract between the plaintiff and the defendant may be implied from the relationship between the parties and/or the circumstances.

J. The Effect of a Statute, Regulation, or Ordinance.

Depending on the law of the forum, an applicable statute, regulation, or ordinance may have any of the following legal effects:

   1. It may give rise to or define the scope of the defendant's duty.

   2. Its violation may be merely admissible as evidence of "fault" or "liability."

   3. Its violation may constitute "negligence *per se*" or make out a *prima facie* case standing alone.

   4. It may create an independent cause of action.

The following list considers only the last effect:

   a. Wrongful death statutes.

   b. Survival statutes (the personal injury action that survives the death of the plaintiff).

   c. Worker's Compensation Acts (plus occupational disease statutes).

   d. Death on High Seas Act, 46 U.S.C. §§ 761-768.

   e. Longshoremen's and Harbor Worker's Compensation Act, 33 U.S.C. § 901 et seq.

   f. Jones Act, 46 U.S.C. § 688 (seamen).

   g. Federal Employee's Compensation Act, 5 U.S.C. § 751 et seq.

   h. Federal Employers' Liability Act, 45 U.S.C. § 51 et seq. (railroad employees).

i. Federal Safety Appliance Act, 45 U.S.C. § 1 et seq. (railroad employees).

j. Boiler Inspection Act, 45 U.S.C. §§ 22 to 23, 28 to 34 (railroad employees).

k. Federal Tort Claims Act, 28 U.S.C. 1291, 1346, 1402, 1504, 2110, 2401, 2402, 2411, 2412, 2671 et seq., and comparable state laws (claims against governmental units).

l. Federal Civil Rights Act, 42 U.S.C. 1981 et seq., and comparable state laws.

m. Dram Shop Acts (liability of tavern for acts of intoxicated patron); also imposed by common law.

n. Safe Place to Work Acts, Scaffold Acts, and other legislation for the benefit of workers.

o. Consumer Product Warranty Act, 15 U.S.C. § 2301 et seq.

p. Direct Action Statutes (allowing suit directly against the defendant's liability insurance company).

q. Counsel should check for state legislation dealing with malpractice, products, and claims arising from automobile accidents (e.g., no fault statute).

Regarding Third-Party Actions and Insurance Actions. Note that the term "third party" action is used for a number of situations, including (1) the action that a worker who is eligible for workmen's compensation from his employer can bring against a party other than his employer who contributed to the causing of his injuries or (2) the action by a defendant who has been held legally responsible against a party who he believes should bear all or a portion of the responsibility.

Third party actions and insurance actions may involve the following:

1. Indemnity (total responsibility of another party to defendant). The right of indemnity may arise from an express or implied contract.

2. Contribution (sharing of liability based on proportionate share of fault or based upon number of defendants).

3. Subrogation (insurer's suit on insured's cause of action).

4. Actions by an insured under life, accident, health, and disability policies.

5. Insurer's liability for failure to inspect properly.

6. Liability of defendant's insurance carrier for payment of judgments which exceed the limits of the defendant's coverage for failing to settle within the limits of the defendant's coverage.

7. Uninsured motorist coverage, Under-Insured Motorists and Unsatisfied Judgment Fund Act.

ANALYSIS BY BASIC FACT SITUATION

Some of the common fact patterns encountered in a tort practice include the following:

A. Vehicles and Transportation.

    1. Private vehicles cases. Counsel should check for special problems with Guest Statutes.

    2. Owner's and/or lessor's responsibilities for the acts of the operator.

    3. Passengers and pedestrians.

    4. Taxis, buses, and other common carriers.

    5. Aircraft.

       a. Commercial.

       b. General.

       c. Military.

    6. Railroads.

       a. Passengers.

       b. Crossing accidents.

       c. Injured workers (statutes relating to workers considered in Parts J.4.h-j above).

B. Premises (Occupiers).

    1. Owner and occupier.

Historically, the defendant's duty will vary according to the classification of the plaintiff's status on the property, viz., trespasser, licensee, or invitee. However, there seems to be somewhat of a trend to abandon distinctions in duties based upon the plaintiff's status and substitute a general duty to use reasonable care under the circumstances. Check for local statutes as they may alter or affect the common law liability of the occupier of land.

    2. Landlord and tenant.

Local statutes may govern or affect the landlord's liability to the tenant for injuries arising from the condition or use of the premises.

    3. Child trespassers.

        a. "Attractive nuisance" doctrine.

        b. "Dangerous instrumentality" doctrine.

    4. Special responsibilities to firemen and policemen.

    5. Injury to persons who have a "right of entry."

    6. Special duties of innkeepers, hospitals, nursing homes, etc.

    7. Liability to abutting owners.

    8. Liability for conditions or activities conducted on premises that injure people off the premises.

C. Contractors and Construction Cases.

Local statutes including but not limited to Workers Compensation Statutes may alter or affect the defendant's liability in a construction case.

    1. Owner's responsibilities.

    2. General and special contractors or subcontractors.

    3. Independent contractors.

    4. Responsibilities to workers and to the public, on and off premises.

5. Design and construction of buildings, viz., the architect's and/or engineer's responsibilities.

6. Statutes requiring a safe place for workers.

D. Products.

Federal and state statutes may alter or affect the common law liability of a defendant in a products case.

1. Potentially culpable activity/omission.

    a. Design (including crashworthiness).

    b. Manufacture/assembly.

    c. Quality control, e.g., inspection and/or testing.

    d. Packaging/labelling/shipment.

    e. Marketing or selling a dangerous product.

    f. Failure to warn.

    g. Instructions for use or maintenance.

    h. Guarantor of quality or performance.

    i. Violation of statute, regulation, ordinance, or standard.

2. Potentially culpable defendants.

    a. Provider of design specifications.

    b. Designer of component or finished product.

    c. Supplier of raw materials.

    d. Manufacturer of basic materials, component part(s), or finished product.

    e. Seller of component part(s) or finished product.

    f. Assembler of component or finished product.

    g. Party responsible for testing and/or inspection (government agency?).

    h. Party responsible for warning and/or instructions for use/maintenance (government agency?).

    i. Author of advertising or marketing literature.

    j. Party responsible for certifying quality and/or performance.

      k. Party responsible for maintenance and/or repair.

      l. Enterprise liability.

E. Malpractice.

    1. Doctors, lawyers, accountants, psychologists, nurses, engineers, etc. Check for local statutes as they may alter or affect the defendant's liability in a malpractice case.

    2. Departure from the standard of care set by like practitioners.

    3. "Captain of the ship" doctrine; *respondeat superior.*

    4. Duty to obtain an informed consent.

    5. In legal malpractice, proof of "case within a case."

F. Aviation Accidents.

    1. Domestic or international transportation (Warsaw Convention).

    2. Airline or general aviation (standard of care).

    3. United States government responsibility for air traffic control and certification of aircraft and crew.

    4. Product liability of aircraft manufacturers.

    5. Responsibilities of airports and fixed base operators.

    6. Federal Aviation Act of 1958, 49 U.S.C. § 1301 et seq. Many states have adopted similar acts.

    7. Federal Aviation Regulations, 14 C.F.R. 1 et seq.

    8. National Transportation Safety Board, Bureau of Aviation Safety, 14 C.F.R. 400 et seq.

G. Admiralty.

    1. Jones Act, 46 U.S.C. § 688 (injuries to seamen or members of crew; based on negligence or unseaworthiness).

    2. Duty of maintenance and cure (common law duty to seamen).

    3. Death on the High Seas Act, 46 U.S.C. § 761, 768 (wrongful death action, in admiralty court).

    4. Longshoremen and Harbor Workers' Act, 33 U.S.C. § 901 et seq.

5. Seaworthiness doctrine (common law responsibility in admiralty to longshoremen and persons doing traditional work of ship's crew).

6. "Twilight doctrine" (consequence of overlapping remedies). See Admiralty Jurisdiction Act, 46 U.S.C. § 740.

7. Ship disasters, collisions, etc. (limitations of liability to value of hull, etc.).

8. Pleasure boats. See Boat Safety Act, 46 U.S.C. § 901 et seq.

9. Ports and Waterways Safety Act, 33 U.S.C. §§ 1221-1227; 46 U.S.C. § 391(a).

H. Sports and Athletic Suits.

1. Actions by participants, spectators.

2. Defenses based upon assumption of risk, contributory fault.

3. Liability of players for intentional torts to other players; liability of manufacturers and lessors of equipment; liability of operators of ski slopes.

I. Toxic Torts.

1. Proof of exposure to and injury by pollutants or other chemicals or radiation sources in the air, water, or land. Counsel should check the numerous federal and state statutes in this area.

2. Latent appearance of injuries and effect upon statute of limitations.

3. Actions based upon product liability, negligence, trespass, nuisance.

J. Governmental Bodies.

1. Federal, state, municipal, or other subdivisions; agencies and commissions; governmental-proprietary distinctions. Special statutes may govern defendant's liability.

2. Schools, hospitals, waterworks, police and firemen, traffic control, public transit, streets and sidewalks.

3. Immunities and effect of insurance.

4. Short period for notice of claim. Note: it is essential for counsel to determine which body is responsible for the service or

facility involved; what time period applies for serving a claim and starting suit; and how the notice of claim is to be made and delivered.

5. Moral claims procedures; special legislative bills for relief.

6. Actions against the U.S. other than under the Federal Tort Claims Act, 28 U.S.C. §§ 1291, 1346, 1402, 1504, 2110, 2401, 2402, 2411, 2412, 2671, et seq.

7. Actions against individuals and/or governmental bodies who violate plaintiff's constitutional rights.

K. Familial Torts and Responsibility.

1. Actions between spouses, child-parent, and other family relations; immunities.

2. Derivative action for loss of services, consortium, and medical expenses.

3. Parental responsibility statutes.

L. Special Plaintiffs.

1. Prenatal injuries; live and still births, concept of viability.

2. Preconception torts (mutagenic substances).

3. Actions for wrongful life.

4. Actions by persons who suffer emotional injuries as a consequence of injury or death of member of family.

5. Incompetent plaintiff.

6. "You take your plaintiff the way you find him"; idiosyncracy, allergy, aggravation of or precipitation of diseases or preexistent injury.

7. Wrongfully fired employees.

ANALYSIS OF PROCEDURAL REQUIREMENTS

Before counsel can properly commence suit, he should give careful consideration to the procedural requirements of the case and make important choices as to theories of law, choice of law, parties, and forum.

A. Choice of Law.

    1. Conflicts of laws rules of the state; place of wrong versus "contacts" or "center of gravity" test.

    2. Substantive versus procedural characterization by court.

    3. "Erie rule" in federal diversity cases.

B. Jurisdiction.

    1. Over the subject matter. In federal court, a minimum jurisdictional amount in controversy and diversity of citizenship is essential or federal question, 28 U.S.C. §§ 1331-32.

    2. Over the "person," viz., proper service; longarm statutes; attachments; publication.

    3. Pendant jurisdiction theory in federal courts.

C. Venue, *Forum Non Conveniens.*

    1. Federal venue requirements, 28 U.S.C. § 1391 et seq.

    2. Dismissal on *forum non conveniens* (inconvenient forum in which to try case), in state courts, or transfer within state.

    3. In federal courts, transfer by change of venue, 28 U.S.C. § 1441.

D. Choice of Forum.

    1. Federal versus state.

    2. Defendant's right to remove case to federal court.

    3. Inferior court versus one of general jurisdiction.

    4. Factors in choosing between courts and states: applicable laws, periods of limitations, types of jurors, judges.

E. Jury.

    1. Under federal rules, demand at time of filing complaint or removal, FED. R. CIV. P. 38.

    2. No jury in Federal Tort Claims Act and admiralty cases.

F. Prior Events in the Case.

    1. *Res judicata.*

    2. Collateral estoppel (mutuality not required).

3. "Law of the case" (prior legal decisions of rulings in same litigation).

4. Prior dismissals; "two dismissal rule" in federal courts, FED.R. CIV. P. 41; dismissal with or without prejudice.

5. Survival and abatement of actions (effect of death of party).

6. Releases and covenants not to sue.

7. Subrogation and intervention.

G. Statute of Limitations.

1. Ascertain the statutes applicable to the cause or causes of action.

2. Ascertain the time the cause of action accrued.

3. Tolling devices (extending the time for the running of the statute).

4. Estoppel to assert.

5. Saving statutes (refiling after dismissal).

6. Laches in cases in equity.

H. Multiple Plaintiffs and Defendants

1. Class actions, FED. R. CIV. P. 23.

2. Multi-district Litigation (MDL), 28 U.S.C. § 1407.

3. Collateral estoppel; enterprise liability.

4. Consolidation within districts.

5. Voluntary co-operation.

ANALYSIS OF POTENTIAL DEFENSES

The following is a selective list of defenses which may be available to the defendant in a personal injury case. Counsel must check local case law and local legislation for a complete and accurate list of potential defenses.

A. Defenses which negate the plaintiff's burden of proof.

1. Wrongful defendant.

2. The defendant is immune from liability.

    a. Statute.

    b. Contract.

3. The defendant has no duty.

4. The defendant did not breach his duty; E.g.:

    a. Exercised due care.

    b. Compliance with custom.

    c. Compliance with applicable statute, regulation, standard.

    d. Compliance with the state of the art; i.e., "unavoidably unsafe."

5. The defendant's acts or omissions did not cause the incident or the plaintiff's injury; e.g.:

    a. Incident not foreseeable.

    b. Subsequent change in condition of product or premises.

    c. Intervening and superseding cause.

    d. The incident was unavoidable or inevitable.

    e. "Act of God."

B. Affirmative Defenses.

    1. Contributory or comparative "fault."

        a. Plaintiff's own.

        b. Imputed.

    2. Assumption of risk.

    3. Open and obvious.

    4. Misuse.

    5. Special statutory defenses.

C. Defenses to Damages.

    1. Liquidated/limited.

    2. Plaintiff's duty to minimize.

    3. Apportionment.

    4. Contribution.

    5. Comparative fault.

6. Release.
7. Set-off/recoupment.
8. Prepayment.
9. Collateral service.
10. Speculative.
11. Not within contemplation of parties.
12. Reduction to present worth.
13. Pre-existent condition.
14. Subsequently occurring incident.

Chapter 3

BASIC MEDICAL ANATOMY

Throughout a lawyer's career, but most particularly during the early years of practice, the medical aspects of a personal injury case can be frightening. Few law schools treat the medical considerations of personal injury law in depth. The basic thrust of tort courses is directed towards theories of liability and defense: this is as it must be, for all the medical knowledge in the world will be to no avail without a basic knowledge of the law of torts. Nevertheless, a significant percentage of the professional life of any personal injury lawyer is spent conferring with doctors, reading medical reports and hospital records, taking medical depositions, and considering, either for settlement or trial purposes, the implications of bodily injuries. Further, to represent an injured client effectively the lawyer must be able to empathize. To do so, counsel must understand the effects of an injury upon an individual; he must understand the workings of a tremendously complex structure, the human body. With some concentrated effort, the young attorney can learn enough about anatomy and the principal functions of various tissues, organs, and systems to enable him to understand medical records and to communicate with doctors. Mastery of the four systems considered in this chapter—skeletal, muscular, nervous, and circulatory—will enable counsel to handle effectively most of his personal injury cases

91

Of necessity, the study of the human body requires a fractionalized approach, that is, a study of its basic units and the various systems independently. A complete understanding of the effects of injury upon the body, however, will come only with the realization that the body is a single and interworking whole. Thus, trauma is inflicted not upon a single cell, tissue, organ, or system, but rather upon an integrated, functioning whole person.

Medical terminology presents a formidable psychological barrier to many young attorneys; nonetheless, a basic medical vocabulary is not difficult to acquire. Medical terms are derived mainly from Greek and Latin. In learning a relatively small number of roots, suffixes, and prefixes, the attorney can acquire a basic understanding of medical terms. For example, the root for nerve is "neur" and the suffix, "itis," means inflammation. Thus the term "neuritis" means inflammation of a nerve.

A facet of the medical language which must be mastered at the outset is the terminology related to the positions, directions, and movements of the body. The following describe positions:
1. Anterior—front.
   Posterior—back.
2. Ventral—front.
   Dorsal—back.
3. Lateral—away from the midline.
   Medial—toward the midline.
4. Proximal—toward the source.
   Distal—away from the source.
5. Cranial—toward the head.
   Caudal—toward the tail.
6. Superior—above.
7. Inferior—below.

The following describe movements:
1. Abduction—away from the center of the body.
   Adduction—toward the center of the body.
2. Flexion—bending of a joint.
   Extension—straightening of a joint.
3. Supination—turning upward.
   Pronation—turning downward.

4. Eversion—turning outward.
Inversion—turning inward.

"Anatomical planes" identify "views" of the body. The more common anatomical planes include:

1. Frontal — a section to the side of the body, passing at right angles to the median plane. This divides the body into anterior and posterior portions.

2. Median or Midline — an imaginary plane which passes from the front to the back through the center of the body, dividing the body into right and left equal portions.

3. Sagittal — a section parallel to the long axis of the body or parallel to the median plane, dividing the body into right and left unequal parts.

4. Transverse — a horizontal plane, passing at right angles to both the frontal and median planes, dividing the body into cranial and caudal parts.

Some anatomical postures to which physicians frequently refer are as follows:

1. Erect — the body is in a standing position.

2. Supine — the body is lying flat on the back.

3. Prone — the body is lying face and trunk down.

4. Laterally recumbant — the body is lying horizontally, either on the right or left side.

BASIC UNITS OF THE BODY

The human body is made up of four basic units: cells, tissues, organs, and systems. Cells are the building blocks of the body; they are the fundamental unit of the body and are not of immediate importance to the trial lawyer. Tissues consist of a collection of cells which are similar in structure and function. The primary tissues are the following:

1. Epithelial — these cover internal and external surfaces of the body.

2. Connective — these hold organs in place and bind all parts of the body together.

3. Muscular — these largely carry out activities of motion.

4. Nervous — these are the most highly specialized in the body; they convey impulses from and to the central nervous system.

Organs consist of different types of tissue which combine to perform a specific physiological task; e.g., the liver, the heart, lungs, pancreas, etc. Organs do not operate independently; they operate within the framework of systems. Systems are groupings of organs which perform specific functions. The body may be divided into ten basic systems:

1. Skeletal.
2. Muscular.
3. Nervous.
4. Cardiovascular.
5. Lymphatic.
6. Gastrointestinal.
7. Genitourinary.
8. Respiratory.
9. Endocrine.
10. Integumentary.

The majority of injuries with which the trial lawyer will deal have their primary effect upon one, or all, of the first four systems.

SKELETAL SYSTEM

A. General Considerations. The skeletal system makes movement possible. This system is made up of some 200 bones and connective fibers. The purpose of the skeletal system is to give support and shape to the body (see Fig. 1) and provide attachment points for bones, muscles, and ligaments.

B. Anatomical Classification of Skeletal System.
   1. The axial skeleton is comprised of those bones lying near the midline of the body, such as the skull and spinal column.
   2. The appendicular skeleton is comprised of those bones which support the limbs.

C. Major Bones. An attorney should be familiar with the following portions of the skeletal systems:
   1. The Skull. (See Fig. 2.)
      (a) Frontal.
      (b) Temporal.
      (c) Parietal.
      (d) Occipital.
      (e) Maxilla.
      (f) Mandible.

SKELETAL System

NOTE: For additional details of skeletal structures, refer to the regional sections in Vols. 1 - 8.

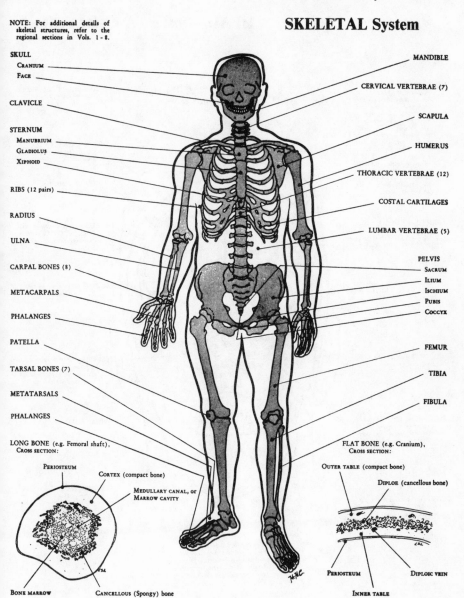

SKULL
  CRANIUM
  FACE

CLAVICLE

STERNUM
  MANUBRIUM
  GLADIOLUS
  XIPHOID

RIBS (12 pairs)

RADIUS

ULNA

CARPAL BONES (8)

METACARPALS

PHALANGES

PATELLA

TARSAL BONES (7)

METATARSALS

PHALANGES

MANDIBLE

CERVICAL VERTEBRAE (7)

SCAPULA

HUMERUS

THORACIC VERTEBRAE (12)

COSTAL CARTILAGES

LUMBAR VERTEBRAE (5)

PELVIS
  SACRUM
  ILIUM
  ISCHIUM
  PUBIS
  COCCYX

FEMUR

TIBIA

FIBULA

LONG BONE (e.g. Femoral shaft),
  CROSS SECTION:

PERIOSTEUM

CORTEX (compact bone)

MEDULLARY CANAL, or
MARROW cavity

BONE MARROW

CANCELLOUS (Spongy) bone

FLAT BONE (e.g. Cranium),
  CROSS SECTION:

OUTER TABLE (compact bone)

DIPLOE (cancellous bone)

PERIOSTEUM

DIPLOIC VEIN

INNER TABLE

© *Berkeley Press* 1964

THE SKELETON
Figure 1

HEAD—Postero-Anterior Series

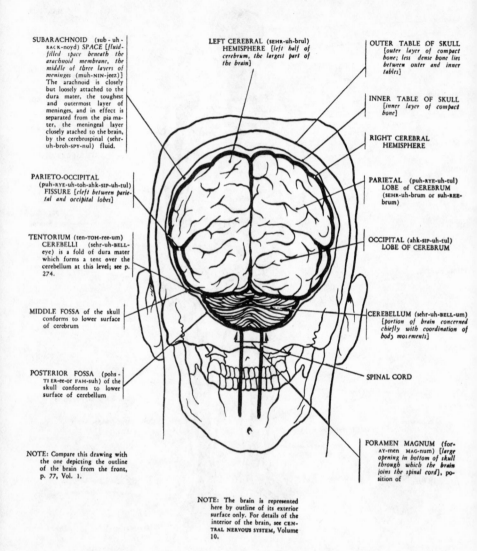

SUBARACHNOID (sub - uh - RACK-noyd) SPACE [fluid-filled space beneath the arachnoid membrane, the middle of three layers of meninges (muh-NIN-jeez)] The arachnoid is closely but loosely attached to the dura mater, the toughest and outermost layer of meninges, and in effect is separated from the pia mater, the meningeal layer closely atached to the brain, by the cerebrospinal (sehr-uh-broh-SPY-nul) fluid.

PARIETO-OCCIPITAL (puh-RYE-uh-toh-ahk-SIP-uh-tul) FISSURE [cleft between parietal and occipital lobes]

TENTORIUM (ten-TOH-ree-um) CEREBELLI (sehr-uh-BELL-eye) is a fold of dura mater which forms a tent over the cerebellum at this level; see p. 274.

MIDDLE FOSSA of the skull conforms to lower surface of cerebrum

POSTERIOR FOSSA (pohs - TI ER-ee-or FAH-suh) of the skull conforms to lower surface of cerebellum

LEFT CEREBRAL (SEHR-uh-brul) HEMISPHERE [left half of cerebrum, the largest part of the brain]

OUTER TABLE OF SKULL [outer layer of compact bone; less dense bone lies between outer and inner tables]

INNER TABLE OF SKULL [inner layer of compact bone]

RIGHT CEREBRAL HEMISPHERE

PARIETAL (puh-RYE-uh-tul) LOBE of CEREBRUM (SEHR-uh-brum or suh-REE-brum)

OCCIPITAL (ahk-SIP-uh-tul) LOBE OF CEREBRUM

CEREBELLUM (sehr-uh-BELL-um) [portion of brain concerned chiefly with coordination of body movements]

SPINAL CORD

FORAMEN MAGNUM (for-AY-men MAG-num) [large opening in bottom of skull through which the brain joins the spinal cord], position of

NOTE: Compare this drawing with the one depicting the outline of the brain from the front, p. 77, Vol. 1.

NOTE: The brain is represented here by outline of its exterior surface only. For details of the interior of the brain, see CENTRAL NERVOUS SYSTEM, Volume 10.

BRAIN, RELATIONSHIP TO SKULL—Anatomy
Figure 2

2. Vertebral Column and Associated Structures. (See Figs. 3, 4, and 5.) The importance of understanding the basic anatomy of the vertebral column and its associated structures cannot be over-emphasized. There are three major areas of the vertebral column: the cervical area, the thoracic or dorsal area, and the lumbar area. The bony structures which make up the vertebral column are known as vertebrae.

The cervical area contains seven vertebrae. The first of these is termed the "atlas." This structure supports the skull. The second cervical vertebra is called the "axis." This provides a point of rotation of the skull on the neck. The thoracic or dorsal area of the vertebral column is made up of twelve vertebrae. The lumbar area has five vertebrae. It is the lumbar area which is responsible for carrying most of the weight of the trunk. Immediately below the lumbar area is the sacrum. This structure consists of five fused vertebrae. Immediately below the sacrum is the coccyx, or "tail bone."

Between each pair of vertebrae there is an intervertebral disc. Anatomically, the outer portion of the disc, or the annulus fibrosus, is made up of cartilaginous substance. Within the annulus fibrosus is a jelly-like substance known as the nucleus pulposus. Functionally, intervertebral discs serve a highly important, cushioning purpose.

3. Upper Trunk. The ribs are made up of twelve pairs of flat curved bones which are attached posteriorly to the thoracic portion of the vertebral column. Anteriorly the first seven pairs are attached to the sternum, the broad flat bone located in the midline of the chest (the "breast bone"). The eighth, ninth, and tenth ribs are joined to the cartilage of the seventh rib. The eleventh and twelfth are unattached anteriorly and are the so called "floating ribs." Basically, the ribs, plus the sternum, comprise the thoracic cage. This bony structure protects the vital organs of the chest and makes possible the movement which permits expansion and contraction in inhalation and exhalation.

4. Upper Extremities.
   (a) Clavicle, the collar bone.
   (b) Scapula, the shoulder blade.

BACK—Postero-Anterior Series

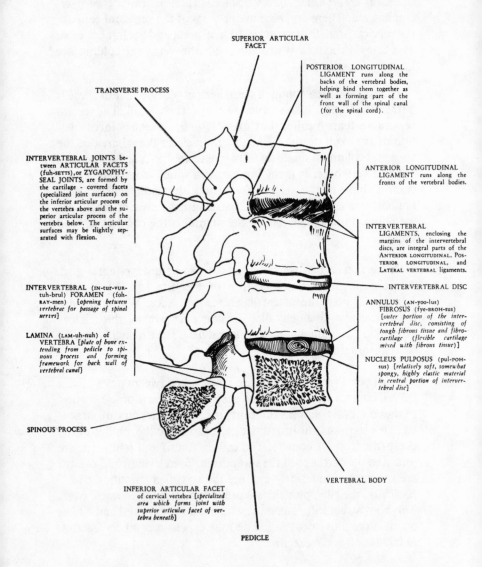

SUPERIOR ARTICULAR
FACET

POSTERIOR LONGITUDINAL
LIGAMENT runs along the
backs of the vertebral bodies,
helping bind them together as
well as forming part of the
front wall of the spinal canal
(for the spinal cord).

TRANSVERSE PROCESS

INTERVERTEBRAL JOINTS be-
tween ARTICULAR FACETS
(fuh-SETTS), or ZYGAPOPHY-
SEAL JOINTS, are formed by
the cartilage - covered facets
(specialized joint surfaces) on
the inferior articular process of
the vertebra above and the superior articular process of the
vertebra below. The articular
surfaces may be slightly separated with flexion.

ANTERIOR LONGITUDINAL
LIGAMENT runs along the
fronts of the vertebral bodies.

INTERVERTEBRAL
LIGAMENTS, enclosing the
margins of the intervertebral
discs, are integral parts of the
ANTERIOR LONGITUDINAL, POS-
TERIOR LONGITUDINAL, and
LATERAL VERTEBRAL ligaments.

INTERVERTEBRAL DISC

INTERVERTEBRAL (IN-tur-VUR-
tuh-brul) FORAMEN (foh-
RAY-men) [opening between
vertebrae for passage of spinal
nerves]

ANNULUS (AN-yoo-lus)
FIBROSUS (fye-BROH-sus)
[outer portion of the intervertebral disc, consisting of
tough fibrous tissue and fibrocartilage (flexible cartilage
mixed with fibrous tissue)]

LAMINA (LAM-uh-nuh) of
VERTEBRA [plate of bone extending from pedicle to spinous process and forming
framework for back wall of
vertebral canal]

NUCLEUS PULPOSUS (pul-POH-
sus) [relatively soft, somewhat
spongy, highly elastic material
in central portion of intervertebral disc]

SPINOUS PROCESS

VERTEBRAL BODY

INFERIOR ARTICULAR FACET
of cervical vertebra [specialized
area which forms joint with
superior articular facet of vertebra beneath]

PEDICLE

INTERVERTERBRAL DISCS—Anatomy
Figure 3

BACK—Postero-Anterior Series

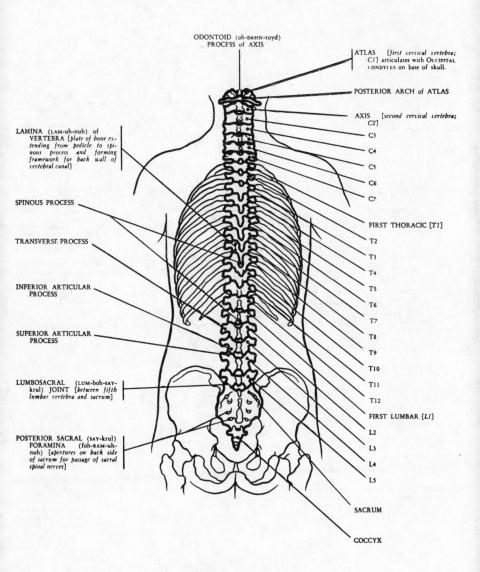

ODONTOID (oh-DAHN-toyd) PROCESS of AXIS

ATLAS [*first cervical vertebra; C1*] articulates with OCCIPITAL CONDYLES on base of skull.

POSTERIOR ARCH of ATLAS

AXIS [*second cervical vertebra; C2*]

C3

C4

C5

C6

C7

LAMINA (LAM-uh-nuh) of VERTEBRA [*plate of bone extending from pedicle to spinous process and forming framework for back wall of vertebral canal*]

SPINOUS PROCESS

TRANSVERSE PROCESS

INFERIOR ARTICULAR PROCESS

SUPERIOR ARTICULAR PROCESS

LUMBOSACRAL (LUM-boh-SAY-krul) JOINT [*between fifth lumbar vertebra and sacrum*]

POSTERIOR SACRAL (SAY-krul) FORAMINA (foh-RAM-uh-nuh) [*apertures on back side of sacrum for passage of sacral spinal nerves*]

FIRST THORACIC [*T1*]

T2

T3

T4

T5

T6

T7

T8

T9

T10

T11

T12

FIRST LUMBAR [*L1*]

L2

L3

L4

L5

SACRUM

COCCYX

VERTEBRAE—Anatomy 1
Figure 4

NECK—Lateral Series

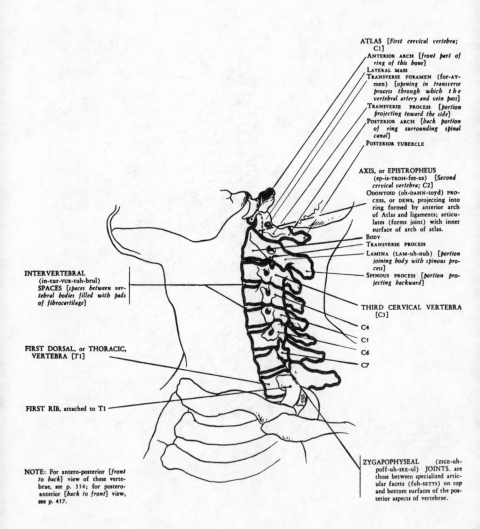

ATLAS [*First cervical vertebra;* C1]
ANTERIOR ARCH [*front part of ring of this bone*]
LATERAL MASS
TRANSVERSE FORAMEN (for-AY-men) [*opening in transverse process through which the vertebral artery and vein pass*]
TRANSVERSE PROCESS [*portion projecting toward the side*]
POSTERIOR ARCH [*back portion of ring surrounding spinal canal*]
POSTERIOR TUBERCLE

AXIS, or EPISTROPHEUS (ep-is-TROH-fee-us) [*Second cervical vertebra;* C2]
ODONTOID (oh-DAHN-toyd) PROCESS, or DENS, projecting into ring formed by anterior arch of Atlas and ligaments; articulates (forms joint) with inner surface of arch of atlas.
BODY
TRANSVERSE PROCESS
LAMINA (LAM-uh-nuh) [*portion joining body with spinous process*]
SPINOUS PROCESS [*portion projecting backward*]

THIRD CERVICAL VERTEBRA [C3]

C4
C5
C6
C7

INTERVERTEBRAL (in-tur-VUR-tuh-brul) SPACES [*spaces between vertebral bodies filled with pads of fibrocartilage*]

FIRST DORSAL, or THORACIC, VERTEBRA [T1]

FIRST RIB, attached to T1

ZYGAPOPHYSEAL (ZIGE-uh-poff-uh-SEE-ul) JOINTS. are those between specialized articular facets (fuh-SETTS) on top and bottom surfaces of the posterior aspects of vertebrae.

NOTE: For antero-posterior [*front to back*] view of these vertebrae, see p. 354; for postero-anterior [*back to front*] view, see p. 457.

VERTEBRAE—Anatomy 1
Figure 5

(c) Humerus, the upper arm bone.

(d) Ulna and Radius, bones of the lower arm.

(e) Carpals, eight wrist bones.

(f) Metacarpals, bones of the palm and posterior hand.

(g) Phalanges, finger bones.

5. Lower Extremities.

(a) Pelvis. The pelvis consists of two hip bones laterally and in front, and the sacrum and coccyx behind. The hip bones are divided into three parts: the ilium, the ischium, and the pubis; these three bones join to form the pelvic girdle.

(b) Acetabulum. This is not actually a bone, but rather a descriptive term for a large cup-shaped socket in the lateral aspect of the hip, into which the head of the femur fits.

(c) Greater and Lesser Trochanters. These are bony prominences located on the lateral and medial sides of the femur. These prominences are for the purpose of attachment of muscles.

(d) Femur. This is the longest bone in the body; it is the bone of the upper leg.

(e) Patella. This is the kneecap.

(f) Tibia and Fibula. These are the bones of the lower leg. The tibia is the larger and is located medially.

(g) The Lateral Malleolus is the lower end of the fibula; the Medial Malleolus is the lower end of the tibia. These are the ankle bones.

(h) Tarsals. These are the seven bones of the ankle.

(i) Metatarsals. These are the five bones in the sole and instep of the foot.

(j) Phalanges. These are the bones of the toes.

D. Joints. Joints are typically dealt with as separate structures; they are in fact the place where bones are held together by various types of connective tissue in a manner so as to permit certain movements while preventing others. Joints may be classified according to the types of connective tissue which holds the bones together or according to the movement permitted. The three major classifications refer to the type of connective tissue:

1. Fibrous (synarthrosi). These are united by fibrous tissues; there are two types:

(a) Sutures. These are connected by several fibrous layers, such as the skull.

(b) Syndesmoses. These are fibrous joints in which the intervening connective tissue is much more than a suture, for example, the tibiofibular syndesmosis, or the joint between the lower ends of the tibia and fibula.

2. Cartilaginous (synchondrosi). These are united by fibrocartilage and serve as growth areas for the bones they join. Eventually, most of them are replaced by the newly formed bone. The joint at the base of the skull beneath the pituitary gland is an example.

3. Synovial (diathrodial). These possess a fluid filled space and are specialized to permit more or less free movements. The articular surfaces are covered with cartilage, and the bones are united by the joint capsule and ligaments. All of the joints of the extremities are examples.

In classifying the joints with respect to movement, there are also three major classifications:

1. Synarthroses. These are immovable, such as the sutures of the skull.

2. Amphiarthroses. These have limited movement, as in the articulations between the vertebrae.

3. Diarthroses. These are freely movable.

(a) Plane Joint. Articular surfaces are slightly curved, and permit gliding or slipping in any direction, like the carpal and tarsal joints of the foot.

(b) Hinge Joint. Uni-axial and permits movement in only one place; an example is a joint between one of the bones (phalanges) of the finger or the toe.

(c) Condylar Joint. Articular area consists of two distinct articular surfaces; the knee joint is an example.

(d) Ball and Socket Joint. The shoulder joint is an example.

(e) Ellipsoidal Joint. Articulating surfaces are much longer in one direction than in another; the radiocarpal joint is an example.

(f) Pivot Joint. Uni-axial; the axis is vertical. The axis-atlas joint of the neck which allows the head to turn is an example.

(g) Saddle Joint. Biaxial joint, for example, the carpo-metacarpal joint of the thumb.

NECK—Lateral Series

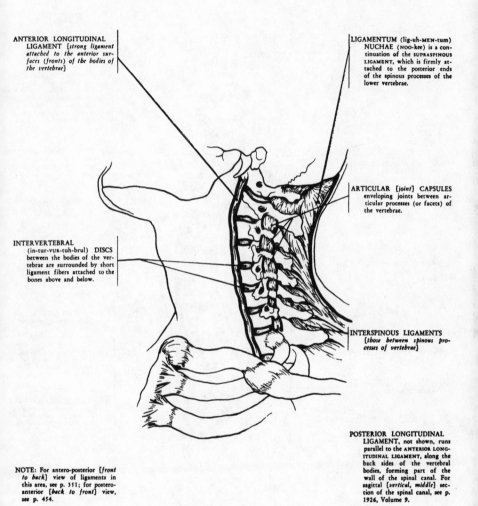

ANTERIOR LONGITUDINAL
LIGAMENT [*strong ligament
attached to the anterior surfaces (fronts) of the bodies of
the vertebrae*]

LIGAMENTUM (lig-uh-MEN-tum)
NUCHAE (NOO-kee) is a continuation of the SUPRASPINOUS
LIGAMENT, which is firmly attached to the posterior ends
of the spinous processes of the
lower vertebrae.

ARTICULAR [*joint*] CAPSULES
enveloping joints between articular processes (or facets) of
the vertebrae.

INTERVERTEBRAL
(in-tur-VUR-tuh-brul) DISCS
between the bodies of the vertebrae are surrounded by short
ligament fibers attached to the
bones above and below.

INTERSPINOUS LIGAMENTS
[*those between spinous processes of vertebrae*]

POSTERIOR LONGITUDINAL
LIGAMENT, not shown, runs
parallel to the ANTERIOR LONG-
ITUDINAL LIGAMENT, along the
back sides of the vertebral
bodies, forming part of the
wall of the spinal canal. For
sagittal [*vertical, middle*] section of the spinal canal, see p.
1926, Volume 9.

NOTE: For antero-posterior [*front
to back*] view of ligaments in
this area, see p. 351; for postero-
anterior [*back to front*] view,
see p. 454.

SPINAL LIGAMENTS—Anatomy
Figure 6

BACK—Lateral Series

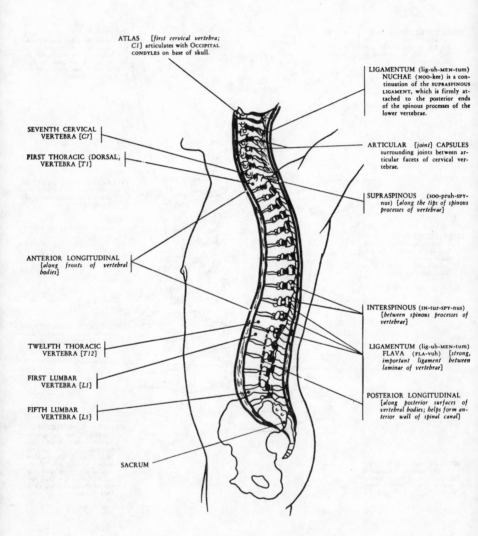

ATLAS   [*first cervical vertebra;
C1*] articulates with OCCIPITAL
CONDYLES on base of skull.

LIGAMENTUM (lig-uh-MEN-tum)
NUCHAE (NOO-kee) is a continuation of the SUPRASPINOUS
LIGAMENT, which is firmly attached to the posterior ends
of the spinous processes of the
lower vertebrae.

SEVENTH CERVICAL
VERTEBRA [*C7*]

FIRST THORACIC (DORSAL)
VERTEBRA [*T1*]

ARTICULAR   [*joint*] CAPSULES
surrounding joints between articular facets of cervical vertebrae.

SUPRASPINOUS   (soo-pruh-SPY-nus) [*along the tips of spinous
processes of vertebrae*]

ANTERIOR LONGITUDINAL
[*along   fronts   of   vertebral
bodies*]

INTERSPINOUS (IN-tur-SPY-nus)
[*between spinous processes of
vertebrae*]

TWELFTH THORACIC
VERTEBRA [*T12*]

LIGAMENTUM (lig-uh-MEN-tum)
FLAVA (FLA-vuh) [*strong,
important   ligament   between
laminae of vertebrae*]

FIRST LUMBAR
VERTEBRA [*L1*]

POSTERIOR LONGITUDINAL
[*along posterior surfaces of
vertebral bodies; helps form anterior wall of spinal canal*]

FIFTH LUMBAR
VERTEBRA [*L5*]

SACRUM

LIGAMENTS—Anatomy
Figure 7

BACK—Postero-Anterior Series

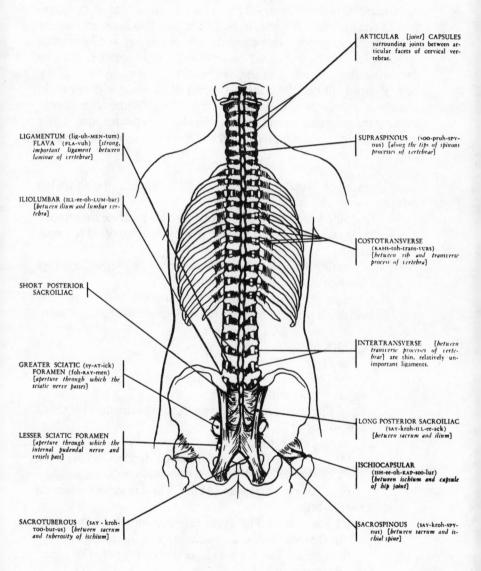

ARTICULAR [*joint*] CAPSULES surrounding joints between articular facets of cervical vertebrae.

LIGAMENTUM (lig-uh-MEN-tum) FLAVA (FLA-vuh) [*strong, important ligament between laminae of vertebrae*]

ILIOLUMBAR (ILL-ee-oh-LUM-bar) [*between ilium and lumbar vertebra*]

SHORT POSTERIOR SACROILIAC

GREATER SCIATIC (sy-AT-ick) FORAMEN (foh-RAY-men) [*aperture through which the sciatic nerve passes*]

LESSER SCIATIC FORAMEN [*aperture through which the internal pudendal nerve and vessels pass*]

SACROTUBEROUS (SAY - kroh-TOO-bur-us) [*between sacrum and tuberosity of ischium*]

SUPRASPINOUS (soo-pruh-SPY-nus) [*along the tips of spinous processes of vertebrae*]

COSTOTRANSVERSE (KAHS-toh-trans-VURS) [*between rib and transverse process of vertebra*]

INTERTRANSVERSE [*between transverse processes of vertebrae*] are thin, relatively unimportant ligaments.

LONG POSTERIOR SACROILIAC (SAY-kroh-II L-ee-ack) [*between sacrum and ilium*]

ISCHIOCAPSULAR (ISH-ee-oh-KAP-soo-lur) [*between ischium and capsule of hip joint*]

SACROSPINOUS (SAY-kroh-SPY-nus) [*between sacrum and ischial spine*]

LIGAMENTS—Anatomy
Figure 8

MUSCULAR SYSTEM

A. General Considerations. All human activity is carried on by operation of the muscles. The human body contains five hundred muscles which are large enough to be seen by the naked eye and thousands more which can be visualized only through a microscope. Muscles constitute about one-half of the weight of the body; the form of the body is largely due to the muscle covering of the skeletal framework. Muscles are made up of tissues composed of long slender cells. In considering the muscular system, one should also consider tendons. These are strong bands which attach muscles to bones or to other structures. (See Figs. 9 and 10.)

B. Movement of Muscles. Basically muscles fall into the following categories with respect to movement:
   1. Prime Movers. These muscles actively produce movement.
   2. Antagonists. These muscles operate in opposition to prime movers.
   3. Fixation Muscles. These muscles steady a part while others execute movement.
   4. Synergists. These muscles control movement of a proximal joint so that a prime mover may obtain movement of a distal joint.

C. Primary Muscles.
   1. The Neck.
      (a) Sternocleidomastoid. This muscle is frequently involved in cervical sprains.
      (b) Paravertebral. These muscles run the length of the spinal column.
   2. The Upper Trunk.
      (a) Trapezius. The triangular shaped muscle is located in the back of the neck and the upper trunk.
      (b) Pectoralis Major and Minor. These muscles are located on the chest.
      (c) Latissimus. This is the broadest muscle on the back.
      (d) Deltoid. This is a muscle capping the shoulder.
      (e) Triceps. This is a muscle located on the posterior aspect of the upper arm.
      (f) Biceps. This is a muscle located on anterior aspect of upper arm.

MUSCULAR System

✓ NOTE: For further details of these muscles, and for illustrations of those beneath the outermost layer, refer to the regional sections in Vols. 1 - 8.

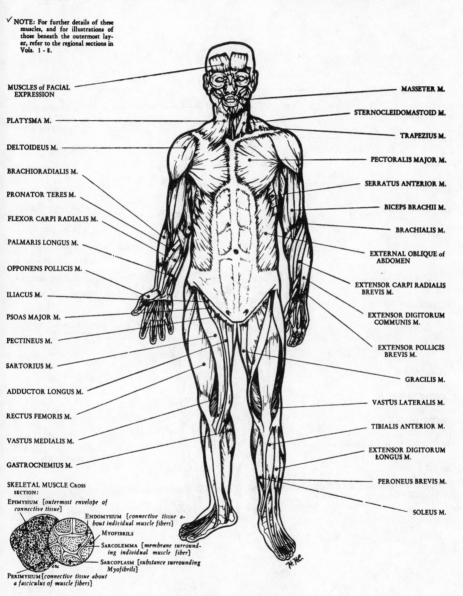

MUSCLES of FACIAL EXPRESSION

PLATYSMA M.

DELTOIDEUS M.

BRACHIORADIALIS M.

PRONATOR TERES M.

FLEXOR CARPI RADIALIS M.

PALMARIS LONGUS M.

OPPONENS POLLICIS M.

ILIACUS M.

PSOAS MAJOR M.

PECTINEUS M.

SARTORIUS M.

ADDUCTOR LONGUS M.

RECTUS FEMORIS M.

VASTUS MEDIALIS M.

GASTROCNEMIUS M.

MASSETER M.

STERNOCLEIDOMASTOID M.

TRAPEZIUS M.

PECTORALIS MAJOR M.

SERRATUS ANTERIOR M.

BICEPS BRACHII M.

BRACHIALIS M.

EXTERNAL OBLIQUE of ABDOMEN

EXTENSOR CARPI RADIALIS BREVIS M.

EXTENSOR DIGITORUM COMMUNIS M.

EXTENSOR POLLICIS BREVIS M.

GRACILIS M.

VASTUS LATERALIS M.

TIBIALIS ANTERIOR M.

EXTENSOR DIGITORUM LONGUS M.

PERONEUS BREVIS M.

SOLEUS M.

SKELETAL MUSCLE Cross SECTION:

EPIMYSIUM [*outermost envelope of connective tissue*]

ENDOMYSIUM [*connective tissue about individual muscle fibers*]

MYOFIBRILS

SARCOLEMMA [*membrane surrounding individual muscle fiber*]

SARCOPLASM [*substance surrounding Myofibrils*]

PERIMYSIUM [*connective tissue about a fasciculus of muscle fibers*]

MUSCLES—Anterior
Figure 9

© *Berkeley Press 1964*

MUSCULAR System

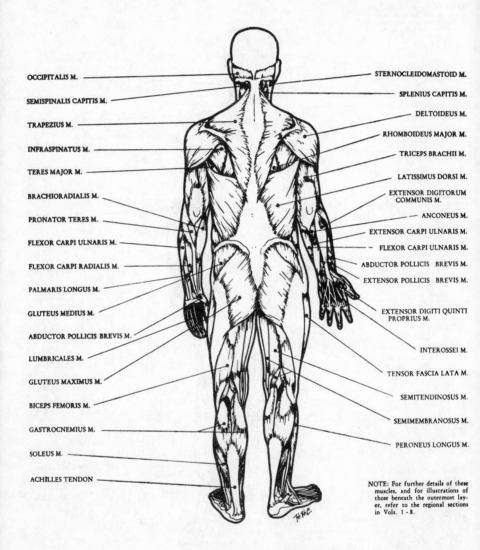

OCCIPITALIS M.

SEMISPINALIS CAPITIS M.

TRAPEZIUS M.

INFRASPINATUS M.

TERES MAJOR M.

BRACHIORADIALIS M.

PRONATOR TERES M.

FLEXOR CARPI ULNARIS M.

FLEXOR CARPI RADIALIS M.

PALMARIS LONGUS M.

GLUTEUS MEDIUS M.

ABDUCTOR POLLICIS BREVIS M.

LUMBRICALES M.

GLUTEUS MAXIMUS M.

BICEPS FEMORIS M.

GASTROCNEMIUS M.

SOLEUS M.

ACHILLES TENDON

STERNOCLEIDOMASTOID M.

SPLENIUS CAPITIS M.

DELTOIDEUS M.

RHOMBOIDEUS MAJOR M.

TRICEPS BRACHII M.

LATISSIMUS DORSI M.

EXTENSOR DIGITORUM COMMUNIS M.

ANCONEUS M.

EXTENSOR CARPI ULNARIS M.

FLEXOR CARPI ULNARIS M.

ABDUCTOR POLLICIS BREVIS M.

EXTENSOR POLLICIS BREVIS M.

EXTENSOR DIGITI QUINTI PROPRIUS M.

INTEROSSEI M.

TENSOR FASCIA LATA M.

SEMITENDINOSUS M.

SEMIMEMBRANOSUS M.

PERONEUS LONGUS M.

NOTE: For further details of these muscles, and for illustrations of those beneath the outermost layer, refer to the regional sections in Vols. 1 - 8.

MUSCLES—Posterior
Figure 10

℗ Berkeley Press 1964

3. Thoracic Wall and Abdomen.

(a) Intercostals. These are located between the individual ribs.

(b) Subcostals. These connect a superior rib to the second and third inferior ribs.

(c) Sternocostals. These connect the breastbone and ribs.

(d) External and Internal Obliques. These support the abdominal contents and arise from the ribs extending to the crest of the ilium.

(e) Rectus Abdominus. These are long, vertical muscles in the front part of the abdomen, one to the right and one to the left of the midline, meeting along the vertical midline in the front of the abdomen. These are the muscles which bend the spine forward; they also support the abdominal wall.

(f) Transversus Abdominis. This girdle holds the abdominal organs in place.

4. Hip and Thigh.

(a) Gluteus Minimus, Medius, and Maximus. These are the three muscles which form the buttock.

(b) Pectineus. Located at the upper part of the thigh, this muscle bends the thigh at the hip joint to bring it toward the other thigh.

(c) Adductor Longus, Brevis, and Magnus. These three thigh muscles all move the thigh to a position closer to the midline of the body.

(d) Quadriceps Femoris. This is a powerful thigh muscle, used in standing and walking, which straightens the leg at the knee joint.

(e) Sartorius. This muscle extends from the hip to the leg. Contracting it causes the thigh to bend at the hip joint and also to rotate outward; in addition, it helps to bend the leg at the knee.

(f) Hamstrings. These are three thigh muscles which bend the leg at the knee joint.

(i) The semimembranosus extends from the hip to the tibia.

(ii) The semitendinosus extends from the back of the hip to the tibia.

(iii) The biceps femoris is in the back of the thigh and extends between the femur and the lower part of the hip.

5. Lower Leg and Foot.

(a) Tibialis Anterior and Posterior. These muscles are in the front and back, respectively, of the leg. They move the foot inward and outward and upward and downward.

(b) Peroneus Longus and Brevis. These are muscles of the leg which turn the sole of the foot outward and lower the front part of the foot.

(c) Soleus. This is a muscle in the calf which extends the ankle joint, such as when the heel is raised to stand on one's toes.

(d) Gastrocnemius. This is an outer calf muscle which bends the leg at the knee and bends the foot downward.

NERVOUS SYSTEM

The human body has a "central authority" which issues orders to the rest of the body. The function of the nervous system, then, is to coordinate all of the activities of body. The basic functional units of the nervous system are neurons. These are specifically designed to carry impulses or messages rapidly over relatively long distances. There are basically two types of neurons: sensory neurons, which conduct impulses from sense organs to the spinal cord and brain, and motor neurons, which conduct impulses from the brain and spinal cord to the muscles and glands.

The nervous system may be divided into three main parts: the central nervous system, the peripheral nervous system, and the autonomic nervous system.

A. Central Nervous System. There is no more important part of the body than the central nervous system. When the body sustains serious trauma to this system, damage will in all probability be extensive. The basic components of the central nervous system are the brain, the spinal cord, and their coverings. Three membranes, known as the meninges, ensheath the central nervous system. The meninges serve supportive and protective roles. The meninges, from the outer to the innermost, are designated as the dura, the arachnoid, and the pia.

1. The Brain. (See Figs. 11 and 12.) The brain comprises 98 percent of the central nervous system and lies within the bony protec-

NERVOUS System

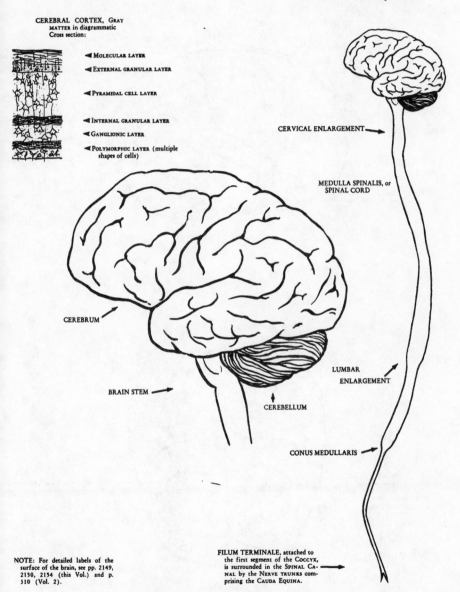

CEREBRAL CORTEX, Gray MATTER in diagrammatic Cross section:

◄ Molecular layer

◄ External granular layer

◄ Pyramidal cell layer

◄ Internal granular layer

◄ Ganglionic layer

◄ Polymorphic layer (multiple shapes of cells)

CERVICAL ENLARGEMENT →

MEDULLA SPINALIS, or SPINAL CORD

CEREBRUM

BRAIN STEM →

CEREBELLUM

LUMBAR ENLARGEMENT

CONUS MEDULLARIS →

NOTE: For detailed labels of the surface of the brain, see pp. 2149, 2150, 2154 (this Vol.) and p. 310 (Vol. 2).

FILUM TERMINALE, attached to the first segment of the Coccyx, is surrounded in the Spinal Canal by the Nerve trunks comprising the Cauda Equina. →

CENTRAL NERVOUS SYSTEM
Figure 11

© *Berkeley Press 1964*

NERVOUS System

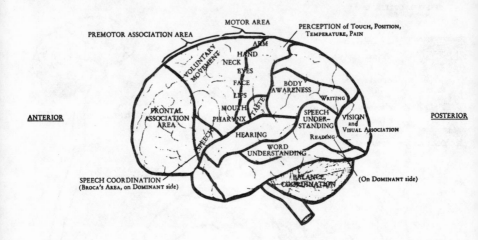

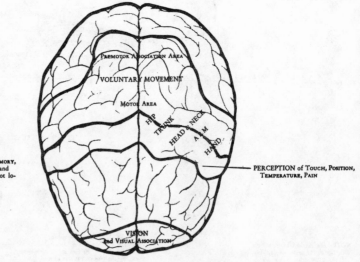

BRAIN—Exterior, Top & Lateral (Cortical Areas)
Figure 12

© Berkeley Press 1964

tion of the skull. One may designate the following major divisions of the brain:

(a) Medulla Oblongata. A truncated cone of nervous tissue continuous above with the pons and below with the spinal cord. It lies anterior to the cerebellum. The medulla contains highly specialized nerve centers regulating heart action, breathing, circulation, and control of body temperature. It is in this area that many of the nerves cross over to the other side of the body. Thus, the right side of the brain controls the left side of the body, while left side of the brain controls the right side.

(b) Pons (meaning bridge). This connects the medulla and the midbrain.

(c) Midbrain. This is the upper part of the brain stem located just above the pons.

(d) Cerebellum. This is the second largest portion of the brain; it is located in the posterior aspect of the skull. The chief function of the cerebellum is to bring balance, harmony, and coordination to motions of the body initiated by the cerebrum. The cerebellum integrates and correlates nerve impulses.

(e) Diencephalon. This is the portion of the brain lying between the midbrain and cerebrum. It contains the following:

(i) Thalamus. The integrating center of the brain where tactile, olfactory, painful, and gustatory impulses are correlated with motor reactions.

(ii) Epithalamus.

(iii) Subthalamus. This regulates the muscles of emotional expression.

(iv) Hypothalamus. This controls emotions that effect the heart beat and blood pressure, as well as body temperature, carbohydrate metabolism, food metabolism, appetite, and sexual reflexes.

(f) Cerebrum. This occupies most of the cranial cavity; it may be divided into cerebral hemispheres, and each hemisphere is, in turn, divided into four lobes:

(i) Occipital. This is visual in function.

(ii) Frontal. This is the center of voluntary movement and is also the seat of intellect and memory.

(iii) Temporal. This is auditory in function.

(iv) Parietal. This is sensory and motor in function.

2. The Cerebral Spinal Fluid. This is a clear transparent fluid found in the spinal canal, more specifically in the subarachnoid space (the area between the arachnoid and the pia). When a history of central nervous system pathology is suspected, physicians will draw out, or "tap," some of the fluid for the purpose of analysis. This fluid surrounds the brain and spinal cord, and it is in large measure, protective in function.

3. The Spinal Cord. One may compare the spinal cord to a highly complex telephone cable. It is enclosed in the vertebral column and has the three membranous coverings: the dura, the pia, and the arachnoid. Cerebral spinal fluid also surrounds the spinal cord.

One may differentiate an "ascending tract" (responsible for conducting impulses to the brain) and a "descending tract" (responsible for conducting impulses from the brain). It is through the spinal cord that the brain maintains its intimate functional relationship with the organs of the body. Thirty-one pairs of spinal nerves which protrude from the lateral aspects of the spinal cord, through the vertebral foramina, or openings, and into the peripheral areas of the body, constitute the specific means of accomplishing this highly complex system of intra-communication. Spinal nerves are attached to the spinal cord by anterior and posterior roots. The nerves, after leaving the cord, are named after their corresponding vertebrae. Thus, the first eight spinal nerves are known as cervical; the next twelve, dorsal; the next five, lumbar; the next five, sacral; and the last pair, coccygeal. (See Fig. 13.)

Actual trauma to the cord itself may produce serious injury. If there is a severing of the cord, the body will function normally above the level of injury, while those portions of the body served by nerves emanating from the spinal cord below the site of injury will be paralyzed.

B. Peripheral Nervous System. The peripheral nervous system is made up of nerves outside of the brain and spinal column. The thirty-one pairs of spinal nerves and twelve pairs of cranial nerves which branch out into the body for the purpose of sending and receiving messages to and from the brain are known as the peripheral nerves. (See Fig. 14.)

BACK—Lateral Series

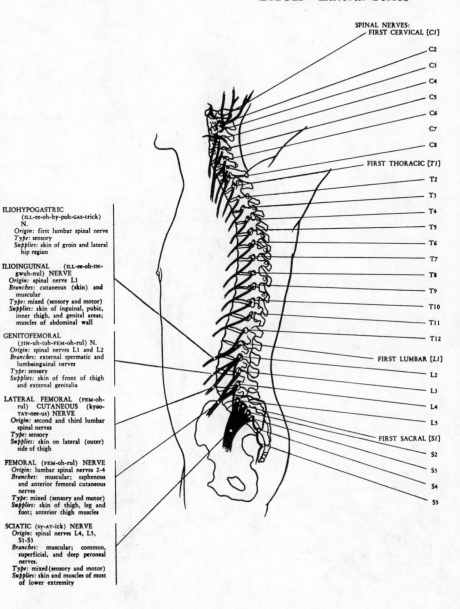

SPINAL NERVES:
FIRST CERVICAL [*C1*]

C2
C3
C4
C5
C6
C7
C8

FIRST THORACIC [*T1*]

T2
T3
T4
T5
T6
T7
T8
T9
T10
T11
T12

FIRST LUMBAR [*L1*]

L2
L3
L4
L5

FIRST SACRAL [*S1*]

S2
S3
S4
S5

ILIOHYPOGASTRIC
(ILL-ee-oh-hy-poh-GAS-trick)
N.
Origin: first lumbar spinal nerve
Type: sensory
Supplies: skin of groin and lateral
hip region

ILIOINGUINAL (ILL-ee-oh-IN-
gwuh-nul) NERVE
Origin: spinal nerve L1
Branches: cutaneous (skin) and
muscular
Type: mixed (sensory and motor)
Supplies: skin of inguinal, pubic,
inner thigh, and genital areas;
muscles of abdominal wall

GENITOFEMORAL
(JIN-uh-toh-FEM-oh-rul) N.
Origin: spinal nerves L1 and L2
Branches: external spermatic and
lumboinguinal nerves
Type: sensory
Supplies: skin of front of thigh
and external genitalia

LATERAL FEMORAL (FEM-oh-
rul) CUTANEOUS (kyoo-
TAY-nee-us) NERVE
Origin: second and third lumbar
spinal nerves
Type: sensory
Supplies: skin on lateral (outer)
side of thigh

FEMORAL (FEM-oh-rul) NERVE
Origin: lumbar spinal nerves 2-4
Branches: muscular; saphenous
and anterior femoral cutaneous
nerves
Type: mixed (sensory and motor)
Supplies: skin of thigh, leg and
foot; anterior thigh muscles

SCIATIC (sy-AT-ick) NERVE
Origin: spinal nerves L4, L5,
S1-S3
Branches: muscular; common,
superficial, and deep peroneal
nerves.
Type: mixed (sensory and motor)
Supplies: skin and muscles of most
of lower extremity

NERVES—Anatomy
Figure 13

NERVOUS System

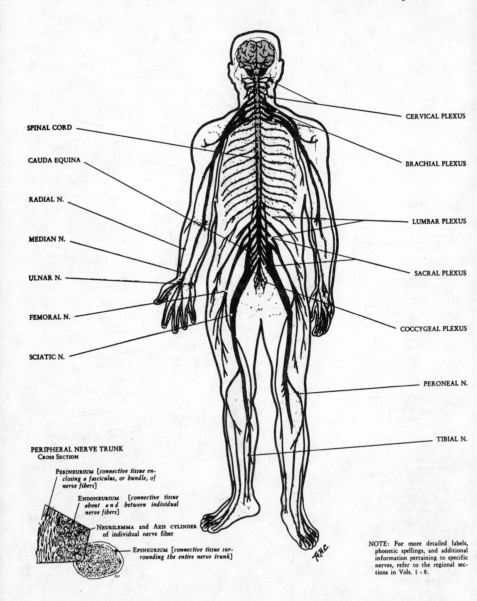

CERVICAL PLEXUS

SPINAL CORD

BRACHIAL PLEXUS

CAUDA EQUINA

RADIAL N.

LUMBAR PLEXUS

MEDIAN N.

ULNAR N.

SACRAL PLEXUS

FEMORAL N.

COCCYGEAL PLEXUS

SCIATIC N.

PERONEAL N.

TIBIAL N.

PERIPHERAL NERVE TRUNK
CROSS SECTION

PERINEURIUM [connective tissue enclosing a fasciculus, or bundle, of nerve fibers]

ENDONEURIUM [connective tissue about and between individual nerve fibers]

NEURILEMMA and AXIS CYLINDER of individual nerve fiber

EPINEURIUM [connective tissue surrounding the entire nerve trunk]

NOTE: For more detailed labels, phonetic spellings, and additional information pertaining to specific nerves, refer to the regional sections in Vols. 1 - 8.

© Berkeley Press 1964

PERIPHERAL NERVES
Figure 14

There are twelve pairs of cranial nerves which arise on each side of the brain. They are as follows:

1. First Cranial Nerve. This is olfactory in function; i.e., it is the nerve for the sense of smell.
2. Second Cranial Nerve. This is the optic nerve.
3. Third Cranial Nerve. This is oculomotor (moves the eyeball) in function.
4. Fourth Cranial Nerve (also called the trochlear nerve). This serves the eye muscles.
5. Fifth Cranial Nerve (or trigeminal nerve). This is the largest of the cranial nerves. It serves both a sensory and a motor function. It has three portions:
    (a) Ophthalmic, serving the forehead.
    (b) Maxillary, serving the upper cheek.
    (c) Mandibular, innervating the jaw and lower face.
6. Sixth Cranial Nerve (also called the abducens). This is visual in function and serves a purely motor function.
7. Seventh Cranial Nerve. This is both sensory and motor in function; it controls the muscles of the face, ears, and scalp.
8. Eighth Cranial Nerve. This is primarily acoustic or auditory. This is the sensory nerve of hearing and equilibrium.
9. Ninth Cranial Nerve. Known as glossopharyngeal nerve; it serves both a motor and sensory function, carrying messages from the pharynx and back part of the tongue to the brain.
10. Tenth Cranial Nerve. This is the vagus nerve, serving both a motor and sensory function to the thorax and abdomen.
11. Eleventh Cranial Nerve. It is a motor nerve which supplies the muscles of the neck and shoulders.
12. Twelfth Cranial Nerve. This is the hypoglossal nerve. It is a motor nerve controlling the muscles of the tongue.

C. Autonomic Nervous System. The autonomic nervous system functions automatically; it activates involuntary, smooth, and cardiac muscles, as well as glands. It serves the vital systems which function automatically, i.e., the digestive, circulatory, respiratory, urinary, and endocrine systems.

The autonomic nervous system is broken down into two major divisions: sympathetic nervous system and parasympathetic nervous system. These two systems work in harmonious opposition and thereby balance and maintain the actions and reactions of various body mechanisms. For example, the sympathetic system dilates the pupils, but, the parasympathetic system contracts them.

The trunk of the sympathetic system lies in close proximity to the vertebral bodies and is composed of a series of ganglia on either side of the spinal column. The ganglia extend from the base of the skull to the coccyx.

The ganglia of the parasympathetic system are located in the mid-portion of the brain and the sacral region of the spinal cord.

CARDIOVASCULAR SYSTEM

There are five principal components of the cardiovascular system: heart, arteries, veins, capillaries, and blood.

A. Blood. Blood is a tissue, fluid in nature, pumped by the heart, which courses through miles of arteries, veins, and capillaries. The function of the blood is to carry oxygen, food, and water to all of the cells of the body and to return carbon dioxide to the lungs for disposal. It is absolutely essential that all living tissue within the body receive a continuous supply of blood which is appropriately enriched with oxygen. When, for some reason, tissue has a relative lack of oxygen supply, the condition is described as "hypoxia." The total lack of oxygen is known as "anoxia."

B. The Heart. The heart is a hollow, muscular pump. It is located in the front of the chest, slightly to the left, between the lungs. A large portion of the heart is located directly behind the sternum. The heart is enclosed in a membranous sac called the pericardium.

The heart is divided longitudinally into left and right chambers by the septum passing through the apex to the base of the heart. Each side of the heart is subdivided into chambers: an atrium above and a ventricle below. (See Fig. 15.)

C. Arteries. Blood is carried from the heart to all of the structures of the body by elastic tubes called arteries. (See Fig. 16.) The arteries branch and rebranch as they course through the body, becoming smaller and smaller, until they are called arterioles. The arterioles feed

CIRCULATORY System

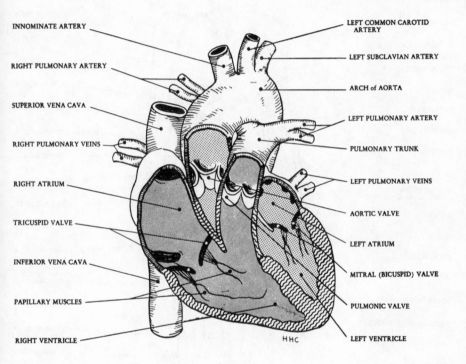

INNOMINATE ARTERY

RIGHT PULMONARY ARTERY

SUPERIOR VENA CAVA

RIGHT PULMONARY VEINS

RIGHT ATRIUM

TRICUSPID VALVE

INFERIOR VENA CAVA

PAPILLARY MUSCLES

RIGHT VENTRICLE

LEFT COMMON CAROTID ARTERY

LEFT SUBCLAVIAN ARTERY

ARCH of AORTA

LEFT PULMONARY ARTERY

PULMONARY TRUNK

LEFT PULMONARY VEINS

AORTIC VALVE

LEFT ATRIUM

MITRAL (BICUSPID) VALVE

PULMONIC VALVE

LEFT VENTRICLE

HHC

HEART—Chambers & Valves
Figure 15

© *Berkeley Press 1964*

CIRCULATORY System

NOTE: Arteries deliver blood *to* tissues, whereas veins drain blood *from* tissues. Veins have TRIBUTARIES (blood flow being from smaller to larger vessels) and arteries have BRANCHES (blood flow being from larger to smaller vessels).

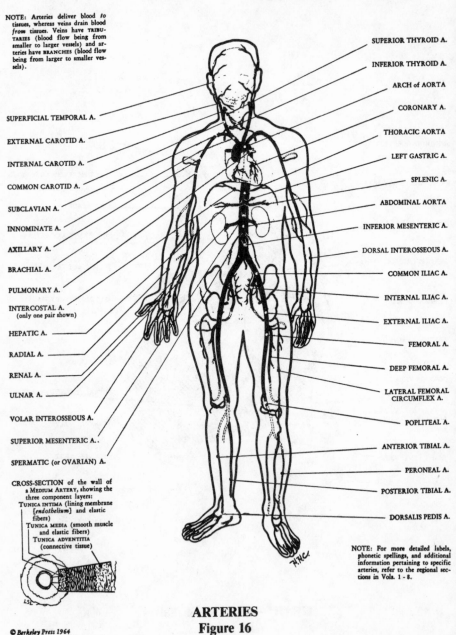

SUPERIOR THYROID A.

INFERIOR THYROID A.

ARCH of AORTA

CORONARY A.

THORACIC AORTA

LEFT GASTRIC A.

SPLENIC A.

ABDOMINAL AORTA

INFERIOR MESENTERIC A.

DORSAL INTEROSSEOUS A.

COMMON ILIAC A.

INTERNAL ILIAC A.

EXTERNAL ILIAC A.

FEMORAL A.

DEEP FEMORAL A.

LATERAL FEMORAL CIRCUMFLEX A.

POPLITEAL A.

ANTERIOR TIBIAL A.

PERONEAL A.

POSTERIOR TIBIAL A.

DORSALIS PEDIS A.

SUPERFICIAL TEMPORAL A.

EXTERNAL CAROTID A.

INTERNAL CAROTID A.

COMMON CAROTID A.

SUBCLAVIAN A.

INNOMINATE A.

AXILLARY A.

BRACHIAL A.

PULMONARY A.

INTERCOSTAL A. (only one pair shown)

HEPATIC A.

RADIAL A.

RENAL A.

ULNAR A.

VOLAR INTEROSSEOUS A.

SUPERIOR MESENTERIC A.

SPERMATIC (or OVARIAN) A.

CROSS-SECTION of the wall of a MEDIUM ARTERY, showing the three component layers:
TUNICA INTIMA (lining membrane [*endothelium*] and elastic fibers)
TUNICA MEDIA (smooth muscle and elastic fibers)
TUNICA ADVENTITIA (connective tissue)

NOTE: For more detailed labels, phonetic spellings, and additional information pertaining to specific arteries, refer to the regional sections in Vols. 1 - 8.

ARTERIES
Figure 16

© *Berkeley Press* 1964

blood directly into the capillaries. As the blood circulates through the capillary net, it gives off oxygen and food to the adjacent tissue and picks up waste products.

The aorta is the largest artery in the body. It arises directly from the left ventricle of the heart, arches upward, and passes down along the spinal column through the diaphragm. All along its route, the aorta branches off into other arteries which supply blood to the head, neck, arms, chest, abdomen; it then divides into arteries which supply the legs and lower body. Some of the larger arteries include the following:

1. Innominate artery.
2. Right subclavian — supplies the right arm.
3. Right carotid — supplies the right side of the head.
4. Internal carotid — supplies the brain and eyes.
5. External carotid — supplies the muscles and skin of the face.
6. Left carotid — supplies the left side of the head.
7. Left subclavian — supplies the left arm.
8. Axillary — supplies the arm.
9. Brachial — supplies the upper arm.
10. Radial and Ulnar — supply the lower arm.
11. Coronary — supplies the heart.
12. Pulmonary — takes blood to be oxygenated.
13. Gastric — supplies the stomach.
14. Splenic — supplies the spleen.
15. Hepatic — supplies the liver.
16. Superior mesenteric — supplies the small intestine and proximal colon.
17. Inferior mesenteric — supplies the lower half of the colon and rectum.
18. Renal — supplies the kidneys.
19. Abdominal aorta — divides into the right and left common iliacs which supply blood to the lower extremities.
20. Femoral—supplies the thigh.
21. Popliteal — is located just behind and supplies the knee.
22. Anterior and posterior tibial — supply the area of the tibia.
23. Peroneal — supplies blood to the lower leg.
24. Dorsalis pedis — supplies blood to the foot.

D. Veins. The veins carry blood back to the heart. (See Figs. 17 and 18.) They are hollow tubes, like arteries, though their walls are much

CIRCULATORY System

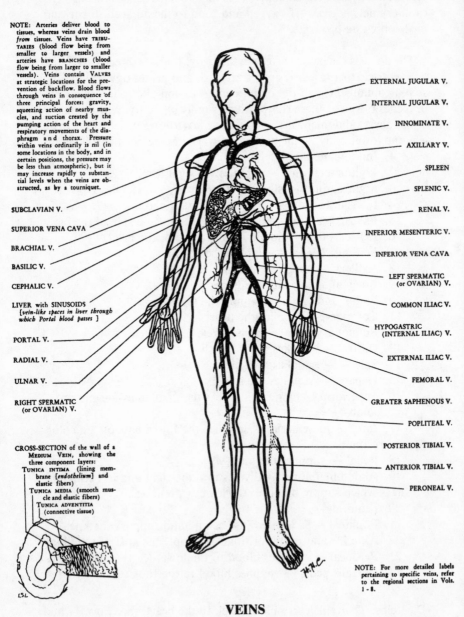

NOTE: Arteries deliver blood to tissues, whereas veins drain blood *from* tissues. Veins have TRIBUTARIES (blood flow being from smaller to larger vessels) and arteries have BRANCHES (blood flow being from larger to smaller vessels). Veins contain VALVES at strategic locations for the prevention of backflow. Blood flows through veins in consequence of three principal forces: gravity, squeezing action of nearby muscles, and suction created by the pumping action of the heart and respiratory movements of the diaphragm and thorax. Pressure within veins ordinarily is nil (in some locations in the body, and in certain positions, the pressure may be less than atmospheric), but it may increase rapidly to substantial levels when the veins are obstructed, as by a tourniquet.

SUBCLAVIAN V.

SUPERIOR VENA CAVA

BRACHIAL V.

BASILIC V.

CEPHALIC V.

LIVER with SINUSOIDS
[*vein-like spaces in liver through which Portal blood passes*]

PORTAL V.

RADIAL V.

ULNAR V.

RIGHT SPERMATIC
(or OVARIAN) V.

CROSS-SECTION of the wall of a MEDIUM VEIN, showing the three component layers:
TUNICA INTIMA (lining membrane [*endothelium*] and elastic fibers)
TUNICA MEDIA (smooth muscle and elastic fibers)
TUNICA ADVENTITIA (connective tissue)

EXTERNAL JUGULAR V.

INTERNAL JUGULAR V.

INNOMINATE V.

AXILLARY V.

SPLEEN

SPLENIC V.

RENAL V.

INFERIOR MESENTERIC V.

INFERIOR VENA CAVA

LEFT SPERMATIC
(or OVARIAN) V.

COMMON ILIAC V.

HYPOGASTRIC
(INTERNAL ILIAC) V.

EXTERNAL ILIAC V.

FEMORAL V.

GREATER SAPHENOUS V.

POPLITEAL V.

POSTERIOR TIBIAL V.

ANTERIOR TIBIAL V.

PERONEAL V.

NOTE: For more detailed labels pertaining to specific veins, refer to the regional sections in Vols. 1 - 8.

VEINS
Figure 17

© Berkeley Press 1964

CIRCULATORY System

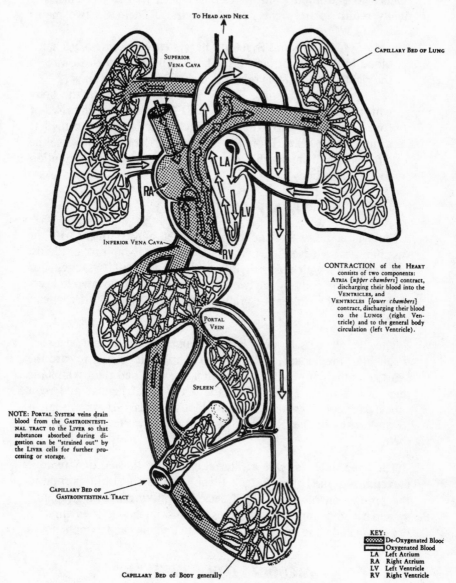

To Head and Neck

Capillary Bed of Lung

Superior Vena Cava

RA

Inferior Vena Cava

LA

LV

RV

Portal Vein

Spleen

CONTRACTION of the HEART consists of two components: ATRIA [*upper chambers*] contract, discharging their blood into the VENTRICLES, and VENTRICLES [*lower chambers*] contract, discharging their blood to the LUNGS (right Ventricle) and to the general body circulation (left Ventricle).

NOTE: PORTAL SYSTEM veins drain blood from the GASTROINTESTINAL TRACT to the LIVER so that substances absorbed during digestion can be "strained out" by the LIVER cells for further processing or storage.

Capillary Bed of Gastrointestinal Tract

Capillary Bed of Body generally

KEY:
De-Oxygenated Blood
Oxygenated Blood
LA   Left Atrium
RA   Right Atrium
LV   Left Ventricle
RV   Right Ventricle

SCHEME OF CIRCULATION
Figure 18

© *Berkeley Press* 1965

thinner and less muscular. The small veins are known as venules; these venules collect blood from the capillary nets, join larger veins, and finally return to the right side of the heart. There are two major systems of veins:

    1. Systemic Venous System. This system carries de-oxygenated blood to the right atrium of the heart. The blood then flows into the right ventricle from where it is pumped into the lungs.

    2. Pulmonary System. These veins are the ones in the body which carry freshly oxygenated blood. This system is comprised of four veins which carry the blood back from the lungs to the left atrium of the heart. From the left atrium, the blood flows to the left ventricle from which it is pumped to the aorta for distribution to the entire body.

LYMPHATIC SYSTEM

The lymphatic system is closely associated and confluent with the vascular system described immediately above. Lymph is an almost colorless fluid which is rich in white blood cells. It is circulated throughout the body by the lymph vessels, which are located in every part of the body except the brain, spinal cord, eyeball, internal ear, nails, and hair.

The lymph vessels and lymph glands form a vast network throughout the body; they collect the lymph and carry it toward the heart, eventually opening into the thoracic duct and right lymphatic duct, which in turn empty into the left internal jugular and right subclavian veins. Lymph vessels, like blood vessels, carry nourishment to the organs of the body and in turn collect waste products from them.

The lymph glands serve a filtering function; that is, they remove bacteria from the lymph system. Lymph glands are also important in the production of white blood cells (lymphocytes). The lymphatic system is highly important in defense against infection. The lymphoid organs include the spleen, tonsils, and thymus, and lymph nodes (glands).

RESPIRATORY SYSTEM

Respiration refers to the exchange of oxygen and carbon dioxide between man and his external world. (See Fig. 19.)

RESPIRATORY System

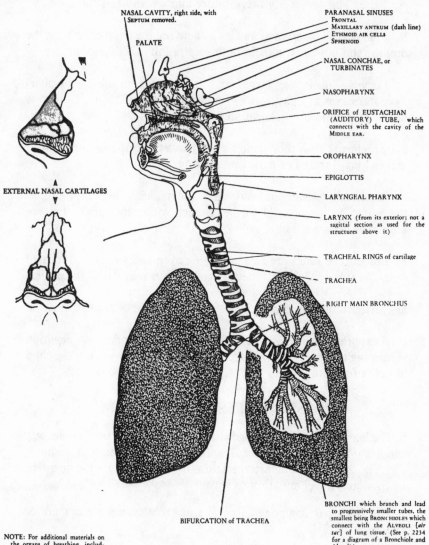

NASAL CAVITY, right side, with SEPTUM removed.

PALATE

EXTERNAL NASAL CARTILAGES

PARANASAL SINUSES
FRONTAL
MAXILLARY ANTRUM (dash line)
ETHMOID AIR CELLS
SPHENOID

NASAL CONCHAE, or TURBINATES

NASOPHARYNX

ORIFICE of EUSTACHIAN (AUDITORY) TUBE, which connects with the cavity of the MIDDLE EAR.

OROPHARYNX

EPIGLOTTIS

LARYNGEAL PHARYNX

LARYNX (from its exterior; not a sagittal section as used for the structures above it)

TRACHEAL RINGS of cartilage

TRACHEA

RIGHT MAIN BRONCHUS

BIFURCATION of TRACHEA

BRONCHI which branch and lead to progressively smaller tubes, the smallest being BRONCHIOLES which connect with the ALVEOLI [*air sac*] of lung tissue. (See p. 2234 for a diagram of a Bronchiole and Alveoli.)

NOTE: For additional materials on the organs of breathing, including many X-rays of PARANASAL SINUSES, TRACHEOBRONCHIAL TREE, and LUNGS, see the regional sections in Vols. 1 - 3.

ORGANS OF BREATHING
Figure 19

© *Berkeley Press* 1964

The principal structures of the respiratory system are as follows:

A. Nose. This serves both respiratory and sensory functions.

B. Pharynx. This serves as an airway between the nasal chambers, the mouth, and larynx. It aids in both respiration and digestion.

C. Larynx. This is the "voice box." It is located just below the pharynx, and serves as a passageway for air, aids in swallowing, and serves in the phonation or vocalization function.

D. Trachea. This is the "wind pipe." It is a tube, approximately four inches long, formed of cartilaginous rings.

E. Bronchi. These are the branches of the trachea which carry air into the lungs. As the bronchi further branch within the lungs, they are known as bronchioles.

F. Lungs. The lungs are two large, closed membranous sacs located on either side of the chest; they are enclosed in a sac called the pleura.

G. Mediastinum. A space which separates the chest into two cavities.

H. Diaphragm. This is a thin, muscular tendinous partition separating the thoracic cavity from the abdominal cavity; it is the chief muscle of respiration.

GASTROINTESTINAL SYSTEM

The gastrointestinal or digestive system includes the alimentary canal and its accessory organs. It extends from the mouth to the anus. (See Fig. 20.) The two major functions of the system are the digestion of food and the elimination of waste.

The principal components of the gastrointestinal system are as follows:

A. Mouth.

B. Pharynx. This is an oval, fibromuscular sac about five inches long. It serves a dual function as a passageway for food and an air passageway.

DIGESTIVE System

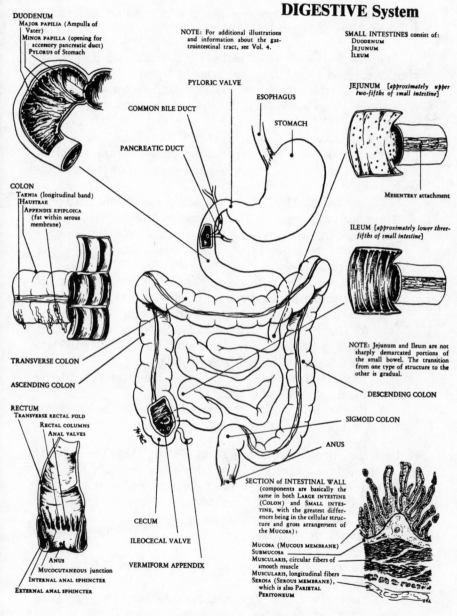

DUODENUM
MAJOR PAPILLA (Ampulla of Vater)
MINOR PAPILLA (opening for accessory pancreatic duct)
PYLORUS of Stomach

NOTE: For additional illustrations and information about the gastrointestinal tract, see Vol. 4.

SMALL INTESTINES consist of:
DUODENUM
JEJUNUM
ILEUM

PYLORIC VALVE

ESOPHAGUS

STOMACH

COMMON BILE DUCT

PANCREATIC DUCT

JEJUNUM [*approximately upper two-fifths of small intestine*]

MESENTERY attachment

COLON
TAENIA (longitudinal band)
HAUSTRAE
APPENDIX EPIPLOICA (fat within serous membrane)

ILEUM [*approximately lower three-fifths of small intestine*]

TRANSVERSE COLON

ASCENDING COLON

NOTE: Jejunum and Ileum are not sharply demarcated portions of the small bowel. The transition from one type of structure to the other is gradual.

DESCENDING COLON

RECTUM
TRANSVERSE RECTAL FOLD
RECTAL COLUMNS
ANAL VALVES

SIGMOID COLON

ANUS

CECUM

ILEOCECAL VALVE

VERMIFORM APPENDIX

SECTION of INTESTINAL WALL (components are basically the same in both LARGE INTESTINE (COLON) and SMALL INTESTINE, with the greatest differences being in the cellular structure and gross arrangement of the MUCOSA):

MUCOSA (MUCOUS MEMBRANE)
SUBMUCOSA
MUSCULARIS, circular fibers of smooth muscle
MUSCULARIS, longitudinal fibers
SEROSA (SEROUS MEMBRANE), which is also PARIETAL PERITONEUM

ANUS
MUCOCUTANEOUS junction
INTERNAL ANAL SPHINCTER
EXTERNAL ANAL SPHINCTER

© Berkeley Press 1964

GASTROINTESTINAL TRACT
Figure 20

C. Esophagus. This is a narrow muscular tube about ten inches long. It connects the pharynx with the stomach.

D. Stomach. This is the widest part of the alimentary canal. It digests masticated food to a fluid consistency and passes it along to the duodenum. There are millions of gastric glands in the stomach and these secrete juices which aid in the chemical breakdown of food.

E. Small Intestine. This is a coiled twenty foot tube which occupies the center and lower parts of the abdominal cavity. The greater part of digestion is completed in the three major divisions of the small intestine; viz:

   1. Duodenum. This is the widest, shortest, and most fixed part. Three accessory organs bear consideration at this point:

      (a) Pancreas. This is a gland extending across the posterior aspect of the abdomen. It empties an alkaline digestive juice into the duodenum.

      (b) Liver. This is the largest gland in the body. It lies in the upper abdomen, under the diaphragm, and above the duodenum. It secretes bile into the duodenum.

      (c) Gall Bladder. This is a sac adhering to the lower aspect of the liver in a hollow space. The main function of the gall bladder is storage and concentration of bile.

   2. Jejunum. The portion of the small intestine which extends from the duodenum to the ileum.

   3. Ileum. This is the longest part of the small intestine. Most of the absorption of food takes place in the ileum.

F. Large Intestine. This organ is about five feet long. The large intestine receives the products of digestion from the small intestine. The major divisions of the large intestine include the following:

   1. Cecum. This is a blind sac located on the lower right side of the abdomen.

   2. Vermiform Appendix. This is a narrow projection attached to the cecum.

   3. Ascending Colon. This long tubular structure is fixed in the right flank.

   4. Transverse Colon. This structure runs across the upper portion of the abdominal cavity.

   5. Descending Colon. This structure runs down the left flank to the brim of the true pelvis.

6. Sigmoid Colon. The sigmoid colon communicates with the rectum.

7. Rectum. This communicates with the anus.

8. Anus.

GENITOURINARY SYSTEM

The genitourinary system is comprised of two major parts: urinary organs and reproductive organs.

A. Urinary Organs. The urinary organs are common to both male and female and are essentially similar in both. The major components of the urinary system are as follows:

1. Kidneys. These are bean-shaped organs situated in the posterior part of the abdomen on either side of the vertebral column.

2. Ureters. These are tubes about fifteen to eighteen inches long, extending from the kidneys down the back of the abdominal cavity and emptying into the urinary bladder.

3. Urinary Bladder. This is a musculomembranous sac lying in the pelvis. It serves as a reservoir for urine.

4. Urethra. This structure serves a different function in the male and female:

(a) In the male, this is a membranous tube running from the urinary bladder to the penis and ending in a foramen. The urethra conveys both urine and the produce of the male reproductive organs.

(b) The female urethra is a short tube extending from the bladder to the anterior portion of the vulva. The function of the urethra in the female is solely for voiding.

B. Reproductive Systems.

1. The Male Reproductive System. The essential organs of the male reproductive system are as follows:

(a) Testes. These are two organs suspended in a sac of skin (the scrotum). The epithelial cells of the testes produce sperm.

(b) Epididymis. This is a cord-like, elongated structure located outside of, but hugging the posterior portion of, the testis. Its function is to store sperm.

(c) Vas Deferens. This tiny tube extends from the epididymis up through the inguinal canal toward the bladder. Its function is to carry sperm to the ejaculatory duct.

(d) Spermatic Cord. Two spermatic cords comprise the vas deferens, arteries, veins, lymphatic ducts, and nerves.

(e) Ejaculatory Duct. This is a short, narrow tube, less than an inch long, which is formed just above the prostate by the union of the seminal vesicles and the vas deferens.

(f) Prostate Gland. This gland secretes a thin alkaline substance which precedes the sperm and secretion of the vesicles during sexual intercourse.

(g) Cowper's Gland. These two structures are yellowish, rounded, lobulated, pea-size bodies on each side of the membranous urethra opening into the urethra.

(h) Urethra. This is a canal about eight inches long which extends from the urinary bladder to the external foramen of the penis.

(i) Penis. This is made up of three masses of tissue.

2. The Female Reproductive System. The essential organs of the female reproductive system include the following:

(a) Ovaries. These almond-shaped organs are approximately an inch and one-half in length and an inch thick. They lie on each side of the pelvis and are responsible for the production of the germ cells.

(b) Uterus (womb). This is a thick-walled, hollow, pear-shaped organ about three inches long and three inches wide at the upper, widest portion. It lies between the bladder and the rectum. It tapers to a lower part called the cervix and projects into the anterior wall of the vagina.

(c) Fallopian Tubes. These are two musculo-membranous tubes about four inches long. They transmit the egg to the uterus where it meets the sperm.

(d) Vagina. This is a fibromuscular tube which extends from the cervix or neck of the uterus to the vulva.

(e) External Genitalia or Vulva.

ENDOCRINE SYSTEM

The complex activities of the body are carried on by the operation of the nervous system and the endocrine system. The nervous system is keyed to act instantaneously through the operation of the nerve impulses. The action of endocrine glands is more subtle, however; they slowly discharge secretions into blood and control the activities of the body more by "inference." The endocrine system is comprised of ductless glands of internal secretion; these glands secrete hormones.

The principal endocrine glands include the following:

A. Thyroid. The thyroid is composed of two pear-shaped lobes separated by a strip of tissue; it is located immediately in front of the trachea. The main function of the thyroid gland is in the secretion of the Thyroid Hormone. The thyroid functions affect growth and metabolism.

B. Parathyroids. These are four glands, two on each side, lying posterior to the thyroid gland and usually found embedded in the thyroid. The parathyroid's function is to secrete hormones which regulate the calcium and phosphorus content of blood and bone.

C. Pituitary. The pituitary gland exercises control over all of the other glands. It is attached to the base of the brain and is divided into an anterior and posterior lobe.

D. Adrenals. The adrenal glands are located on top of each kidney. These glands secrete hormones which are active in metabolism and sex development. The adrenal glands also secrete adrenalin which acts as a stimulant to many bodily functions.

E. Gonads. The female ovaries and male testes produce hormones important for the functioning of the reproductive system.

F. Pineal. This gland is located near the base of the brain; its exact functions are not understood.

G. Thymus. This gland is situated in the front of the trachea, partly in the neck and partly in the thorax. It is believed to be associated with immunological activities.

H. Pancreas. This gland is the only gland in the body which functions both with and without a duct. It secretes digestive juices which are delivered into the alimentary canal through a duct. The pancreas also contains specialized cells, called the Islets of Langerhans, which secrete insulin directly into the bloodstream.

INTEGUMENTARY SYSTEM

The Integumentary System includes the skin, hair, nails, mammary glands, sweat, and sebaceous glands. Its main function is protective.

ANNOTATIONS.

Treatises

Bender's Anatomy Charts—Commentary by Marshall Honts.
Gray, Attorneys' Textbook of Medicine—Third Edition.
Schmidt, Attorneys' Dictionary of Medicine—Eleventh Edition.
Courtroom Medicine Series:
  The Law Book—Vols. 1, 1A, 1B
  The Neck—Vols. 2, 2A, 2B
  Death—Vols. 3, 3A, 3B
  Pain and Suffering—Vols. 4, 4A, 4B
  Shoulder and Elbow—Vols. 5, 5A
  The Skin—Vols. 6, 6A, 6B
  Hip and Thigh—Vols. 7, 7A
  Head and Brain—Vols. 8, 8A
  Knee and Related Structures—Vol. 9
  Abdominal Injuries—Vol. 10
  Chest, Heart and Lungs—Vol. 11
  Psychic Injuries—Vol. 12
  Cancer—Vol. 13
  The Eye—Vol. 14
Honts, Proving Medical Diagnosis and Prognosis.

Am Jur Trials

Presenting plaintiff's medical proof—common injuries and conditions, 6 AJT 1-107.

Am Jur Proof of Facts

Abrasions, 1 POF 27-32
Allergy, 1 POF 463-474.
Amputations, 12 POF 1-119.
Ankle Injuries, 1 POF 641-649.
Atrophy, 2 POF 211-220.
Back injuries, 2 POF 291-420.
Bladder injuries, 2 POF 547-555.
Blood tests, 2 POF 585-606.
Brain injuries, 2 POF 693-771.
Burn injuries, 3 POF 97-115.
Chest injuries, 3 POF 195-214.

Chapter 4

MEDICAL EXAMINATION AND TESTING

This chapter will describe some of the more common medical tests which physicians employ in examining patients with head and neck injuries and injuries to the lumbar spine.

HEAD AND NECK

When a physician is presented with a neck injury (cervical), the examination and testing is initially centered on the neurologic pathology, i.e., the symptoms that indicate impairment of the nerves in the area. This pathology may manifest itself in the upper extremity by appearing as muscle weakness, altered reflexes, or pain. Since these symptoms may be the result of interference with the peripheral nerves at the level of the cervical spine or may involve the brachial plexus or other nerves, an expanded neurologic examination is needed. This provides a more comprehensive interpretation of the integrity of the brachial plexus and of pathologic signs and symptoms in the upper extremity as well.

The cervical spine serves to support and stabilize the head, allow for the range of motion of the head, and provide housing, protection, and transport for the spinal cord and vertebral artery.

135

The physician inspects the patient by noting the posture and attitude of the head. Normally, the head is held erect, perpendicular to the floor, and it moves in smooth coordination with body motion.

Palpation of Bony Structures

When the examination begins, the neck should be palpated to examine the bony structures of the neck. The anterior (frontal) aspect of the cervical region (see Fig. 1) is composed of the hyoid bone which is a horseshoe-shaped structure and is situated above the thyroid cartilage. The patient is asked to swallow; when he does so, the movement of the hyoid bone becomes palpable.

Thyroid cartilage. This cartilage (see Fig. 1) is commonly known as the "Adam's Apple," and it marks the level of the C4 vertebral body, while the lower portion designates the C5 level.

Cricoid. The first cricoid ring (see Fig. 1) is situated just below the thyroid cartilage, opposite C6. It is immediately above the site for emergency tracheostomy.

The C1 transverse process, which lies between the angle of the jaw and the skull's styloid process, just behind the ear, has little clinical significance, but it serves as an easily identifiable point of orientation.

Palpation of Soft Tissues

When the physician examines the soft tissues of the neck, he begins with the area known as the anterior triangle, defined laterally by the sternocleidomastoid muscles, superiorly (upward toward the head) by the mandible, and inferiorly (downward toward the feet) by the suprasternal notch.

Sternocleidomastoid Muscle. This muscle is frequently stretched by hyperextension-hyperflexion (see Figs. 2 and 3) injuries of the neck during automobile accidents. The patient is asked to turn his head to the side opposite the muscle to be examined. This stretches the muscle so that it will stand out sharply near its tendonous origin. If the physician can palpate a localized swelling within the muscle, the cause may be due to hematoma and may result in the head turning abnormally to one side (torticollis). Tenderness elicited during palpation may be associated with hyperextension-hyperflexion injury of the neck.

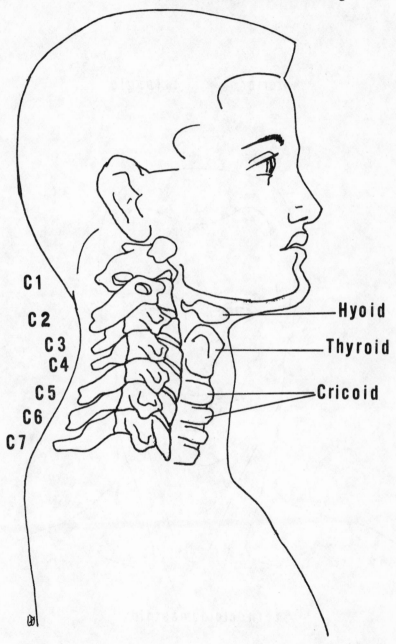

C1
C2
C3
C4
C5
C6
C7

Hyoid
Thyroid
Cricoid

Fig. 1

Anterior   Triangle

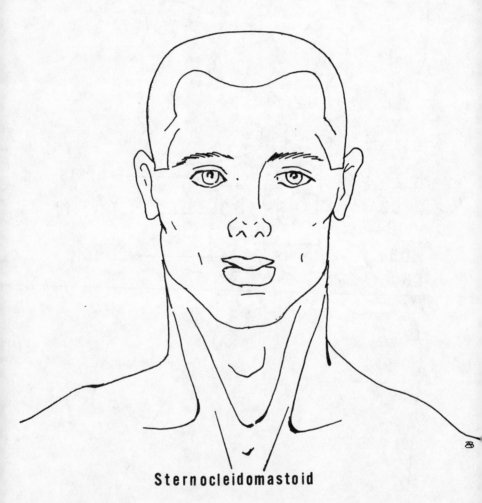

Sternocleidomastoid

Fig. 2

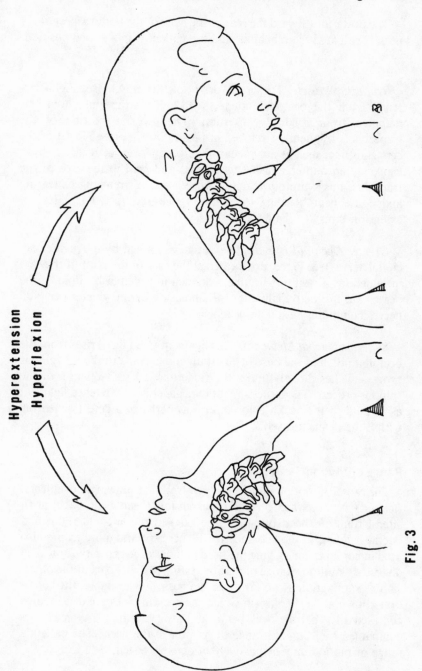

Hyperextension
Hyperflexion

Fig. 3

The posterior (toward the rear or the back of the body) aspect of the neck is palpated from behind, and the patient is in a seated position.

Trapezius Muscle. The broad origin of this muscle (see Fig. 4) extends from the occipital notch to T12. The trapezius should be palpated from origin to insertion. The superior portion of the trapezius is frequently stretched in flexion injuries (see Fig. 3) of the cervical spine, such as may occur in automobile accidents. The physician may encounter unusual tenderness and pain in the area of the trapezius; this symptom is due to the excessive stretching or tearing and consequent bleeding (hematoma) that results from a flexion-extension injury to the neck.

Greater Occipital Nerves. The muscles supplied by the greater occipital nerves (see Fig. 5) are located at the base of the skull. If they are inflamed (as a result of trauma sustained in "whiplash" injury), the nerves are distinctly palpable. Inflammation of the greater occipital nerves commonly results in headache.

Superior Nuchal Ligament. This ligament (see Fig. 5) rises from the occipital notch at the base of the skull and extends to the C7 spinous process. It lies directly under the fingertips during palpation of the spinous process. Tenderness might indicate either a stretched ligament as a result of the neck flexion injury or, perhaps, a defect or tearing within the ligament itself.

Range of Motion Testing

The range of motion in the neck involves the following movements: flexion (chin forward on chest), extension (head bent backward), lateral rotation (head turned to the side) to the left and right, and lateral bending to the left and right. These specific motions are also used in combination, giving the head and neck the capacity for widely diversified motion. Range of motion testing is a vital part of the physician's examination of an injury to the neck. For example, the condition known as Torticollis (in which the neck muscles are distorted or contracted so that the neck bends and the head tilts) is typically accompanied by a limited range of motion in the neck. The patient's range of motion may be passively or actively tested.

Palpation

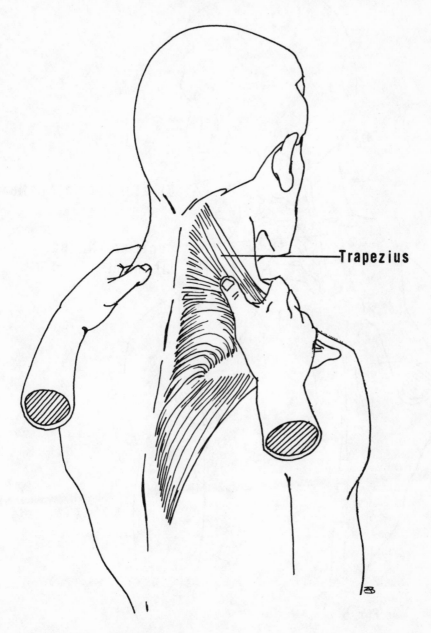

Trapezius

Fig. 4

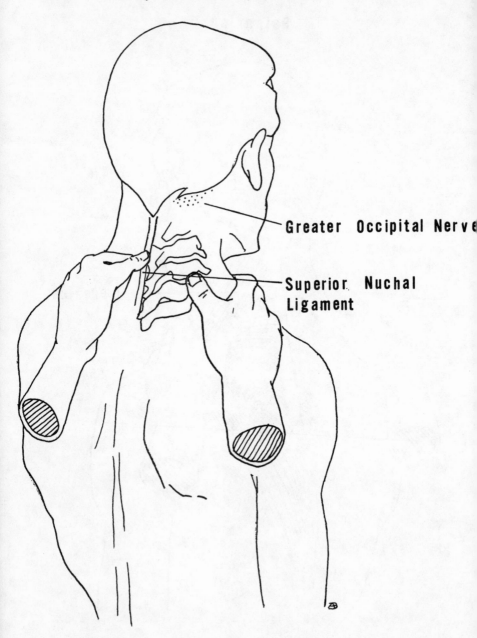

Greater Occipital Nerve

Superior Nuchal Ligament

Fig. 5

Motion Testing—Passive

Flexion and Extension. (See Fig. 6.) To test flexion and extension of the neck, the patient should be instructed to nod his head forward in a "yes" movement. He should be able to touch his chin into his chest (normal range of flexion) and to look directly at the ceiling above him (normal range of extension). If there is injury in the cervical area due to soft tissue trauma, this may result in a limitation in the range of motion and a disruption of the normal, smooth arch.

Rotation. The patient should be able to move his head far enough to both sides (see Fig. 7) so that his chin is almost in line with his shoulder. The motion should proceed with ease and in a smooth arch.

Lateral Bending. The patient in this test should try to touch his ear to his shoulder (see Fig. 8), making certain that he does not compensate for limited motion by lifting his shoulder to his ear. Normally, he should be able to tilt his head approximately 45° toward each shoulder. Enlarged cervical lymph nodes may limit motion, especially in lateral bending.

Motion Testing—Active

In order to test the nerve innervation to the muscles of the neck, the same motions of flexion-extension, lateral rotation-lateral bending are again repeated, except this time the physician will place his hand or hands in a position as to prevent the rotation of the head or flexion or extension in order to determine the ability of the muscles to contract and maintain adequate strength. If there is a limitation or a giving way of the muscle strength, this is an indication of nerve pathology.

Flexion. The primary flexor muscles are the sternocleidomastoids, the scalenus muscles, and the paravertebral muscles, which are innervated by the spinal accessory or cranial nerve XI. These muscles and nerves are tested (see Fig. 9) by placing the hand on the patient's forehead resisting forward flexion of the head and noting the maximum resistance he can overcome.

Extension. Primary extensors are the paravertebral extensor muscles, i.e., splenius, semispinalis, capitus, and trapezius, also innervated by the spinal accessory or cranial nerve XI. The test for this (see Fig. 9) is done similarly except that the physician places his hand on

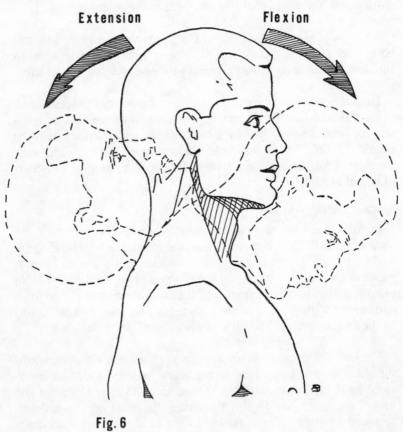

Fig. 6

Rotation

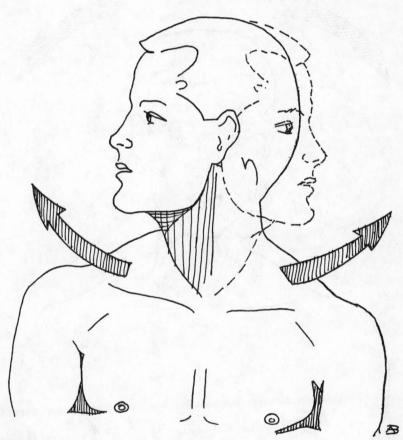

Fig. 7

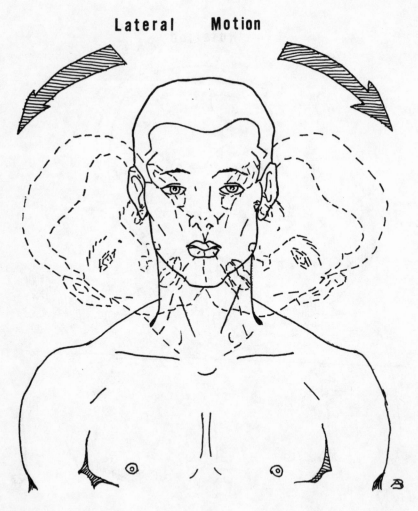

Lateral   Motion

Fig. 8

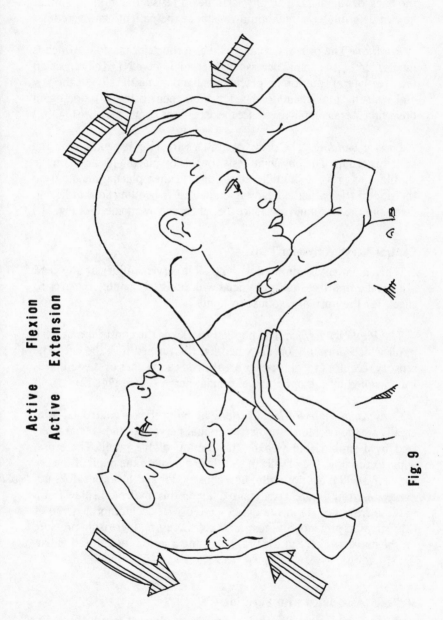

Active Flexion

Active Extension

Fig. 9

the back of the head. The physician again resists the motion, so that he can determine the maximum resistance the patient can overcome.

Rotation. The primary rotator is the sternocleidomastoid, which is innervated by the spinal accessory or cranial nerve XI. The physician tests for lateral rotation by placing his hand along the side of the jaw and resisting movement to the right and then to the left side again observing the maximum resistance the patient can overcome. (See Fig. 10.)

Lateral Bending. The primary muscles for lateral bending are the scalenus group. The physician tests for this by placing his hand on the shoulder to prevent shoulder elevation and then placing his hand on the side of the patient's head; again he resists bending so that he can determine the maximum resistance the patient can overcome. (See Fig. 11.)

Central Nervous System Testing

When a patient is admitted with possible cervical injury or any head injury, the first test that a physician will do is to examine the eyes to check for the normal response to light.

The Pupillary Reflex. The pupillary reflex is the constriction of the pupil which normally occurs when light is flashed into the eye. The sensory receptors for this reflex are the rods and cones of the retina. It is controlled by the optic nerve, cranial nerve II (see Fig. 12).

Consensual Light Reflex. Consensual light reflex is controlled principally by the occulomotor nerve, cranial nerve III, and is characterized by a similar, but weaker constriction of the pupil. Therefore, when examining, the physician will flash a light on the pupil of the eye to see if it will react normally, i.e., constriction. If this reflex does not exist, i.e., pupils are fixed and dilated, this indicates some brain pathology, either (1) in the optic nerve or the occulomotor nerve or (2) increased pressure on the brain and, therefore, increasing pressure on the nerves which exit the brain, causing a serious and life threatening situation.

Reflexes Associated with Focusing

When the eyes are directed to an object close at hand, three different reflex responses are brought into co-operative action:

Active   Rotation

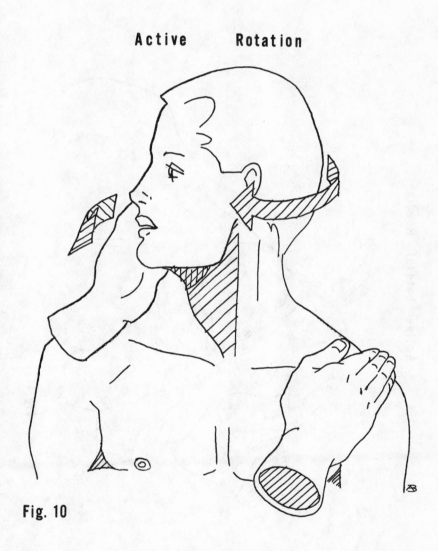

Fig. 10

Active Lateral Bending

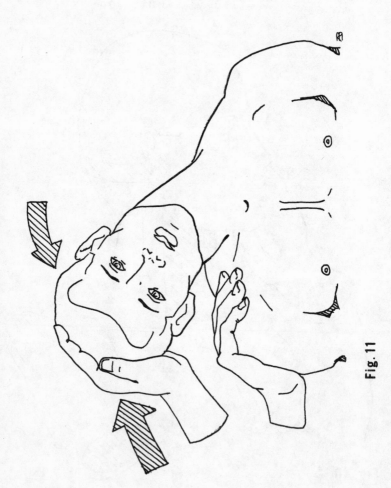

Fig. 11

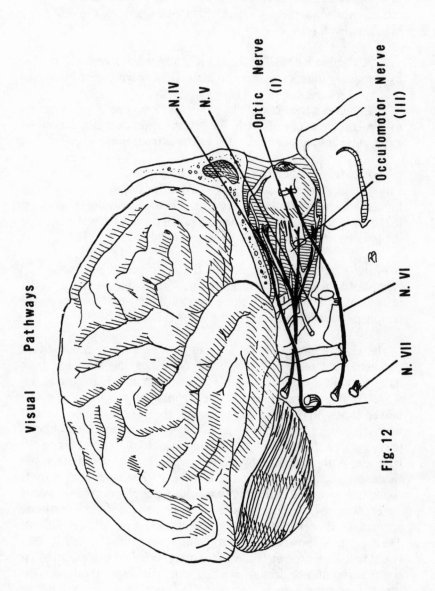

Visual   Pathways

N. IV

N. V

Optic   Nerve
(I)

Occulomotor Nerve
(III)

N. VI

N. VII

Fig. 12

1. Convergence. The medial recti muscles contract to move the eyes into alignment so that images in each eye focus on the same part of the retina. Otherwise, the two images cannot be fused and diplopia (double vision) will result.

2. Accommodation. The lenses are thickened as a result of tension by the ciliary muscles in order to maintain a sharp-focused image.

3. Pupillary constriction. The pupils are narrowed as an optical aid to regulate the depth of focus. The constriction does not depend on any change in illumination and is separate from the light reflex.

Protective Reflexes. If an object is quickly thrust in front of the eyes without warning, it causes a blink. This reflex response cannot be inhibited voluntarily. Impulses are sent in certain neurologic pathways in the brain and exit the facial nerve (cranial nerve VII), which activate the muscles around the eyelid to close the lid. (See Fig. 12.)

Visual Field. Destroying one of the optic nerves blinds the eye. Atrophy of the optic nerve affects some fibers but spares others, and, instead of total blindness, there usually is loss of function in the peripheral parts of the field of vision of each eye.

The visual fields (see Fig. 13) can be measured in detail with a perimeter, but there is a simple way of examining them for gross defects. While the subject fixes his gaze straight ahead, an object is introduced at some point beyond the normal periphery of vision and moved slowly toward the line of vision. (See Fig. 14.) The point at which the object is first seen is noted, and after repeating the process in several directions, an estimate of the extent of the field of vision can be made. With optic atrophy there may be a reduction of both visual fields, or a centrally located patch of visual loss (scotoma) may be found in each eye. Restricted visual fields without any organic lesions are encountered in some psychoneurotic patients to whom everything appears as if viewed through twin-barrelled guns (tunnel vision). These patients, however, do not stumble over objects, and if their visual fields are accurately measured on repeated occasions, gross inconsistencies may be demonstrated. Tunnel vision may result from injury to the optic chiasma (point where the optic nerves join behind the eye) and may occur without loss of consciousness.

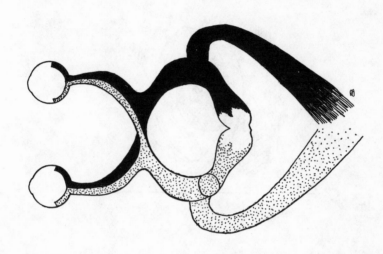

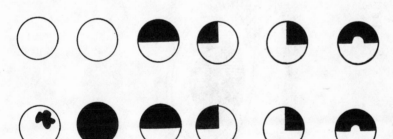

Fig. 13

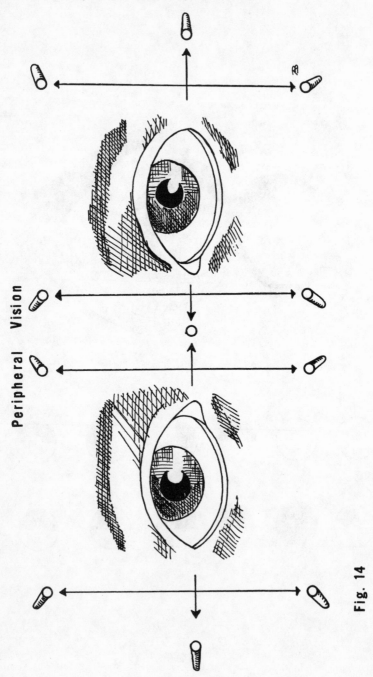

Peripheral Vision

Fig. 14

Vertigo. Vertigo is another common problem which may be seen in cervical or head injuries. The ability to maintain balance and to maintain a sense of direction and motion is controlled by the vestibular branch (see Fig. 15) of the acoustic nerve or cranial nerve VIII. The vestibular branch is connected to the semicircular canal and gives the sense of equilibrium. Vertigo is a sensation of whirling. The individual himself may have a subjective feeling of rotation, or it may seem to him that external objects are spinning around. Feelings of giddiness, faintness, and light-headedness may be vaguely described in somewhat similar terms, but they should not be mistaken for true vertigo.

Meniere's Syndrome. Meniere's Syndrome is a disease of uncertain nature which is characterized by periodic attacks of severe vertigo, often accompanied by nausea and prostration. Tinnitus (whistling or ringing in the ears) and impairment of hearing are included in this syndrome. Meniere's Syndrome may be associated with exposure to loud noises or simple head trauma.

Petechial hemorrhages. Acceleration-deceleration injuries with cervical involvement may cause microscopic or petechial hemorrhages in the brain (see Fig. 16). These small hemorrhagic areas will not elicit any gross brain pathology as can be diagnosed by neurologic testing, but have been reported to cause headaches and discomfort.

Peripheral Nerve Testing in the Upper Extremity

Another problem which arises from a hyperextension-hyperflexion injury to the cervical region is a herniated disc. (See Fig. 17.) This is frequently diagnosed because of decreased motor function, decreased reflexes, and areas of altered sensation (pain) in the arm and shoulder. The upper extremity is innervated by cervical nerves C5 through T1. These nerves, exiting through intervertebral foramina (holes) in the cervical spine, form a plexus (grouping of nerves) in the shoulder referred to as the brachial plexus. The following diagnostic tests will help determine whether there is a relationship between upper extremity neurologic problems and a primary source in the neck.

In order to understand the tests that are performed for neurological injuries to the brachial plexus, one must first review and understand the components and functions of the brachial plexus. (See Fig. 18.) The brachial plexus originates chiefly from branches and divisions of the cervical nerves C5-C8 plus the first thoracic nerve. These branches

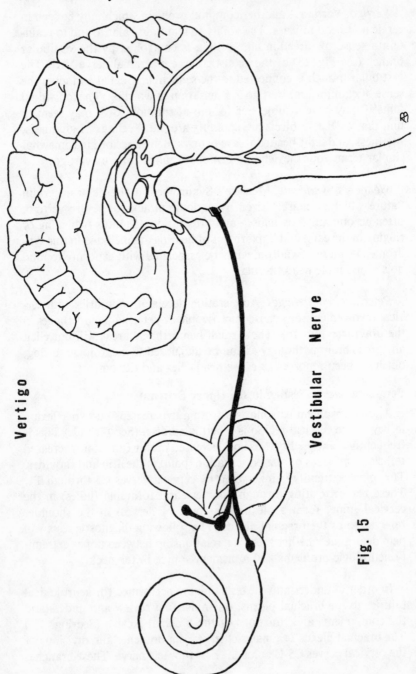

Vertigo

Vestibular Nerve

Fig. 15

Petechial Hemorrhages

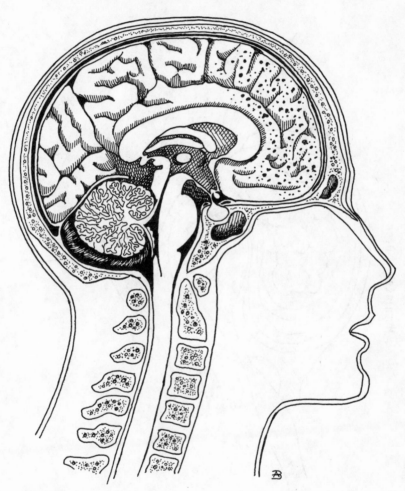

Fig. 16

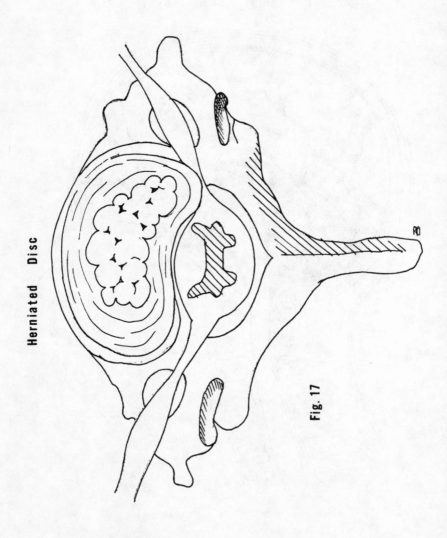

Herniated   Disc

Fig. 17

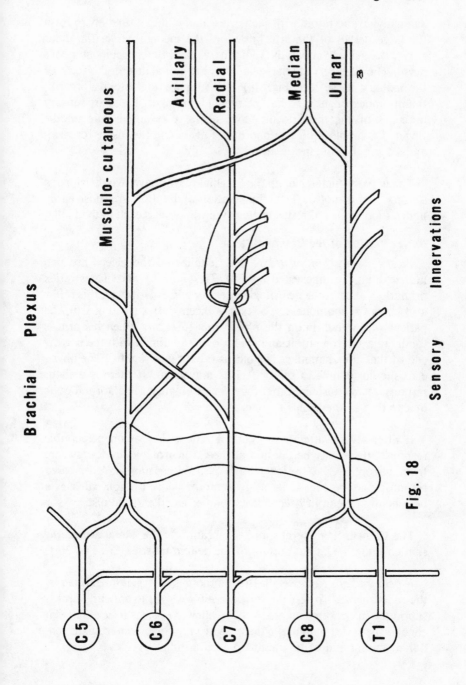

Fig. 18

again divide and rejoin with each other many times ultimately to form the large nerves of the arm known as the median nerve, the ulnar nerve, the axillary nerve, the radial nerve, and the musculocutaneous nerve. The fifth cervical nerve supplies the lateral arm in the form of the axillary nerve (see Fig. 19). C6 supplies the lateral forearm, thumb, index finger, and half of the middle finger. These are sensory branches of the musculocutaneous nerve. C7 supplies the middle finger, C8 supplies the ring and little fingers and the inside forearm, and T1 supplies the inside arm.

The nerves which make up the brachial plexus have two divisions: a sensory and a motor. Their innervation and action are most easily understood by use of reflex testing. We will discuss each individually.

Reflex Testing of the Brachial Plexus

Biceps Reflex Testing (C5). The deltoid and the biceps are two muscles that are innervated by C5. (See Fig. 19.) The biceps reflex primarily indicates the neurologic integrity of C5. However, this reflex also has a C6 component. To test the biceps reflex (see Fig. 20), the patient's arm rests upon the physician's forearm. When his arm is totally relaxed, the physician taps his own thumbnail with the narrow end of the reflex hammer. The biceps should jerk slightly. The physician should be able to see or feel its movement. If there is a slight response, it is considered that the C5 neurologic level is normal in its innervation of the biceps muscle.

If after several attempts to elicit a reflex, there is no perceptible response, there may be a lesion at the C5 neurologic level anywhere from the root at C5 to the innervation of the biceps muscle. A decreased response may be caused by a lower motor neuron lesion, such as a peripheral nerve injury secondary to a herniated cervical disc.

The C5 neurologic level supplies sensation to the lateral arm in the skin covering the lateral portion of the deltoid muscle. (See Fig. 20.)

Brachioradialis Reflex (C6). Brachioradialis muscle is innervated by the radial nerve. To test the reflex (see Fig. 21), the patient's arm is supported in the same manner used to elicit the biceps reflex. The flat edge of the reflex hammer is then used to tap the brachioradialis tendon at the far end of the radius to elicit a radial jerk.

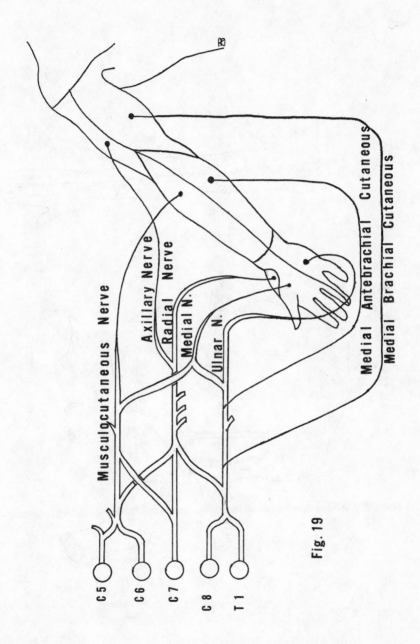

Fig. 19

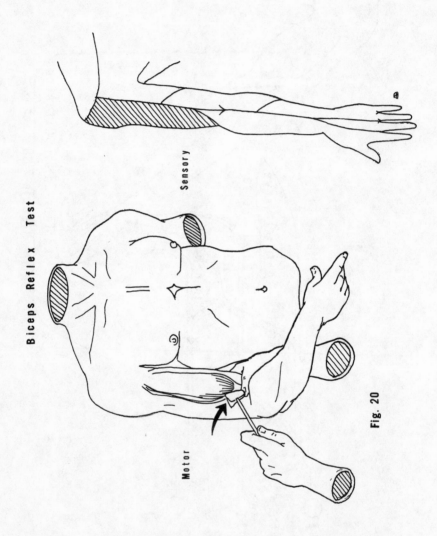

Biceps Reflex Test

Sensory

Motor

Fig. 20

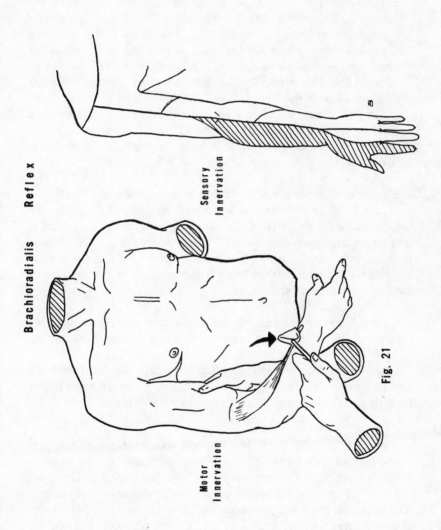

Brachioradialis Reflex

Sensory Innervation

Motor Innervation

Fig. 21

C6 supplies sensation to the lateral forearm, the thumb, the index, and one-half of the middle finger. To easily remember the C6 sensory distribution, it is often referred to as the "six shooter."

Triceps Reflex (C7). The triceps (see Fig. 22) is innervated by the radial nerve. The reflex is largely a function of the C7 neurologic level. The physician keeps the patient's arm in the same position used for the two previous tests. The patient is asked to relax his arm completely. When the physician is certain that it is relaxed (he can feel the lack of tension in the triceps muscle), he taps the triceps tendon where it crosses the back of the elbow with the narrow end of the reflex hammer. The physician should be able to see the reflex or to feel it as a slight jerk on the supporting forearm. C7 supplies sensation to the middle finger. Occasionally, middle finger sensation is also supplied by C6 and C8.

Testing of C8. Since C8 has no motor reflex, muscle strength and sensation tests are utilized to determine its integrity. The muscles involved are the finger flexors, namely flexor digitorum superficialis and flexor digitorum profundus. The flexor digitorum superficialis receives innervation from the median nerve, while the flexor digitorum profundus receives half its innervation from the ulnar nerve and half from the median nerve.

To test finger flexion (see Fig. 23), the physician curls or locks his fingers into the patient's left fingers and tries to pull them out of flexion.

C8 supplies sensation to the ring finger and little fingers of the hand and to the distal half of the forearm (ulna side). The ulna side of the little finger is the purest area for ulnar nerve sensation.

Testing of T1. Since T1, like C8, has no identifiable reflex, it is evaluated for its motor and sensory components by checking for finger abduction. The finger abductors are innervated by the ulnar nerve. They are the dorsal interossei and the abductor digiti quinti. The physician evaluates abduction by squeezing (see Fig. 24) the abducted fingers together and having the patient try to open them.

The sensation is supplied to the medial arm by the medial brachiocutaneous nerve.

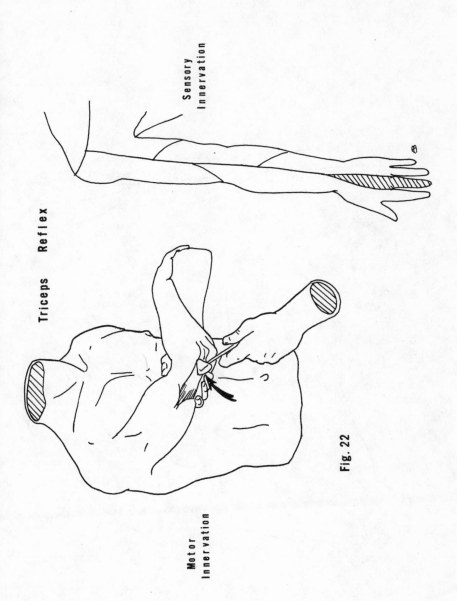

Triceps Reflex

Sensory Innervation

Motor Innervation

Fig. 22

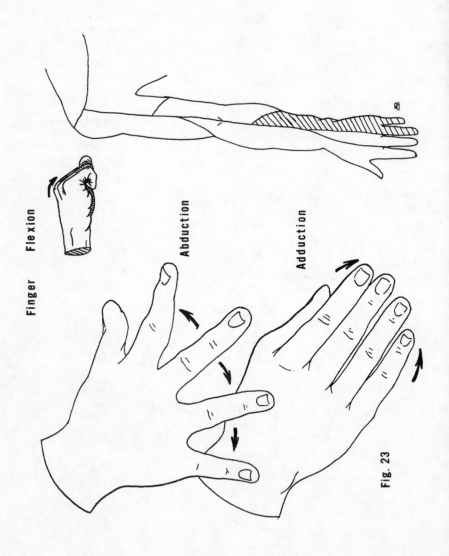

Finger   Flexion

Abduction

Adduction

Fig. 23

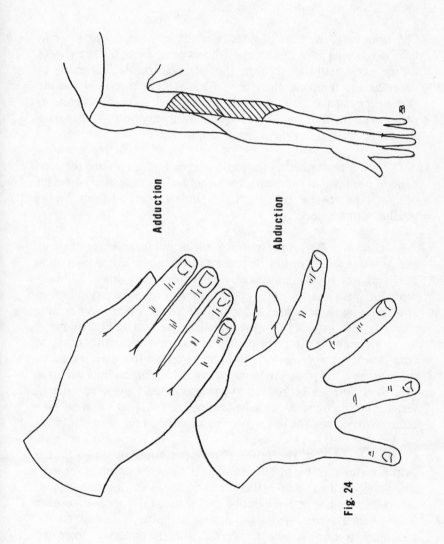

Adduction

Abduction

Fig. 24

Other Tests for Upper Extremity

In addition to the tests which have been previously described, there are about five other tests which are directly related to the cervical spine. These will be described in detail.

Distraction Test. This demonstrates the effect that traction may have in relieving pain. Distraction relieves pain caused by a narrowing of the nerve pathway through the vertebrae (neural foramen) by widening the foramen, therefore relieving nerve root compression. Distraction also relieves pain of the cervical spine by decreasing pressure on the joint capsules. In addition, it may help alleviate muscle spasms by relaxing the contracted muscles.

This test is performed by the physician (see Fig. 25) placing the open palm of one hand under the patient's chin and the other hand upon his occiput. The physician then gradually lifts the head to remove the weight from the neck.

Compression Test. A narrowing of the neural foramen, pressure on the vertebral joints, or muscle spasms can cause increased pain upon compression. In addition, the compression test may faithfully reproduce pain referred to the upper extremity from the cervical spine, and, in doing so, may help locate the neurologic level of any existing pathology. This test is performed by the physician (see Fig. 26) pressing down upon the top of the patient's head while he is either sitting or lying down. If there is an increase in pain in either the cervical spine or the extremity, the physician notes the exact distribution. In a variation of this test, the head is rotated to one side (usually away from the injured side thereby stretching the cervical nerves), and the same procedure is repeated. The test is more sensitive when the head is rotated.

The Valsalva Test. The Valsalva Test is performed by having the patient hold his breath and bear down as if he were moving his bowels. The physician then asks whether the patient feels any increase in pain, and if so, whether he can describe the location. If a space-occupying lesion, such as a herniated disc is present in the cervical canal, the patient may develop pain in the cervical spine secondary to increased pressure. Pain may also radiate into the arm. (See Fig. 27.)

Adson Test. This test is used to determine the state of the subclavian

Distraction   Test

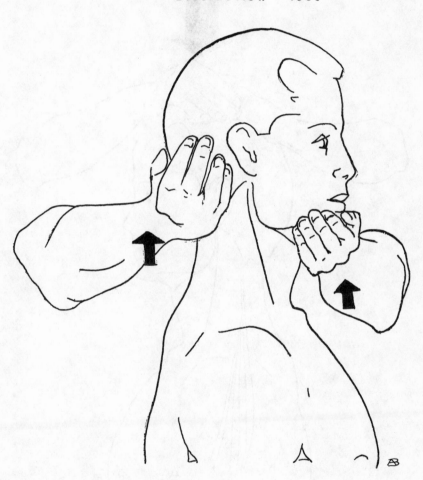

Fig. 25

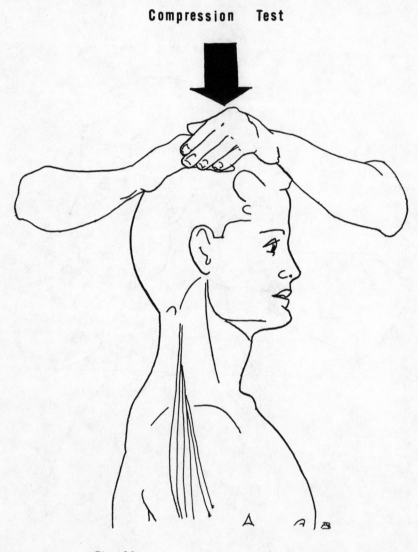

Fig. 26

Valsalva   Test

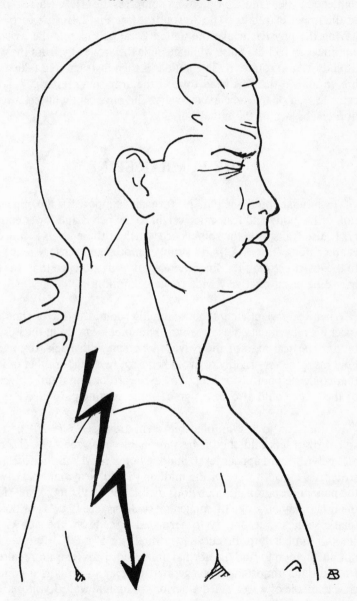

Fig. 27

artery, which may be compressed by an extracervical rib or by a tightened scalene muscle which can compress the artery where it passes to the upper extremity. The Adson test (see Fig. 28) is performed by having the physician take the patient's radial pulse at the wrist. He continues to feel the pulse while he pulls the arm away from the body, extends it, and rotates it. The patient is then instructed to take a deep breath and to turn his head toward the arm being tested. If there is compression of the subclavian artery, the physician will feel a reduction or absence of the radial pulse.

THE LUMBAR SPINE

The lumbar spine (see Fig. 29) furnishes support for the upper portion of the body and transmits weight to the pelvis and lower extremity. It also transports the spinal cord which at these levels is called the cauda equina (horse tail) and supplies motor and sensory perception to the lower extremities. Since there are no ribs attached to it, the lumbar spine has a relatively wide range of motion.

When the patient enters the examining room, the doctor should inspect his movements, posture, and spatial relationship in the horizontal and vertical axes of the pelvis. A patient with back trouble may hold his spine very rigidly to avoid bending, twisting, or other motions that could be painful for him. Any awkward or unnatural movement of the spine could also be a sign of some existing pathology.

Posture can give a graphic representation (see Fig. 30) of many spinal disorders and should be thoroughly analyzed. The shoulders and pelvis should appear level, and the bony, as well as the soft, tissue structures on both sides of the midline should be symmetrical. When the patient is standing, an obvious inclination or listing to one side or the other may be a sign of congenital scoliosis (see Fig. 31) or possible sciatic scoliosis, secondary to herniated disc. From the side view, a smooth lumbar lordotic curve is normal (see Fig. 30). However, it is not uncommon to find the normal lumbar lordosis (curvature) altered. In addition, abnormally exaggerated lumbar lordosis is a common characteristic of a weakened anterior abdominal wall. Kyphosis is the abnormality of increased convexity in the thoracic spine as viewed from the side, i.e., hunchback.

Adson Test

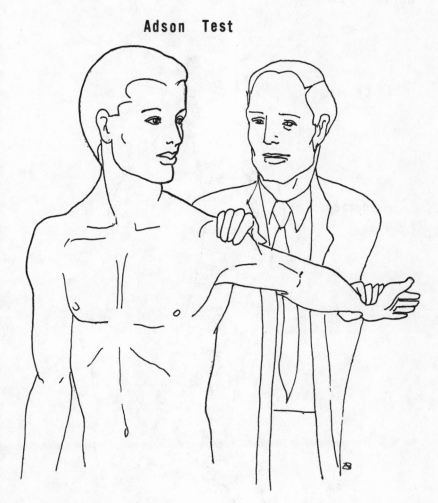

Fig. 28

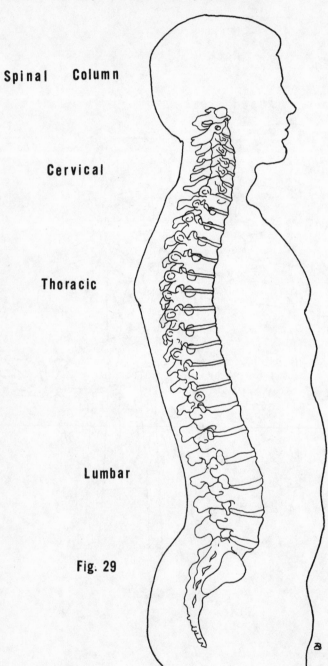

Spinal   Column

Cervical

Thoracic

Lumbar

Fig. 29

Posture

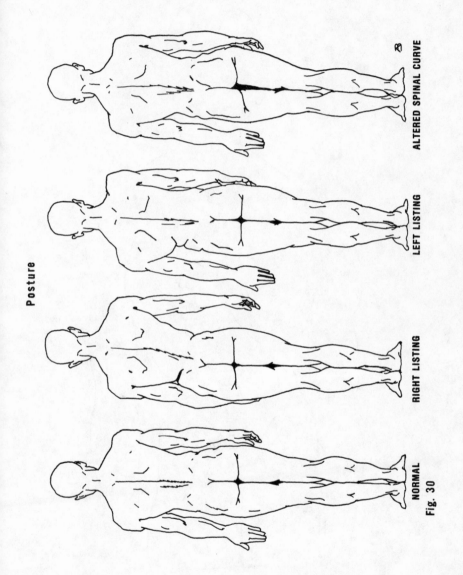

NORMAL   RIGHT LISTING   LEFT LISTING   ALTERED SPINAL CURVE

Fig. 30

Scoliosis

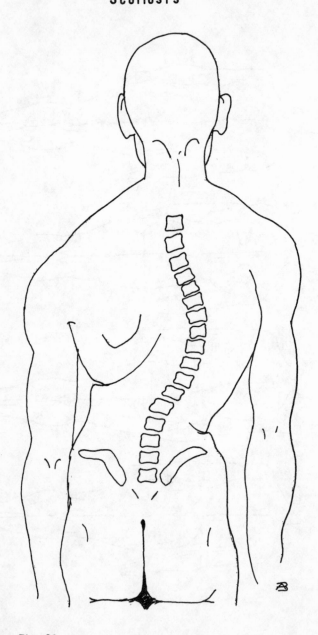

Fig. 31

All the bony protuberances of the vertebrae and the pelvis should be palpated and examined closely. If upon pressing or palpating any of the vertebrae pain is experienced by the patient, this may be an indication of a defect in the spine such as a lumbar herniated disc. (See Fig. 32.) A visible or palpable step-off from one bony process to another may be an indication of spondylolisthesis (forward slippage of one vertebra over the body of another—most often L5 on S1, or L4 on L5). Spondylosis is a general term for degenerative changes due to osteoarthritis. These conditions may cause pain in the back. In conjunction with these defects, there is the likelihood that a nerve root has been stretched or compressed or a disc herniated, with accompanying pain down one or both legs.

Range of Motion Testing

The bodies of the lumbar vertebrae are separated by elastic, segmental intervertebral discs, which are composed of an annulus fibrosis (tough outer part) and a nucleus pulposus (spongy inner part). (See Fig. 32.) Vertebral motion is greatest where the discs are thickest and the joint surfaces largest. Both of these conditions exist in the lower lumbar region between L4, L5, and S1. Where there is more motion, however, there is more chance of a breakdown, and herniated discs and osteoarthritis are found in the lower spine much more often than in the upper lumbar spine. Since there are no restraining ribs in the lumbar spine, more flexion, extension, and rotation can take place than in the thoracic spine. Tests which are intended to demonstrate the range of motion in the low back and hips are routinely performed where there is a likelihood that the patient has sustained an injury to the lumbar spine.

Flexion. Major motion, such as flexion (see Fig. 33), primarily involves motion in the hip; only an insignificant amount of movement actually takes place in the spine itself.

Flexion is tested by having the patient bend as far forward as he can with his knees straight and try to touch his toes. If he cannot, measure the distance from his fingertips to the floor.

Extension. Extension (see Fig. 34) is tested by the physician placing one hand on the patient's back so that his palm rests on the lower back. Then the patient is instructed to bend backward as far as he can using the physician's hand for a fulcrum for his motion.

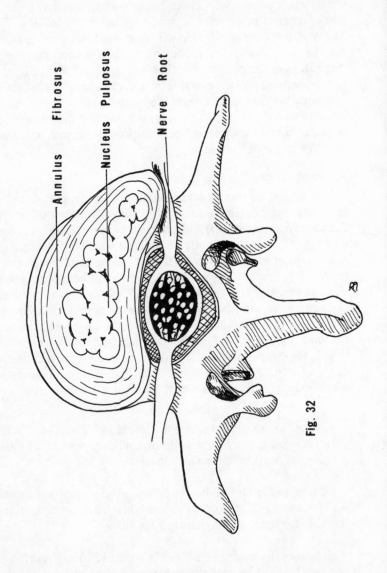

Lumbar Herniated Disc

Annulus Fibrosus

Nucleus Pulposus

Nerve Root

Fig. 32

Flexion

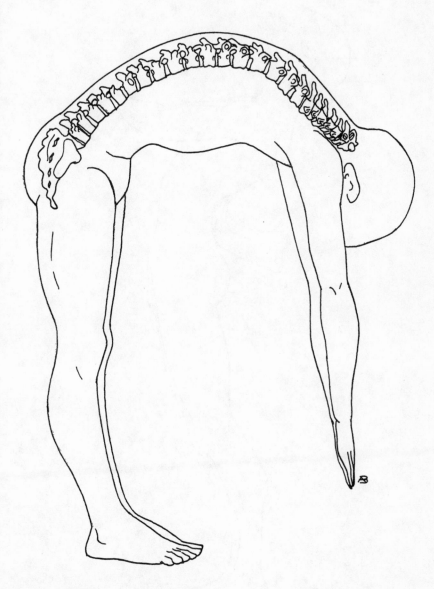

Fig. 33

Extension

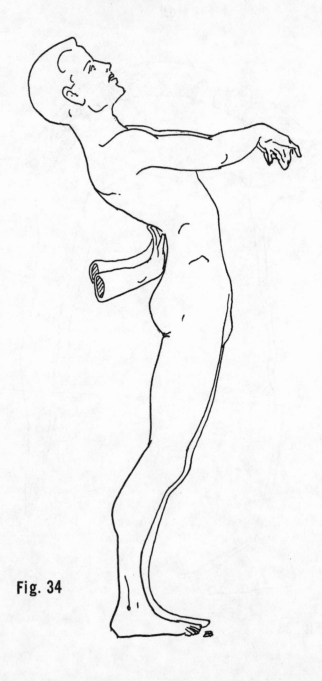

Fig. 34

The range of extension achieved should be estimated and recorded. Spondylolisthesis causes increased back pain upon extension; patients with this condition may find some relief in flexion.

Lateral bending. Lateral bending in the lumbar spine is not a pure motion, for it must occur in conjunction with elements of spinal rotation. Lateral bending (see Fig. 35) is tested by first stabilizing the iliac crest and then asking the patient to lean to the left and then to the right as far as he can. The physician notes how far he can bend to each side and compares the ranges of motion. Any discrepancy in the ranges of active and passive lateral bending of the low back should be noted.

Rotation. To test rotation (see Fig. 36) in the lumbar spine, the physician positions himself behind the patient and stabilizes his pelvis by placing one hand on the iliac crest and the other on the opposite shoulder. Then he turns the trunk by rotating the pelvis and the shoulder posteriorly.

Neurologic Examination

The neurologic examination of the lumbar spine includes an examination of the entire lower extremity, since the spinal cord or cauda equina pathologies, such as herniated discs and nerve root damage, are frequently manifested in the extremity itself in the form of altered reflexes, sensation, and muscle strength. Therefore, this examination describes the clinical relationship between the various muscles, reflexes, and sensory areas in the lower extremity and their particular spinal cord levels, so that detection and location of spinal cord problems can be accomplished with relative accuracy and ease.

In addition to testing each vertebra and the movement and rotation of the vertebrae, the pelvis and all of its bony components should be palpated and checked very carefully. (See Fig. 37.) This may be done either with the patient standing or lying down, whichever is more comfortable. However, some portion of this exam should be done while he is standing, since the pelvis is a weight-bearing structure, and in this position pathology might become apparent under the stress of weight.

Iliac Crest. The iliac crests are the bony protuberances at the waist. The physician places his hands at this level and palpates the iliac crests

Lateral   Bending

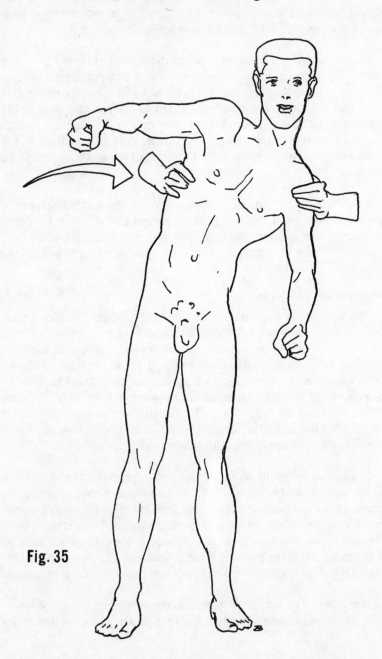

Fig. 35

Rotation

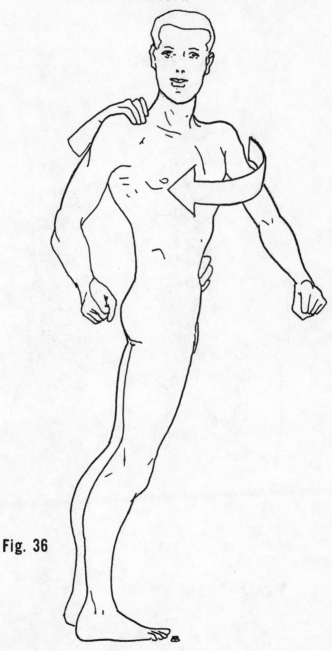

Fig. 36

Palpations

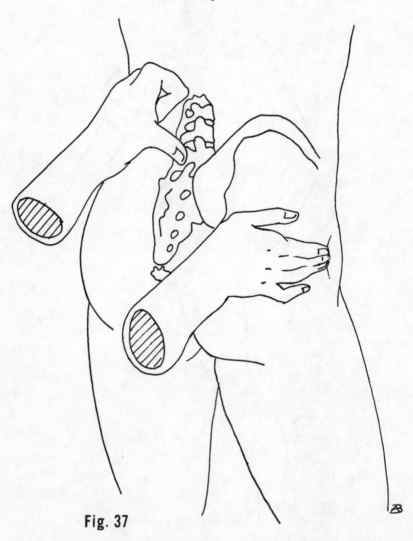

Fig. 37

in order to see if they are level in relationship to each other. When they are not level, it is usually because of some pelvic or vertebral abnormality. (See Fig. 38.)

Greater Trochanter. The physician can palpate the greater trochanter (see Fig. 39) by sliding his hands down the iliac tubercles; he will feel the posterior edge of the greater trochanter, which is felt as a bulge in the hip area. By pressing and palpating this area, the physician can detect if there has been a congenital dislocation of the hip or a hip fracture that has healed in a poor position. If either one of these two pathologies exist, the level of the trochanters may be unequal.

Posteriorly, it is important for the physician to palpate and detect the level of the ischial tuberosity. It is located in the middle of the buttocks at the approximate level of the gluteal fold (crease formed by the back of the thigh and the lower buttock). The importance of testing or locating and palpating the ischial tuberosity and the greater trochanter is that the sciatic nerve is located midway between these two bony projections. (See Fig. 40.) Once the physician has located these two, if he presses firmly into the soft tissue depression at the midpoint, he may be able to feel the sciatic nerve underneath the fatty tissue. Tenderness of the nerve may be due to a herniated disc at the lumbar region, a muscle spasm, or direct trauma to the nerve itself.

There are no individual reflexes for the T12, L1, L2, L3 levels, and their integrity can only be evaluated from muscle and sensory tests.

Muscle Testing—Lumbar Spine

The muscles will be tested in functional groups: flexors, extensors, abductors, and adductors. Each functional group receives innervation from a different peripheral nerve and, in most instances, from a different neurologic level.

Flexors. Iliopsoas muscle—the main flexor of the hip. It is innervated by the femoral nerve, a combination of T12, L1, L2, L3. This muscle is tested (see Fig. 41) by having the patient sit on the edge of the examining table with his legs dangling. The physician stablizes the pelvis by placing his hand over the iliac crest and asks the patient to raise his thigh actively from the table. The physician then places his hand over the distal femoral portion of the patient's knee and asks

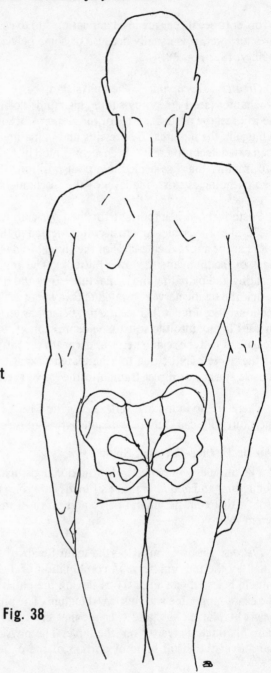

**Abnormal
Iliac Crest
Level**

Fig. 38

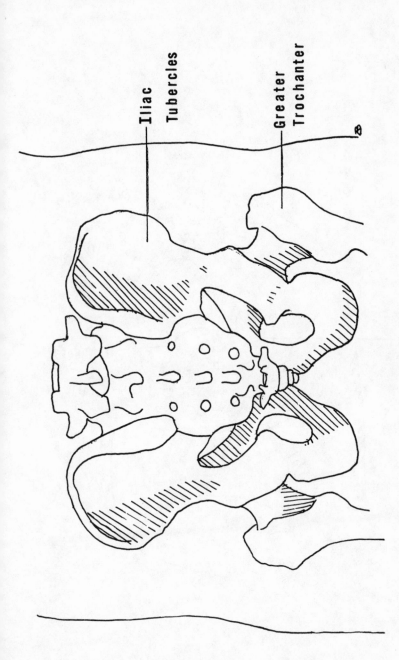

Iliac
Tubercles

Greater
Trochanter

Fig. 39

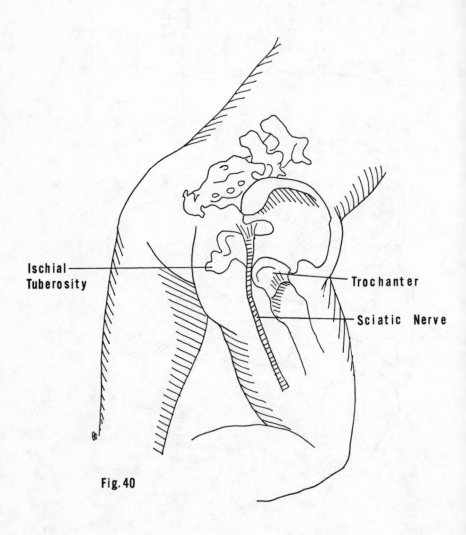

Fig. 40

Flexor   Testing

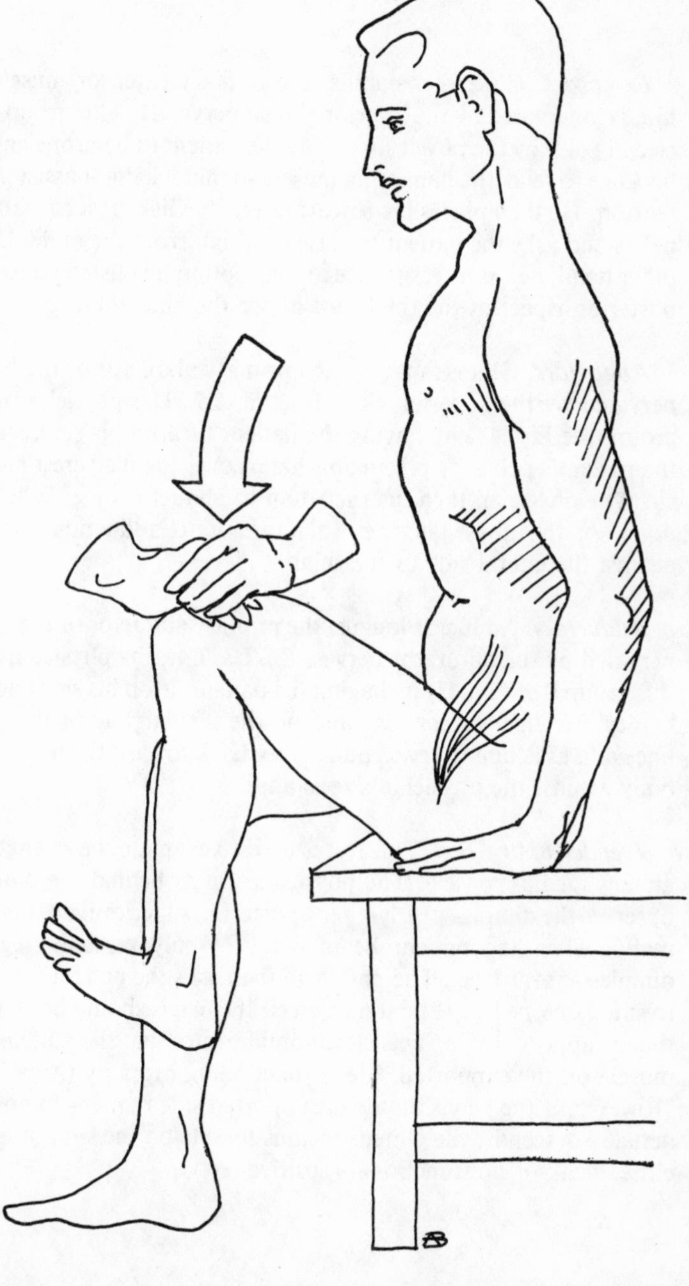

Fig. 41

him to raise his thigh further while the physician resists this motion. After determining the maximum resistance he can overcome, the test is repeated for the opposite iliopsoas muscle.

Extensors. Gluteus maximus, the primary extensor muscle of the hip, is innervated by the inferior gluteal nerve, S1. This group is tested (see Fig. 42) by the physician asking the patient to lie prone and to flex his knee to relax the hamstring muscle so that it cannot assist in hip extension. He then places his forearm over the iliac crest to stabilize the pelvis and asks the patient to raise his thigh from the table. Using his other hand, he offers resistance to this motion by pushing down on the posterior aspect of the thigh just above the knee joint.

Abductors. Gluteus medius, the primary abductor of the hip, is innervated by the superior gluteal nerve, L5. The physician tests this group (see Fig. 43) by having the patient turn on his side, stabilizing the patient's pelvis by placing his hands over the iliac crest and tubercle. The physician then instructs him to abduct his leg. When he has done so, the physician tries to return it to adduction by pushing against the lateral side of the thigh.

Adductors. Adductor longus, the primary adductor of the hip, is innervated by the obturator nerves, L2, L3, L4. The physician tests for this group (see Fig. 43) by having the patient lie on his side and abduct his leg. He then places his hand on the medial side of the patient's knee and asks him to try to pull his leg back toward the midline of the body against the physician's resistance.

Trendelenburg Test. This test is used to evaluate the strength of the gluteus medius muscle. The physician stands behind the patient and observes the dimples overlying the posterior-superior iliac spines. Normally, when the patient bears weight evenly on both legs, these dimples appear level. The physician then asks the patient (see Fig. 44) to stand on one leg. If he stands erect, the pelvis should be elevated on the unsupported side. This elevation indicates that the gluteus medius muscle on the supported side is functioning properly (negative test). However, if the pelvis on the unsupported side remains in position or actually descends, the gluteus medius muscle on the supported side is either weak or nonfunctional (positive test).

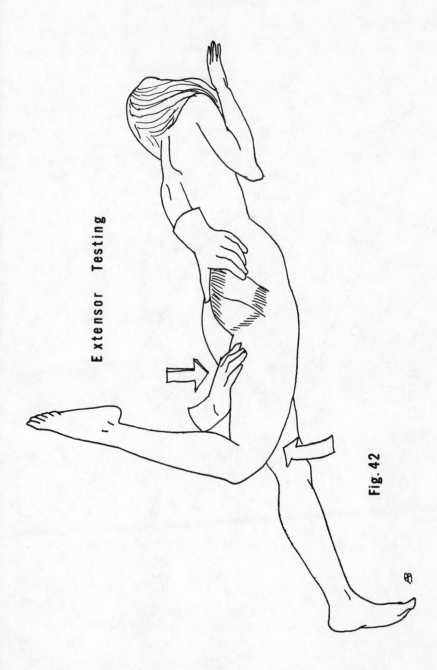

Extensor Testing

Fig. 42

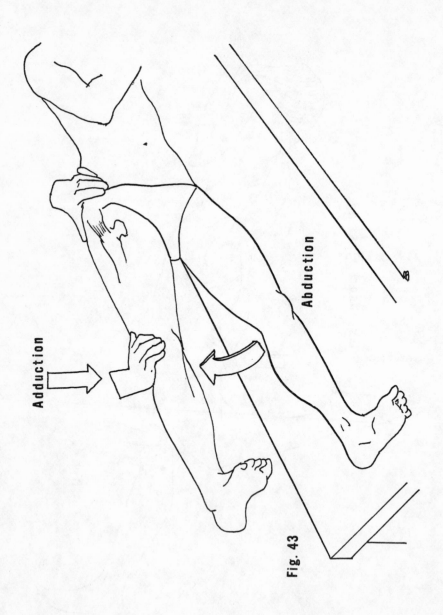

Fig. 43

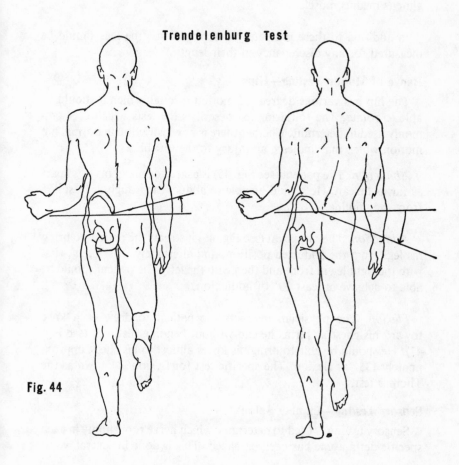

Trendelenburg   Test

Fig. 44

Fractures of the greater trochanter or a slipped femoral epiphysis can cause the muscle to become weak. Another possibility is a congenital dislocation of the hip, which not only brings the muscle's origin closer to its insertion, but also destroys the normal fulcrum around which it functions. In addition, neurologic problems including a nerve root lesion within the spinal canal, may cause paralysis of the gluteus medius muscle.

In addition to these previously described tests, the legs should be measured for any discrepancy in their length.

Range of Motion Testing—Hips

The hip has various degrees of motion through which it should be able to rotate. The following list describes the tests which are commonly used to determine whether there is any restriction in normal hip motion which may indicate an injury to the low back.

Abduction. The patient (see Fig. 45) is asked to spread his legs apart as far as he can. He should be able to abduct each thigh at least 45° from the midline.

Adduction. The physician (see Fig. 46) instructs the patient to bring his legs from the abducted position, and alternately cross them, first with the right leg in front and then with the left. The patient should be able to achieve at least 20° of adduction.

Flexion. The physician instructs the patient to draw each knee toward his chest as far as he can without bending his back (see Fig. 47). He should be able to bring his knees almost to his chest, approximately 135° of flexion. The specific test for flexion is known as the Thomas test.

Sensory Testing—Lumbar Spine

Sensory testing is used to determine which nerve root supply in each specific dermatome has been damaged. This is done in several ways:

1. The physician will drag a wisp of cotton across the skin to see if the patient can perceive any touch sensation. (See Fig. 48.)

2. He will use a pin prick to see if the patient has any pain sensation. (See Fig. 49.)

Abduction

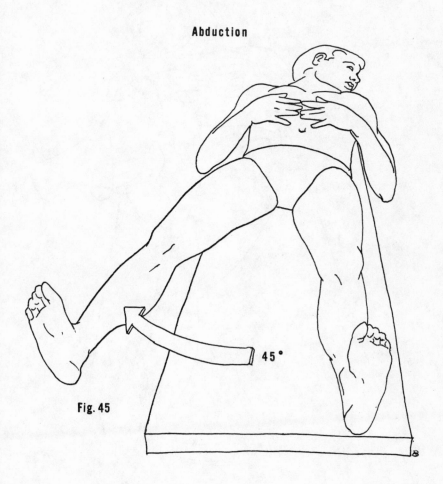

45°

Fig. 45

Adduction

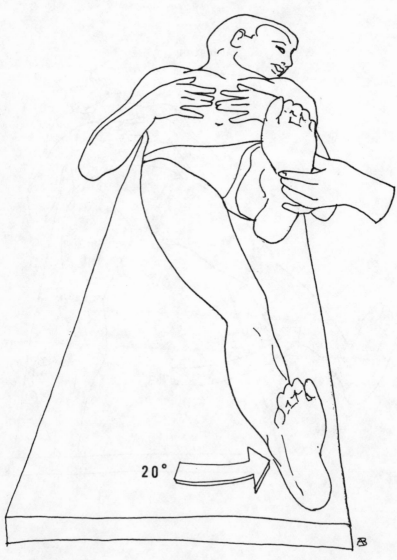

20°

Fig. 46

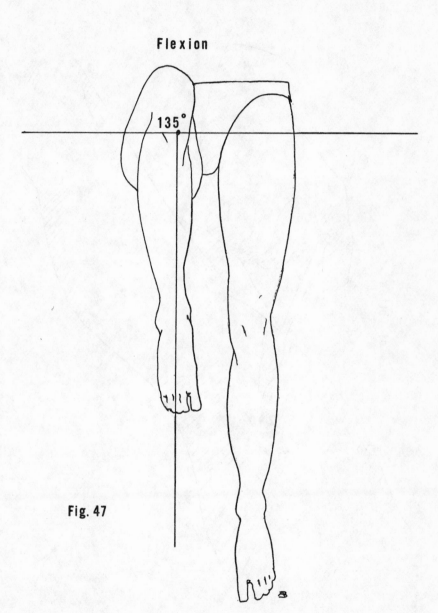

Flexion

135°

Fig. 47

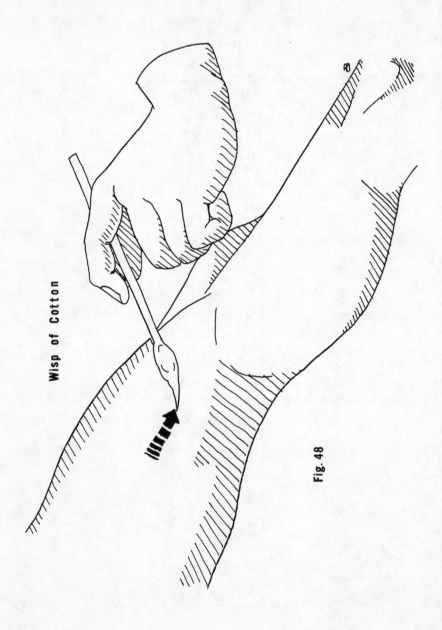

Wisp of Cotton

Fig. 48

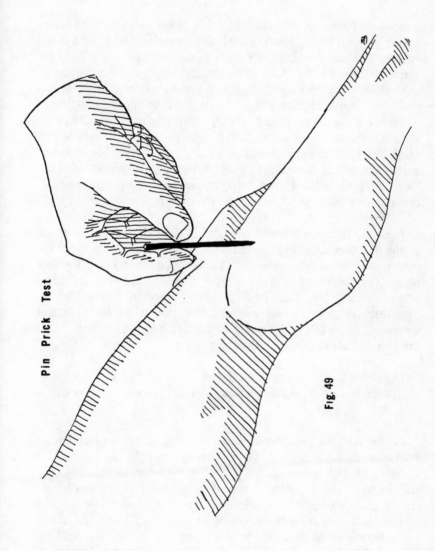

Pin Prick Test

Fig. 49

3. He will use the two point discrimination test in which he will use two pin points next to each other in order to determine the ability to discriminate between two points of pain. (See Fig. 50.)

Sensation is supplied to the hip, pelvic region, and thigh by nerves taking origin from the roots in the lower thoracic, lumbar, and sacral spines. The areas supplied by each particular neurologic level are broadly defined as bands, or dermatomes, which cover certain areas of skin. (See Fig. 51.) The dermatomes of the anterior abdominal wall run in transverse, slightly oblique bands; the strip approximately level with the umbilicus is supplied by T10, the strip immediately above the inguinal ligament is supplied by T12, and the area in between is supplied by T11. The sensory area of L1 lies immediately below the inguinal ligament and parallel to it on the upper anterior portion of the thigh. An oblique band immediately above the kneecap represents L3, and the area between L1 and L3 on the mid-thigh is supplied by L2.

The cluneal nerves (divisions of L1-2-3) cross the posterior portion of the iliac crest and supply sensation over the iliac crest between the posterior-superior iliac spine and the iliac tubercle and over the buttocks. The posterior cutaneous nerve of the thigh (S2) supplies sensation to a longitudinal band on the posterior aspect of the thigh, extending from the gluteal crease to beyond the popliteal fossa. The lateral cutaneous nerve of the thigh (S3) supplies sensation to a broad, oval area on the lateral aspect of the thigh.

The dermatomes surrounding the anus are arranged in three concentric circles, receiving innervation from S2 (the outermost ring), S3, and S4.

Reflex Testing. The patella reflex (see Fig. 52) is a deep tendon reflex, mediated through nerves emanating from the L2, L3, and L4 nerve roots, but predominately from L4. The patella reflex is considered an L4 reflex; however, even if the L4 nerve root is totally cut, the reflex is still present in significantly diminished form, since it receives innervation from sources other than L4. To test this reflex, the patient is asked to sit on the edge of the examining table with his legs dangling free, or the physician may have him sit on a chair with one leg crossed over his knee. In these positions, the infrapatellar tendon is stretched and primed. The reflex is elicited by tapping the ten-

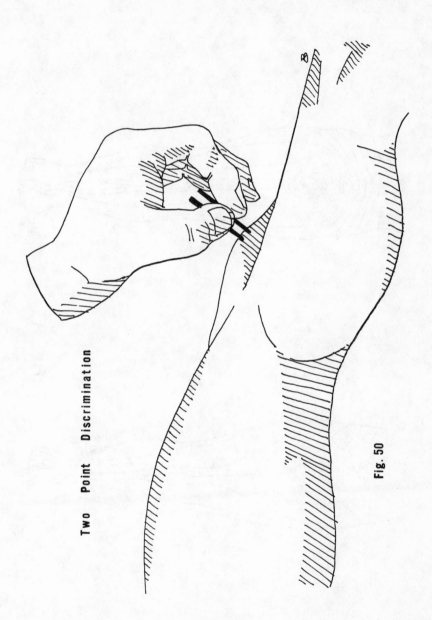

Two Point Discrimination

Fig. 50

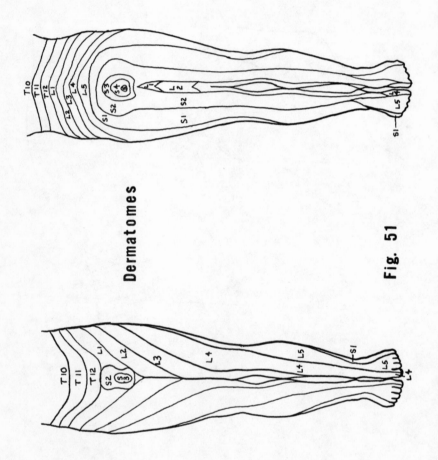

Dermatomes

Fig. 51

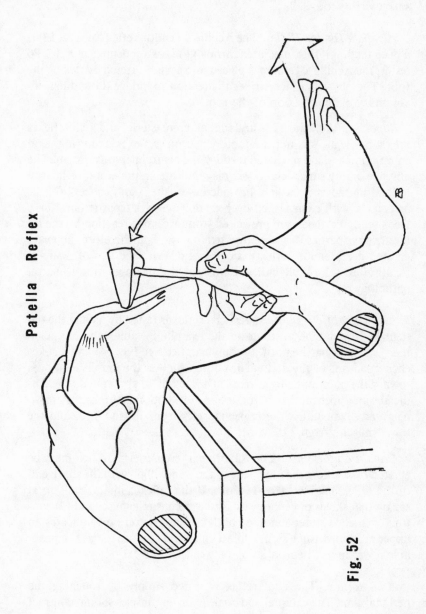

Patella Reflex

Fig. 52

don with a reflex hammer at the level of the knee joint, using a short, smart wrist action.

Achille's Tendon Reflex. The Achille's Tendon reflex (see Fig. 53) is a deep tendon reflex, mediated through the gastrocnemius muscle. To test it, the Achille's Tendon is placed into a slight stretch by flexing the foot. The physician then strikes the tendon to induce the sudden, involuntary plantar flexion of the foot.

Superficial Reflexes. The abdominal, cremasteric, and anal reflexes are superficial, or upper, motor neuron reflexes requiring skin stimulation and are mediated through the central nervous system. The absence of any superficial reflex may indicate an upper motor neuron lesion; an absence which has increased the significance of it is associated with exaggerated deep tendon reflexes (spastic paralysis). Deep tendon reflexes are prevented from excessive reaction by the inhibitory properties of the central nervous system; therefore, an exaggerated deep tendon reflex in combination with the loss of a superficial reflex is a double indication of cerebral or upper motor neuron pathology.

Abdominal Reflex. The superficial reflex is tested by having the patient lie in a supine position on the examining table. The physician then uses the sharp end of a reflex hammer (see Fig. 54) and strokes each quadrant of the abdomen, noting whether the umbilicus moves toward the point of being stroked. The lack of an abdominal reflex indicates an upper motor neuron lesion. The abdominal muscles are innervated segmentally, the upper muscles from T7 and T10, and the lower muscles from T10 to L1.

Cremasteric Reflex. The superficial cremasteric reflex may be elicited by stroking the inner side of the upper thigh with the sharp end of the reflex hammer. (See Fig. 55.) If the reflex is intact, the scrotal sac on that side is pulled upward as the cremasteric muscles (T12) contract. Absence or reduction of both cremasteric reflexes indicates an upper motor neuron lesion, while a unilateral absence suggests a probable lower motor neuron lesion between L1 and L2.

Anal Reflex. The anal reflex is tested simply by touching the perianal skin. The external and anal sphincter muscles should contract in response (S2, S3, S4).

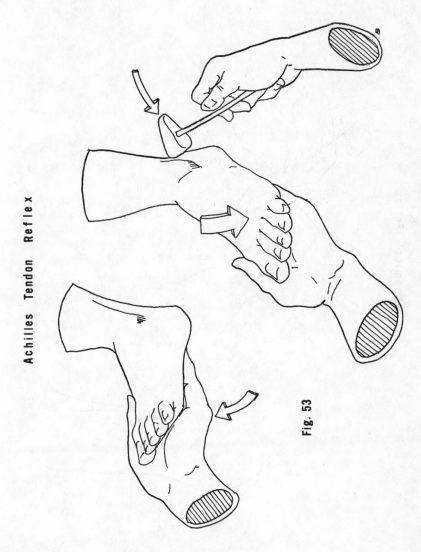

Achilles Tendon Reflex

Fig. 53

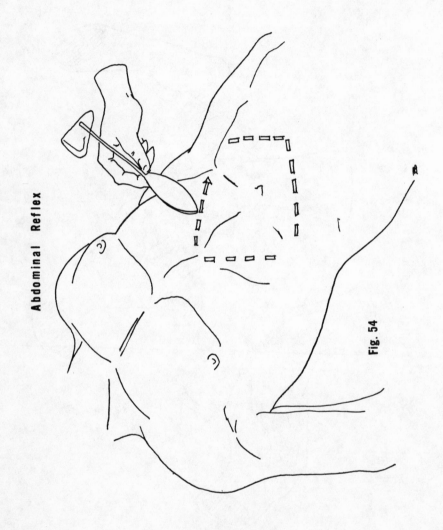

Abdominal Reflex

Fig. 54

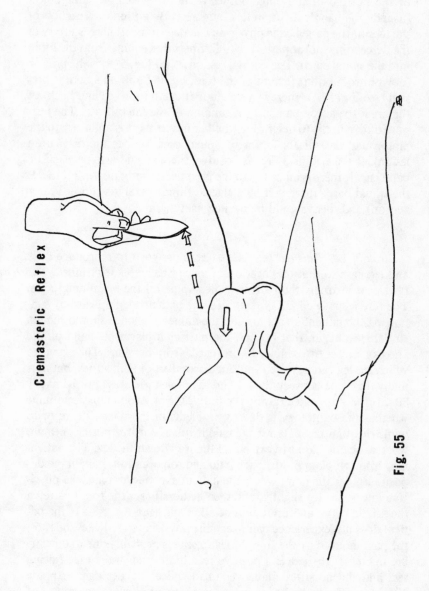

Cremasteric Reflex

Fig. 55

Babinski Test. The Babinski Test (see Fig. 56) involves the stroking of the bottom of the outer border of the foot with a blunt object (usually the handle of the reflex hammer). By noting the reaction of the toes of the patient, the physician can determine if there is injury to the descending motor pathways (i.e., fibers descending from the brain into the spinal cord). The normal response (see Fig. 57B) is the plantar (downward motion) flexion of the toes, but if Babinski's Sign is present (see Fig. 57A), there is a slow dorsiflexion (upward and back) of the great toe accompanied by a fanning of the lateral toes. The purpose of this test is to determine whether or not there is an injury to the motor pathway of the brain or spinal cord (upper motor neuron lesion). If the Babinski Sign is positive, there should also be a spastic paralysis. If there is an injury to the peripheral motor nerve as it leaves the spinal cord, there will be a flaccid (limp) paralysis (lower motor neuron) and there should be no Babinski Sign.

Straight Leg Raising Test. This test is designed to reproduce back and leg pain so that the location of its cause can be determined. The physician instructs the patient to lie supine on the examining table. The physician (see Fig. 58) then lifts the patient's leg upward by supporting the patient's foot around the ankle. The knee should remain straight; to insure that it does, the physician places his hand on the anterior aspect of the knee to prevent it from bending. The extent to which the leg can be raised without discomfort or pain varies, but normally the angle between the leg and the table measures approximately 80°. If the straight leg raising is painful, the physician must determine whether the pathology is due to problems in the sciatic nerve or to hamstring tightness. Hamstring pain involves only the posterior thigh, whereas sciatic pain can extend all the way down the leg. The patient may also complain of low back pain and, on occasion, pain in the opposite leg. At the point where the patient experiences pain, the physician lowers the leg slightly, and then he dorsiflexes the foot to stretch the sciatic nerve and reproduce sciatic pain. (See Fig. 58.) If the patient does not experience pain when the physician dorsiflexes the foot, the pain induced by the straight leg raising is probably due to hamstring tightness. If there is a positive reaction to the straight leg raising test and the dorsiflex maneuver (also called the Lessuge test), the physician asks the patient to locate, as nearly as possible, the source of his pain.

Babinski Test

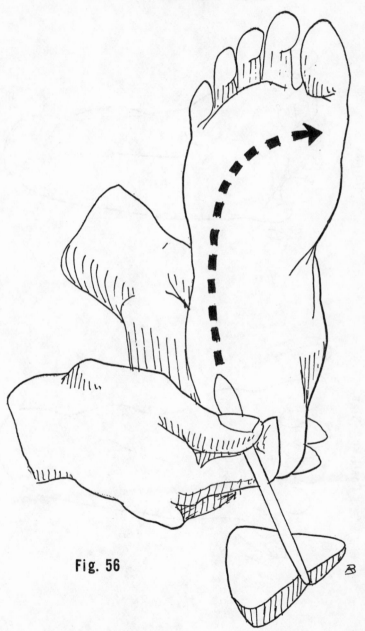

Fig. 56

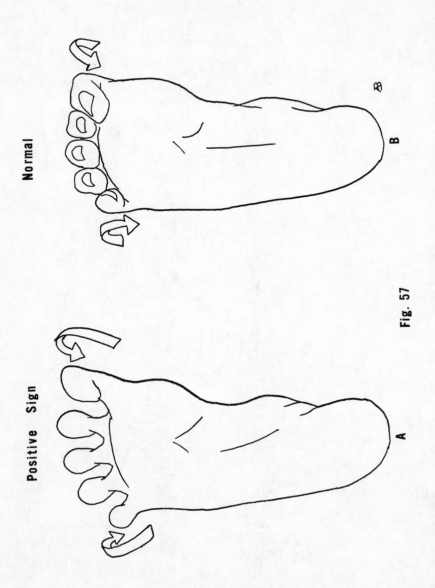

Fig. 57

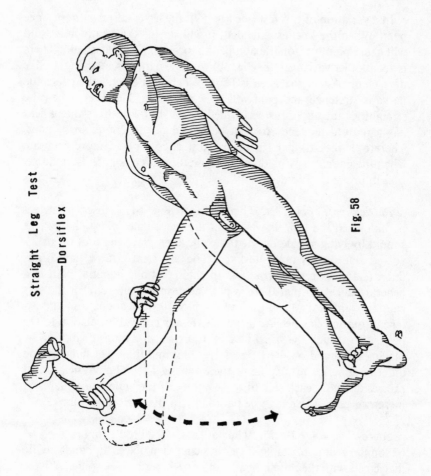

Straight Leg Test

Dorsiflex

Fig. 58

Next, with the patient lying in a supine position, the physician raises the uninvolved leg. If he complains of back and sciatic pain in the opposite (involved) side, there is presumptive evidence that there may be a space occupying lesion such as a herniated disc in the lumbar area. This test is also referred to as the positive cross-leg-straight-leg raising test.

In a variation of this test (see Fig. 59), the leg is raised with the knee bent. When the knee is extended, it will stretch the sciatic nerve and will cause pain, or dorsiflexion of the toes will also cause pain. There is yet another variation (see Fig. 60) with the patient seated on the edge of a chair. Again the knee is bent. When it is extended, the sciatic nerve is stretched and pain will be experienced. However, when the straight leg raising test is performed in the sitting position the patient has a natural tendency to lean back and not to complain of pain. Therefore, the straight leg raising test is considered more accurate when the patient is lying down because the patient's back is immobilized in prone position.

Patrick or Faber Test. This test (see Fig. 61) is used to detect pathology in the hip, as well as in the sacro-iliac joint. The patient should by lying supine on the table and then place the foot of his involved side on his opposite knee. The hip joint is now flexed, abducted, and externally rotated. In this position, inguinal pain is a general indication that there is pathology in the hip joint or the surrounding muscles. When the end point of flexion, abduction, and external rotation has been reached, the femur is fixed in relation to the pelvis. To stretch the sacro-iliac joint, extend the range of motion by placing one hand on the flexed knee joint and the other hand on the anterior-superior iliac spine of the opposite side. The physician then presses down on each side of these points. If the patient complains of increased pain, there may be pathology in the sacro-iliac joint.

Sacro-Iliac Joint Testing. The patient is asked to lie supine (see Fig. 62) on the examining table. The physician then places his hands on the iliac crests with the thumb on the anterior-superior iliac spine, with his palms on the patient's iliac tubercles. The physician then forcibly presses the pelvis toward the midline of the body. If the patient complains of pain around the sacro-iliac joint, there may be pathology in the joint itself, such as infection or problems secondary to trauma.

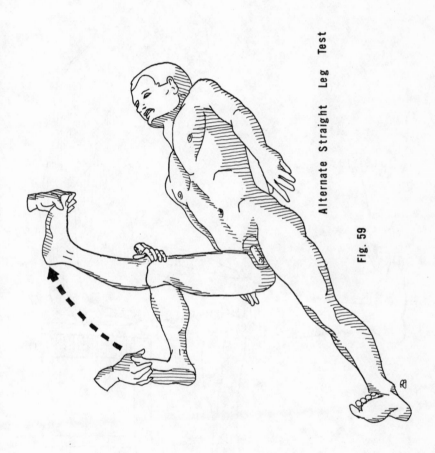

Alternate Straight Leg Test

Fig. 59

Seated
Straight Leg Test

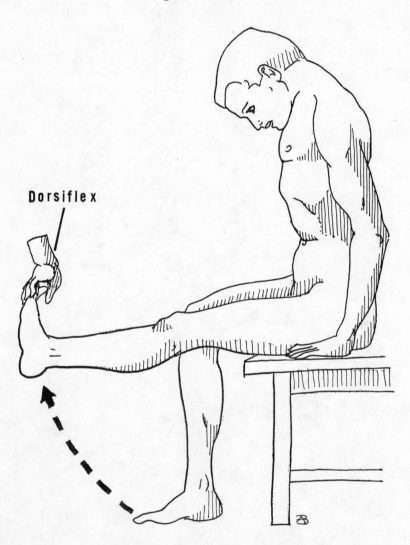

Dorsiflex

Fig. 60

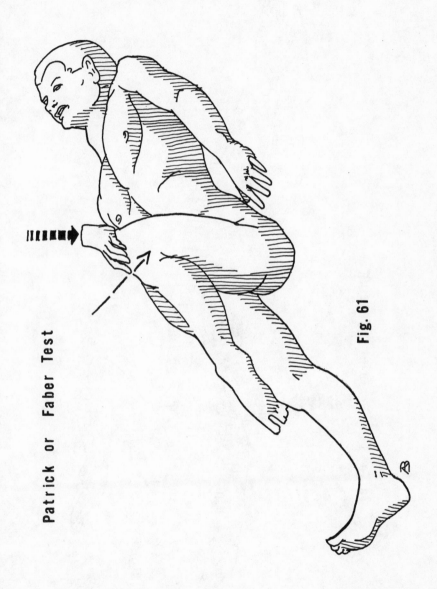

Patrick or Faber Test

Fig. 61

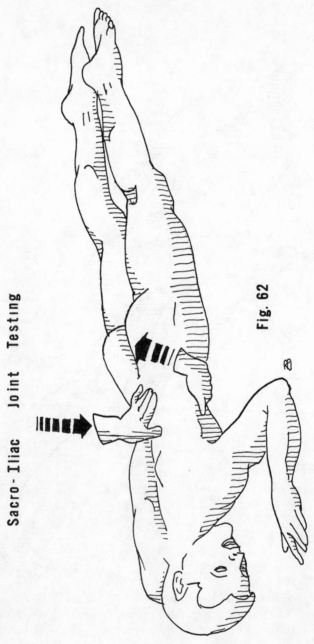

Sacro - Iliac   Joint   Testing

Fig. 62

Chapter 5

DISCOVERY PROCEDURES

INTRODUCTION

The increase in the importance of pretrial discovery is one of the most radical developments that affects the practice of the modern trial lawyer. Two factors have had the greatest impact on bringing about this change:

1. The almost universal adoption of expansive discovery procedures permitted by the modern discovery rules.

2. The increasing complexity of litigation.

The modern trial lawyer spends a good bit more time and effort implementing pretrial discovery procedures than his predecessor. This is as unavoidable as it is necessary.

Adequate consideration of discovery requires a familiarity with both the state rules or statutes governing discovery and the Federal Rules of Civil Procedure, the latter having served as a model for many state codes. However, the following discussion will center on and assume the applicability of the Federal Rules of Discovery (hereinafter the "Rules"). The authorities that construe these Rules will be persuasive if not controlling in most court jurisdictions.

The oft stated purposes of discovery include "to eliminate surprise," "to limit the issues in litigation," "to expedite the termination of litigation by settlement or summary judgment," and "to ex-

pedite the course of the trial if attempts at settlement are ineffective."
Each is an accurate statement; each statement is interrelated.

The plaintiff's counsel should always remember that pretrial
discovery is a two-edged sword. Just as the plaintiff can obtain
valuable information from a defendant, the defendant can obtain
significant disclosures from the plaintiff. Thus, in deciding how to
conduct his discovery, plaintiff's counsel must consider not only how
to perfect his case, but also how his case may be damaged by discovery
initiated by the defendant. Furthermore, the pursuit of extensive
discovery may actually be counterproductive; it will point out to the
defendant areas of his liability of which he might not be fully aware
and ultimately result in strengthening his defenses. If counsel can investigate and prepare his case from sources and materials that do not
require utilization of the Rules of Discovery, he would be well advised
to do so. Plaintiff's counsel should not employ the discovery Rules as
a substitute for independent research and plain old "leg work." It is,
however, true that in a number of cases a good bit of information can
only be acquired from the defendant.

From a practical standpoint, the basic purpose of discovery is to
collect evidence. From the earliest possible stage, counsel should
outline the points of proof he needs to establish a *prima facie* case. He
should then carefully distinguish the points of proof he can establish
from outside sources from those points of proof that require
discovery. The second of these divisions is the object of this discussion. No lawyer is prepared to begin to use the tools of discovery until
he outlines his case and knows what evidence he has and what
evidence he needs to acquire.

THE PURPOSE OF THE DISCOVERY RULES
IN THE CONTEXT OF MODERN LITIGATION

It is submitted that both (1) the express language of the Rules and
(2) judicial interpretation of the Rules unequivocally establish a *strong
policy* favoring *full disclosure* as the intended consequence of the implementation of the Rules of Discovery. This policy of full disclosure is
poignantly applicable and vitally necessary in a technically and factually complex case (such as a products liability case or a claim of professional negligence). This is true in part because of the huge disparity

between the plaintiff and the defendant in their relative knowledge of technical information and access to resources essential to a fair preparation and presentation of the case.

A rather large percent of modern litigation is relatively complex—factually and/or technically. This is typically true regardless of the plaintiff's legal theory of recovery. Whether the complaint sounds in negligence or in strict liability, the plaintiff should be prepared to prove that the defendant is responsible for having created an unreasonable risk of harm. The evidence of that pivotal proposition frequently involves not only a knowledge of technology (with which the plaintiff and his attorney are typically unfamiliar) but also customarily involves factual data that is exclusively in the possession of the defendant. Therefore, the necessity of the court's applying the discovery Rules so as to promote and fulfill the underlying policy favoring full disclosure is uniquely applicable in modern complex litigation.

CAVEAT: DO NOT ABUSE

A number of legal authors in recent years have discussed the problem of abuse of discovery which can result from a needless over-utilization of the Rules. Most of these discussions deal with commercial litigation between corporate clients and corporate firms in which teams of lawyers employ the discovery rules like weapons in a punitive war. Only a limited number of these discussions are applicable to the efforts on the part of the plaintiff to obtain discovery in a personal injury case. However, counsel should be aware that in recent years the judiciary has been exposed to a conservative sentiment regarding discovery. It is perfectly true that discovery can be abused in personal injury cases. However, in these cases the greatest source of abuse results from the unjustified refusal to respond to necessary and legitimate discovery efforts rather than from over-utilization.

Counsel for plaintiff is, however, advised again to be as careful and as precise as possible in the conduct of his formal discovery.

It is the clear intendment of the Rules that when either party requests relevant information, discovery *should take place* unless and except there is some specific and persuasive reason to the contrary! As we will see, it is the intent of the Rules that discovery should be accomplished affirmatively and voluntarily, that is, by and between the parties without the intervention and compulsion of court orders.

THE UNDERLYING POLICY
OF THE DISCOVERY RULES

The scope of discovery is governed by Rule 26(b) and permits discovery of information that is "relevant" and "not privileged."[1] The ambit of Rule 26(b) extends to each of the five methods of discovery available under the Rules.

A number of authors have urged the Court to redefine and to restrict the definition of relevance so as to limit discovery only to certain issues. To date, the Supreme Court has rejected this approach; however, in the recently adopted Amendments to the Federal Rules of Civil Procedure the Court did incorporate an important change permitting a discovery conference early in discovery at which time a statement of the issues as they then appeared would be drafted.[2] Preceding the discovery conference, the parties and the scope of discovery would continue to be governed by the prevailing definition of relevance.

The very meaning and usage of the word "relevant" is different in "discovery" and "admissibility."[3] The tests of relevance as they relate to information sought in discovery are considerably less stringent than the general relevancy requirements that govern admissible evidence at the trial stage.[4]

The courts have alternately held that relevance in discovery "has a very broad meaning"[5] and that its application should be liberally construed.[6]

---

[1] "The basic philosophy of the present federal practice is that prior to trial every party to a civil action is entitled to disclosure of all relevant information in the possession of any person, unless the information is privileged," 8 Wright and Miller, FEDERAL PRACTICE AND PROCEDURE: Civil § 2001 at 15 (cited herein as Wright and Miller).

[2] See FED. R. CIV. P. 26(f).

[3] As to the definition of "relevancy" within the context of admissible evidence, see the FED. R. EVID. 401 and Lehrman v. Gulf Oil Corp., 464 F.2d 26 (5th Cir. 1972).

[4] Ibid., Lehrman; See FED. R. EVID. 401.

[5] Heathman v. U.S. Dist. Ct., 503 F 2d 1032 (9th Cir. 1974).

[6] Bowman v. General Motors Corp., 64 F.R.D. 62, 69 (E.D., Pa. 1974.)

Burden on Resisting Party

The party resisting discovery on the grounds of relevancy has the burden of showing the court that the information sought is "clearly irrelevant"[7] or that the evidence sought "has no possible bearing" on the subject matter.[8]

There are two pivotal observations which affect the utilization and application of the discovery Rules which emphatically illustrate their underlying policy:

First, the limitation on discovery that prevailed under the old common law as evidence—that the information sought must be admissible as evidence—is no longer applicable; in fact, it is not only expressly rejected by the language of the Rules themselves[9] but also is in absolute opposition to the underlying policy and purpose of discovery under present day practice.[10]

Secondly, the Rules are designed to operate so as to effect discovery "extra-judicially"; that is, without the utilization and necessity of hearings and rulings by the court unless and except some specific objection is raised upon which the parties cannot agree.

The new Amendments to the Rules permitting a discovery conference underscore the obligation of both parties to proceed with discovery voluntarily in that Amended Rule 26(f) requires a statement that the attorney requesting the conference has made a reasonable effort to reach agreement with his opposition as to the unresolved matters of discovery. Furthermore, and of significance, is the fact that the drafters of Rule 26(f) thought it necessary and appropriate to insert an express statement within the text of the Rule that all parties have an *obligation* to participate in discovery in good faith.

Both the express language of the Rules and the cases construing them support the underlying policy that if the information sought is

[7]Independent Productions Corp. v. Loew's, Inc., 30 F.R.D. 377, 381 (S.D., N.Y. 1962).

[8]Hercules Powder Co. v. Rohm & Haas Co., 3 F.R.D. 302 (D.C., Del. 1943); La Chemise La Coste v. Alligator Co., Inc., 60 F.R.D. 164 (D. Del. 1973). See also 8 Wright & Miller, §§ 2035, 2036, 2174, 2214, 2285.

[9]E.g. See the last sentence of Fed. R. Civ. P. 26(b)(1).

[10]Wright and Miller, § 2008 at 41, et seq.

truly relevant, the parties should respond by voluntarily *permitting discovery!*

The Express Language of the Rules

With regard to the filing of objections, the wording of the Rules themselves states that the court should *permit* discovery *unless* the party resisting carries the burden of establishing that his objections are "substantially justified."[11]

The express language of the discovery rules clearly establishes that it is the intendment of the Rules that full and complete discovery shall voluntarily take place *unless* there exist good and substantial reason to the contrary. The Rules provide in pertinent part as follows [emphasis added]:

1. FED. R. CIV. P. 33(a) — Interrogatories.

   Each interrogatory *shall* be answered separately and *fully* in writing under oath, unless it is objected to, in which event *the reasons for objection shall be stated in lieu of the answer.*

2. FED. R. CIV. P. 34(b)—Production of Documents and Things.

   The response shall state, with respect to each item, or category, that inspection and related activities *will be permitted as requested, unless* the request is objected to, in which event *the reasons for objection shall be stated.* If objection is made to part of an item or category, the part shall be specified.

3. FED. R. CIV. P. 36(a)—Request for Admissions.

   If objection is made, *the reasons therefor shall be stated.* The answer shall *specifically* deny the matter or *set forth in detail the reasons* why the answering party cannot truthfully admit or deny the matter. A denial shall fairly meet the substance of the requested admission, and when good faith requires that a party qualify his answer or deny only a part of the matter of which the admission is requested, he shall specify so much of it as is true and qualify or deny the remainder. An answering party may not give lack of information or knowledge as a reason for failure to admit or deny *unless* he states that he has made reasonable inquiry and that the information known or readily obtainable by him is insufficient to enable him to admit or deny. A party who considers that a matter of which an admission has been requested presents a genuine issue for trial may not, on that ground alone, object to the request; he may, subject to the provisions of Rule 37(c), deny the matter or set forth reasons why he cannot admit or deny it. . . .

[11]See, e.g., FED. R. CIV. P. 36(a) and FED. R. CIV. P. 37(a)(4).

Unless the court determines that an objection is justified, it *shall* order that an answer be served.

4. FED. R. CIV. P. 37(a)—Sanctions.

(3) For purposes of this sub-division an evasive or incomplete answer is to be treated as a failure to answer.

Sub-division (4) of Rule 37 is a decisive expression of the policy that the Rules are designed to work extra-judicially by the voluntary cooperation of the parties. It provides (within the context of the present discussion) that if the plaintiff is seeking discovery and the defendant has filed a motion seeking a court order to compel discovery and that if that motion is granted the court *"shall* require the defendant to pay the plaintiff the expenses incurred in obtaining the order (including attorney's fees) *"unless the court finds that the opposition to the motion was substantially justified* or that other circumstances make an award of expenses unjust." [Emphasis added.]

Most trial courts are loath to grant sanctions no matter how egregious the defendant's arbitrary refusal to respond. In view of the new Amendments and a recent Supreme Court case exhorting the trial courts to do more to control discovery, it is possible that this reluctance may change.[12]

Judicial Decisions

Appellate courts have expressed an identical policy with regard to the scope of discovery:[13]

[Rule 26] apparently envisions generally unrestrictive access to sources of information, and the courts have so interpreted it.[14]

This Rule [26(b)] has been generously construed to provide a great deal of latitude for discovery.[15]

The utmost liberality should prevail in allowing a wide scope to the legitimate use of interrogatories.[16]

---

[12]See, Herbert v. Lando, 441 U.S. 153 (1979).

[13]"The courts have recognized the utility of the discovery rules and have construed them liberally so that they may achieve the purposes to which they are intended." 8 Wright and Miller, § 2001 at 17.

[14]Horizons Titaniun Corp. v. Norton Co., 290 F.2d 421, 425 (1st Cir. 1961).

[15]Harris v. Nelson, 394 U.S. 286, 297 (1969).

[16]Arktiebolaget Vargos v. Clark, 8 F.R.D. 635, 636 (D.C. 1949).

There are many reasons supporting the strong, clear underlying policy of liberality inherent in the discovery Rules. Probably the first and most compelling is the simple observation that the single objective of the entire judicial process is to determine the truth of a disputed matter.[17] Restrictions on the disclosure of relevant information inherently diminish the probability of an accurate determination of the truth.

The civil trial system has been faced with increasing criticism in recent years that cannot be lightly disregarded. One of the most poignant criticisms comes from observers who attack the system of trial by jury on the basis that it is not an adequate *truth finding process.* The chief ground of this attack is that often a lay jury charged with the duty of determining the truth in a complex and technical matter is provided inadequate information and expertise to resolve the dispute fairly. Full and proper discovery averts this. How can there be a legitimate objection to attaining more light in which to visualize truth?

Dean Roscoe Pound once noted that the greatest criticism of the American Judicial System was with "... our American exaggerations of the common law contentious procedure. The sporting theory of justice... is probably only a survival of the days when the law was a fight...."[18]

The Supreme Court of the United States employed some rather strong language on this subject, tantamount to a philosophical rejection of this concept when it said in *Hickman v. Taylor,* "No longer can time honored cry of 'fishing expedition' serve to preclude a party of inquiring into facts underlying his opponent's case."[19]

Plaintiff's Particular Need

Within the framework of a complex personal injury case there are at least four factors which make it particularly urgent for the courts to apply this underlying policy of liberality to the plaintiff's discovery efforts. These factors reflect the relatively unequal positions and status of knowledge of the plaintiff and the defendant:

[17]Chief Justice Robert C. Underwood of the Illinois Supreme Court, 20 TRIAL LAWYER'S GUIDE 152 (Summer, 1976).

[18]Address by Dean Roscoe Pound, The American Bar Association Convention, August 26, 1906, reprinted 35 F.R.D. 241, 281 (1964).

[19]Hickman v. Taylor, 329 U.S. 495, 507 (1947).

1. Typically, the defendant already has a basic knowledge of the relevant technology. The plaintiff and his lawyer have to acquire an education in a previously unfamiliar field.

2. Typically, the defendant has in his possession the relevant information and documentation pertaining to the facts of the particular case. The plaintiff has to acquire them—often *from the defendant!*

3. Typically, the defendant has ready access to both the relevant technical information and qualified experts. Usually, no such expert is in the employ of the plaintiff and qualified experts are expensive and hard to find.

4. Typically, the defendant possesses relatively greater financial resources to commit to the preparation and defense of the action. The overwhelming majority of plaintiffs in personal injury cases are individuals with limited resources.

In summary:

1. Both the express language of the Rules and the judicial decisions construing their intent announce a strong policy of liberal discovery.

2. This policy is uniquely important and applicable to the plaintiff's efforts in a factually and/or technically complex case.

3. The parties' response to discovery inquiries for relevant information should be affirmative and voluntary.

4. The party objecting to the movant's discovery efforts carries a heavy burden to sustain his objection.

SOME SPECIFIC PRINCIPLES OF LAW APPLICABLE TO DISCOVERY

Form of Request

The plaintiff is often faced with a dilemma: if he is precise in his description of the needed information, the defendant will rely upon some insignificant detail in the language of the request to justify his failure to respond; whereas, if the plaintiff frames his inquiry generically, the defendant replies that the designation is so broad that it is meaningless. In both instances the result is the same—no disclusre of vital information.

In keeping with the general rule of liberal interpretation, the courts have held that as to the form of inquiry "considerable latitude" rather than exactness of definition is permitted.

> 1. Interrogatories. "In fact the courts have given parties considerable latitude in framing interrogatories. Rather general language has been permitted so long as the interrogatories give the other party a reasonably clear indication of the information to be included in its answer."[20]
>
> 2. Request for Production. "Even a generalized designation should be sufficient when the party seeking discovery cannot give a more particular description and the party from whom discovery is sought will have no difficulty in understanding what is wanted."
>
> "The goal is that the designation be sufficient to apprise a man of ordinary intelligence what documents are required and that the court be able to ascertain whether the requested documents have been produced."[21]
>
> 3. Request for Admission. "Each request for an admission should be phrased simply and directly so that it can be admitted or denied without explanation."[22]

Counsel must not approach discovery with the attitude that the court will accept a liberal policy toward discovery as a justification for sloppy work. Particularly in view of the recent Amendments which permit a discovery conference, it is incumbent on plaintiff's counsel to frame his discovery efforts with as much precision as his best informed knowledge permits. Although the new Amendments do not redefine so as to restrict the definition of "relevancy" it is perfectly clear both from the background of the Amendments and the Advisory Committee's Notes, that courts will be increasing inclined to identify the issues involved in the case and to channel discovery accordingly.

Use of Definitions

It may be wise to insert a Table of Definitions as an attachment preceding the actual interrogatories or requests for production or ad-

---

[20]8 Wright and Miller, § 2168 at 515. See Struthers Scientific and Int'l. Corp. v. General Goods Corp., 45 F.R.D. 375, 379 (S.D. Tex. 1963).

[21]8 Wright and Miller, § 2211 at 629. See Ibid., at 631-634; 8 ALR2d 1134.

[22]8 Wright and Miller, § 2258 at 721-722.

mission. The definition and clarification of various terms which are contained in the actual request for information may be helpful in avoiding the trap that lies in language that is either too precise or too broad. It also provides a vehicle for conveying to the opposition the overall objectives of counsel's attempt at discovery. The use of such a procedure has the added benefit of avoiding needless repetition within the body of the formal request.[23]

Response—The Duty to Make Reasonable Inquiry

Request for Admission. Rule 36(a) expressly provides that a party may not give "lack of information or knowledge" as a ground of objection unless he states he has made "reasonable inquiry and that the information known or readily obtainable by him is insufficient to enable him to admit or deny." The cases hold that a party is required to admit or deny, even though he lacks personal knowledge, if the means for the acquisition of the information are reasonably available to him.[24]

Interrogatories. Likewise, the rule governing a party's answers to interrogatories is that he must furnish information that is reasonably available to him.[25]

There is an old adage to the effect that a party cannot ordinarily be forced to "prepare his opponent's case" or be compelled to engage in "extensive research." However, this vintage maxim has its obvious limitations [emphasis added]:

> It would be a mistake, however, to suppose that the fact that answering interrogatories would require research by the interrogated party is enough to bar the interrogatory in every case. It is not. In order to justify sustaining an objection to an interrogatory on this ground, it must be shown that the research required is *unduly burdensome and oppressive.* An interrogatory will not be held objectionable as calling for research if it relates to details alleged in the pleading of the interrogated party, about which he

---

[23]See Diversified Products Corp. v. Sports Center Co., 42 F.R.D. 3 (D. Md. 1967); Harlem River Consumers Co-op., Inc., v. Associated Grocers of Harlem, Inc., 64 F.R.D. 459 (S.D. N.Y., 1974).

[24]FED. R. CIV. P., Advisory Committee Note, 48 F.R.D. at 487, 533 (1970); see also, Hise v. Lockwood Grader Corp., 153 F. Supp. 276 (D. Neb. 1957); 4A MOORE'S FEDERAL PRACTICE § 36.04 (2d ed. 1966); 8 Wright and Miller, § 2261 at 731.

[25]Pilling v. General Motors Corp., 45 F.R.D. 366, 369-370 (D. Utah 1968).

presumably has information, or if the interrogated party would gather information in the preparation of his own case.[26]

Request to Produce. Similarly, a Rule 34 request may be appropriate if the party to whom the request is made has the legal right to obtain the document, even though at the time of the request he does not physically possess a copy—the key is "control."[27]

Response—Objection That Response Would Be "Burdensome"

It is entirely possible that the adequate response to a request for discovery may require a substantial commitment of time and effort from the defendant. This is no more than another way of saying that the preparation which a case requires may unavoidably involve the location and production of a relatively large amount of information. That fact standing alone does not pretermit discovery. A contrary rule would simply forbid the plaintiff from maintaining a complicated case which necessarily involves extensive discovery. The obvious injustice of such a rule is particularly evident in cases where much of the relevant information is in the defendant's exclusive possession, available for examination and use by the defendant's employees and experts but only available to the plaintiff through discovery.

Rule 26(c) indicates the test for the efficacy or this objection: *"undue* burden of expense..

> The mere fact that compliance with an inspection order will cause great labor and expense or even considerable hardship and possibility of injury to the business of the party from whom discovery is sought does not of itself require denial of the motion.[28]

Discovery should be required unless the opposing party persuades the court that the "hardship is *unreasonable"* when balanced against the need for the materials and information being sought.[29]

[26]8 Wright and Miller, § 2147 at 554-555. See Dusek v. United Air Lines, Inc., 9 F.R.D. 326 (N.D. Ohio 1949).

[27]See 8 Wright and Miller, § 2210 at 622, et seq.; see E.G. Hantscho Co. v. Miehle-Goss-Dexter, Inc., 33 F.R.D. 332 (S.D. N.Y. 1963); 47 ALR3d 676.

[28]8 Wright and Miller, § 2214 at 647.

[29]Burke v. Fire Underwriters Ass'n, 21 F.R.D. 583, 584 (W.D. Mo. 1958); Uitts v. General Motors Corp., 58 F.R.D. 450 (E.D. Pa. 1972); Kozlowski v. Sears, Roebuck & Co., 73 F.R.D. 73 (D. Mass. 1976); Clark v. General Motors Corp., 20 Fed.R. Serv.2d 679 (D. Mass. 1975).

The defendant's duty to make inquiry in order to respond to discovery and the "burdensome" objection would be appropriate topics for the discovery conference now permitted by Rule 27(f). Plaintiff's counsel is well advised to come to the discovery conference prepared to support his contention that the material and information he seeks is both relevant and needed.

An Amendment to Rule 33(c) has been adopted that is intended to avert the problem created by a response that simply refers the questioner to a body of documents in lieu of giving a specific answer; the Amendment requires a more detailed specification of the material to which the questioner is referred so as to permit the questioner to ascertain the answer as readily as the responder. The Amendment to Rule 34(b) requires the responder either to produce the requested documents in the same order as they are kept in the usual course of business or to organize and label them so as to correspond to the requested items. Coupled together, these two amendments should prove helpful in eliminating the "dump truck" abuse.

DISCUSSION OF THE VARIOUS METHODS OF DISCOVERY

The following is a discussion of the various methods of discovery permitted by the Federal Rules. Most states have adopted similar provisions. For the purpose of discussion, the various methods are discussed separately but that does not imply that only one method may be pursued at a time; in fact, the preferred practice is initially to file a set of carefully drafted interrogatories along with a request for production and a request for admissions. Hopefully, the defendant's response to these three discovery devices will both refine the issues in dispute and limit the need for expensive depositions.

With regard to the plaintiff's initial discovery efforts, two rules should govern counsel:

1. Carefully—even painstakingly—draft your original interrogatories, requests for production, and requests for admission. In complex litigation this will necessarily require hours—possibly tens of hours—of research and consultation with experts to insure that the form and the substance of your efforts is on target. The failure to ex-

tend this advance effort not only dooms your efforts to almost certain futility, it is very likely to result in a rebuke from the court at the discovery conference.

2. Begin early! It is at best difficult and at worst impossible for the average plaintiff's lawyer to match the defendant's discovery efforts in complex litigation. The typical defense firm in complex litigation simply has greater staff available than the average plaintiff's firm. This fact, coupled with the previously mentioned advantages inherent in the defense position, make "catch-up" discovery a disastrous approach.

Interrogatories

Rule 33 and similar provisions in most states establish a procedure by which one party may require the adverse party to answer written questions known as interrogatories.

If only because of considerations of expense and simplicity, the bulk of discovery in routine lawsuits should be accomplished by the use of interrogatories. Again, at the outset, it is extremely important for counsel to take great care not only in drafting the questions he propounds to the defendant but also in providing full response to the defendant's interrogatories. In view of the obvious objectives of the discovery conference, the significance of this approach cannot be over-emphasized. It is doubtful that in the future trial courts, in ruling on motions for protective orders or motions to compel sanctions, are going to permit a game of "hide and seek."

Availability—Procedures for Use. Interrogatories may be served on the defendent along with the summons and complaint or thereafter on counsel of record for the defendant. The required answers must be made under oath and in writing.

It is possible that both the number of questions and/or the scope of permissible inquiry may be limited by local procedure. Therefore, counsel for plaintiff should closely examine any applicable local rules before propounding interrogatories to the defendant.

Although counsel may obtain valuable ideas by reference to the various form books which set out proposed interrogatories for various types of cases, form or "canned" interrogatories must not be used unless each individual question is actually applicable to the facts of the particular case. However if a question is truly applicable, the fact that it has been used and tested may in and of itself be extremely helpful. (A list of typical topics about which the plaintiff should inquire is outlined in Form No. 4.)

The very process of drafting interrogatories to the defendant can and should provide plaintiff's counsel with an opportunity to visualize and outline his entire case.

It would be an excellent practice for counsel, immediately after he drafts his initial interrogatories and requests for production and admission, to dictate a memorandum summarizing his analysis of the case. This memorandum should reflect a preliminary identification of the issues likely to be involved in the case, and it should contain a list of the factual information counsel will need to prepare his case. He can refer to such a memorandum in assessing the adequacy of the defendant's answers and generally in guiding his subsequent investigation and discovery.

There are two specific advantages to discovery by written interrogatories in contrast to oral depositions:

1. They permit the attorney to carefully choose the best possible language in which to phrase his question; and,

2. They are inexpensive.

The obvious disadvantage of interrogatories is that they do not permit immediate rejoinder to an evasive answer.

If the defendant fails to answer or furnishes an incomplete or evasive answer or offers an unfounded objection, counsel for the plaintiff should immediately file a motion seeking relief. Assuming that the topics of counsel's inquiry are truly relevant and that the language of the question fairly communicates the desired objectives, the court should insist on a full and fair response from the defendant. Both because the Rules so command and in order to create a favorable contrast, counsel for plaintiff should furnish full and fair response to the defendant's interrogatories rather than point to the defendant's lack of good faith as justification for his own inadequate answers.

If the defendant objects to an interrogatory, nothing further will happen unless the plaintiff moves under Rules 37(a) to compel an answer. It is noted that Rule 37(a)(4) provides that expenses normally are to be assessed against the losing party on a motion of this kind, unless there was substantial justification for the defendant's objection. Thus, a party who makes an unjustified objection and forces his opponent to go to court to compel an answer can and should be made to pay expenses. By the same token, if the objection is well taken, the moving party may be required to pay expenses. The burden under Rule 37(a) motions is on the objecting party!

Ordinarily, the motion to obtain complete answers to interrogatories should be filed before resorting to oral depositions, if only to continue the effort to avoid the added expense. There are at least two important exceptions to this approach:

1. Where time is of the essence either because of a pending trial date or a discovery cut-off date; and

2. Where it may be advisable to make a record in support of counsel's positon on the Rule 37(a) motion.

Opinions, Contentions, and Conclusions. Rule 33(b) states that an interrogatory is not necessarily objectionable because the answer involves an opinion that requires the application of law to fact. The Rule does not totally eliminate this kind of objection; it merely states that such an interrogatory is not necessarily objectionable for this reason.

Counsel for the plaintiff should propound well drafted "contention" interrogatories. In all probability the court will permit the defendant to delay responding to contention interrogatories until after the discovery conference or after the pretrial conference.

It is perfectly permissible and usually advisable for counsel to file a request for production and a request for admissions simultaneously with the filing of interrogatories.

The use of interrogatories may, as previously stated, result in a substantial savings, either by eliminating the necessity for some depositions or by limiting the scope of inquiry of any particular deposition. However, interrogatories are not intended as a substitute for oral depositions—particularly with regard to discovery from non-party witnesses. In fact, the plaintiff may choose to propound a few carefully drawn interrogatories after a deposition in order to clear up certain key points.

The use at trial of the defendant's answers to interrogatories may be governed by local rules. In many jurisdictions the answers can be read in evidence at the trial. In every jurisdiction, interrogatory answers can be used at the trial to impeach the defendant's testimony. In either event, it is most effective to read to the jury the defendant's sworn answer to a well drawn interrogatory.

When the defendant serves interrogatories upon the plaintiff, counsel should take great care in drafting answers. Many a plaintiff's case has been seriously damaged by poorly prepared responses to interrogatories. Counsel for plaintiff should immediately determine how much time he has to answer the questions. This date should be recorded. It is absolutely essential that counsel set up and implement an inter-office system that insures that timely responses are prepared and filed. Most jurisdictions permit counsel to take leave past the original time.

If one or more of the defendant's questions are improper, counsel must either object or move to strike the offending question within the prescribed period. The failure to take timely action may result in the waiver of the grounds of objection, though otherwise well taken.

In preparing the answers to the interrogatories, counsel should call the plaintiff into his office and go over each question in detail. This interview must take place far enough in advance of the time for filing answers to permit such additional investigation as may be necessary to furnish full and accurate answers. Counsel should *not* rely solely upon the plaintiff's memory; many questions will call for information reflected in medical records, investigative reports, and other sources acquired for counsel's investigation.

Counsel is reminded that Rule 26(e) requires that answers to certain topics of inquiry must be supplemented should additional information be subsequently obtained.

Requests for Production

Rule 34 and analogous provisions in many states provide for the production of documents and things and entry upon land for inspection and other purposes. The obvious purpose of the Rule is to make relevant and non-privileged material available to the parties before trial thereby eliminating surprise and for the added purpose of simplifying the issues to be tried.

The scope of discovery permissible under the Federal Rule is defined by Rule 26. Discovery is not limited merely to matters that would be admissible at trial. Rather, any document or thing that is relevant to the subject matter involved may be inspected unless it is privileged or has been prepared in anticipation of litigation. Counsel should, of course, consult local statutes for additional limiting language.

As has been stated with reference to interrogatories, counsel for plaintiff should draft his request for production with great care keeping in mind the anticipated issues of the particular case. As in the case of interrogatories, form books are helpful reference sources but should not be slavishly followed. (Some typical topics are set forth on Form No. 5.)

It is usually preferable to file a motion to produce before taking oral depositions. This permits counsel to examine and analyze the needed documents at a time when he can carefully reflect on the questions those documents suggest. There are many instances, however, in which it would be advisable to secure the production of documents at the same time of the oral examination. This approach may be accomplished by the use of a *subpoena duces tecum* rather than a request for production.

It is noted that the very fact that the document has been procured in response to a request for production does, in and of itself, satisfy the element of authenticity.[30]

Should the defendant file a request for production, counsel must file a timely response or suffer the sanctions permitted by Rule 37—including the waiver of objections. If the defendant's request for production will require research or inquiry that cannot be completed within the prescribed time, counsel must seek and obtain an appropriate extension.

[30]See Alabama Power Co. v. Tatum, 293 Ala. 500, 508, 306 So.2d 251 (1975); see FED. R. EVID. 901, 902.

Requests for Admissions

Many jurisdictions have adopted a rule similar to Rule 36 which provides a procedure by which one party may request his adversary to admit the truth of certain facts or genuineness of certain documents. Every case involves undisputed facts. Some of these plaintiff's counsel will prefer to prove by testimony as part of the persuasive development of his case before the jury. As to such facts, stipulation or formal admissions might interfere with the development of the evidence. On the other hand, there are usually a number of factual points which can and should be admitted. Admissions prior to trial reduce the expense, time, and inconvenience of proving matters not actually in dispute. At the very least, an exchange of requests for admissions will focus on the facts which really are disputed.

Strictly speaking, however, a request for admissions is not a discovery procedure. Plaintiff's counsel merely tries to have the defendant concede certain facts so as to narrow the scope of disputed issues and thereby to expedite the trial. A request for admission with respect to the genuineness of a document often eliminates the necessity for tedious proof of facts constituting the foundation for admitting the document as evidence at trial.

As a general rule, the request should be phrased so that the answer can be a simple "yes" or "no" or "admitted" or "denied." A suggested manner of phrasing a request is as follows: "You are requested to admit the truth of the following statements of fact, pursuant to Rule X, under the terms of which these matters will be deemed admitted if you do not serve a response in accordance with such rule on or before _____, (1) That ... (2) That ... (reciting a single fact in each paragraph)." Copies of documents referred to in a request for admission should be attached as exhibits to the request.

As stated earlier, the party upon whom the request is served must answer the request even though he has no personal knowledge of the facts if the means of obtaining the necessary information is available to him. An affirmative answer to a request for admission is similar to a judicial admission and is regarded as conclusive upon the party making it.

If the responding party denies a request and the party requesting the admission proves the genuineness of the document or the truth of the fact at trial, the requesting party may apply to the court for an order requiring the other party to pay him the reasonable expenses incurred in the making of the proof—including, in some situations, reasonable attorney fees. Unless the court finds that there were good reasons for the denial, the motion for monetary relief will be allowed. Requests for admissions are potentially very valuable tools. Plaintiff's lawyers typically do not utilize the procedure nearly as often as they should.

Depositions Taken by the Plaintiff

Purpose for Taking. The deposition is the most effective, albeit the most expensive, weapon in the trial lawyer's arsenal of discovery procedures. Depositions serve at least four functions: (1) to discover information; (2) to serve as a basis for impeachment of the deposed witness should he appear at the trial and should his testimony differ at the trial from his deposition testimony; (3) to obtain admissions from a party for use as affirmative proof in trial; and (4) to preserve testimony of an important witness or party who is not likely to be available at the time of trial.

Relationship to Other Discovery Devices. The relationship of their use to other discovery devices, such as written interrogatories and motions for production of documents, will determine the timing for the taking of depositions. Most plaintiff's attorneys do not initiate the discovery process with the use of depositions because due to their importance they require the extensive preparation. Many plaintiff's lawyers prefer to defer taking depositions until they have completed their investigation, have made full use of written interrogatories to the adverse party, and have filed a motion to produce documents where pertinent. They believe that depositions can be truly effective only after these procedures have been completely accomplished. Of course, when preservation of testimony is the primary purpose for taking the deposition, the health and availability of the witness will govern the timing of the taking of the deposition. Many plaintiff's counsel advocate taking early depositions of hostile witnesses, for their recollections are fresher and less apt to be affected by the testimony or suggestion of others or by attempts to mold their memories.

Time for Taking. The time for taking depositions may also be affected by the rules affecting priority. In many jurisdictions, the defendant may take the plaintiff's deposition at any time, but the plaintiff must wait a set period of time after filing his action before he may serve notice to take the defendant's. The timing may also be affected by the rules of the jurisdiction concerning the use of supplementary depositions and the availability of other discovery devices. Counsel will be less hesitant in taking the deposition of the adverse party early in the case when he knows that he can follow it with interrogatories or a supplementary deposition at a later date.

The order in which depositions are to be taken is also significant. Generally, the person to be deposed first by the plaintiff is the party or hostile witness believed to be the person with the most information. His testimony may be all that is needed, or he may provide the key to the case and indicate how other critical information may be obtained. After taking the principal deposition, other short ones may be all that is necessary to round out and complete the process.

Obviously, a dishonest witness or party can be greatly aided in planning his testimony if there has been an opportunity to study the deposition testimony of others. Even a witness who is only included to stretch the facts or to exaggerate may be influenced by reading the testimony of others before he is deposed. It is generally advantageous to avoid allowing depositions to be taken of the plaintiff's witnesses, or of the plaintiff, substantially in advance of the deposing of adverse witnesses. Further, it is also generally advisable to take the depositions of all adverse witnesses as close together as possible.

Pre-Action Depositions. Rule 27 and similar rules in most states permit the taking of testimony before the case is filed. That is, before the lawsuit is filed, the attorney may file a motion with the court to seek permission to depose either a potential party or a potential witness. If testimony of an important witness must be preserved and it appears that this witness will be later unavailable, in many jurisdictions that witness' deposition will be permitted even though suit has not been filed. In some jurisdictions, the court will permit pre-action depositions if the plaintiff's attorney can show that he has a potential cause of action but needs information to draft a complaint, determine the nature of his cause of action, or identify the proper defendant.

Place for Taking. Depositions of parties and lay witnesses are generally taken in the office of the attorney who initiates the taking of the particular deposition. Generally, depositions of medical witnesses are taken in the doctor's office. In some instances, counsel may prefer to take depositions at the scene of the accident. When such a procedure is employed, the witnesses can view the accident scene and give more accurate testimony.

Scope of Examination. As stated, the Federal Rules (and the rules of most states) allow a broad scope of examination during deposition. Under the federal practice, the deponent can be examined on any non-privileged matter which is relevant to the subject matter of the litigation, whether it relates to the claim or defense of the examining party or any other party. The scope of the examination is not limited by the language of, or the issues framed by, the pleadings. The fact that the question does not seek to elicit testimony which would not be admissible at trial is not in and of itself an appropriate basis to forbid the answer.

Person to Depose. The persons most likely to be deposed by the plaintiff are (1) the defendant, (2) hostile witnesses, and (3) friendly witnesses. The primary usefulness of taking depositions from the defendant or adverse witnesses is discovery; plaintiff's counsel wishes to know what the witnesses or defendants will say so that he can appraise the adversary's case and better understand his own. Another goal of taking depositions of the defendant or adverse witnesses is to get them committed on all material matters. Should the defendant or witness change his story at the time of trial, plaintiff's counsel can use the deposition during cross-examination to impeach him. Finally, depositions of the defendant and the adverse witnesses will aid plaintiff's counsel in developing impeaching evidence and in preparing plaintiff's witnesses to meet the defense version of the facts.

Deposition of Defendant or Hostile Witness. Some argue against taking the adverse party's deposition on the ground that his attorney may gain insight into the plaintiff's case from the questions asked the defendant. *Rarely* is there a sound justification for failing to depose the defendant, since the information received by the plaintiff's counsel will invariably be more important than any information given the defendant. By taking the defendant's deposition, plaintiff's counsel can determine definitely whether he has sued the right party and can, in some situations, gain important admissions which can be used at the trial. In addition, the deposition provides an opportunity to evaluate the defendant's effectiveness as a witness. (A sample outline for the deposition of the individual defendant is contained in Form No. 1.)

The defendant's deposition may also serve as a jumping off point for settlement negotiations. If settlement discussions are unproductive, the defendant's deposition will frequently serve as a basis for future investigation and preparation for trial. Once plaintiff's counsel knows the tenor of the defendant's testimony, he can plan his cross-examination in trial and direct his efforts toward marshalling his evidence to discredit and disprove the defendant's testimony.

Pragmatically, a function of the deposition of the defendant and of the hostile witnesses is to advise the injured plaintiff of the case for the defense. Some plaintiffs seem to remember only the most advantageous aspects of their cases and in many instances do not realize that the defendant also has a case. After taking the deposition of the defendant and hostile witnesses, plaintiff's counsel can concretely show his client the position that the defense is taking and awaken the plaintiff to the problems inherent in litigation. This may increase the possibility of settlement.

One important factor militating against plaintiff counsel's taking depositions of the defendant or the hostile witness is their possible unavailability at the trial. Thus, if it appears that the defendant or a key defense witness will not be available to testify at the time of trial, it is not to the plaintiff's advantage to preserve their testimony by deposition.

Since taking the deposition of one witness often leads to action by the counsel for defendant regarding deposing of other witnesses in the case, some consideration should be given to (1) whether the plaintiff's initiation of depositions may lead to others which might otherwise not be taken; and (2) whether in this instance development of the entire group of depositions is to the advantage of the plaintiff. In some situations, plaintiff's counsel may find it better to wait for his adversary to initiate depositions and take advantage of the chance that he may fail to do so. In most jurisdictions, taking the deposition of a witness does not necessarily make him plaintiff's witness. Thus, plaintiff may be permitted to examine the defendant and expert witnesses retained by the defendant as if upon cross-examination. If this rule does not prevail, the practical disadvantage of making the witness the plaintiff's on deposition must be considered in determining whether to take his deposition. Little will be lost if the witness will be available at trial, but if there is any doubt concerning his availability, the potential danger is great.

Deposition of a Friendly Witness. The primary reason plaintiff's counsel has for taking the deposition of the plaintiff or a favorable witness is to preserve his testimony, insuring its availability in the event of death, illness, or unavailability at the trial. Also, the plaintiff may wish to take the deposition of a favorable witness to protect against the hazards of faulty memory, an unexplainable change of heart, or the influence of a clever adversary. Nonetheless, the usefulness of a deposition of the plaintiff or favorable witness is ordinarily more than counterbalanced by the usefulness of the deposition to the defendant. Thus, the plaintiff should generally not initiate the taking of a deposition of the plaintiff or a favorable witness unless it is absolutely essential to making out a case and it is reasonably certain that the deponent will not be available at trial.

Deposition of Plaintiff's Doctor. For a number of reasons, counsel for the plaintiff may want to or have to take the deposition of his client's physician. The physician either may not be available, or, if he is compelled to attend the trial, he may be hostile. Increasingly, doctors request (insist) on giving their testimony by a deposition scheduled at their office. Counsel may wish to wait to see if the defendant will take this deposition. (A suggested outline for the deposition of the plaintiff's doctors is set forth in Form No. 2.)

Because a deposition is taken it does not follow that plaintiff's counsel should order it transcribed and filed. Where the purpose of a deposition is preservation of testimony, transcription and filing is virtually mandatory; where the purpose is discovery, however, much cost can be saved by taking extensive notes. Frequently, when plaintiff's counsel deposes the defendant, he does not have the deposition written up until immediately before the trial. Likewise, when the defendant takes the plaintiff's deposition, it is not necessary for the plaintiff's counsel to have the deposition written up until it appears certain that the case will go to trial. Thus, judiciously taking notes can usually save money.

Method of Examination. The form of questioning will necessarily be a reflection of the purpose for which the deposition is taken. If the purpose of the deposition is mainly to achieve discovery, the examiner's questions will tend to be broad in scope, the subjects far-reaching, and the likely answers rambling and discursive. Such an examination pursues information in an attempt to discover what the deponent knows, without serious concern for the form in which the information is received or its later admissibility. If, on the other hand, a deposition is being taken for the purpose of preserving testimony, the questions will have to be much like those asked at the trial. If the questions and answers are not in admissible form, the testimony becomes useless and the necessary evidence will be lost.

Questions on depositions, like those during the examination of the witness at the trial, should be simple and clear. The deposition, which may be used later at the trial for impeachment purposes, serves its purpose much better if it is clear to the jury that the witness was not confused or misled by the questions, but understood them and intended the obvious meaning of his answers.

The usefulness of the method of sudden and frequent changes in the subject matter of the questions is a subject of some disagreement. The technique is considered effective when used on the hostile witness or the defendant. This is especially true when more detailed and orderly inquiry is used following the use of the "skipping-around" technique. It is believed that this technique is more likely to elicit spontaneous, truthful answers from a hostile witness than an orderly, logical inquiry in which the witness can anticipate the questions and plan his answers accordingly. Sudden shift in subject matter throws the witness off balance, but it also makes that particular part of the deposition less useful for impeachment at the trial. Thus, during the initial portion of the deposition of the hostile witness or the defendant, many advocate that plaintiff's counsel skip about frequently so as to gain the most information, then switch to orderly questioning, in which all the prior admissions are consolidated. At the trial, the latter part of the deposition can be used for impeachment should the witness change his testimony. The disadvantages in the use of this device (sudden and frequent changes of subject, supplemented by more detailed later questioning) are the greater length and increased cost of the deposition.

Where it is relatively certain that the plaintiff-initiated deposition of the hostile witness or the defendant will not be used as evidence at the trial, plaintiff's counsel should encourage the witness to talk as much as possible, for the greater the length of the testimony the more the examiner will know. Thus, the hostile witness should not be discouraged from volunteering answers, and the general prohibition against asking him the "why" question should be put aside. Where the possibility exists that the deposition will be used as evidence at the trial, plaintiff's counsel should seek to keep the witness under control in his deposition.

When deposition testimony relates to certain documents, the examiner should make sure that the questions and answers relating to them clearly identify the documents being used. Similarly, the examiner should make clear precisely what language he is asking about, what page it is on, and, indeed, the specific line on which it is found. Vague references to "this letter" or "the report" may be clear to those attending the deposition but will often be meaningless in the typed transcript. Before the examiner asks any questions concerning the contents of a document on deposition, he should have it marked as an exhibit so that he, as well as the witness, can refer to it by the exhibit number.

When taking the deposition of the defendant or hostile witness, the plaintiff's counsel should remember that he need not play all his cards. That is, he may find it wise to save certain impeaching material until the time of the trial if it appears likely that the witness will appear at the trial and the purpose of the deposition is mainly for discovery. Should plaintiff's counsel show his full hand and impeach the witness at the deposition, the witness will have time to prepare testimony in mitigation of the damaging disclosure prior to the time of the actual trial.

Most lawyers adopt a more friendly attitude toward an adverse witness or defendant during a deposition taken for the purpose of discovery than they may have during examination at the trial. The theory supporting this practice is that a friendly atmosphere will appeal to the finer instincts of the witness, causing him to testify more freely and openly. In the taking of the deposition, however, there may come a time when it is necessary to press the witness relentlessly in the face of evasion, even at the expense of losing his "friendship": an ambiguous or evasive answer will be of little value for discovery or impeachment purposes. An aggressive attitude may upset and unnerve the deponent and cause him to make statements which can be easily impeached at the trial.

Even the most experienced attorneys can use an outline or check list when conducting a deposition. In the case of a deposition of a hostile witness or the defendant, the outline need not dictate the sequence of questioning. If the questions are asked in a logical forseeable pattern, the witness may be ready for each question as it is asked. The outline is used most effectively as an aid in assuring that no important subjects of inquiry are omitted.

Depositions Taken by the Defendant

Preparing the Plaintiff. Most attorneys agree that preparing the plaintiff for his deposition is just as important as preparing him to testify at the trial, if not more so. Though the amount of time needed to properly prepare the plaintiff for the deposition varies according to the complexity of the case, the memory and intelligence of the client, and the client's ability to relate his experiences, one hour is the usual absolute minimum. To obtain the maximum benefit from this predeposition conference an instruction sheet which describes the deposition procedure should be sent to the client. (See Form No. 3.)

Plaintiff's counsel should always advise his client to be completely honest and candid. He should inform him that in most instances the defense will know, or will have the facilities to find out, everything which is adverse to the plaintiff's case. The plaintiff should be made to understand that nothing can be more harmful to his case than to be caught lying or exaggerating. The client should also be told to listen carefully to the questions being asked, to answer only those questions which he understands, and to answer as briefly and concisely as is possible. Plaintiff should be further advised that there is no need to rush into an answer and that he has the prerogative of asking the defense counsel to repeat the question or to make it more clear if he does not understand it.

The plaintiff should be told that it will be his duty to answer all questions and that it will be the job of counsel to make objections. The client should also be told that there is nothing dishonest or reproachful in failing to remember something, and that the statement, "I do not remember," where true, is a perfectly acceptable answer. For the same reasons, if a witness does not know the answer to a question, the only truthful response he can make is, "I don't know."

He should attempt to give brief, factual answers and should be told to avoid expressions such as, "I assume," "I guess," or "I suppose." The plaintiff must be informed that his only duty is to answer questions, *not* to volunteer information. Many plaintiffs look upon the deposition as a preliminary trial, and feel that they should reveal all the evidence that is favorable to their case. The plaintiff should be made to understand that the time to present all his favorable testimony will come at a later date. He should be told to say the minimum commensurate with his obligation to tell the truth. He should be told to avoid uncalled for explanations and cautioned not to provide background or illustrative anecdotes.

The plaintiff must also be warned to keep his temper at all costs; he should be told that some examiners will try to anger and excite him in order to handicap his reasoning powers and to gain irrational statements which will be harmful. An angry or irritated witness is usually a less alert and effective one. The plaintiff also should be told that when objection is made by plaintiff's counsel, he should *not* respond further or make *any* statement until he is told by counsel to answer the question.

Prior to taking the deposition, it is absolutely mandatory that plaintiff's counsel go over every aspect of the case with his client to refresh his recollection. That is, all facts of liability must be discussed and all aspects of the injury and all items of damage reviewed. In preparing a client, counsel will rely heavily on the plaintiff's initial statement, the police report, the hospital record, the doctors' record and any other pertinent information he has in his file. The preparation needed to equip a client for the taking of his deposition will vary from case to case. Failure by the attorney to prepare his client fully will, in almost every instance, be disastrous to his client's case.

Plaintiff's counsel must make every effort to put his client at ease prior to the deposition. Most plaintiffs are very nervous prior to deposition, and this can cause them to become confused and forgetful. The client should be told at the outset of the pre-deposition conference that it a routine procedure, that he will be fully prepared prior to the taking of the deposition, and that his lawyer will be with him during the entire procedure. He should also be told that there is nothing to be nervous about and that it is in his best interest to relax.

Making Objections. In every stage of the plaintiff's deposition, his counsel should be alert for questions which are improper in form or outside the scope of the permissible inquiry. If, by rule of the jurisdiction, all objections except as to form of the question are preserved until the time of trial, plaintiff's counsel's principal concern will be identifying defects of form. Examples of such defects would be argumentative, ambiguous, or multiple questions. Occasionally, in lieu of formal objections, plaintiff's counsel will merely request that defense counsel clarify the question to prevent the plaintiff's being confused. Such participation, if not overdone, can be helpful in maintaining an accurate, non-misleading record.

In situations where the plaintiff's counsel feels the defense lawyer is going beyond the permissible scope of deposition examination and that the matters of which he is inquiring would be prejudicial, plaintiff's counsel may instruct the plaintiff *not* to answer the question. Initial instinct should argue against such instruction if another course is open. Refusal to answer gives the examiner the option to adjourn the deposition in order to obtain a court ruling as to the permissibility of the question. Thus, the deposition may be halted and valuable time, effort, and expense consumed in motion proceedings. Although the examining party may suspend questioning when an instruction to refuse to answer is given, in most jurisdictions the examining party will usually continue the deposition on all other matters. Frequently, he will obtain the desired information with other questions, in connection with other subjects. If at the conclusion of the deposition he feels the question to have been left unanswered, where the answer is important, he may go to court to obtain a ruling.

Cross-Examination. Generally, when the plaintiff's deposition is taken by the defendant, plaintiff's counsel does not examine his own client. Unless there is some special reason for asking questions of the plaintiff, the best cross-examination upon deposition is *no* cross-examination. There are exceptions to this rule: if the plaintiff seems to be confused about some of the questions or has made some misleading or incomplete statement, it may be wise to clarify this at the deposition—if local rules permit the plaintiff's counsel to ask questions of the plaintiff after the defendant has closed. Inquiry along these lines by the plaintiff's counsel of his own client will protect against the defendant's argument that the supplementary testimony offered at trial was the product of ingenuity, exercised after the deposition had been completed, rather than fact. Some consider it helpful if plaintiff's counsel examines the plaintiff after the defendant has concluded if any aspect of his injury or damages was not thoroughly covered by the defense. The plaintiff can rarely get into trouble on deposition by being too thorough about his injury and damages. The temptation to engage in extensive examination of plaintiff when the defendant has elicited some apparently damaging but explainable testimony demands determined resistance. Although the natural inclination of counsel and plaintiff may be to refute and rebut the defendant's case and to assert the rightfulness of the cause, the time for making such a presentation is normally at trial, not at the plaintiff's deposition.

Video Taped Depositions

The recent amendments to the Federal Rules permit video tape transcriptions of depositions. This may be accomplished either by agreement or by the grant of a motion requesting permission to video tape the proceedings. The advisability of video taped testimony varies too greatly to be the subject of extensive discussion in this book. The procedure is relatively expensive and would ordinarily be done only when it is extremely important to convey a visual impression of the witness (good or bad) to the jury.

Medical Examination

In most jurisdictions, one of the most important pretrial discovery tools available to the defendant is the defense medical examination. Under this procedure, the defendant can have the plaintiff in a personal injury case examined by a physician of the defendant's choice. If the case is on file in a jurisdiction where the rules, statutes, or decisions give the defendant the right to have a physical examination performed, the penalties provided should the plaintiff refuse to submit are so severe that there is rarely any question as to whether the plaintiff will comply with a proper request that he be examined. In some jurisdictions the examinations will be made by a court appointed doctor if the plaintiff objects to the doctor suggested by the defendant. As a general rule, many lawyers consider it better from the plaintiff's point of view to allow an examination by a doctor named by a defendant than to resist such a request and submit to an examination by a doctor appointed by the court. A jury will be far more likely to accept the findings of a court appointed physician.

In principle, the Rule is equally available for use by the plaintiff; practically, however, the need to do so rarely arises.

It is absolutely mandatory that plaintiff's counsel meet with the plaintiff prior to the examination. At this conference, plaintiff's counsel should review every aspect of the plaintiff's medical history, injury, and other related problems. If the client's memory is not refreshed, he may forget or overlook certain key information, thereby distorting the history which he gives to the defense examiner. The plaintiff's counsel should use the hospital records, the reports of the plaintiff's treating and examining physicians, and all memoranda in his file to refresh his client's memory. It may be advisable for plaintiff's counsel or a member of his firm to accompany the plaintiff to the defense examiner's office and, local practice permitting, to accompany the plaintiff into the examining room. If a representative of the plaintiff's law firm is permitted to enter the examining room and observe the examination, he should take notes as to the questions asked by the examiner, the tests performed, the apparent results of the tests, and the length of time the examination takes. He should subsequently dictate his notes as a memorandum. Such notations may be particularly valuable should the case reach trial and plaintiff's counsel be forced to cross-examine the defense examiner.

The increasing tendency of the defense to request an examination of the plaintiff to determine his candidacy for rehabilitation presents serious questions as to whether Rule 35 can be used for this purpose.

CONCLUSION

In summary, it can be seen that there are many pretrial discovery tools which can assist both the plaintiff and the defendant in preparing their cases. Before taking an aggressive stand regarding the use of such tools, plaintiff's counsel should seek to determine whether extensive discovery (1) is really necessary and (2) would help his case as much or more than the defendant's. Plaintiff's counsel should always remember that the discovery initiated by the defendant is as important as the discovery initiated by the plaintiff. He must take great care to prepare the plaintiff for deposition and to answer interrogatories. Many cases have been lost either because of inadequate discovery initiated by the plaintiff or because of sloppy response to discovery initiated by the defendant.

Form No. 1

CHECK LIST FOR DEPOSITION OF INDIVUDAL DEFENDANT

1. Identification and Biography.
   - Correct Legal Name.
     — Is summons correct?
     — Guardian/ward, spouse, personal representative?
   - Address at present and last five years.
   - Telephone number at present and last two years.
   - Employer now and last five years.
   - Education—if relevant.
   - Experience—if relevant.
   - Criminal charges.
   - Prior similar incidents.

2. Relation to Other Defendants.
   - Agency.
   - Ownership of vehicle/product.
   - Interest of any kind in purpose of activity.
   - Control over method of activity.
   - Anyone else potentially responsible?
     — Obstruction contribute to cause?
     — Product contribute to cause?

3. Facts of Incident.
   - Establish basic facts of jurisdiction and venue and statute of limitations.
   - Correct date and place of incident.
   - Chronological narrative.
   NOTE: Relate time/place/speed to both plaintiff and defendant at all points in chronological narrative.

4. Any and All Statements.
   - Plaintiff.
   - Defendant.
   - Any other person.
   - Who, what, when, where?

- Written/oral? Who, where copy?
- Re: liability and/or damages.

5. Injuries.
   - Plaintiff appear injured or not?
   - Defendants?

6. Identify Any/All Potential "Witnesses."
   - Who, what, when, where?
   - Re: liability and/or damages.
   - Including any and all investigations of incident.

7. What Did Plaintiff Do Wrong?

8. Do You Plan to Use Expert?
   - Who, what, why?
   - Re: liability and/or damages.

Form No. 2

CHECKLIST FOR DEPOSITION OF DOCTOR

1. Identification and Qualifications.
   * Specialty?
   * Education?
   * Experience?
   * Special Boards—or Professional Associations?

2. Initial Examination.
   * When, where, why?
   * Referral?
   * History?
     — Who, what, why?
   * Clinical records? (Produce, examine, copy, attach to deposition)

3. Initial Diagnosis.
   * What? (lay language)
   * Basis?

Q: Is the trauma of the incident reported in the history (1) a competent producing cause of injuries of the type you have described in your diagnosis and (2) a precipitating cause of the injuries you described in your diagnosis, in your best medical judgment?

4. Treatment Prescribed.
   * What and why?
   * Clinical records? (Produce, examine, copy, attach to deposition)

5. Subsequent Visits/Exams.
   * Chronological narrative.

6. Development of Symptomology and Present Status?

7. Complications.
   - That have occurred?
   - That may occur?

8. Prognosis.
   - Anatomical vs. personal (E.g., individual vocational and personal life)
   - Physical vs. emotional, mental, psychic, etc.
   - Recommended future surgery, treatment, therapy, limitations of activity, etc.

9. Authoritative Treatise?

10. Bills and Expenses.
    - Medically needed and advisable for treatment of injuries described in diagnosis?
    - Fair and reasonable amount for treatment described?
    - Value of nursing service rendered by members of family.

Form No. 3

YOUR DEPOSITION

Introduction

One of the lawyers on the other side of your lawsuit has given formal notice of his intention to take your testimony at the time and place listed below:

Time:

Place:

We want you to come by the office before the time listed above so that we can explain to you in some detail what this procedure is likely to involve. Please immediately telephone the lawyer in this office who is handling your case (or his secretary) and make this important appointment.

The rest of this little pamphlet is designed to explain in advance some of the questions that our clients in the past have asked us about the deposition practice.

Question: What Is a Deposition?

The lawyer representing the other side in your lawsuit will ask you a number of questions about the issues in your case. Your answers will be given under oath; they will be written up later and will be available as testimony at the time of trial. Under the rules of practice in this state, each side in a lawsuit has the right to take the discovery deposition of the opposing party. Therefore, when you become either a plaintiff or a defendant in a lawsuit the opposing party may require you to appear at a specified time and place and give oral testimony under oath. The procedure is very informal; it will be done either in our office or in the office of the opposing counsel. We will be there with you during the time the other side questions you. We think we have a pretty good idea of the questions he is likely to ask you. The taking of depositions is a routine with which we have had a good deal of experience. One of the reasons we have asked you to make an appointment before the time the other side has set for your deposition is to give us an opportunity to tell you what questions we expect the other side to ask. You will be asked to take an oath to tell the truth, and a court reporter will be present taking down everything you say—therefore, it is extremely important that everything you say be accurate and truthful.

Question: What Is the Purpose of a Deposition?

The purpose of a deposition is to discover what the witness knows about the issues in the case. This information helps the lawyers in the preparation and trial of the lawsuit. The lawyers for both sides have to have this information in order to evaluate the case for settlement purposes. We want you to understand that it is normal and customary for lawyers to take discovery depositions; it is done in most cases like yours.

Question: How Should I Dress?

You should wear neat, clean clothing. It is not necessary to "dress-up"; we would advise that you avoid radical or faddish styles. If you have to take time off from work to attend the deposition, give yourself enough time to go home and freshen up and get out of your work clothes. It is extremely important that you make a good impression upon opposing counsel. The overall rule is simply that you should appear at your deposition dressed the same as you would expect to dress if you were actually going to court to appear before the jury.

Question: Should I Bring Anything to Your Office Before the Deposition?

There may be a number of documents or exhibits that we need to examine together before you give your testimony. When you call our office, be sure and specifically discuss this topic. The following is a list of some of the items we may need. We may want or need your help in getting these items, so be certain to ask when you call to make your appointment.

1. Statement of time lost from work.
2. Statement of lost wages.

3. Income tax returns.
4. Doctor bills (whether or not paid by insurance).
5. Hospital bills (whether or not paid by insurance).
6. Medical appliances.
7. Estimates of property damage or bills for repairs.
8. Copies of your own insurance policies.
9. Photographs.
10. Copies of any statement you have made regarding the incident.

If you have or know about any document that you might be questioned about, be sure to call it to our attention.

We are not suggesting that you will be questioned about everything on this list, but it is necessary that we know *everything* about which you *might be questioned!*

Question: Is There Any Particular Way I Should Act During the Deposition?

The following guidelines are based on our experience in the past—the fact that we list the things below does not suggest that we have any question that you would not do these things naturally. The following list is merely a summary of important guidelines:

1. Tell the truth!

2. Tell the truth even if you think your answer will hurt your case.

3. Be humble and respectful. If your answer is in the affirmative, say "yes, sir" or "yes, ma'am"; if it is in the negative say "no, sir" or no ma'am"—even if the lawyer asking the questions is younger than you are.

4. Never argue or lose your temper.

5. You must answer by speaking out. Do not shake your head "yes" or "no"; the court reporter must be able to hear and understand what you say.

6. Speak slowly and clearly.

7. If you do not understand the question, ask that it be repeated or explained.

8. Answer all questions directly giving concise answers and then stop talking! You are not required to volunteer information nor is it advisable. If you can answer the question with a simple "yes, sir" or "no, ma'am," do so and then stop. If the question requires an explanation then give it, but do not provide an unnecessary explanation.

9. Testify only to the facts as you personally know them. On one hand, do not attempt to give opinions or estimates of time and distance unless you have good reason for knowing that those opinions or estimates are accuarate. On the other hand, if you are sure of your position, do not qualify your answer by saying "I think" or "I believe" or "I guess" or "maybe" or "possibly." It is better to be positive. If you have some doubt then say, "as I recall" or "in my best judgment."

10. If you do not know the answer to a question, admit it. Some witnesses think they have to have an answer for every question simply because a lawyer is asking them and their answers are given under oath. You cannot know all the facts, and you do yourself a disservice if you attempt to testify to facts with which you are not acquainted. We repeat—do not guess at something you do not know. If you do not know the answer, it is perfectly permissible simply to say so.

11. Do not try to write down and memorize your recollection of this incident. Justice only requires that a witness tell his story to the best of his ability.

12. With regard to your injuries, we want you to give a full and fair description of all of your injuries and losses. However, the facts will speak for themselves, and it is not necessary for you to magnify or exaggerate any aspect of your loss. We can and will bring in doctors and other people who know you if it is necessary to fully acquaint the jury with each and every loss you have suffered. For example, do not say

"I can't do thus and so" if the truth is that you are simply not able to do "thus and so" as well now as before your injury or that you choose not to do it because of pain or discomfort. "Can't" means a physical impossibility; that is, you can't move your hand if you do not have a hand.

13. If you have had any injuries before the occurrence of the incident involved in the lawsuit, *be sure to tell the opposing lawyer about those injuries if he asks.* He is almost certain to ask. Search your recollection carefully so that you can tell him about every previous accident or injury or disease that you have ever suffered, even if you do not think they are related! If they are not related, we should be able to persuade the jury of that fact. If you do not mention some previous injury or disease there is a very good likelihood that the opposing side will learn of its existence, and the proof of its existence before a jury when you have not mentioned it will greatly increase the implication that we are trying to cover something up that is important. Not telling everything on this point could mean that your case will be lost. If you need to call a doctor that treated you for some prior injury or disease, be sure and do so before your deposition.

SPECIAL NOTE: It is possible that matters which you consider to be private and personal may legally be the subject of the other side's inquiry. For instance, a prior conviction in a criminal matter or a former divorce may under certain circumstances be legally relevant. In no event should you deny such matters without talking to your lawyers first. If you deny it and the other side is permitted to bring it out at trial, the results could be disastrous. If you tell your lawyer and the topic is truly irrelevant, your lawyer can take the proper steps to prevent inquiry into that topic.

REMEMBER, the single most important aspect of your lawsuit is YOU YOURSELF, the appearance you make, and the impression you convey of earnestness, fairness, and honesty. Our experience has confirmed over and over again that the jury's evaluation of a lawsuit is greatly influenced by their acceptance of the credibility and candor of the individual plaintiff.

Thank you for taking the time to read this carefully.

Please remember to make an appointment to come in before your deposition. We look forward to seeing you then.

_____

(Firm or Attorney's Name)

Form No. 4

TOPICS FOR INTERROGATORIES

1. Are all defendants correctly named?
2. Identify other potential defendants.
3. Establish agency.
4. Establish facts of incident.
5. Identify all "witnesses."
   a. Liability.
   b. Damages.
6. Any/all statements.
   a. Liability.
   b. Damages.
7. Experts.
   a. Liability.
   b. Damages.
8. Defense contentions.
   a. Liability.
   b. Damages.

See Form No. 1 for more details.

Form No. 5

TOPICS FOR PRODUCTION

1. Statements of plaintiff.
2. Statements of "witnesses."
3. Photographs.
   a. Vehicles/product.
   b. Scene.
   c. Incident.
   d. Parties.
4. Liability insurance contracts.
5. Evidence of ownership/interest in vehicle/product/activity.
6. Evidence of maintenance of or prior use of vehicle/product.
7. Material re: plaintiffs injuries.

Form No. 6

TOPICS FOR ADMISSION

1. Plaintiff named correctly.
   (Attach documentary evidence of representative capacity as Exhibit.)
2. All defendants named correctly.
3. Service/jurisdiction/venue proper.
4. Basic facts correct.
5. Agency admitted.
6. Plaintiff's expenses.
   a. Services medically necessary.
   b. Amount fair and reasonable.
   (Attach documentary evidence as an Exhibit)
7. Authenticity of documents.
   (Attach as Exhibit)
8. Truth of documents.
   (Attach as Exhibit).

ANNOTATIONS

Treatises

Bender's Forms of Discovery (Vols. 1-19).
Sann and Bellman, Deposition—Strategy, Law and Forms.

Am Jur Trials—Articles

Discovery—written interrogatories, 4 AJT 1-118.
Discovery—oral depositions, 4 AJT 119-184.
Request for admissions by plaintiff, 4 AJT 185-214.
Requests for admissions by defendant, 4 AJT 215-222.
Motions for production and inspection, 4 AJT 223-252.

Am Jur Trials—References

Discovery in Federal Tort Claims Act proceedings, 8 AJT 699-708.
Discovery in railroad trespasser accident litigation, 9 AJT 272-280.
Discovery in child-pedestrian accident cases, 9 AJT 450-460.
Discovery in exploding bottle litigation, 10 AJT 403-411.
Discovery in blasting damage case, 11 AJT 376-381.
Discovery in litigation under the Federal Employers' Liability Act, 11 AJT 565-587.
Discovery in products liability cases, 12 AJT 97-120.
Discovery in dram shop litigation, 12 AJT 777-782.
Discovery in boiler explosion cases, 12 AJT 397-406.
Discovery in light aircraft accident litigation, 13 AJT 692-712.
Discovery in liquified petroleum (LP) gas fires and explosion cases, 14 AJT 383-395.
Discovery in drug products liability cases, 17 AJT 81-136.
Discovery in power press accident cases, 17 AJT 458-481.
Discovery in rear-end collison cases, 19 AJT 623-651.
Discovery in burn injury cases, 22 AJT 199-346.
Discovery in automobile fuel tank fire cases, 23 AJT 428-442.
Discovery in gas pipe line explosion cases, 25 AJT 455-462.
Discovery in dental malpractice litigation, 25 AJT 553-562.

Am Jur

Discovery, Am Jur 2d, Depositions and Discovery, §§ 1 et seq.

ALR Annotations

Disclosure of name, identity, address, occupation, or business of client as violation of attorney-client privilege, 16 ALR3d 1047.

Scope of defendant's duty of pretrial discovery in medical malpractice action, 15 ALR3d 1446.

Pretrial examination or discovery to ascertain from defendant in action for injury, death, or damages, existence and amount of liability insurance and insurer's identity, 13 ALR3d 822.

Discovery and inspection of articles and premises in civil actions other than for personal injury and death, 4 ALR3d 762.

Who is a "managing agent" of a corporate party (to civil litigation action) whose discovery-deposition may be taken under Federal Rules of Civil Procedure or state counterparts, 98 ALR2d 622.

Discovery, inspection, and copying of photographs of article or premises the condition of which gave rise to instant litigation, 95 ALR2d 1061.

Discovery and inspection of article or premises the condition of which is alleged to have caused personal injury or death, 13 ALR2d 657.

Who is "employee" with statute permitting examination, as adverse witness, of employee of party, 56 ALR2d 1108.

Pretrial discovery of engineering reports of opponent. 97 ALR2d 770.

Pretrial deposition-discovery of opinions of opponent's expert witnesses, 86 ALR2d 138.

Right to elicit expert testimony from adverse party at pretrial discovery proceedings, 88 ALR2d 1190.

Discovery and inspection in action under Federal Tort Claims Act, 1 ALR2d 222.

Discovery and inspection of income tax returns in actions between private individuals, 70 ALR2d 240.

Pretrial examination or discovery to ascertain from defendant in action for injury, death, or damages the existence and amount of liability insurance and the insurer's identity, 13 ALR3d 822.

Names and addresses of witnesses to accident or incident as subject of pretrial discovery, 37 ALR2d 1152.

Pictures of litigant taken by opponent or latter's investigator as subject of pretrial disclosure, production, and inspection, 95 ALR2d 1084.

Pretrial discovery to secure opposing party's private reports or records as to previous accidents or incidents involving the same place or premises, 74 ALR2d 876.

Statements of parties or witnesses as subject of pretrial or other discovery, production, or inspection, 73 ALR2d 12.

Privilege against disclosure of matters arising out of transaction or relationship between accountant and client, 38 ALR2d 670.

Privilege of communications or reports between liability or indemnity insurer and insured, 2 ALR2d 659.

Privilege of custodian, apart from statute or rule, from disclosure, in civil action, of official police records and reports, 36 ALR2d 1318.

Privilege or immunity as affecting statements of parties or witnesses as subject of pretrial or other disclosure, production, or inspection, 73 ALR2d 84, 133.

What preliminary data gathered by public department or officials constitutes "public records" within the right of access, inspection, and copying by private persons, 85 ALR2d 1105.

Discovery or inspection of trade secrets, formula, or the like, 17 ALR2d 383.

Work product or confidential privilege as affecting discovery, inspection, and copying photographs of article or premises the condition of which gave rise to instant litigation, 95 ALR2d 1063.

Construction and effect of Rule 30(b)(d), 31(d) and similar state statutes and rules, relating to preventing, limiting, or terminating the taking of depositions, 70 ALR2d 685.

Time and place, under pretrial discovery procedure, for inspection and copying of opposing litigant's books, records, and papers, 83 ALR2d 302.

Time for filing and serving discovery interrogatories, 74 ALR2d 534.

Party's duty, under Federal Rule of Civil Procedure 36(a) and similar state statutes and rules, to respond to requests for admission of facts not within his personal knowledge, 20 ALR3d 756.

Identity of witnesses whom adverse party plans to call to testify at civil trial, as subject of pretrial discovery, 19 ALR3d 1114.

Pretrial testimony or disclosure on discovery by party to personal injury action as to nature of injuries or treatment as waiver of physcian-patient privilege, 25 ALR3d 1401.

Use of videotape to take deposition for presentation at civil trial in state court, 66 ALR3d 637.

Recording of testimony at deposition by other than stenographic means under Rule 30(b)(4) of Federal Rules of Civil Procedure, 16 ALR Fed 969.

Applicability of discovery order as "final decision" under 28 USCS § 1291, 36 ALR Fed. 763.

Discovery, in medical malpractice action, of names of other patients to whom defendant has given treatment similar to that allegedly injuring plaintiff, 74 ALR3d 1055.

Discovery of hospital's internal records or communications as to qualifications or evaluations of individual physician, 81 ALR3d 944.

Pretrial discovery of facts known and opinions held by opponent's experts under Rule 26(b)(4) of Federal Rules of Civil Procedure, 33 ALR Fed. 403.

Chapter 6

SETTLEMENT

INTRODUCTION

No lawyer can guarantee what kind of verdict the jury will award. The specific objective of the individual plaintiff is to obtain compensation for his injury. If this can be achieved by settlement, then plaintiff's counsel should make every effort to settle the case. Settlement avoids delay, expense, and risk of loss; further it provides the client with the money he deserves at the earliest time possible. 95 percent of all personal injury cases are settled.

No lawyer has either the time or the stamina to try all of his cases. Despite this fact, lawyers receive a disproportionate amount of training and advice on trial techniques and relatively little on settlement. In contrast, insurance companies and claims agencies train their personnel extensively in settlement techniques. The preparation and evaluation of a case for settlement take substantial work, even equal to that required for trial.

Evaluation typically requires the knowledge and the insight of an experienced attorney. This frequently is the most valuable advice and assistance an attorney provides to his client. For example, in a case of clear liability, the client could actually win a verdict by himself. If, however, he were left without the assistance of competent counsel to determine the proper amount of damages to which he is entitled, he would almost certainly receive an inadequate award.

Any attorney who diligently prepares his case can acquire the necessary skill to conduct successful settlement negotiations.

FACTORS THAT AFFECT EVALUATION

The Plaintiff

Will a jury identify positively or negatively with the plaintiff? Will the age, sex, race, marital status, economic status, personality, attitudes, and mannerisms of the plaintiff cause a jury to think favorably of the plaintiff and sympathize with him, or will a jury dislike the plaintiff and disfavor him?

The Defendant

The question is again one of identification. Will a jury respond favorably or unfavorably towards the defendant? If the defendant is an individual, counsel must analyze the same personal attributes in his efforts to anticipate the jury's reaction.

If the defendant is a corporation, well established and well regarded in the local community, a jury may identify positively with it. If the corporation is a national or international concern, the jurors' attitudes may be negative or ambivalent.

Liability

How good is the liability? What is the probability of winning or losing the case? Counsel, through experience and familiarity with the courts of his jurisdiction, should have some rough idea as to the probability of success on the issue of liability. This consideration and review depends upon many factors, such as whether it is a products liability case, whether there are catastrophic injuries, whether the liability issues are highly technical, and so on. These factors may be conceptually divided into three categories:

1. Difficult liability.

    a. On the merits.

    b. Factually and/or technically complex.

2. Simple liability.

    a. On the merits.

    b. Factually and/or technically simple.

3. Aggravated circumstances.

Obviously, the liability in the case of a defendant who runs a stop sign and strikes a plaintiff who has the right-of-way is much simpler than the liability of a manufacturer of a stamping press who sold his equipment with a guard that was subsequently removed by the plaintiff's employer.

Aggravated circumstances generally refer to some quality of wrong-doing on the part of the defendant which requires corrective deterrence or punishment. Counsel must consider whether it is probable that the jurors will feel directly threatened by the conduct of the defendant because they themselves are potential victims of the same conduct and injury. If the jurors are angered or offended by the defendant's conduct or personally identify themselves (or their families) as objects of the defendant's conduct, this is likely to find expression in their verdict.

Practical Considerations

The character and credibility of the plaintiff, as well as that of the plaintiff's witnesses, are factors to be weighed in the settlement equation. The character and credibility of the defendant and defense witnesses must also be taken into account. The difficulty of proving the plaintiff's case is also a factor. Strong, live witnesses usually enhance the likelihood of success more than the reading of dull depositions. Unfortunately, in many cases where witnesses are beyond the subpoena power of the court or unwilling to testify live, deposition witnesses must be used.

Type of Case

Some cases are better received by juries than others. For instance, jurors generally will be more favorably inclined to find for a plaintiff that is hurt on the job than for the plaintiff in a professional malpractice suit.

Damages

Damages which are easily understood and readily perceived are more susceptible to a dollar evaluation. For example, the loss of an arm is easier to evaluate than mental anxiety. Counsel must also consider problems such as aggravation of pre-existing condition of injury or subsequent injury. The effect of specific injuries to particular plaintiffs must also be considered. The loss of a finger to a violinist is far more valuable than to a night watchman. In considering injuries, one must look to the prognosis for medical complications and disabling effects in the future. Is the plaintiff likely to get better, stay the same, or get worse?

Economic Loss

Economic damages can be categorized as hard or soft. Hard damages are those actual losses which are readily verifiable, such as medical bills, lost wages, and property damage. Soft damages include loss of future profits, loss of future earnings, likelihood of loss of one's job in the future, and diminution of earning capacity.

Speculative Damages

Most jurisdictions allow recovery for some types of intangible damages: for example, loss of enjoyment of life, mental anguish, and pain and suffering. These are difficult to evaluate for purposes of settlement negotiation. However, they must be taken into consideration in evaluating a plaintiff's claim. Some guidance can usually be obtained from a review of settlements and verdicts in similar cases. Inexperienced counsel can obtain this type of information from various publications that report settlement and verdict results.[1]

Trial Forum

While counsel must become acquainted with the verdict experience in the jurisdiction where his case will be tried, he must also consider the potential for damages in this particular case. The verdicts in one area may historically tend to be more conservative than in another. Nevertheless, counsel must review carefully what the jury verdict range will be in his case if it is tried well.

The Judge

The attitude and actions of the trial judge are important considerations. While theoretically, all judges are impartial, they are also human. Counsel must consider what effect, if any, the qualities and characteristics of the particular judge before whom his case will be tried may have on the outcome of the case.

Quality of the Defense

Has the defendant's case been prepared adequately? Is the defendant's lawyer exceptional or merely capable? Are there any peculiar strengths in the defendant's case? Such factors must be taken into consideration as having a significant effect on the verdict range in any case.

[1]For instance, see ATLA *Law Reporter.*

Financial Responsibility

Even the best trial lawyer cannot get blood from a stone. The limits of an individual's insurance coverage may govern settlement negotiations to a great extent. In cases of clear liability in which there are very low limits and large damages, counsel should have little difficulty in quickly obtaining a tender of the policy limits. If defense counsel or the defendant's claims adjuster has all the information reasonably necessary to evaluate liability and damages and if it is clear that the value of the case exceeds the policy limits, plaintiff's counsel should make sure that the settlement demand preserves a possible claim for a future bad faith action.[2]

Specific Questions of Law

In considering what a case is worth, counsel must evaluate how the court will rule on particular issues of law or evidence. For example, one might have excellent proof that the defendant redesigned the intersection two days after the plaintiff's accident occurred. However, if this evidence is not admissible, it should not be considered in determining the value of the case.

Specific Issues

If evidence of the plaintiff's involvement with some moral taboo (e.g., "drinking" or "living together but unmarried") is likely to be admitted. Counsel must anticipate the probable reaction of the jury. Attitudes and reactions to particular taboos may vary from one community to another, e.g., rural versus cosmopolitan. Only certain types of individuals may respond negatively; if so counsel may be able to strike all such persons from the venire if he has a sufficient number of peremptory challenges.

APPROACHES TOWARD SETTLEMENT

Topics to Discuss with the Client

Indeed, it is the rare client who will demand that his case be tried regardless of the offer of settlement. Most clients want their cases settled before trial in order to avoid the attention, aggravation, and embarrassment they foresee as inevitable in the courtroom environment. It is generally unwise in the initial client interview to suggest what settlement value is appropriate to the case. Clients often have a one-sided view of the value of their case. Whether that opinion overvalues or

[2]See Harrison and Langerman, *Actions Against Insurer for Bad Faith Failure to Settle Claims,* 21 AJT 229-452 (1974).

undervalues the claim is not nearly as significant as the fact that the client's initial evaluation is simply inaccurate.

When attempting to discuss the value of a case with a client, many attorneys structure the discussion around three basic issues: liability, damages, and financial responsibility. The lawyer tells his client that the issue of liability involves the question of who's right and who's wrong; what percentage of responsibility for plaintiff's injuries can reasonably be charged to the defendant, and what portion is the plaintiff's own fault. This analysis obviously will be different in jurisdictions with comparative negligence than in those with traditional contributory negligence.

Counsel should discuss the recoverable elements of damages permitted under the law of his jurisdiction. It is wise to explain the difference between tangible and intangible damages and the difficulty of assigning precise values to the latter. Most lawyers speak in terms of "ranges of recovery"; however, one should not suggest what a reasonable range of recovery would be until careful review of the actual evidence is in hand. Reliance on representations from the client can backfire if subsequent discovery shows that the client's perceptions of his own case were significantly inaccurate.

Financial responsibility often translates into the amount of the defendant's insurance coverage. In most cases, the outside limit of settlement recovery is fixed by the limits of liability insurance. Plaintiff's counsel should tell his client that the client will make the ultimate settlement decision and that he, the attorney, will simply offer his advice and recommendations. He will keep his client regularly informed of the progress of settlement negotiations and will secure authority and consent of the client before any final settlement is fixed. An attorney can create serious problems for himself and his client if he formally represents to the defendant's counsel or liability insurance carrier that he has authority to settle for a specific figure when, in fact, he does not. He should determine whether oral or written authority to accept a specific settlement figure is required in his jurisdiction in order to bind the parties.

Who Initiates Negotiation and When

Who should initiate settlement discussions—the plaintiff or the defendant? If the plaintiff's attorney believes he has a duty to try to settle his client's case, then it is appropriate for him to initiate settlement discussions.

In most instances the best time to do so is at the earliest point possible. There are several factors which favor early initiation of settlement discussion. These include the fact that the defendant's insurance company needs to set reserves to cover the claim. If the liability and damage pictures are clear, an early settlement demand can set up the defendant for a future claim for excess liability or bad faith. Early settlement negotiations also force the plaintiff's attorney to evaluate and prepare his case promptly.

Some situations militate against commencing early negotiations. These include the possibility of making the plaintiff appear too eager to settle, resulting in the defendant's refusing to offer a fair settlement amount. If the client wants and deserves a jury trial, then early settlement negotiations would be inappropriate. If plaintiff's counsel "puts his cards on the table" too early in the case, the defense may realize that the plaintiffs consider their case to be worth a lot less than defendant originally anticipated. This again could result in a psychological disadvantage which might diminish the likelihood of a reasonable settlement.

There are certain situations in which settlement should not be discussed until immediately before or even during trial. These include situations involving a defense attorney who has not evaluated his case until right before trial or an insurance company which does not make its best offer until the last possible moment. Many trial lawyers believe they make better settlements just before or even after the start of trial. This is certainly true of those insurance companies which arbitrarily increase their reserves on a claim after the case is set for trial or after the trial has begun. Late negotiations immediately before trial might also catch the defense counsel unaware and lead to his revealing weaknesses of which plaintiff's counsel would not otherwise be aware.

Initiating settlement discussion late in a case might be undesirable. Counsel should consider the cost involved in the preparation of a claim and the net benefit to his client. If it is unlikely that the settlement offer will be significantly higher late in the case than it is early on, delay may result in additional expense to the client and a lower net recovery. Late initiation of settlement discussion may foreclose the possbility of an excess liability claim. Late consideration of settlement may also cause plaintiff's counsel to defer a hard evaluation of his claim and subsequently mislead him or his client as to the true value of the lawsuit.

THE OFFER TO SETTLE

How to Determine the Offer

The ultimate question is, of course, the actual dollar figure which you tell the defendant your client will accept in settlement. The determination of the precise amount of your final offer is beyond the scope of this chapter. Obviously it will depend on unique facts and factors affecting the particular case. In general, the decision of the precise amount of your settlement offer is determined by the answer to the following questions:

1. How strong is your case on liability?
2. How large are your damages?
3. Can you prove 1 and 2?
4. Can you collect the probable verdict?

How to Communicate the Offer

You must consider the individuals with whom you are negotiating. A defendant's attorney may prefer to receive an offer which he knows is excessive and then work to an eventual settlement which is a compromise below the original figure. On the other hand, he may be the type of individual who prefers a straight, honest, good-faith demand and works to settle the claim for that figure without forcing the plaintiff to "negotiate against himself" as the case proceeds. There are also defense attorneys who, regardless of what demand the plaintiff makes, will counteroffer an extremely low figure in an effort to out-bargain the plaintiff into a low range settlement. In settlement negotiations, it is wise to find out with what kind of defense counsel you are working and how he has handled claims in the past.

If you are dealing with a representative of the defendant's insurance company, another factor may come into play. The insurance adjustor's primary objective may not be to settle the case. Instead, he may merely be trying to get information and to commit the plaintiff to a figure which the defendant's lawyer can subsequently negotiate downward in later discussions. On the other hand, many insurance carriers want to avoid exposure to large verdicts and will seriously negotiate a reasonable settlement from the start.

When dealing directly with a defendant corporation, as opposed to an insurance company, one must consider the company's experience with litigation. An inexperienced company may refuse to admit that it is at fault and insist on a jury trial. There is little point in engaging in serious negotiations with such a defendant. On the other hand, an inexperienced company may be fearful of the risk of a large verdict and therefore be willing to negotiate a settlement. Still other companies with extensive claims experience have their own claims department; railroads and power companies often fall into this category. If you know your defendant has its own claims department or has an insurance carrier that negotiates in good faith, you might consider writing the defendant's home office before filing suit. You might be able to negotiate a reasonable settlement quickly and with minimal expense to your client.

The Form of the Offer

Some attorneys like to make their settlement demand in the form of a letter. Others use settlement brochures which include actual exhibits, such as photographs, medical bills, and hospital records. Still others prefer to use videotapes and "Day in the Life" films. The nature of the plaintiff's injuries and the size of the case should dictate which approach is appropriate. In a case involving minor injuries, a "Day in the Life" film is both an unnecessary expense and an inappropriate approach to settlement. On the other hand, in a case involving serious injuries, a "Day in the Life" film might well be worth the expense and also be quite appropriate.

TYPES OF SETTLEMENT

Settlements fall into three basic categories: simple complete settlements, partial settlements, and structured settlements.

Simple Complete Settlements

Simple complete settlements usually involve cases where there is only one defendant and the damages are not catastrophic. The case is settled for a specific figure, the parties execute complete releases and/or covenants not to sue, and any pending action is dismissed with prejudice, or a stipulated judgment is filed and the case is concluded.

Partial Settlements

Partial settlements usually involve cases where there are multiple defendants. The rules vary around the country as to the effect of covenants not to sue, partial releases, "Mary Carter" agreements, and the like. It is absolutely imperative for counsel to check the status of the law applicable to such agreements. Some types of partial settlement may be forbidden; some types may have the effect of releasing the remaining defendants. Local statutory law and case law will also control the effect in trial on other defendants of partial settlements regarding such issues as admissibility, contribution, set off or reduction from final verdict.

Structured Settlements

In large damage cases, structured settlements might be appropriate. If a structured settlement is considered, careful consideration must be given to the ethical, economic, and tax considerations. Plaintiff's counsel should consider consulting an experienced economist or comparable individual to evaluate the variables. When minors are involved, counsel must see that their interests are fully protected. Local practice should be determined and followed carefully, for example, appointment of guardians *ad litem,* necessity of court approval, and appointment of trustees.

The structuring of the actual settlement must be planned so as to provide for the needs of the client over his foreseeable lifetime. Counsel would be ill advised to rely solely on the defendant's analysis of the advantages and disadvantages of a particular settlement proposal. The plaintiff's own economic experts should carefully review and analyze the terms of the settlement before it is finally accepted.

The tax consequences of a settlement must also be considered so that the client's best interests are protected. (See Bibliography for more detailed references.)

SPECIAL CONSIDERATIONS

Settlements in wrongful death cases are generally governed by local statutes and case law. Counsel must comply strictly with the requirements of the law of his jurisdiction regarding the authority to settle, the approval of the settlement, the award of attorney's fees, and the identity of persons to whom distribution is made.

In claims involving minors or incompetents, again local statutory and case law must be reseached and followed before the case is settled for a specific figure, monies are disbursed, and fees are paid.

Before counsel recommends any settlement to a client, he should know the identity of the insurance companies involved and the layers of coverage. This is true both in simple automobile cases where uninsured motorist coverage, underinsured motorist coverage, or stacking coverage may be involved and in cases involving catastrophic injuries where there are multiple insurance companies carrying excess insurance beyond base policy limits.

CONCLUSION

A good, just, and fair settlement is one that is the product of complete and realistic evaluation of all liability factors, careful consideration of all elements of damages, and a complete discovery of the financial responsibility of the defendant.

ANNOTATIONS

Treatise

Herman, Better Settlements Through Leverage.

Am Jur—Articles

Settling the case—plaintiff, 4 AJT 289-378.
Settling the case—defendant, 4 AJT 379-410.
Sample settlement brochure, 4 AJT 411-439.
Predicting personal injury verdicts and damages, 6 AJT 963-1042.

Am Jur Trials—References

Settlements in Miller Act litigation, 7 AJT 338, 339.
Settlements in swimming pool accident cases, 7 AJT 677-680.
Settlements in airline passenger death cases, 8 AJT 209-212.
Settlements in motor vehicle collision cases involving an agency relationship, 8 AJT 29-32.
Settlements in Tort Claims Act proceedings, 8 AJT 698-699.
Settlements in falls from scaffolds cases, 9 AJT 43-45.
Settlements in seamen's injuries cases, 9 AJT 718-722.
Settlements in exploding bottle litigation, 10 AJT 412, 413.
Settlements in trip-and-fall cases involving premises liability, 10 AJT 274-276.
Settlements in blasting damage cases, 11 AJT 382, 383.
Settlements in litigation under the Federal Employers' Liability Act, 11 AJT 588, 589.
Settlements in uninsured motorist claims cases, 11 AJT 154-159.
Settlements in wrongful death actions, 12 AJT 388-390.
Settlements in glass door accident cases, 14 AJT 168-172.
Settlements in drug products liability cases, 17 AJT 140.
Settlements in cosmetic surgery malpractice cases, 18 AJT 667-676.
Failure to settle, action against insurer for bad faith, 21 AJT 229-452.
Settlements in comparative negligence cases, 21 AJT 747-750.
Settlements in dental malpractice litigation, 25 AJT 563-566.

Am Jur

Settlement, Am Jur 2d, Compromise and Settlement, §§ 1 et seq.

ALR Annotations

Federal Tort Claims Act: judgment against or settlement with negligent employee as releasing United States, or vice versa, 42 ALR2d 960.

Avoidance (or) compromise of personal injury claims on ground of fraud or mistake as to extent or nature of injuries, 71 ALR2d 82, 167.

Specific performance of compromise and settlement agreement, 48 ALR2d 1211.

Settlements with or release of person directly liable for injury or death as releasing liability under civil damage act, 78 ALR2d 988.

Power and responsibility of executor or administrator to compromise claims due estate, 72 ALR2d 191.

Power and responsibility of executor or administrator to compromise claim against estate, 72 ALR2d 243.

Construction of provision, in compromise and settlement agreement, for payment of costs as part of settlement, 71 ALR3d 909.

Legal malpractice in settling or failure to settle client's case, 87 ALR3d 168.

Chapter 7

PSYCHOLOGY OF TRIAL

INTRODUCTION

Trial advocacy can be divided into three interrelated components: procedural law, substantive law, and persuasion. These three components are interdependent. With respect to persuasion, there are psychological principles which have been generally recognized by trial practitioners as having special importance. Persuasion is the art of moving human beings to action. Communications experts and language psychologists generally agree, "what the mind attends to, it considers. What the mind does not attend to, it dismisses. What the mind tends to continually, it believes; and what the mind believes, it ultimately does."[1]

In order for jurors to listen to your case and believe it, it is necessary to focus their attention on the crux of your case from the very start of the trial. Many successful trial practitioners have been able to get the jurors' attention and hold it through the selection of a motif or theme. This can be done by selecting a narrow target, focusing on it, keeping it highly visible, and relating the main points of a trial to this continuing theme.

Many jurors have difficulty understanding and paying attention to what goes on during the trial because they are unfamiliar with court-

---

[1]Professor Ormond Drake, New York University.

room procedures and are unable to absorb large portions of what goes on in the courtroom. They are first interrogated by lawyers during voir dire; they hear conflicting opening statements of what the testimony will be; witnesses contradict each other, etc. As a result, much of the content of the trial is lost and what remains is essentially an impression. The jurors are then required to debate among themselves and arrive at a verdict. Because jurors are people, and people are different, they come with different societal values, predispositions, and feelings. It is no wonder then that different jurors respond differently to the same perceived communication. Yet, there are certain patterns of perceived communication that have general application.

The process of influencing others can be analyzed under the headings of attention, comprehension, and acceptance. The influencing process starts the first moment counsel and client come into contact with the jury. From that moment until the jury room door closes, everything that occurs in the presence of the jury influences persuasion.

JURY EXAMINATION

Objectives

When counsel stands to address prospective jurors in voir dire, his objective is to aid the court in selecting a fair and impartial jury. His further objective as an advocate is to obtain necessary information to exclude those jurors who, based on their biases and prejudices, might be unable to respond favorably to his client's case. Counsel also seeks to establish his credibility with the prospective jurors in order that they might be predisposed to decide the case in favor of his client.

Methods of Analysis

Much has been written on the analysis of jury selection. Trial lawyers would do well to stay abreast of a large body of literature published in this area. Many attorneys believe that there are particular personality profiles which can generally be excluded because of their inability to respond favorably to any type of personal injury action. Many experienced trial attorneys believe that there are definite verbal and nonverbal communications which can cue an attorney to a favorable or unfavorable disposition of a juror. In certain select cases, counsel might well consider using some form of communications specialist or jury psychologist to analyze his case and discover what types of jurors might respond favorably or unfavorably to it. Whatever practice or procedure an attorney uses in trying to determine what kind of jurors would be suitable or unsuitable for a particular case, it is generally agreed that necessary information can be obtained either through a pretrial investigation and/or observation of verbal and nonverbal communications during the voir dire process itself.

Pretrial investigation of jurors can sometimes be accomplished by obtaining a published list before trial of the venire panel from which the particular jury will be selected. In those jurisdictions where the list is available a reasonable time before the commencement of the trial, at least an elementary pretrial investigation can be conducted. Counsel can check addresses, occupations, and other basic information. More sophisticated analyses include, for example, the use of a specialist to determine community attitudes on key issues in the case or the outcome of similar litigation.

During voir dire, the lawyer should observe both the verbal and nonverbal reactions of prospective jurors to questions posed. This is true both of questions which you ask as well as questions asked by opposing counsel. It is possible to design questions which are specially gauged to indicate stress levels and acceptance levels on the part of prospective jorors. If a particular case warrants the effort and expense, a trained psychologist or communications specialist could be positioned in the courtroom to aid counsel in this process.

Selection Guidelines

Counsel should realize that in the overwhelming majority of cases, it would be impractical to conduct community attitudinal surveys or to investigate the background of prospective jurors before trial. Nevertheless, the three following guidelines may be useful in the selection of any jury:

1. Consider carefully what a juror says in response to your question;

2. Observe how he says it; and

3. Look for clues in body codes when he says it.

For example, when analyzing the response to the standard question, "Mr. Jones, what is your profession or occupation and by whom are you employed?" you should consider the content—that is, what he says, how he says it, and what his body is doing as he is speaking. Mr. Jones may tell you that he is a leader, a passive person, or generally a reasonable follower. This type of analysis can be characterized as: "big I, the little i, and the no i" analysis. If Mr. Jones responds, "I am an architect, and I own my own company," he's likely to have a strong assertive personality. If he responds, "I am a mechanic for a local telephone company," he might well be an ordinary follower. If he simply responds, "Stock boy in a local department store," he may have no particularly strong identity. If the president of a local bank is a member of the jury, he might exercise substantial influence in relationship to his position on the jury. If a juror has a specialized knowledge or experience which involves issues in your case, he might exercise disproportionate weight in the decision-making process because of special authority given to his opinions. Further, a juror's occupation or social status may strongly influence his social and economic values and could dispose him favorably or unfavorably toward the plaintiff or defendant.

Studies of jury deliberations have indicated that jurors who have exercised the most influence and control in jury deliberations are traditionally in the following order: proprietors and white collar professionals, clerical workers, skilled laborers, and unskilled laborers. Counsel should be warned, however, that there are exceptions to every rule in every case. Familiarity with local conditions in one's jurisdiction should always be given high priority.

JURY ACCEPTANCE

Reaction Analysis

Over the past twenty years, there has been a large body of literature developed on how individuals respond and react to the communications of others. The interaction of people in the process of communication has been formalized into a number of different analytical frameworks. One of the more popular is known as "transactional analysis." Transactional analysis is a method of observing, characterizing, and analyzing relationships between or among two or more people through their verbal and nonverbal interactions.[2] Simple transactional analysis is concerned with stimulus and response. A stimulus is the original communication from you to a prospective juror; the response is the reaction to that communication by the juror. The stimulus-response can be characterized methodically in various ways. One of the more popular is parent, child, or adult. These response patterns are not roles as much as they are mental states which condition the evaluation of particular information as received, accepted, or rejected. There are also verbal and nonverbal cues to help identify transactional responses as parent, child, or adult. These cues include gestures, facial expressions, and body movements. The goal is to be able to identify the individuals on the jury as to how they relate to your case, to the defense, and to each other. The jurors may attempt to mask their personal biases; they may do this consciously or unconsciously. The verbal and nonverbal communicative technique mentioned above will help to identify and analyze prospective jorors' verbal responses as consistent or inconsistent with their body language.

Verbal and Nonverbal Communication

We all know that to understand what a word means we sometimes have to read the entire sentence. The same is true about gestures. To understand gestures, you have to fit them into clusters and interpret them in a context. If gestures are consistent with one another, they may well reflect an attitude of a juror. If verbal and nonverbal communications of a particular juror are inconsistent, the nonverbal communication is probably more authentic and reliable.[3] For example, in a negligent knockdown case, if you ask a juror if he likes children, and he says yes, but at the same time crosses his arms and legs and cups his hand under his chin, these gestures are incongruent with his verbal message and probably indicate that he is masking a bias against children. If the person to whom you are speaking casts his eyes down and turns his face away, he may already have turned you off. If his mouth is relaxed and his chin is forward, he may be considering what you are saying. If he looks directly at you with a slightly one-sided smile, it is probable that he is going to accept what you are saying. If he looks at you directly in a relaxed manner, he probably accepts your

[2]Generally: E. BERNE, THE GAMES PEOPLE PLAY (1964); T. HARRIS, I'M O.K., YOU'RE O.K. (1967); J. MENNINGER, SUCCESS THROUGH TRANSACTIONAL ANALYSIS (1973).

[3]G. NIERENBERG and H. CALERO, HOW TO READ A PERSON LIKE A BOOK (1971).

position.[4] It is impossible to catalogue each movement in body language, especially as it relates to a courtroom environment; however, many body cues and codes do exist. A good trial practitioner should develop a sensitivity to these signals and take advantage of them.[5]

Establishing Credibility

It is also essential from the beginning of trial to establish credibility with the jury. How effective a communication is and how well it is received depends not only on the attitudes of the receiver but also on who initiates it and how it is communicated. Much of the communication that occurs in a courtroom is nonverbal. Much nonverbal communication influences whether a juror accepts you and your case as believable. A juror's initial impression of your appearance, style, and delivery has a strong influence on the credibility he attaches to what you say during trial. The more credible you are perceived to be, the more successful you are likely to be in motivating the jury to act in a manner consistent with success for your client.[6]

Clothing

While clothes do not make the man or the woman, they do affect how people judge the wearer's status, character, and expertise.[7] The business suit is still generally considered a positive authority symbol in the courtroom. Darker suits usually transmit more authority than do light colored ones. Style of dress varies with community. Counsel should know what is traditionally worn by trial lawyers in his area. Generally speaking, however, it could be said that (1) dark blue and medium blue solids project credibility to middle-class jurors in the United States,[8] (2) it is preferable not to wear jewelry or clothing which reflects personal, political, religious, or social attitudes, and (3) women attorneys do well to wear solid colored two-piece suits, conservative shoes, conservative jewelry, and conservative makeup.

[4]T. SANNITO, A PSYCHOLOGIST'S VOIR DIRE (1979); E. DEMBY, BIASES AND PREJUDICES AMONG JURORS (1970).

[5]Ibid.

[6]C. HOVLAND AND I. JANIS, PERSONALITY AND PERSUASABILITY 11-12 (1959).

[7]J. MOLLOY, DRESS FOR SUCCESS 187-198 (1975).

[8]A pre-publication summary of a study by Litigation Sciences of Los Angeles indicated that suit color does not significantly affect juror's perception of a lawyer, although jurors do rate a lawyer as far more competent, sincere, and powerful when he wears a suit rather than a sport coat. In the preliminary data analysis of this study, the *brown* suit had the highest overall rating: 3:81, as opposed to 3.77 for the dark blue suit. Litigation Sciences, Lawyer Apparel Study: Pre-Publication Summary (June, 1981).

Clients and witnesses should wear conventional dress which is consistent with their age, occupation, social position, and the community where the case is being tried.

OPENING STATEMENT

Primacy

Opening statement is the first time a jury hears a coherent explanation of the case. It is pivotal in creating fundamental impressions. Because it comes first, it is primary. "Primacy" means that people tend to believe most deeply what they hear first. Which side of an issue is presented first should have an influence on opinion formation. At the start of a civil trial, the plaintiff has the advantage of primacy. Plaintiff's counsel speaks first; therefore, he persuades first. Some trial attorneys believe that many jurors make up their minds on the issue of liability after opening statement and rarely change their minds during the remainder of the trial.

Order of Presentation

The order of presentation of facts and the order of presentation of words strongly influence a juror's perception of evidence. In a recent study using college students, one group was asked to give their impression of an individual who was described as intelligent, industrious, impulsive, critical, stubborn, and envious. The other group was asked to describe an individual who was characterized as envious, stubborn, critical, impulsive, industrious, and intelligent. Group 1 concluded that the individual was an able person with minor shortcomings. Group 2 concluded the individual had serious problems and personality difficulties. By simply reversing the order of words in the description, the impression and interpretation of the groups was altered.[9]

Persuasive Communication

Persuasive communication should engender belief and stimulate action. The persuasive communication therefore should (1) command the attention of the jury; (2) produce the understanding you intend; (3) be perceived as credible and accurate; (4) be consistent with the jurors' values of what is right and wrong; and (5) stimulate the jurors to act favorably towards your position. The juror should be persuaded that a wrong was committed and that it is their role to right that wrong

[9]Lawson, *Experimental Research on the Organization of Persuasive Arguments: An Application to Courtroom Communications*, 1970 ARIZONA ST. L. J. 463-481.

by their verdict. The plaintiff's attorney should present the basic facts in his opening statement in a positive and forceful manner. During his case in chief, his evidence must affirm the truth and believability of what he set forth in his opening statement. His closing argument must then motivate the jury to return a verdict that is just, right, and consistent with the position that he has put forth throughout the case.

Structure, Clarity, and Repetition

The principle of primacy relates also to the order of proof and the structure of closing argument. Brief exposure to ambiguous testimony may result in the jurors' forgetting what was said. It is important that critical testimony be presented with clarity and that the jurors be exposed to it for a sufficient period of time so that its importance is firmly established. Therefore, a trial attorney should see that key facts essential to a case are strategically repeated in a clear and unambiguous fashion in the course of a trial.

PRE-EMPTION

Adverse Evidence

In the psychology of persuasion, it is often to one's advantage to diffuse the psychological effects of adverse evidence before the opposition has an opportunity to present it. For instance, if the plaintiff suffered previous injury to the same part of his body, this could be mentioned in opening statement and covered in the direct testimony of the medical expert. The plaintiff himself could also testify to these facts on direct examination. Psychologists generally consider it more advisable to present one's favorable evidence first to evoke favorable response and then present unfavorable testimony which may evoke avoidance at some later point. When jurors hear favorable testimony first, it tends to strengthen a commitment to plaintiff's position.

Direct Examination

During direct examination, if you are permitted by the court in your jurisdiction, you should consider standing by the jury rail across the courtroom from the witness. This technique enables you to develop an identity with the jury as well as to force the jury's attention on the witness. It also enhances the importance of the witness by expanding his physical territory in the courtroom by requiring him to look and speak to the jury in order to respond to you. By this technique, you compel your witnesses to develop stature and status before the jury. Conversely, when dealing with defense or adverse witnesses, it is possible to cut off their territorial space in the courtroom and their contact with the jury by moving closer to the witness box during cross-examination.

Cross-Examination

During cross-examination, you should try to blunt the persuasive effect of your opponent's case. This can be accomplished (1) by attacking the testimony of the witness, (2) damaging other defense testimony through the witness, and (3) attacking the witness himself. Cross-examination can also be used to corroborate testimony presented in your case. Confrontation between the cross-examiner and the witness can be influenced by nonverbal communication. For example, (1) when the cross-examined witness gives an answer that is favorable to your case, you can so indicate by facial expression or gesture; (2) when a witness concedes a point, you can indicate this to the jury by moving closer to the witness box and reducing his sphere of influence; and (3) by using volume and intonation in sequencing your questions, you can suggest to the jury that you are succeeding in your attack. One should be cautioned, however, that excessive interruptions by opposing counsel can blunt the effectiveness of direct and cross-examination. If you feel that objections are being made simply to blunt the effectiveness of your cross-examination, you might consider, if appropriate to your jurisdiction, requesting the court to advise counsel of his duty to make objections in good faith and only when necessary. You will at least alert your opposing counsel to the fact that you are aware of the technique he is using, and it might reduce the impact of his effort.

Final Argument

The plaintiff goes first in voir dire and, in most jurisdictions, speaks first and last in final argument. "Recency" is the principle that states that people remember best and most vividly what they hear last. It involves memory, not depth or intensity of belief. The psychological objective in opening statement was to establish credibility. A primary objective in final argument is to motivate the jury first, to return a verdict for the plaintiff, and second, to return one that provides adequate compensation. In opening statement, plaintiff's counsel tells the jury what he will prove. In his case in chief he proves it, and in final argument he tells the jury that he has done so. Persuasiveness of final argument depends in large measure upon the order of presentation as well as the manner of presentation. In order to structure final argument, counsel must be keenly aware of the complexity of the factual issues involved in the case as well as the intelligence of the jury. The more complex the issues, the more need there will be to explain. Counsel should not presume that the jury will remember the key points in a case, and it is wise to emphasize them in closing, if time permits. One should not presume too high an intelligence level for a jury. It is important to structure one's argument so that the last impression left with the jury is the most significant and is the one upon which they are likely to act when they convene in the jury room.

There are many approaches to structuring final argument. One approach is the two-sided, pro-con type which considers the psychological importance of primacy and recency. It is advisable to present the pro arguments first in order to evoke agreement and then to present the con arguments for contrast. Some experts suggest further that the final note again should be repetition of the pro arguments so that the last impression given the jury is a positive one. Counsel should touch on negative points if he fears that opposing counsel may suggest to the jury that you intentionally avoided a negative argument because you are trying to deceive the jury or because the argument is dispositive of the case.

Another structural approach to closing argument is that of the climax or anti-climax order. The climax approach places the strongest argument last. In civil cases, many trial lawyers who know they will be followed by opposing counsel will use the climax approach, presenting their strongest argument last in order to force their opponents to respond to it. In criminal cases, the reverse approach may be appropriate. The anti-climax order is used because the effort is to reverse the thought processes of the jury as quickly as possible away from the views presented by the prosecution.

Language has been classified as powerful or powerless.[10] In closing argument, powerful language suggests competency, trustworthiness, and credibility. One's argument should be structured to avoid weak words and weak grammatical forms. A closing argument that hedges,

[10]Conley, O'Barr, and Lind, *The Power of Language: Presentational Style in the Courtroom,* 1978 DUKE L.J. 1375, 1379-1385.

hesitates, or apologizes does not suggest credibility or trust. Strong language should complement positive body language during closing argument. If the two are inconsistent, subconsciously jurors will sense this. In order to avoid a disjunction between one's verbal and nonverbal communication, pretrial preparation should include the careful planning of closing argument. Many great trial lawyers practice their closing arguments in front of a mirror before they present them to the jury.

Jury Instructions

A jury trial is a contest between opposing sides, each contending that its characterization of the evidence is correct. While counsel's primary concern is his message to the jury, he should closely observe the judge while he reads the instructions. If the court's reading of the charges to the jury appears to be prejudicial, counsel should so note in the record. If his case is prepared and presented well, the jury will believe him and, "What the mind believes, it ultimately does."[11]

[11]Professor Ormond Drake, New York University.

Chapter 8

VOIR DIRE EXAMINATION
AND JURY SELECTION

INTRODUCTION

Purpose

The purposes of the voir dire examination of the jurors include, but are not limited to, the identification and striking of those persons who are disqualified by statute from serving, those who have some relationship to the lawyers on either side of the case to be tried, those who have prior knowledge of the parties or case and who have formed opinions about the case, and those who have some preconceived bias, notion, or prejudice arising from their background, occupation, business, or environment. These things add up to the selection of a jury that will be fair and impartial to all parties. The conduct of the voir dire examination necessarily imparts information. It would be impossible not to impart information since to identify bias one must frankly question the jurors about matters that could be bias-creating factors, such as "The plaintiff in this case had consumed two martinis before he was hit by the defendant who ran the red light. Would you hold that aginst the plaintiff if you find that had nothing to do with causing the collision?" Thus, voir dire is a discovery process and a decision-making time for the lawyer. He decides, based on questions asked the jurors, their oral responses, and personality manifestations, who are the most qualified jurors for that particular case.

Voir dire is *not* opening statement, and it is *not* the time or place to argue the case!

293

Desirability of a Jury Trial

The question of whether or not to demand a jury trial should be addressed in every case. Most often, a jury trial is desirable. Sometimes, however, because of the nature of the case on liability or damage issues or because of the nature or appearance of the client or the client's background, you may not want to demand a jury trial.

Challenging Jurors

Virtually every jurisdiction has statutes or rules which provide counsel an opportunity to eliminate jurors who they believe are not fit or qualified to hear their client's case. Although a near-infinite variety of local rules exist, there are in general two types of challenges: challenges to the array and challenges to the polls. Challenges to the array are directed at the entire jury panel and are designed to question the validity of its makeup; they are based on claims of defects or irregularities in the selection of jurors from the jury lists or in the summoning of the jurors. This type of challenge is used very infrequently. Challenges to the polls are addressed to individual jurors. There are two types of challenges to the polls: (1) a challenge for cause and (2) a peremptory challenge. A challenge for cause may be based upon a statutory disqualification, in which case nothing is left to the discretion of the court, or it may be based upon an allegation that the particular juror is biased in favor of one of the parties, in which case the court must exercise its discretion to rule on the challenge. There is no limit to the number of challenges for cause made by counsel. The peremptory challenge, on the other hand, is limited—only a specific number of prospective jurors can be eliminated by each side. When he executes a peremptory challenge, counsel need *not* give his reason. Counsel's exercise of a peremptory challenge does not involve the trial judge's discretion.

In Federal Court

Voir dire in Federal Court is limited by some U.S. District Court judges. This limitation on voir dire severely and unnecessarily restricts the need and the necessity for counsel for both sides to learn of the existence of some prejudice or preconceived bias on the part of the jurors that will literally control the outcome of the case despite the law and the facts. In a recent case the U.S. Court of Appeals for the Fifth Circuit stated:

...the real issue is whether the voir dire examination uncovers possible prejudice and bias of any juror so that a fair and impartial jury may be impaneled. Peremptory challenges are worthless if trial counsel is not afforded an opportunity to gain the necessary information on which to base such strikes.

and further:

...we must acknowledge that voir dire examination in both civil and criminal cases has little meaning if it is not conducted by counsel for the parties.[1]

THE VOIR DIRE EXAMINATION

Purpose

Voir dire is the examination of prospective jurors to determine who among the panel will be selected to sit on a jury in a particular case. More accurately, the jury makeup is determined by a process of elimination rather than by selection, as jurors are stricken rather than chosen. The voir dire examination serves two judicially recognized purposes: (1) to test the statutory qualifications of the individual veniremen, and (2) to afford the attorneys a procedure by which they may obtain information about the prospective jurors which they *must* have if they are intelligently and fairly to exercise their challenges for cause and their peremptory challenges.

Limitations

The right to examine prospective jurors in order to test their legal qualifications is granted by statute in almost every jurisdiction, but some judges are reluctant to allow extensive voir dire examinations because of a fear of "losing control" over the proceeding. Good reasons to curtail voir dire drastically *cannot* be advanced except where inexperienced or over-eager counsel use the procedure as a means of arguing the case before the trial begins. While the argument that restricted voir dire will save time has superficial plausibility, it makes no more sense than limiting all trials to one day, closing arguments to ten minutes, or each side to one witness. There are many ways to shorten the trial, but justice should never be sacrificed in the name of speed. A proper voir dire examination, on the other hand, can actually *save* time by bringing into focus the issues of the case.

Because the point is so terribly important we repeat it. The exercise of peremptory challenges is a matter of right granted by statute. It is

---

[1]U.S. v. Ledee, 549 F.2d 990, 993 (5th Cir. 1977).

an important right; it is inseparably related to the right to trial by an unbiased jury. Therefore counsel must be granted a reasonable time to make inquiries of the prospective jurors under oath. In order for counsel to strike prejudiced veniremen intelligently, he must have some knowledge, insight, or information concerning the juror's beliefs and prejudices.

In every jurisdiction which permits voir dire examination, the limits of the examination are subject to the trial court's discretion. If counsel, prior to trial, believes the trial judge will drastically curtail the examination he may wish to file a written motion requesting the privilege of conducting a voir dire examination. The motion may contain a list of the questions to topics the counsel wishes to cover, or, as an alternative, may request the court to make the necessary inquiries. Counsel may also wish to file a brief citing the authorities which support the position that a wide latitude of inquiry is permitted during voir dire examination. Should the court, at the time of the examination, limit counsel, cutting off his inquiry before counsel is satisfied, the attorney should take exception so that he will have a proper record for appellate review.

MOTIONS IN LIMINE

Purpose

Before voir dire, counsel should consider whether there are any facts harmful to the plaintiff's case which would not be admissible in evidence under the rules of his jurisdiction. Examples include (1) the plaintiff was operating a vehicle without a valid driver's license, (2) the plaintiff was issued a traffic citation as a result of the collision, (3) the plaintiff had a long record of traffic violations prior to the collision, (4) the defendant was not issued a traffic citation, (5) the plaintiff's medical bills were paid by Blue Cross or some other collateral source, (6) the plaintiff was paid his regular wages while absent from his job as a result of sick leave or vacation benefits, or some form of insurance, (7) the plaintiff's medical care was rendered free of charge, (8) the plaintiff, prior the collision, was convicted of a crime which did not involve moral turpitude, (9) the plaintiff was arrested and charged with the commission of a crime, (10) the plaintiff had a prior claim involving injury to the same are of the body injured in the case on trial, and (11) the spouse prosecuting a death action remarried prior to the date of trial. Having determined that such facts exist, counsel should make a motion to forbid the mentioning of such facts prior to the voir dire examination. (This motion may be denominated a "motion to suppress," "motion to quash," or "motion in limine.") Although counsel may make the motion orally in the presence of the court reporter, it is better practice to file the motion in writing with a brief which cites the cases which support the proposition that the facts or matters specified are not admissible in evidence.

If prejudicial matters are brought before the jury, no amount of objection or instruction can remove the harmful effect, and the plaintiff is powerless unless he wants to forego this day in court and ask for a mistrial. Once the questions are asked, the harm is done. Thus, counsel should state in the motion that if the matter designated were brought to the attention of the jury, the plaintiff would be irreparably prejudiced, even though the court were to sustain an objection and instruct the jury to disregard the evidence. It should be made clear to the court that the purpose of the motion is to prevent a mistrial. Should the motion be granted, defense counsel will be prohibited—by order of the court—from making any reference to the facts during the voir dire examination or opening statement or making any inquiry during his examination of witnesses which might tend to bring out the suppressed matter.

Court's Authority to Grant

The power of the trial court to grant such a motion is inherent in its authority to control the conduct of the proceedings so as to insure a fair trial and in the court's right to admit or exclude evidence; this practice may not be specifically mentioned in the official rules of procedure. The use of the motion is limited only by the rules of evidence and the ingenuity of counsel.

OBTAINING INFORMATION PRIOR TO VOIR DIRE

Sources

Prior to the voir dire examination, many lawyers advise gathering information on the prospective jurors. In some jurisdictions jury lists are published in advance of the date of trial. Where this is the case, counsel has the right to make an investigation of prospective jurors as long as he does not actually approach those summoned for jury duty.

There are many sources for obtaining information concerning prospective jurors prior to the trial. Official jury lists (which are sometimes published by the clerk of court), may contain the name, address, and occupation of each prospective juror. In some metropolitan areas, there are jury investigating services which publish bulletins containing information about prospective jurors. If counsel is able to obtain the names of the prospective jurors prior to the time of trial, he may conduct a private investigation. Such a procedure is very expensive and is undertaken only in cases with large potential. (The investigator who is employed should be carefully cautioned not to make any effort to contact the prospective jurors either directly or indirectly.) Public records may be of great value in providing information concerning prospective jurors. Among the records which may be valuable are voter lists, city directories, court indexes, and police records. Credit bureaus can generally provide a great deal of information concerning prospective jurors. In rural areas, where the population is small and stable, local politicians and officials may know the members of the prospective panel personally. In jurisdictions in which jurors hear more than one case in a term of court, trial lawyers who have previously tried cases to members of the panel are a most valuble source. Frequently, after a verdict has been rendered, the lawyers in the case will meet with all or some of the members of the jury to discuss the verdict with them. Much information about the true philosophy of each juror can be gained in this way. Counsel who is about to try a case before a panel which has heard another case may gain much valuable information by meeting with the plaintiff's lawyer who tried the previous case to the panel.

Possible Information

Some of the facts which counsel may wish to know about each juror are as follows:

Name	Education
Age	Prior litigation, results
Occupation	Previous jury service, criminal
Marital status	or civil, results
Spouse's age	Lodge or union affiliation
Spouse's ocupation	Sickness in family
Number of children	Disability in family
Residence address	Injuries
Home owner or tenant	Credit rating
House valuation	Prior employment in claims
Religious affiliation	investigation
Autos, number and date	Relationship with insurance

Light or heavy drinker
Relationship with neighbors

industry, employment, or
ownership of stock

Much of this information can be obtained at the time of voir dire examination. The amount of pretrial investigation of the prospective jurors will necessarily be conditioned by the prospective value of the case.

CONDUCTING THE VOIR DIRE

Initial Contact

Counsel meets the jury for the first time during the voir dire. The conduct of the examination requires that counsel acquaint the jury with the general nature of the case. The jurors' response to the particular type of case involved will form the basis for the judgments counsel will have to make concerning the exercise of his challenges. He also has the opportunity to introduce himself to the jury and, hopefully, create a favorable impression in their minds toward himself, his client, and the case he is about to present. Plaintiff's counsel, who generally addresses the jury first, has the benefit of the psychological principle of "primacy," that is, people tend to believe what they hear first about any given matter.

It is imperative that counsel have his theory of the case firmly settled in his mind before he plans the voir dire examination, for his goal is to select the best possible jurors for the particular case being tried. It is only when he understands the theory of his case that he can make sound judgments concerning the type of persons who will make "good" jurors and the type to be eliminated. Once counsel has made some determination of the type of juror he wishes to have empaneled, he should list the topics of inquiry indicated for the particular case. He may wish to draft a number of specific questions for use during examination. Some lawyers make the mistake of asking the same set of "pat" questions in every case. However, each case is different; consequently, the content and conduct of each voir dire should be different. Counsel should exercise as much creativity and imagination in the planning and conduct of his voir dire as he does in the presentation of his case in chief.

How to Avoid Giving Offense

There is always the danger that some of the prospective jurors will be offended by the questions asked on the voir dire examination and consider them as unnecessary intrusion into their private lives. Plaintiff's counsel may wish to explain to the entire panel at the beginning of the voir dire that his purpose in asking questions is not to pry into their personal lives or to embarrass them; he should explain also that both he and defense counsel are granted the right to interrogate the jurors and that the procedure is used in every case tried to a jury and is of ancient origin. Counsel should state that in conducting the examination he is acting as the attorney for the plaintiff and as an officer of the court and that his goal is to aid in the selection of the twelve jurors best suited for the particular case being tried. Counsel may wish to explain that only one-half of the veniry will actually serve on the final jury and if it turns out that they have the opportunity to serve on this particular case, that fact does not mean that the lawyers for either the plaintiff or the defendant consider them to be "unfit" in any general sense. Counsel may tell the veniry that every human being, by reason of environment and personal experiences, probably has some preconceived tendencies which favor one side or the other. Counsel may add that it is a mark of courage and fairness for a person to admit that he may have difficulty in being totally impartial in his hearing of a particular case. It should be emphasized that a fair trial can only be had if each juror will be outspoken and frank in stating whether or not he can be completely fair, impartial, and unbiased with regard to the parties and the issues involved in the particular case. Statements of this type will not necessarily insure that the prospective jurors will honestly admit feelings of possible bias or prejudice, but they may be of some aid.

Atmosphere

Many jurors will probably be sitting in the jury box for the first time and will be nervous and uncertain. They will appreciate it if counsel establishes a casual atmosphere in which they are allowed to relax. Plaintiff's counsel should, however, be cautious in his use of humor.

Conflicting Relationships

The judge in all likelihood will ask the entire panel if any of them are related to or know any of the parties or their attorneys. If the court does not make such inquiry, this should be counsel's first question. He may also ask the jurors whether they have any acquaintanceship, either professional or social, with any of the witnesses who he expects will testify for each side.

The Nature of the Case

Though voir dire examination is not the appropriate time for a detailed discussion of the case, it is proper for the jury to be told something about the nature of the case as a preliminary basis for asking them specific questions. Once the jurors have been told what the case involves, they should be asked whether they have been involved in a situation similar to that of the plaintiff or defendant. Each juror should also be asked whether he has been involved in any accidents which produced injury, whether he has been a plaintiff or defendant in any lawsuit, and whether he has had any injuries similar to those claimed by the plaintiff. Counsel should ask whether any members of the juror's immediate family have been injured as the result of accidents, been sued or filed claims, or had injuries similar to those claimed.

Connections with the Insurance Industry

Counsel for plaintiff will generally ask each juror whether he has ever been involved in the investigation or evaluation of claims and whether he has been employed by, held office, or owned stock in an insurance company which writes casualty or liability insurance. (Before counsel for the plaintiff asks any question which relates to the insurance industry, he must carefully check the law of his jurisdiction to determine what is permissible.)

Extended Trial

When plaintiff's counsel expects that the case will take more than a few days to try, he should ask the jurors whether an extended trial would be a major inconvenience. Frequently, counsel will determine that certain jurors are reluctant to serve because of the pressures of business or other commitments; where such reluctance appears, it is better to exclude the juror from service because an impatient juror will generally not be attentive. Both sides may consent to dismissing such a juror for cause. Neither plaintiff nor defendant wants a juror who cannot concentrate on the evidence.

Confronting Problems in Plaintiff's Case

When the plaintiff's case has a major problem, generally it would be wise to discuss it openly during voir dire examination if he is relatively certain that the defendant knows of it and intends to exploit it. When the plaintiff brings out the problem on voir dire, he may steal some of the defendant's thunder and give the jurors reason to believe that he and his client are open and honest. Equally important, he has the opportunity to secure from each of the jurors assurance that the problem in itself will not necessarily affect their judgment and prevent them from being fair and impartial jurors. For example, suppose a key witness for the plaintiff is an ex-felon. The jury could be told the following:

> This accident was witnessed by John Doe. That is a fact over which the plaintiff had no control. It could have happened in the presence of any citizen in this community. It is proper for you to know that earlier in his life Mr. Doe made a mistake for which he was imprisoned and for which he has paid his debt to society. That is also a fact over which plaintiff had no control. Can any of you tell me now that I cannot win this case for my client solely because Mr. Doe who saw this accident has a criminal record?

Other "problems" which plaintiff's counsel may wish to expose on voir dire include (1) plaintiff was under the influence of alcohol at the time he was injured, (2) plaintiff belongs to a minority group, (3) defendant belongs to a profession which is held in high esteem, (4) plaintiff is suing a member of his family, (5) plaintiff is suing the driver of a car in which he was a guest passenger, (6) plaintiff was at one time convicted of a crime, (7) plaintiff has other lawsuits involving the same injury, (8) plaintiff has prior or subsequent injuries to the same part of the body which is the subject of the claim, (9) plaintiff was using drugs at the time he was injured, and (10) plaintiff was riding a motorcycle when he was hit.

Professional Negligence Cases

If the case involves claims of professional negligence (such as medical or legal negligence) an effort must be made to find out if the jurors believe that doctors or lawyers should be held to the standard of care required under the circumstances. Negligence is negligence whether it arises from a layperson running a stop sign and injuring someone else, a doctor leaving a surgical instrument in a patient's abdomen, or a lawyer letting a statute of limitations run.

Products Liability Cases

If the case involves a claim that a defective product caused an injury, counsel needs to ascertain that the jurors have no quarrel with the law on strict liability or breach of express and implied warranty. So much has been written in the news on this subject that inquiry about preconceived notions in this area should be made.

Jury Co-operation

Another question that counsel must have in mind is how the individual jurors will affect each other. Will one person dominate their deliberations or can they work together in a spirit of co-operation to insure that justice is the result?

Explaining Objections

If counsel foresees that he may be forced to make repeated objections to offers of evidence by the defendant, he will wish to explain to the jury during voir dire examination that objections are based on exclusionary rules of evidence established by the courts and that lawyers are required to "play the game" by the rules. He may also wish to explain further that he may have to make objections in an effort to discharge his obligation to his client. He can then ask the jury whether they will hold it against either lawyer if he makes objections during the course of the trial.

Cases Based on Unpopular Legal Standard

When counsel for the plaintiff is basing his case upon a statute or rule with which he believes the public is not in sympathy, it is wise to tell the jurors during voir dire that he believes the court will so charge them. He should state the law or rule upon which he is relying. he will then ask the jurors whether, assuming the court so charges, they will have any problem in following this law. Counsel should obtain the assurance of each juror that he will accept the court's instructions of law whether or not those instructions comply with the juror's ideas as to what the proper legal standards should be.

Burden of Proof

The average juror's exposure to court proceedings ordinarily comes from television and newspapers. By and large, jurors are exposed to criminal trials and to the special standard of burden of proof of the criminal law—beyond a reasonable doubt. Thus, many prospective jurors have the mistaken idea that the plaintiff in a personal injury case must prove his case beyond a reasonable doubt. Counsel for plaintiff must meet this problem head-on at the outset of the trial. It may be handled in the following manner.

> As you know, this is a civil case and not a criminal case. In a civil case, the plaintiff has the burden of proof. Because this is a civil case, I believe that the judge will tell you when he charges you on the law that the plaintiff must prove his case by a preponderance

or greater weight of the evidence. You will not hear the court tell you that the plaintiff must prove his case beyond a reasonable doubt. This is the standard of the criminal law and *not* the standard which will be used in this case. If the judge instructs you that the plaintiff must prove his case by a preponderance of the evidence and need *not* prove his case beyond a reasonable doubt, will any of you have problems in applying this law or will you be reluctant to do so?

Experienced Jurors

When voir dire examination indicates that a prospective juror has served on a jury in another case, the following questions may be indicated:

Is there anything that occurred in the other case in which you have served that would make it difficult for you to be completely fair and impartial in this case?

Do you think that you could decide this case which is being presented today on its own facts regardless of the different situations and testimony you have seen in the other case you have heard?

High Damage Cases

In a case involving serious injuries in which the plaintiff's counsel is seeking a large sum of money, it is wise to inquire during voir dire as to whether any of the jurors have any preconceived notion or belief that would prevent them from returning a large verdict. Many jurors have read newspaper or magazine articles attacking high verdicts. Some believe that a high verdict will be reflected in their own insurance rates. Counsel may handle the matter in the following fashion:

If you are satisfied that my client is entitled to a verdict in this case, would you be willing to award damages that are fully commensurate with the injuries proved even though they meant returning a verdict for a large sum of money, or would you resist returning such a verdict simply because by the process of arithmetic and the law of damages you would arrive at a substantial sum? In other words, would you reduce the amount of the verdict you arrived at just because when it is all added up it seems like a lot of money?

Counsel should recognize that today there is a constant stream of articles and publications which cast a dark shadow upon persons seeking money damages for personal injury. There can be little doubt that propaganda of this sort has influenced many members of the public.

Many jurors are skeptical of people who seek legal redress and pray for compensation for a personal injury. Plaintiff's counsel should ask whether any of the jurors have ever read or heard anything about personal injury claims which would, for any reason, prevent them from reaching a verdict based solely upon the law and the evidence. Counsel may wish to ask the jurors whether they have any preconceived notions that people who employ the courts to seek damages for personal injuries are not entitled to an award.

In short, he should seek to determine whether any of the jurors have *any* preconceived notions unfavorable to the plaintiff and his effort to obtain redress and compensation for his loss.

EXERCISING CHALLENGES

Statutory Disqualification

Legal qualifications for jury service vary from jurisdiction to jurisdiction. Before counsel enters the court room he should check these qualifications carefully. There are two general categories of qualifications. The first is concerned with requirements for citizenship, residency, age, and criminal record. The second concerns itself with relationship by blood or marriage to the attorneys and parties and business relationships which would tend to give the juror an interest in the outcome of the ligitation. If a juror is disqualified by statute, counsel or the court on its own motion will generally strike the juror for cause.

Bias

As noted above, statutory disqualification is not the exclusive criteria for the exercise of a challenge for cause. If voir dire examination indicates that there is any matter which would probably affect the juror's attitude and influence his decision making ability so that he would not be objective and impartial, a challenge for cause is indicated. That is, a juror who, during voir dire examination, admits that he has a bias or a feeling which he believes would keep him from being completely fair and impartial may generally be stricken by a challenge for cause.

Since the number of peremptory challenges is limited, it is *not* suggested that counsel use one if the objectionable juror can be excused by a challenge for cause. Not infrequently, the juror himself, if his sense of what is fair and right is properly addressed, will excuse himself. This does not mean that counsel should ask the juror whether he would be prejudiced against the plaintiff. Such an inquiry will invariably be met by a negative response. But jurors will frequently admit that they have certain feelings and preconceived notions which may influence their judgment. When plaintiff's counsel encounters a juror who admits that he would have some problem in accepting the law of the court or in awarding substantial damages or some preconceived notion which might prevent him from being fair and impartial, counsel may handle the matter as follows:

> Juror X, you are aware from what I have stated before that I, defense counsel, and the court are seeking the twelve best possible jurors for this particular case. You have candidly told me that you have some feeling which you believe might prevent you from being the best particular juror in this case. I am sure that all of us here in court greatly appreciate your candor and honesty. Because of your feelings, would you prefer to step down and be allowed to sit on another jury? Putting it another way, would you feel more comfortable if you were not required to pass judgment on this particular case.

By handling the matter in this fashion, counsel may be allowing the juror to excuse himself, thereby saving one of his peremptory challenges.

Types of Jurors to Avoid

Although it is impossible to state categorically what type of person will make a good plaintiff's juror and what type will make a poor one, some generalizations can be made. Counsel for the plaintiff should have second thoughts about accepting the spouse of a physician, a nurse, or a policeman. Many doctors view complaints of their patients with a jaundiced eye, transmitting such attitudes to their spouses. Nurses and policemen, by virtue of their work, are constantly exposed to human suffering and probably have developed psychological mechanisms to blot out human misery and suffering.

In selecting the jury for the trial of a case in which expert evidence is to be used, counsel is wise to strike a juror who, by reason of his background or occupation, has some particular knowledge of the subject to which the expert witness is going to testify. The witness may announce an opinion in some casual matter which is at variance with the juror's opinion, and it may nullify everything else the witness has said. Further, the expert on the stand may evoke a combative or competitive impulse in this type of juror. Also, if it should appear that there is someone on the jury who is likely to dominate his fellow jurors, either by virtue of his position, expertise, or personality, it may be well to strike him. The fundamental purpose of the jury system is defeated by a "one person jury."

Where the plaintiff is an attractive young woman, older female jurors may be unsympathetic. Jurors who have themselves been sued may tend to view all claimants with cynicism. Jurors who own commerical properties or operate small businesses may regard a personal injury case as a threat to their own insurance premiums; they are particularly dangerous in a case in which a plaintiff is suing a landowner for negligent maintenance of property. Small home owners are generally viewed as unfavorable jurors in actions against municipalities, for it is possible they will fear that their taxes will be increased if a large verdict is returned. Accountants and engineers are generally considered undesirable jurors for the plaintiff. Persons living in areas where racial or religious strife is known to have occurred should be examined carefully upon voir dire in a case in which the plaintiff is a member of a minority group.

A juror who has sustained an injury similar to the one claimed by the plaintiff may be considered as "an authority on the subject" by his fellow jurors. Such a juror is particularly suspect if he has accepted a relatively small award under workmen's compensation or from the government.

Jurors' Attitudes Toward Counsel

Counsel's decision as to which jurors he will strike is based not only on the verbal information gathered during the voir dire but also upon his instinctive impressions of the jurors. As the prospective jurors enter the jury room and fill the jury box, counsel should focus his entire attention upon them. He should observe their walk, speech, and manner. If counsel's immediate reaction to a juror is unfavorable, he should observe closely how the juror reacts to him personally and to his adversary. If at the conclusion of voir dire, counsel still intuitively senses a negative reaction to a particular juror—an indefinable but pervasive sense of antagonism—he may safely assume the juror feels the same way about him. Counsel should strike him.

Some lawyers recommend that early in the voir dire a prospective juror be given an insignificant command, such as, "Now sit back and relax," to test the juror's reactions. If he does appear to relax, counsel may assume that the juror is personally receptive to him; if he appears to sit up straighter in his seat, counsel can assume that there is a certain resistance which may make him less receptive to counsel's position and contentions.

Announcing Challenges

At the conclusion of the voir dire examination, the plaintiff's counsel is required to announce his challenges for cause before the defense attorney has to proceed with his examination. Generally, plaintiff's counsel is not required at that time to exercise his peremptory challenges. In most jurisdictions, the plaintiff may wait until the defense counsel has completed his examination before he has to make his peremptory statutes.

The manner of exercising peremptory challenges varies from jurisdiction to jurisdiction. In some courts, counsel rises and states the name or number of the juror whom he wishes to excuse. In others, peremptory challenges are exercised in writing so that the juror stricken and the remaining jurors are not informed as to which lawyer is striking which jurors. It is hazardous to use all of your peremptory challenges without any inkling as to whether the replacements will be more desirable than those challenged. Thus, before counsel uses his peremptory challenges, he must analyze the relative desirability of the juror who will replace the challenged juror.

CONCLUSION

Finally, once the jury has been selected, counsel should view the panel with a positive frame of mind and appear completely confident and satisfied that the best possible jurors have been selected for the case being tried.

ANNOTATIONS

Treatise

Wagner, Jury Selection.

Am Jur Trials—Articles

Selecting the jury—plaintiff's view, 5 AJT 143-246.
Selecting the jury—defense view, 5 AJT 247-284.

Am Jur Trials—References

Voir dire and jury selection in motorboat accident litigation, 7 AJT 100-108.
Voir dire and jury selection in contact sports injury cases, 7 AJT 247-250.
Voir dire and jury selection in elevator accident cases, 7 AJT 414-418.
Voir dire and jury selection in child-pedestrian accident cases, 9 AJT 473-480.
Voir dire and jury selection in products liability cases, 12 AJT 150-158.
Voir dire and jury selection in boiler explosion cases, 13 AJT 415-418.
Voir dire and jury selection in glass door accident cases, 14 AJT 172-183.
Voir dire and jury selection in skiing accident litigation, 13 AJT 283-284.
Voir dire and jury selection in drug product liability and malpractice cases, 17 AJT 150-153.
Voir dire and jury selection in child death or injury cases, 20 AJT 674-687.

Am Jur Proof of Facts

Bias or prejudice of juror, 2 POF 495-525.
Proof of prejudice of prospective juror, 20 POF 241-244, 250-258.
Systematic exclusion, 9 POF2d 407-494.

Am Jur

Impaneling, examining, and challenging jurors, 47 Am Jur 2d, Jury §§ 195-212.

ALR Annotations

Social or business relationship between proposed juror and nonparty witness as affecting former's qualification as juror, 11 ALR3d 859.

Counsel's use on voir dire examination, in relation to damages in personal injury or wrongful death case, of blackboard, chart, diagram, or placard not introduced in evidence, 86 ALR2d 241.

Propriety of inquiry on voir dire as to juror's attitude toward amount of damages asked, 82 ALR2d 1420.

Voir dire inquiry, in personal injury or death case, as to prospective jurors' acquaintance with literature dealing with amounts of verdicts, 89 ALR2d 1177.

Previous knowledge of facts of civil case by juror as disqualification, 73 ALR2d 1312.

Professional or business relations between proposed juror and attorney as ground for challenge for cause, 72 ALR2d 673.

Relationship of juror to witness in civil case as ground of disqualification, 85 ALR2d 851.

Prejudicial effect of reference on voir dire examination of jurors to settlement efforts, 67 ALR2d 560.

Propriety and effect of asking prospective jurors hypothetical questions, on voir dire, as to how they would decide issues of case, 99 ALR2d 7.

Political prejudice of proposed juror as proper subject of inquiry or ground of challenge in voir dire in civil case, 72 ALR2d 912.

Bias, prejudice, or conduct of individual member or members of jury panel as ground for challenge to array or to entire panel, 76 ALR2d 678.

Economic prejudice of prospective juror (based on occupational grounds, i.e. labor union or corp.) as proper subject of inquiry or ground of challenge on voir dire in civil case, 72 ALR2d 913.

Claustrophobia or other neurosis of juror as subject of inquiry on voir dire, 20 ALR3d 1420.

Membership in racially biased or prejudiced organization as proper subject of voir dire inquiry, 63 ALR3d 1052.

Juror's voir dire denial or nondisclosure of acquaintance or relationship with attorney in case, or with partner or associate of such attorney, as ground for new trial or mistrial, 64 ALR3d 126.

Use of peremptory challenge to exclude from jury persons belonging to a class or race, 97 ALR3d 14.

Religious belief, affiliation, or prejudice of prospective juror as proper subject of inquiry or ground for challenge on voir dire, 95 ALR3d 172.

Chapter 9

OPENING STATEMENT

INTRODUCTION

Flexibility

The fundamental key to the delivery of an effective opening statement is flexibility. Each case requires a slightly different approach, a different technique, and perhaps even a different style of delivery. The trial lawyer must experiment and find the style and technique which is comfortable for him, which fits his personality, and which suits the particular case he is trying.

Content

The opening statement of the plaintiff generally follows the completion of the impaneling of the jury. It is at this stage of the trial that the plaintiff's counsel is permitted to address the jury directly and present his client's claims. That is, he can give a factual outline of what he intends to prove in the way of liability, injury, and damages. (It should be noted at this juncture that in some jurisdictions opening statements are not permitted. Although this situation is rare, the prudent trial lawyer will check the local rules each time he tries a case before he plans an elaborate opening statement.)

Length

When opening statements are permitted, a time limit is rarely imposed on either party. The typical practice is to permit a "reasonable

311

time." This is in sharp contrast with closing arguments where specific limitations are usually imposed. It is therefore appropriate for counsel to fully express his client's position in the opening statement. Counsel should always exercise caution to avoid boredom and repetition.

Primacy and Recency

Although both plaintiff's counsel and defense counsel are permitted to make opening statements, as a general rule the plaintiff is entitled to make his first. The significance of the opportunity to make the first opening cannot be overemphasized. The jurors, having sworn well and truly to try the case, eagerly anticipate the unfolding of the case they have been selected to hear. At this point, they have the highest communal level of interest they will exhibit throughout the trial. The plaintiff's attorney holds a potent weapon, characterized by psycholigists as "primacy." That is, what we first learn about any subject we tend to believe most deeply and resist altering most firmly. Primacy stands in contrast to "recency," the principle that we remember most easily the last thing learned about any subject. Recency only relates to ease of memory and not to intensity of belief, which is the attribute of primacy.

Some lawyers believe that the effect of the psychological principal of "primacy" as it relates to the opening statement is extremely important. Some even believe that many jurors make up their minds after opening statements. This does not mean that the opening statement alone can win the case, but it does emphasize the potential and the powerful influence of the principal of primacy.

Even so, the trial lawyer should not be overly impressed by the advantages of primacy. Exaggeration in the opening statement can destroy what otherwise might be a solid case. The opening should present what the lawyer expects to prove; it can be characterized as his promise to the jury of things to come. It is essential that the plaintiff's counsel not break the promises he makes on opening. If he does, the defense counsel will most likely bring this breach to the jury's attention during his closing arguments—with devastating effect. Thus, counsel should only make representations or claims which he is reasonably certain can be established by the admission of competent evidence.

GENERAL CONSIDERATIONS

Style

The style of the opening statement should not be argumentative, although it should be persuasive. An argumentative opening will inevitably be met by an objection. Even though the jury may not know why the objection was made or why the lawyer was stopped, an objection will interrupt the smooth presentation of the opening statement. It may be difficult to recover from this sudden interrruption and to resume with an effective presentation. Further, following the objection, the jury may fail to pick up the renewed presentation. Its members may still be contemplating what happened.

The opening statement is the time for more subtle forms of persuasion than argument. It is the goal of the opening statement to make the jury believe that the plaintiff has been wronged by another, has suffered, and deserves compensation. The jury should be approached as if the trial lawyer were conversing with a group of friends who are gathered in his home. They are interested in knowing what happened to his client and why he thinks the defendant is at fault. By persuasive, polite exposition, he tries to create interest and belief in his case, gain the jurors respect and friendship, and establish an identity with and empathy for his client.

Etiquette and Demeanor

The opening statement must be marked by the observance of courtroom etiquette. Counsel should address the court first, "May it please the court," and the jury last, "Ladies and gentlemen." These preliminary statements should not be mumbled or presented while the plaintiff's lawyer shuffles through his notes. His manner and attitude will be gauged by the jurors from the moment they enter the courtroom. During the opening, counsel should stand before the jury box and concentrate on its members. He may not address them by name, but he should establish eye contact with each juror at least once. If it can be avoided, he should not turn his back to the judge. Although counsel's demeanor may not save a bad case, it can damage a good one. Neatness, courtesy, and a manner which suggests that the lawyer wishes to impart knowledge to the jury will be his most effective weapons.

Language

Choice of language is critical in any opening statement, as it is at every stage of the trial. On the whole, jurors are lay people. Communication can best be established through the use of everyday nontechnical language which can be readily understood but which does not convey the impression that the lawyer is "talking down" to them. An exposition of the facts should be given in direct and forceful language. Having once stated, at the outset of the exposition, "We expect the evidence to show" or "We believe that the evidence will prove," the lawyer should turn to more forceful language, such as, "We will show," "We will prove," and "We will put on a witness who will tell you."

The opening should be a positive statement of what will be proved. Throughout the opening, plaintiff's counsel should attempt to use words which will have a positive impact upon the jury. He should speak of the "collision," not the "accident," for the word accident tends to connote an *unavoidable* event to the lay public; that is, an event not caused by the defendant's wrongdoing. He should speak of "fault" and "wrong" when discussing the conduct of the defendant and, during his discussion of damages, should speak of "fair compensation" rather than "damages." In an effort to make his client seem more human and to gain understanding for his client's cause, plaintiff's counsel should refer to his client by name and not by the sterile term, "plaintiff."

Preparation and Organization

The key to an effective opening statement in every case is preparation and organization. Though a good opening statement is the byproduct of a well-prepared case, careful thought must be given to the organization and structure of the statement and the development of an approach tailored to fit the particular case. Only the extraordinary person can make a clear, concise, effective, and positive opening statement without the most careful preparation and organization. In preparing his opening, counsel may wish to write the statement out in detail to insure that it is complete and in the form intended, but he should never read the manuscript at the time of presentation. Many lawyers, in delivering the opening as well as the closing argument, work from an outline. Such an outline may be easily prepared once the lawyer has carefully planned and prepared the entire statement. An outline helps the attorney to avoid wandering from his intended plan during presentation, and it can serve as a check list to assist in insuring that he has not overlooked a critical point. It may also be invaluable as a confidence builder. The lawyer with the skill and experience to give the perfect opening statement without the aid of notes is to be envied, not emulated.

Establishing a *Prima Facie* Case

In planning and delivering the opening, counsel must note that in some jurisdictions the opening statement must establish a *prima facie* case. Failure to comply with this requirement will result in removal of the case from the jury and the entry of a judgment for the defendant. Counsel may readily overcome this hurdle by reading his affirmative pleading to the jury, but it is hard to conceive of a less effective method of making an opening statement. If the lawyer has carefully prepared and organized his opening, he should have no trouble in satisfying this legal requirement. If he has any doubt as to whether he has stated a *prima facie* case by the conclusion of his statement, he may approach the bench and request permission to incorporate his affirmative pleadings in his opening statement. If permission is granted, instructions to the court reporter to incorporate the pleadings in the record will provide a sure way of fulfilling the legal requirement of stating a *prima facie* case without boring the jury by reading their contents. In that rare instance where plaintiff's counsel finishes his opening statement and defense counsel makes a motion for directed verdict, the lawyer should request leave of court to reopen his opening statement for the purpose of adding sufficient pleadings or remarks to state a case. Such leave is usually, although not always, granted.

Referring to Legal Principles

It is often virtually impossible to state the nature of plaintiff's claim clearly without reference to certain legal principles. For example, in a case tried in a jurisdiction which has an automobile guest statute, in which it is claimed that the plaintiff was not a guest of the driver of the automobile but a paying passenger, it is impossible to frame the issue without some reference to the "guest statute."

When plaintiff's counsel feels that it is necessary to refer to a rule of law during his opening, he should be careful to preface his remarks on the law by stating to the jury, "Just as the evidence will come from the witness stand and not from the mouths of counsel, matters of law are the concern of the judge. The law of the case will be explained to you, the jurors, at the conclusion of the case by the judge.'' Counsel should make it clear that his discussion of the law is only an attempt to help the jurors better understand the issues in the case. He might further indicate that they are to rely solely on the judge's statement of the law given at the conclusion of the case, even if it differs from what the counsel has stated during his opening. Prefatory remarks of this nature make it more likely that a brief exposition of necessary legal principles will not be interrupted by the court or counsel for the defense. Any stipulated or agreed facts should be mentioned in the opening statement to make the jury understand that proof of such is unnecessary and to make the record so reflect. Any fact judicially noticed or established by Requests for Admissions should be treated in the same fashion.

Meeting Defense Arguments

Counsel may have no reason to state what he expects the defense to claim. Nonetheless, the plaintiff's lawyer must be aware of the potential defenses and attempt to meet them during his exposition of the facts. Thus, it is often not enough merely to state the facts relating to the defendant's conduct. In a case in which it is anticipated that contributory negligence will be put in issue by the defendant, the reasonableness of the plaintiff's conduct must also be impressed upon the jury during the opening. For example, if he anticipates that the defense is going to make an issue of the speed of the plaintiff's car, counsel for the plaintiff should tell the jury the speed at which the plaintiff was traveling prior to the collision and explain how this speed will be proved. Put simply, then, the jurors must understand at the conclusion of the opening statement that the defendant was at fault and that the plaintiff was free of fault. Generally, if counsel for the plaintiff carefully prepares his opening, he can meet the defense arguments without opening himself up to the objection that he is attempting to usurp the defendants privilege to state his own case.

Comparative Negligence

Where the case involves comparative negligence, counsel must determine whether or not to discuss it at all in the opening. Generally, most attorneys would not inject it into the opening statement if it were a minimal factor. On the other hand, if it will be a major issue, plaintiff's attorney should take the lead by discussing the issue immediately.

Counterclaims

Where a counterclaim exists, counsel has two alternatives. First, he may ignore its existence and in effect treat it as a meaningless, even contemptuous, afterthought of defendant. To choose this approach, counsel must take an extremely positive approach to his own case. As a second alternative, many attorneys mention it "in passing"; they acknowledge its existence as a fact in the case but minimize its significance and continue to emphasize their own case. It is usually not a good tactic to highlight such a counterclaim. Thus, a discussion relating to the fact that the burden of proof would be on the defendant for such counterclaim would be considered highlighting and should usually be avoided.

Crossclaims

Where cross claims are filed between or among defendants, it is usually advisable to mention such fact in plaintiff's own opening statement. (This assumes that it is a proper subject for the opening statement and that issues concerning such claims will be submitted to the jury by way of instruction.) Cross claims are often construed by jurors as admissions against such cross claimants and plaintiff.

Confronting Problems in Plaintiff's Case

One of the most important aspects of plaintiff's opening statement is the opportunity it gives him to expose the weaknesses or problems of his case in such a manner as to minimize their deleterious effect. As was mentioned in the previous chapter, counsel may wish to disclose these matters in voir dire. Disclosures not made during voir dire will often be made in opening statement because counsel has more liberty at that time to make them in a manner which renders them less harmful.

The value of stealing the defendant's thunder by exposing your own weaknesses deserves repeating. The problem or weakness can be put in its best light, and the jury will be favorably impressed with plaintiff's counsel because of his honesty. Jurors realize that there are two sides to every story, and they will be suspicious of the perfect case. Thus, by exposing the weaknesses in the case during the opening, the sting of the exposure can be minimized, and the plaintiff's version of the entire case can be made to appear more credible. But, while the value of exposing plaintiff's own weaknesses cannot be over-emphasized, a word of caution must be interjected. There is no need to expose weaknesses or problems which the plaintiff's counsel is reasonably sure the defense does not intend to exploit during the course of the trial. Stated otherwise, counsel should only disclose those harmful facts which he believes the defendant does intend to exploit to his advantage.

Often, a fact which seems to indicate a weakness in plaintiff's case can be turned into a strength by its proper handling during the opening statement. If the plaintiff's claim involves injury to an area of the body previously injured, the plaintiff should admit that his client had a prior injury. He then should go on to state how it will be proved through medical testimony that, although this prior injury was causing the plaintiff no problems prior to the accident, it made the area in question more prone to injury and impeded the healing process the body normally carries out.

In a cervical or lumbar soft tissue injury case, the plaintiff will frequently have arthritic changes of the spine which pre-existed the trauma. Counsel can turn this apparent weakness into a strength by presenting the fact properly in opening statement. He should point out that the pre-existing arthritis was not causing the plaintiff any pain or disability prior to the collision and that it had an effect upon the extent of injury and the nature of his client's recovery. In a fracture case in which the fracture itself has healed perfectly prior to trial and the plaintiff still has complaints, the plaintiff can anticipate that the perfect healing of the bone will be the focal point of the medical defense. This problem should be met during counsel's opening statement by an explanation of the mechanics of bone fracture, a discussion of the damage to the soft tissues around the fracture site, and an explanation of the fact that, although bone heals to a point where it is often "as good as or better than new," the injured soft tissues heal with scar tissue. It must be emphasized that before plaintiff opens in this manner he must be certain that he has the medical testimony to back up his every word.

Visual Aids

The plaintiff's counsel may find it desirable to use visual aids, such as a prepared chart, a photograph, or a blackboard. In some jurisdictions the legality of the use of such aids is not clear. The lawyer should check local case law on the point. If there is no law on the subject, the matter can best be handled by a bench conference with the trial judge before the opening statement. During the bench conference counsel should make it clear to the judge that the purpose of visual aids is perfectly consistent with the purpose of the opening statement, that is, to assist the jurors in their initial perception and understanding of the evidence in the case. If he reminds the trial judge that the purpose of opening statement is to provide the jury with an integrated overview of the evidence, and if the judge is convinced that the visual aids will expedite an understanding of the issues, their use should be (and usually is) permitted.

Many lawyers prefer to use blackboard and chalk or pad and marker pencil rather than a prepared visual aid. An advantage of the pad over the blackboard is that the individual pages may be torn off and saved for later reference. Those who choose the pad or blackboard technique over the prepared aid believe that the jurors tend to identify a speaker at a blackboard or pad with a schoolteacher—in short, with the truth. Even so, when the plaintiff's lawyer takes the chalk or marker pen in hand he must be extremely careful, for distortion or exaggeration, though innocent, may leave the plaintiff open to a successful attack by the defense counsel.

Presence of Witnesses

Two schools of thought exist as to whether plaintiff's counsel should encourage his prospective witnesses to sit in the courtroom during the opening statement, assuming the court has not ordered, or will not order, witnesses excluded during trial. The first contends that witnesses, other than the plaintiff, should be encouraged to remain outside the courtroom so that when they later appear and testify they will convey the impression to the jury that they are speaking spontaneously and not following any script prepared for them by the plaintiff's counsel. The second school maintains that it is helpful to have one's witnesses in the courtroom during the opening so that they can see where they fit into the oveall picture of the plaintiff's case. It is further hoped that a forceful presentation will build up an incentive for them to deliver their testimony more effectively when their turn comes to testify.

Keeping a Record

In those jurisdictions in which a court reporter is not automatically present at the outset of the trial, plaintiff's counsel should make the necessary arrangements to have the opening statements officially recorded. Only by keeping a proper record can prejudicial references made by defense counsel during opening statement be preserved and used on appeal. Further, just as plaintiff's counsel's opening statement constitutes a promise of what is to come, so does the defense counsel's statement. Plaintiff's counsel should listen carefully and take notes during the defendant's opening statement. If the case has been properly prepared, counsel will know at once which of defendant's promises he will have difficulty keeping. Key defense representations that have not been fulfilled by the close of the evidence should be transcribed by the stenographer so that the defendant's failure to deliver can be forcefully driven home during plaintiff's final argument.

BEGINNING THE OPENING STATEMENT

Summary of Case

Most attorneys prefer to open the statement by introducing themselves and their client to the jury. Subsequent to this introduction, many experienced attorneys choose to give a capsulized picture of their case so that at the beginning the jury will have some understanding of the nature of the plaintiff's case. As part of the overall summary most attorneys at this point, in cases involving substantial damages and injuries, will briefly describe the broad nature of the injury (such as paralysis or an amputation,) and leave detailed development of these for later in the opening statement. This acquaints the jury quickly with the magnitude of the case and pricks their curiosity as to how and why such severe injuries occurred. This brief statement of the theme of the plaintiff's case should be designed to get the attention of the jurors, to acclimate their thinking in terms of the defendant's fault and the harm he has caused the innocent plaintiff.

Purpose

Following this brief statement of the plaintiff's claim, counsel should give the jury some explanation of the purpose of his opening statements. He should inform the jury that the opening statement is not an argument to convince, but a brief description of the claims of the parties which is meant to aid the jury in hearing and evaluating the evidence. It should be explained to the jury that, because of the rules of evidence and the availability of witness, it is not always possible for either lawyer to offer his evidence in a perfectly logical or chronological sequence. Because evidence may be admitted in apparently unconnected bits and pieces, it is helpful for the jurors to have a bird's eye view of the claims of both parties at the outset. Just as it is easier to assemble a complicated jigsaw puzzle if one can see the finished picture, so the jurors have a better chance to arrive at the truth if they have a sketch of what is to be proved before the evidence is presented.

Just before the opening statements are given, the judge ordinarily explains to the jury that the opening remarks of counsel are not evidence; it should not, therefore, be necessary for counsel to repeat this observation. In fact, repeated reference to this may be taken by the jury as an expression of weakness on the part of counsel—as if counsel is not certain what he may prove.

Explanation of Roles

During the introductory portion of the opening statement, many lawyers briefly explain the function of the jury, the judge, and both lawyers. In discussing the juror's role counsel should make it clear that jurors are the sole judges of the facts. He should attempt to communicate his belief in their ability to do this job properly. In discussing counsels' roles, he may wish to explain that lawyers serve both as officers of the court and as the legal representative of their clients; that it will be their respective jobs to bring forth the evidence necessary for the jury to make a full and fair determination of the facts. He may wish to explain that the trial judge is the impartial representative of society who can not and will not take sides and who will preside over the trial and state the applicable rules of law at the conclusion of the case. Such an explanation may accomplish two ends. First, the trial lawyer reflects confidence in his own case when he expresses confidence and trust in the ability and integrity of the jury and the judge. He conveys the point that all he and his client want is a fair trial because they believe that a fair trial will necessarily result in a just verdict for his client. Second, he strikes a chord of fairness and sincerity at the outset of the case. It is believed that a jury will listen carefully to a lawyer who they believe is genuinely interested in justice.

Burden of Proof

During the introductory portion of the opening statement, it may be advisable to discuss the order of the trial and thereby explain to the jury why the plaintiff speaks first during the proceedings. Some jurors may think it strange or even unfair that the plaintiff is given the first opportunity to ask questions on voir dire, to give opening statement, and to present evidence. Counsel can dispel any doubt or question along these lines at the outset by telling the jury that the order of trial is established by law and explaining that the plaintiff goes first because he has the burden of proof.

Mentioning the burden of proof gives counsel an opportunity to define the difference between a civil and criminal case and to explain the significance of this distinction. It is important to impress the significance of this distinction on the jury *as soon as possible* so that by the time they retire for deliberations, any false notions that they may have had at the outset about the burden of proof on the plaintiff in a *civil* case will be totally dispelled. Accustomed to watching television and reading newspaper accounts of sensational criminal trials, jurors are conditioned to the phrase "beyond a reasonable doubt." It should be explained in *opening* that this is the standard of the criminal law and that the judge will instruct them that the plaintiff in a civil case need only prove his case by a preponderance of the evidence. If this point is first communicated to the jury at the conclusion of the case—after they have heard the evidence—it may be too late. A discussion of the distinction between a criminal and a civil lawsuit (which does not involve punitive damages) also gives plaintiff's counsel an opportunity to explain the plaintiff is not seeking to punish the defendant but is only seeking that which the law permits—fair compensation.

Defendant's Right to an Opening Statement

Plaintiff's counsel should make it clear that the defendant also has a right to give an opening statement following the conclusion of plaintiff's statement. Such a comment may force defense counsel to open and expose his defense strategy after plaintiff concludes his own opening. If defense counsel chooses to make an opening which exposes nothing, he will, in all likelihood, leave the jury with a negative impression and bolster the strength of plaintiff's opening. If he chooses to make no opening statement, the jury may wonder what it is that he has to hide or conclude that he has nothing to say.

Importance of the Case to Plaintiff

The importance of the case to the plaintiff is another important theme to introduce during the opening statement. Most jurors know little more about litigation than what they read in the newspaper. In the average civil suit, they may start out with the attitude, "Why is the plaintiff wasting my time for such a small amount of money?" This attitude must be met head-on and changed if the plaintiff is to receive full justice. During his opening statement, the plaintiff's counsel should make it clear that the case being heard is neither sensational nor important to the newspapers but that it is *very* important to his client. This is his client's "day in court," his one opportunity to come before his fellow citizens and seek justice for the wrong that has been done him by the defendant. This theme should be emphasized whenever counsel has the opportunity to speak directly to the jury.

HANDLING LIABILITY ISSUES

Fault of the Defendant

Following the introductory section of the opening statement, the plaintiff's lawyer should concentrate on liability if it is disputed. Many experienced trial lawyers believe liability is won or lost on the opening statement. In dealing with the liability issues, it is essential that plaintiff's counsel emphasize "what the defendant did wrong" or "how the defendant was at fault" and "why it is fair for him to be held accountable." As lay people, jurors think in terms of fault, not in terms of hyper-technical violations or "legalese." When an automobile collision occurs, one of the first questions you will hear a bystander ask is, "Whose fault was it?" Thus, even in a case where there is a clear technical liability, the plaintiff should address himself to the fault of the defendant in his opening statement. The plaintiff's claim should not be phrased in terms of the defendant's failure to obey a particular traffic law but rather in terms of the defendant's failure to pay attention to traffic, his driving too fast, his following too closely, etc. Jurors may not be impressed by what seems to be a technical liability based on violation of a statute of which they have never heard; they may be impressed by fault, carelessness, recklessness, and negligence. This is not to say that plaintiff's counsel should ignore a statutory violation during his opening statement, where such a violation is involved. Rather, the statutory violation *per se* generally should not be the central theme of his opening on liability.

It should be relegated to a position secondary to the fault of the defendant.

Using the Court's Language

Many lawyers, especially in the more complicated products liability or malpractice cases, like to use the language of the court's instruction during the opening statement. Obviously, counsel must know what language the court will use. Where, for example, defendant in a malpractice case left a scalpel in the abdomen after surgery, counsel might state that the evidence will show that the defendant carelessly left a scalpel in plaintiff's abdomen and in so doing "failed to use that degree of skill and learning ordinarily used under the same or similar circumstances by members of defendant's profession." By using the language of the courts instruction, he makes the jury familiar with it, and they will quickly recall it when the judge later reads the instruction to them. Similarly, in a products liability case involving a defective tire, counsel might state that the evidence will show that the defendant "manufactured and marketed a defective tire which was unreasonably dangerous when put to its ordinary and customary use" and that the plaintiff suffered his injury as a consequence of the defect in the tire. The purpose of using the court's language is to familiarize the jury with it and adopt it as a recurring refrain throughout the trial.

Theme

The opening statement is an ideal time to attempt to establish an identity between the jury and either the plaintiff or the plaintiffs "cause." A theme or appealing phrase that aptly describes the case may be effective in achieving this. Thus, one might describe the case as "the case of the poisonous pills" or "the case of the exploding gas tank." The theme might be put in the form of a question: "Will the public hold the Power Company accountable for the hazard it created and controls?"

Malpractice Cases

In more complicated cases, such as malpractice or products liability, some special techniques may be useful. In a malpractice case, for instance, the cause of action may be described as one based on professional error or omission because such language tends to soften juror resistence against returning a verdict based on "malpractice."

Products Liability Cases

The opening statement in a products liability case may also be useful to illustrate how to advise a jury as to those elements which are *not* a part of the case. Generally, one accentuates the positive in an opening statement, but there are occasions when the jury must be made aware at the outset that certain matters will not bar plaintiff's recovery. For example, in a products liability case, counsel for plaintiff may tell the jury in the opening statement that this case is based on strict liability. The law of strict liability does not focus on the defendant's *conduct* (whether careful or careless); rather, it focuses on the quality of the defendant's *product* and that even if the defendant carefully made a dangerous and unsafe product he is still accountable for the harm it causes. Likewise, the jury must be made aware that "intent" is not involved so that whether defendant intended the product to be free from defect is immaterial.

Statement of Facts

The opening on liability should be a clear and concise statement of the essential facts which the plaintiff will prove (and must prove). Although it is good to emphasize key facts, some "surprises" might be saved for the actual testimony. It is not advisable for the plaintiff's counsel to state every fact he intends to prove or to name each witness he will call. Predictably, the jury would be "turned off" by an opening statement which simply named each witness and detailed his testimony. When there is a key witness there is nothing wrong with telling the jury who he is, where he was at the time of the occurrence and what the vital part of his testimony is. Similarly, it may be valuable on opening to highlight the key testimony which will be given by an expert witness and to give his qualifications, if impressive.

If there is a clear point or issue in dispute which is essential to the plaintiff's case, counsel may wish to rapidly cover the evidence which supports his position, using the blackboard or large note pad to summarize the superior weight of plaintiff's evidence. The theory behind this technique is that the battle may well carry the war. If the jury is impressed at the outset that the fact focused upon is pivitol and is convinced at the conclusion of the trial that the plaintiff's lawyer has proved his position, the case for plaintiff may be principally won on this alone. The danger of employing such a tactic is evident. Failure to win on the battleground selected by counsel may be devastating to his client's case.

DISCUSSING INJURIES AND DAMAGES

Mechanics, Nature, and Effect of the Injury

After the liability portion of the plaintiff's opening statement is completed, the issue of injuries and damages must be considered. The opening should explain the mechanics of the injury; that is, how the particular incident caused the plaintiff's problems. In a soft tissue injury case, for example, this aspect may be extremely important if there was only a slight impact to plaintiff's automobile. In such a situation, the jurors must be made to understand medically and mechanically how the plaintiff sustained an injury to the ligaments and muscles of his neck or low back. Counsel should also explain the nature of the injury and the effect the particular injury has had on the person of the plaintiff and will likely have in the future. It is essential that the jury understand how the injury affected the plaintiff's every day life and altered his capacity to earn, his ability to enjoy his family, and to participate in favored activities and caused personal suffering. In this phase of the opening, the plaintiff's lawyer must impress jurors with the fact that the plaintiff is a person much like themselves, a person with their troubles, their joys, and their ambitions. If empathy and understanding are to be achieved, the jury must see the plaintiff as a real person, with real problems, all brought about through the fault of the defendant. If the jurors empathize with the plaintiff's plight during the opening statement, the defendant will find it difficult to dispell this perspective during the remainder of the trial.

Explaining Medical Terms

When discussing the nature of plaintiff's injury, plaintiff's counsel should explain the technical medical terms which will be used during the course of testimony. Counsel should make an effort not to sound erudite, but he should give an accurate account of the injury and the resultant condition. He should next point out that he will ask the expert physicians to fully explain the medical terms in words that both he and the jury can understand. If this technique is employed, the jurors will gain some familiarity with the medical terms and their relation to the plaintiff's problems. They will not feel that the plaintiff's lawyer is either trying to practice medicine or impress them with his expertness.

Categories of Damages

In discussing damages, counsel should itemize the various legal categories or types of damages for which the law permits recovery. During the opening statement, he should introduce the jury to the fact that the plaintiff is seeking to recover his reasonable medical expenses, both past and present; his lost earnings to date; compensation for the diminished value of his ability to earn money in the future, and a sum representing compensation for the pain, discomfort, disability, and aggravation, both mental and physical, that the injury has caused in the past and will cause in the future. The jury should be made aware that they have the power to award the figures suggested by counsel or whatever amount they believe is adequate to restore the loss. No jury should be made to feel they must award either the amount suggested by plaintiff's counsel or nothing. It should be emphasized that future damages should never be discussed in the opening statement unless counsel has talked to the medical witnesses and assured himself that their testimony will provide the evidential basis to support such a claim.

Discussing Dollar Amounts

Attorneys disagree as to whether the opening statement is the most advantageous time for the plaintiff to indicate the sum of money he is seeking. In larger cases, many believe it is good to condition the jury early and often to the fact that a substantial sum of money is involved. Other experienced lawyers believe that in both the larger and smaller cases more is to be lost than gained by discussing dollar amounts in the opening statement. Money discussions early in the case may cause the jury to lose rapport with the plaintiff or set the stage for the defense to launch a successful attack against the plaintiff based on greed, avarice, and exaggeration of damages. Those holding this belief feel that the translation of injury and loss into dollars should be saved for final argument. If counsel for the plaintiff does choose to mention a sum of money in his opening statement, his comments should be coupled with an explanation that the jury cannot award any sum unless plaintiff proves his case and that the plaintiff is asking no more and no less than full justice.

CONCLUDING THE OPENING STATEMENT

The conclusion of the opening provides an opportunity for plaintiff to reinforce on the jury two impressions which should have been made during the introductory portion of the statement: namely, the plaintiff's lawyer's confidence in the ability of the jury to try the case fairly and the fairness and sincerity of the plaintiff's lawyer. Plaintiff's counsel should emphasize that he is certain that the jury will listen carefully to all the evidence to make sure that the claims made are fulfilled. He is confident the jury will consider all the evidence and give a fair trial to all concerned. Plaintiff's counsel should also emphasize that he is not soliciting their sympathy, only seeking full justice—nothing more and nothing less. The conclusion of the opening statement should leave the jury with the strong feeling that the plaintiff's lawyer is fair, that he is confident in his own case, and that he is confident that the jury will weigh all the issues completely and make a determination in his client's favor.

ANNOTATIONS

Am Jur Trials—Articles

Opening statements—plaintiff's view, 5 AJT 285-304.

Opening statements—defense view, 5 AJT 305-330.

Am Jur Trials—References

Opening statements in anesthesia malpractice suit, 12 AJT 295-300.

Opening statements for action against attorney for professional negligence, 14 AJT 294-299.

Opening statements in automobile collision case involving divider line, 10 AJT 522, 532-538.

Opening statements in exploding bottle litigation, 10 AJT 417-422.

Opening statements in action under Federal Employers' Liability Act, 11 AJT 407, 595-606.

Opening statements in federal tort claims, 8 AJT 713-735.

Opening statements in trip and fall case, 10 AJT 285-297.

Opening statements in glass door accident case, 14 AJT 183-188.

Opening statements in light aircraft accident case, 13 AJT 722-732.

Opening statements in reference to pain and suffering, 5 AJT 300, 989-991.

Opening statements as to applicability of res ipsa loquitur, 13 AJT 726.

Opening statements in stairway accident case, 11 AJT 288-290.

Opening statements in skiing accident litigation, 15 AJT 285-306.

Opening statements in drug products liability and malpractice cases, 17 AJT 155-163.

Opening statements in child death or injury case, 20 AJT 687-693.

Am Jur

Opening statements of counsel generally, 75 Am Jur 2d, Trial §§ 202-209.

ALR Annotations

Proprietary and prejudicial effect of reference by plaintiff's cousnel, in jury trial of personal injuries or death action, to amount of damages claimed or expected by his client, 14 ALR3d 541.

Reference in opening statement to settlement efforts or negotiations, 67 ALR3d 650.

Prejudicial effect, in counsel's opening statement in civil case, of remarks disparaging opposing counsel, opponents, or opponent's case or witnesses, 68 ALR2d 999.

Chapter 10

THE CASE IN CHIEF

INTRODUCTION

The "case in chief" refers to that portion of the trial in which the plaintiff is permitted to examine his witnesses directly and offer the evidence he chooses to introduce.

Importance

The case in chief is by far the single most important aspect of the plaintiff's presentation. The plaintiff must carry both the legal burden of proof and the practical burden of persuasion. That is, the plaintiff must introduce sufficient evidence to support the requisite elements of his case (including liability and damages), and he must do so in a fashion that persuades the jury of the "justness" of his client's claim. If at the end of the presentation of the plaintiff's case in chief both judge and jury are not favorably impressed, the plaintiff's chances of obtaining an adequate award are minimal. The case in chief should be prepared and presented with all the care of a professionally produced stage drama. The plaintiff's case must have a definable beginning and ending (opening statement and final summation), lead and supporting characters (the plaintiff and his witnesses), and a carefully developed theme (order of proof)—all supporting the central message (the "justness" of plaintiff's prayer for redress). It should be presented in an honest yet interesting and thought-provoking manner. Care should be taken lest too much attention be given to details not essential to the central theme. The jury's attention must be kept at all times.

Analysis and Preparation

Long before the time of actual trial—indeed, during the initial interview—plaintiff's counsel should begin to analyze his fact situation and select the legal basis upon which he will rest his contention that his client is entitled to recovery. Every case will present certain "problems" and certain favorable points which will affect the preparation and presentation of the plaintiff's affirmative case. Counsel should identify these points as early as possible.

As the time of trial approaches, counsel should carefully (and continuously) reconstruct the overall picture of plaintiff's case as it will be presented to the court and jury; he should have clearly in mind his overall theory and the facts which are essential to a fair, complete and concise presentation of the case. He should prepare and consider the instructions to be submitted to the court, for they provide the skeletal framework around which the plaintiff will build his affirmative proof.

SELECTION AND ORDERING OF WITNESSES

In most instances, plaintiff should be prepared to present his entire case by the direct examination of the plaintiff and his own witnesses. There are situations where it is necessary to call an adverse witness in order to prove an essential element of the plaintiff's case. Most states have adopted statutes or rules that permit the plaintiff to call and cross-examine an adverse witness. Counsel must carefully check the terms of the local rule and the court's construction of the rule regarding the direct examination of "hostile" or adverse witnesses. In any event, most lawyers agree that the cross-examination of a hostile witness is less predictable than the direct examination of a friendly witness. Thus, it is best not to rely on cross-examination of your adversary's witness in order to supply the necessary elements of plaintiff's claim, especially when such information can be obtained by direct examination of a co-operative witness. On the other hand, if the testimony of an adverse party or hostile witness is essential to get past a motion for a directed verdict, such an examination is, of course, necessary.

Generally, witnesses may be divided into two groups: expert and non-expert or lay witnesses. Plaintiff's counsel usually has a great deal of discretion in selecting his expert witnesses (with the notable exception of medical witnesses) and relatively little discretion in the non-expert witnesses he will present.

THE EXPERT WITNESS

The increasing complexity of modern litigation requires that counsel carefully consider using an expert, either as a consultant to assist in preparation or as a witness at trial. Whereas an expert may be extremely helpful—indeed in some cases, they are literally indispensible—many experienced attorneys feel the popular tendency is to use an expert more than is actually necessary.

Very early in his case analysis, counsel for the plaintiff must determine whether the services of an expert will be required.[1] The potential topics on which an expert witness might be called to testify are obviously too numerous to discuss in detail. The following are a few general suggestions:

1. Counsel must list the basis for each and every opinion of his expert. He must be certain that he can prove the factual basis of his expert's opinions.

2. Should the direct examination of the expert involve the introduction of exhibits, these must be labeled and organized in advance so that they may be utilized and offered into evidence without interrupting the course of the examination.

3. The direct examination of experts typically invites more objections than the examination of lay witnesses. These evidentiary questions must be anticipated and briefed in advance of the trial.

4. Counsel should spend a great deal of time preparing his expert for cross-examination. It is occasionally but unfortunately true that the low point of the plaintiff's case is the cross-examination of an expert witness. This can only be avoided by anticipation and preparation.

NON-EXPERT OR LAY WITNESSES

This group of witnesses may be divided into two categories: eye witnesses and lay medical witnesses.

---

[1] H. PHILO, LAWYERS DESK REFERENCE (7th ed. 1980).

Eye Witnesses

The plaintiff in a tort case (unlike the plaintiff in a contract action) does not typically have the opportunity to select people of his choice to witness the incident. As an unwilling victim of a traumatic event, he must simply make the best possible use of the people who by chance were present and witnessed the incident. While the eye witness to the collision may be a convicted felon, he may also be the only witness available. Similarly, although the plaintiff himself may be inarticulate and make a poor witness, his testimony will obviously be necessary.

Lay Medical Witnesses

One exception to the observation made above is the "lay medical witness," that is, a person called to testify concerning the effects of an injury on the plaintiff's life. With a minimum of investigative effort, plaintiff's counsel should be able to locate an appropriate number of lay medical witenesses to provide such "before and after" testimony. Since plaintiff's counsel must avoid the appearance of over-trying his case, he will undoubtedly *not* want to call more than a few such witnesses. Carefully, he should select the one or two lay medical witnesses who can most vividly and effectively portray the effects of the injury upon the person and life of the plaintiff. Such witnesses should make a good appearance, be well-spoken, relate favorably to people, and be unimpeachable on collateral subjects. If plaintiff's counsel carefully selects his lay medical witnesses, there will generally be little cross-examination. Barring the unforeseeable, defense counsel wants an effective lay medical witness off the stand and out of the courtroom as fast as possible. A lengthy cross-examination probably means that counsel has selected the wrong lay witness.

Lay witnesses may be selected from such categories as fellow employees, close friends or neighbors, fellow members of civic groups, or the plaintiff's church (if the plaintiff was truly active) or family. A lay witness who is a member of plaintiff's family must be chosen with care as he is obviously "interested" in the plaintiff's claim.

A person who is engaged in the same type of work in which the plaintiff was employed before his injury is often a very good lay witness on the question of the plaintiff's ability to perform the duties of such work. If the witness is engaged in a supervisory capacity (such as a foreman) he may be qualified to give testimony in connection with the availability of work for a person in the plaintiff's condition.

ORDER OF PROOF

Contents and Structure

After plaintiff's counsel has selected the legal basis of liability and determined which witnesses he will call, he must then consider the order in which he will present his proof and plan the "production" of his case in chief. This order of proof should include not only his direct proof but also anticipated rebuttal testimony. It should be sufficiently detailed to ensure that the plaintiff will make a *prima facie* case. The following items should be included:

1. Selected portions of the defendant(s)' Answers to Interrogatories and Responses to Requests for Admissions;

2. A list of witnesses (including those who will testify by deposition);

3. A list of exhibits and demonstrative aids; and

4. A list of all "Special Damages," including lost wages, medical expenses and property damage.

After the order of proof has been prepared in writing it should be discussed with other attorneys who are participating in the case from the standpoint of strategy and any necessary adjustments should be made. No two lawsuits are alike; each case has its own peculiarities calling for a particular ordering of witnesses. Frequently, for example, expert witnesses will have prior commitments which necessitate calling them "out of order." Even so, counsel should try to present his affirmative case in a logical and coherent sequence. His case should be organized so that the proofs will be presented in a concise, fast moving, and interesting fashion.

Ordering Witnesses

While it is impossible to formulate any specific rules on ordering witnesses, several general suggestions may be helpful. Plaintiff's counsel should try to begin and end with strong witnesses; common sense and the psychological laws of primacy and recency so advise.

Leading Off with the Plaintiff. If the plaintiff will make a good impression upon the jury and will stand up well under cross-examination, many plaintiff's counsels like to lead off with their client's testimony.

If the plaintiff is timid or equivocal in his description of the occurrence of the incident or his injuries, it may be better to call him *after* he has heard the testimony of his eye witnesses and/or his physician. Permit him to sit for a day or two and watch the trial to gain some familiarity with the procedures of the courtroom, so that he will be better prepared when he is called to testify. Further, holding the plaintiff's testimony in abeyance until late in the trial focuses the jury's attention more vividly upon his testimony. After all, plaintiff is at the center of the controversy.

Calling Defendant as an Adverse Witness. Some urge calling the defendant immediately for cross-examination or, if the rules of procedure in the particular court permit him to do so, reading pertinent portions of the defendant's deposition testimony. This beginning is particularly effective if the defendant makes an unfavorable impression either because of his appearance or the content of his testimony or if he has made significant admissions in his deposition. To call the defendant to the stand at the inception of the trial and obtain significant admissions on the issue of liability is certainly an auspicious beginning for plaintiff's case. Moreover, some defense lawyers handle a large volume of cases and thus do not have the time to adequately prepare the defendant before the start of the trial. The defendant's counsel may count on the noon or evening recess to fully prepare the defendant for cross-examination. Plaintiff's counsel has a real advantage if he can subject the defendant to a searching cross-examination before he has been prepared by his lawyer.

However, there are obvious disadvantages to calling the defendant as an adverse witness early in the case. If the defendant is a clean-cut, likeable, articulate witness, he may make a very favorable impression on the jury. The effect of this will not be easy to overcome. Furthermore, the defense attorney may seize the opportunity of having his client on the witness stand to present his side of the case in a very convincing fashion at the very beginning of the trial. This is an opportunity that the defendant does not ordinarily have and only has if the plaintiff gives it to him by calling the defendant's client out of turn as a hostile witness.

Liability and Damages as Structure

Plaintiff's counsel should consider the classical division between "liability" and "damages" as providing the structure for the presentation of his case. First, prove those elements necessary to establish the responsibility of the defendant; and, second, demonstrate the "debt" the defendant owes. For example, in a relatively simple automobile case, in which no experts other than doctors are to be employed, plaintiff's counsel *could* decide to order the witnesses as follows:

1. The investigating officer (to set the scene);

2. The defendant (only if significant admissions can be obtained);

3. Eye witnesses;

4. Any other witnesses or evidence bearing upon the liability issue;

5. The medical records;

6. Doctors;

7. Lay medical witnesss; and

8. The plaintiff.

Number of Witnesses and Length of Testimony

Three or four witnesses should not be called on a particular point when one can cover the subject just as well. The more witnesses plaintiff's counsel calls, the greater the risk that one of them will become confused, make mistakes, offer testimony that conflicts with testimony of another plaintiff's witness, or offer testimony which is detrimental to the client's case. Similarly, the longer any one witness is on the stand, the greater the probability that he may become confused or tired or may utter the unexpected. It is better for plaintiff's counsel to prove the necessary elements of his case as quickly as possible, amplify one or two points, and then rest.

Preparing Witnesses

Plaintiff's counsel should take the time with each witness to explain the mechanics of being a witness and something about what will happen in court to put the witness at ease. Many reluctant and uncertain witnesses will have their confidence bolstered by a simple explanation of relevant trial procedures, coupled with a realization that several other persons no more familiar with the law than they will be witnesses in the same trial. While such explanation is no more than common courtesy, it will also help ensure a well prepared, flowing presentation—an event possible only if witnesses are reasonably at ease while testifying.

The plaintiff, as well as other witnesses, should be prepared on the factual aspects of his testimony with great care. Well in advance of trial, counsel simply must set aside the time necessary for the preparation of his client and his witnesses. Some lawyers find it helpful to make an outline briefly listing the major topics to be covered in the examination of the witness. This outline should accurately reflect the conversation between the witness and the attorney and should provide the structure for the attorney's questioning of the witness at trial. Under no circumstances should the witness be given a copy of any type of outline (or any summary of his testimony). The use of the outline merely allows the plaintiff's attorney to present matters in a logical sequence and thereby make it less likely for the witness to become confused.

The following areas should be covered with every witness, whether expert or non-expert.

Truth, Accuracy, and Brevity. Initially, plaintiff's counsel should emphasize to every witness that, above all, he is expected to tell the truth, to testify as accurately as possible and to the best of his recollection. When a witness makes such an effort, the chances of opposing counsel "crossing him up" are slight. Each witness should also be cautioned to be certain he understands every question before attempting to answer it. Explain that there is no stigma attached to asking counsel to repeat a question. The witness should understand, too, that he does *not* have to answer quickly, that he should give each question whatever thought he feels necessary for an accurate and complete response. He should be told that if he does not know the answer to a particular question, he should feel at liberty to admit it. Most importantly, the witness should be instructed to answer only the single question that was asked and then stop. Witnesses should be told that judges and jurors do not apppreciate long, rambling dissertations which inevitably result in long, boring trials.

Objectives. Advise each witness to leave all objections to counsel; a witness who himself objects to questions and tries to avoid answering them will create an impression that he is biased and unwilling to make a full disclosure.

Demeanor, Dress, and Etiquette. All witnesses should realize that they will be under the watchful eye of the jurors at all times, both while on the stand and while sitting in the courtroom. The demeanor of witnesses in and around the courtroom is crucial, and witnesses should be cautioned against discussing the case with anyone while they are in the courthouse. The importance of appropriate dress should also be discussed. Ladies should be cautioned about excessive use of jewelry, makeup, or inappropriate dress. Police officers should be encouraged to appear in uniform. Each witness should be instructed to sit up in the witness chair and address the jury, court and counsel in a clear and distinct voice. Witnesses also should be requested to be polite. Jurors are human beings who respond to and are favorably impressed by a witness who addresses both lawyers courteously, for example, "Yes, ma'am," and "No, sir," and shows similar respect for the court by addressing the judge as, "Your Honor."

All witnesses should be cautioned not to lose their tempers, exhibit anger or attempt to argue or fence with opposing counsel. While a witness may gain some personal satisfaction by matching wits with opposing counsel or finding humor at his expense, he will almost certainly alienate the jury. Similarly, since lawsuits are serious matters and should be regarded as such, witnesses should not joke.

Qualifying Language. Whenever possible, a witness should answer positively. Phrases such as "I believe," "I think," or "in my opinion," should not be used to preface every answer. Jurors realize that witnesses can testify only to the best of their recollections and abilities, and the members of the jury need not be reminded of this fact by a *caveat* to every answer. On the other hand, point out to witnesses that there is no requirement that they answer each question with absolute certainty.

PREPARATION FOR A CROSS-EXAMINATION

Leading Questions

Both the plaintiff and his witnesses should be told to expect the defendant's lawyer to use "leading questions" in their cross-examination. They should be advised that a "leading question" is one in which the question itself suggests (or compels) a certain answser. Inform them that although the use of leading questions is perfectly permissible in cross-examination, no witness has to agree with the suggestion such a question implies or affirms the truth of any fact with which he, the witness, differs. It is usually a good idea to pose examples of leading questions that can be readily anticipated to illustrate that the witness may respectfully differ with the content of a question that does not accurately reflect his knowledge.

Counsel should tell witnesses about some of the "stock" cross-examination questions, such as: "Have you talked to Mr. X, the plaintiff's counsel, about the case?" If the witness is prepared for such questions, they should not present a problem.

Avoiding References to Insurance

All witnesses should also be cautioned about making reference to the defendant's "insurance" or the "adjuster"; the mention of "insurance" may cause a mistrial.

Discussion of Plaintiff's Injuries

But, while each witness should know all the above, there are certain additional instructions to be given the plaintiff in a personal injury lawsuit. At some point during the plaintiff's testimony, he will undoubtedly be asked to discuss the injuries he sustained and the effect of these injuries upon his life. Psychologically this is a crucial point in the plaintiff's attempt to establish a firm rapport with the jury. The plaintiff should be admonished not to over-play his injuries or expound on his plight at great length. There are two reasons why testimony regarding the plaintiff's injuries must be handled with delicacy. First, some members of the jury may sense that they are intruding into a personal and intimate area of the plaintiff's private life. Second, the very concept of suffering is unpleasant and people do not normally like to or want to vicariously experience unpleasant ideas. Plaintiff's counsel should obtain from his client a fair, clear, and complete account of his injuries and their effects. When testimony concerning the injuries can be elicited from witnesses other than the plaintiff, the resulting effect upon the jurors is more favorable.

PRESENTATION OF MEDICAL TESTIMONY

Proper preparation and presentation of the testimony of the plaintiff's treating and examining physicians is of great importance. Medicine is generally beyond the expertise of most jurors. Therefore, plaintiff's counsel must take particular care to make understandable the medical aspects of the case.

Pretrial or Deposition Conference

Some physicians are reluctant to testify as a witness in court. This may be due to an anxiety resulting solely from unfamiliarity with the trial procedure, or it may simply be due to a continuous commitment to a demanding medical practice. For these or any of a number of reaons, it may be necessary to present the doctor's testimony by deposition. Before either deposition or trial, plaintiff's counsel should telephone the doctor's office and arrange for an appointment to meet with the doctor personally. Counsel should make every effort to schedule this interview at a time during which the doctor will not be pressed for attention to other matters. The best practice may be simply to make an office appointment like any other patient. This conference must not be conducted in a hurried, harried way, for the medical witness must be prepared to face both direct and cross-examination. Plaintiff's counsel should call the doctor far enough in advance of the trial, so that the doctor may arrange his schedule to include a pretrial conference *and* time to come to court. It is unfair to ask the doctor to donate his time; at the outset, plaintiff's counsel should make it clear to the doctor that he expects to compensate him fairly for time lost from his practice.

The pretrial or predeposition conference with the doctor should cover each of the areas in which he will be examined. Topically divided, these areas usually include the following:

1. Qualifications;
2. History;
3. Examination;
4. Treatment;
5. Diagnosis;
6. Prognosis;
7. Medical expenses; and
8. Medical literature.

Either in advance or at the betinning of the interview, counsel should request and read the doctor's office records. The doctor should be given a copy of the client's authorization to counsel along with this request. Counsel may wish to advise the doctor that it is permissible if not advisable to bring his file to court when he testifies and to point out that no one expects him to remember all the details it contains—the doctor should feel free to refer to his records to refresh his recollection.

Qualifications

When qualifying the doctor, plaintiff's counsel should bring out the doctor's educational and professional qualifications, including internships and residencies, his licensed right to practice medicine, the length of time he has been so licensed, whether he is a specialist and board certified, including the length of time he has held that honor, as well as the length of time he has practiced his specialty. Plaintiff's counsel should also question the doctor on any professional honors he has received, publications he has authored, various medical associations of which he is a member, teaching positions he may hold or has held, and the names of hospitals with which he is associated.

The sloppy qualifying of an expert medical witness is a very serious mistake. Never call the doctor to the stand and casually ask, "Tell us a little bit about your educational background and professional attainments." Such an approach reveals a lawyer with embarrassingly little tact or sensitivity to a courtroom situation, for it places the doctor in an awkward position. If the doctor is highly qualified and explains in some length his justly earned qualifications, he will appear conceited. If he underplays his qualifications, he will not impress the court or jury with his just stature. Plaintiff's counsel should develop the doctor's qualifications on a question and answer basis. It is much better to have the jury receive the impression that the doctor is a relatively modest man, only fully setting forth all of his qualifications at the insistence of counsel.

History

Physicians typically acquire a case history of the patient. Such a history usually covers three topics:

1. A brief and general description of the incident that caused or precipitated the patient's symptomology.

2. A summary of the patient's present symptoms.

3. A short review of prior and relevant medical history.

Counsel must take care to ascertain that the doctor's history is factually accurate. The doctor's concern with the description of the incident is merely to acquire some insight into the direction, type, and force of the blow. His concern relates solely to the effect such knowledge may have in assisting him in his diagnosis and choice of treament. The doctor is neither trained to conduct nor concerned with conducting an interrogation for the purpose of determing legal liability. If there is an apparent conflict between the history and the plaintiff's factual account of the incident, counsel should undertake to learn why and to resolve the conflict if possible. The case history is not always taken by the physician; the contents of the history may not have been provided by the plaintiff but by some well intentioned but uninformed bystander, family member, or police officer.

Counsel should always learn who referred the patient to the doctor. Point out to the doctor, if appropriate, that there is nothing to fear if the attorney himself referred the patient to him for expert treatment.

Examination

Plaintiff's counsel should next ask the doctor to discuss the first examination he conducted. (During the pretrial conference with the doctor, plaintiff's counsel should point out that the doctor should describe the type and manner of the examination he conducted. Counsel should ask the doctor to list the subjective symptoms initially reported by the plaintiff and to explain to the jury what subjective symptoms are. Counsel should further point out that he would like to have the doctor explain to the jury that physicians not only consider it medically proper but that they routinely consider subjective symptoms in making a diagnosis, and that it is, in fact, essential to do so. Counsel should then ask the doctor to relate the objective symptoms he discovered on physical examination and to explain the significance of these findings. It is usually wise to tell the doctor simply and candidly why some defense lawyers seek to make an important distinction between "objective" and "subjective" symptoms; namely, to suggest that the plaintiff is exaggerating his injury or is just plain lying. The doctor may want to confirm that his patient is a reliable informant and that his medical diagnosis is in all respects consistent with his patient's symptoms—both objective and subjective. The distinction between "objective" and "subjective" symptoms is significant only to veterinarians and defense lawyers.

If the doctor performed the standard neurological or orthopedic tests [see Chapter 4], counsel should ask the physician to explain these tests to the court and jury. If the tests were positive, their significance should be explained. Indicate to the doctor that your questions will be liberally sprinkled with "whys" and "hows." Point out to the doctor that the jurors are laymen, and tell him that medical terms will have to be defined and explained in simple language. The use of charts may be very helpful in illustrating these tests; if so, their use should be discussed with the physician so that he can affirm their accuracy and assistance in conveying his testimony.

Diagnosis

After the first examination has been covered, counsel will ask the doctor to give his initial diagnosis and to state whether it was definitive or tentative. If the doctor's initial diagnosis was tentative, counsel will want him to explain when, if ever, he reached a definitive diagnosis and then what that diagnosis was.

If appropriate, charts, drawings, and X-rays can be utilized during the direct examination of the doctor. Visual aids may serve to help the doctor explain the injuries and their effects upon the plaintiff to the jury. Before such aids are employed, the doctor should be asked whether they will be of assistance. The doctor should be given an opportunity to review any aid that is to be used so that he can become familiar with it.

Treatment

Having covered the doctor's examination and diagnosis, counsel's next area of inquiry should be treatment. If the plaintiff was hospitalized, plaintiff's counsel should see to it that the hospital records are offered in evidence and that the physician is prepared to bring out the details of the hospitalization; the doctor should narrate these details step-by-step. The course of treatment from the first visit to the time of trial should also be covered thoroughly.

If the case has taken several years to come to trial and the doctor has not seen the patient for some time, it may be advisable to request the plaintiff to make a visit to the physician just prior to the time of trial. If plaintiff does, counsel should, of course, bring out the fact that the doctor recently examined the plaintiff for the specific purpose of learning his present condition. The doctor should be asked to relate his most recent findings regarding the condition of the plaintiff and his prognosis based upon his findings, the patient's history, and the present symptoms.

Plaintiff's counsel should carefully prepare the testimony which reflects the limitations on the everyday life of the patient caused by the injuries. For example, the doctor might be asked to describe how or why the injury he diagnosed prevented the plaintiff's return to work. The doctor should explain precisely the disability the injury produced, what he means by "disability,"and how long the disability lasted or will likely last.

Causation

Keeping in mind the evidentiary requirements of his jurisdiction, plaintiff's counsel should carefully prepare the questions with respect to causation. The doctor is not just a factual witness who describes his findings; he is an expert witness who renders opinions based upon his expertise. The doctor can—and must—render an opinion which establishes the necessary causal relationship between the trauma and the injury. Some states require that the doctor be able to formulate this causal relationship to a degree of "reasonable medical certainty," while others require no more than a "reasonable medical probability." (If plaintiff's counsel is in a jurisdiction which requires "reasonable medical certainty," the doctor should be made aware of this requirement. Plaintiff's counsel should carefully explain to the doctor the meaning of the legal standard and the difference between medical and legal causation.)

Prognosis

After the topic of causation has been covered, plaintiff's counsel then is prepared to ask the doctor to render his prognosis, that is, what the future is likely to hold for this particular person with this particular injury. The prognosis will typically involve such topics as the likelihood of complications, the need for additional treatment or surgery, and the percentage and permanency of any aspect of the plaintiff's injury. Again, plaintiff's counsel must be aware of the evidentiary requirements of his jurisdiction. If appropriate, he should ask the doctor to relate the permanent injurious effects to either or both the occupation and the everyday activities and avocations of the plaintiff.

Medical Expenses

Finally, plaintiff's counsel will wish to cover the number of visits to the doctor, the amount of the bill for the services rendered, the reasonableness of the charges for these services, and the fact that the services were necessarily incurred as a result of the injury. Further, plaintiff's counsel should solicit the doctor's opinion on the probable expenses of future medical treatment.

Cross-Examination

The plaintiff's counsel should prepare his examining or treating physicians not only for direct examination but also for cross-examination. Counsel should discuss with the doctor the lines of attack the defense counsel will likely employ; he should point out that defense counsel will undoubtedly phrase his questions in such a way that the answer will call for a "yes" or "no." He should instruct the doctor to answer the question in this way, if possible. He should also inform the doctor that, if he feels answering in this fashion would convey an incorrect impression, he should state that he does not feel he can fairly answer the question without giving an explanation. Counsel should explain to the doctor that there will be redirect examination in which the attorney for the plaintiff can then ask him questions to clarify his previously limited answer.

Plaintiff's counsel should also point out to the doctor that in most jurisdictions he may not be cross-examined through the use of medical books and treatises unless he first agrees that a particular work is "authoritative." If he does not know the work, or if he does not recognize the author as authoritative, he should state this.

Defense counsel will frequently attempt to play down the injuries suffered by the plaintiff by flattering the doctor and asking him if it is not a fact that he obtained a "marvelous" result with his treatment. The doctor, while he may agree that he got good results, should point out the substantial difference between a good *functional* result and a good *anatomical* results.

Medical Literature

Counsel for the plaintiff may wish to support or illustrate some aspect of his client's injury by reference to medical literature. He may wish to authenticate a medical treatise to use in the cross-examination of a hostile doctor he anticipates the defense will call, or counsel may merely wish to strengthen his own doctor for cross-examination. Whenever counsel anticipates that a question of medical literature may arise, he should conduct a survey, prepare a bibliography of the relevant treatises and periodicals, and furnish actual copies to the doctor with a request that he read and acquaint himself with the contents of this material.

DEMONSTRATIVE EVIDENCE

Many trials end with no evidence having been offered other than what witnesses say on the stand. Oral testimony is, in some ways, the least convincing type of evidence that can be offered. It is subject to all the frailties and human errors of observation, memory, and expression. The lawyer who has introduced effective exhibits has a distinct advantage in convincing the jury of his case; thus, the adage, "One picture is worth a thousand words." It is, therefore, a good practice to make judicious but creative use of physical or demonstrative evidence. Careful attention—and some imagination—in searching for such evidence will disclose that more is available than is employed. Before counsel seeks to introduce any exhibit, he should examine it with care to make certain that there are no facets of the exhibit which are likely to damage his case.

It is not the purpose here to discuss in detail the use of demonstrative evidence; there are, however, several types of demonstrative evidence that should be considered. Carefully prepared diagrams which the jury can see may convey far more than even an articulate witness could express in words. A well constructed model may communicate information that would otherwise be impossible to convey to the jury. Enlargements of charts, pages from books, photographs, etc., may be highly effective. Aerial photographs sometimes provide indispensible information in that they make it possible to present an overview of the entire scene. Transparent overlays are very effective to make vital comparisons and to portray a sequence of events. Movies and videotapes may be used to illustrate movement and action that cannot be conveyed by a single photograph. If counsel has had a test or demonstration performed, he may wish to introduce such evidence by a movie or videotape along with oral testimony establishing the accuracy of the film and the similarity of the conditions.

THE TRIAL NOTEBOOK

The case in chief can be organized in many ways. Each attorney must adopt the practice that suits his individual needs. There is, however, one important consideration that overrides all others. The plaintiff's case in chief should be completely prepared in its entirety well prior to trial. It must be logically arranged and easily accessible. The trial notebook is a very useful tool because it is easy to handle, it facilitates change or adaptation, and it is compact. A typical trial notebook may be divided into the following sections:

1. Matters Preleminary to Trial.
2. Topics or Questions for Voir Dire.
3. Opening Statement.
4. Order of Proof.
5. Interrogatories, Admissions, and Portions of Depositions to Introduce.
6. Witness Outlines (By Topics).
7. Exhibits to Introduce.
8. Deposition Summaries, and/or Witness Statements.
9. Questions or Topics for Defendant's Witnesses.
10. Law Points.
11. Points for Argument.

THE STYLE OF EXAMINATION

During direct examination, counsel should only ask one question at a time. Compound questions are difficult to understand and follow, and answers to such questions are likely to be incomplete or ambiguous. It is best to make each question as brief as possible so that both the witness and the jurors are able to remember the question and understand its significance. The question should be framed in simple language for it is absolutely essential that all of the jurors understand both the question and the answer. This consideration requires language used in everyday conversation by average people in the community, although this is not to say that slang or bad grammar should be employed. Simply stated, the questions should be clear. It is not enough that the lawyers and the witness understand—the *jury* is the arbiter of the facts presented. Since the jurors are less familiar with the facts and circumstances than either the attorney or the witness, hurriedly asked questions are likely to pass over their heads. When it is anticipated that hypothetical questions will be used, counsel should prepare them carefully in advance; there is nothing more disconcerting than hearing a lawyer stumble through the phrasing of a long hypothetical question.

OUTLINE:
DIRECT EXAMINATION OF PLAINTIFF'S DOCTOR

NOTE: Prior to taking the stand, the physician should be asked to acquire and to assemble (1) any notes or records he may need to refer to in the course of his testimony and (2) any exhibits that will be offered in evidence such as X-rays, diagrams, hospital charts, bills, medical literature, etc.

I. QUALIFICATIONS.
   Q. Name and occupation?
   Q. Type of specialty? (Defined)
   Q. Educational background as it relates to his practice?
   Q. License to practice medicine in the state?
   Q. Experience—type of practice and how long?
   Q. Staff of hospital?
   Q. Medical societies, etc.?
   Q. Board certified? (Describe procedure and significance.)
   Q. Publication of articles?
   Q. Any professional honors?
   Q. Teach in any university?

II. RELATIONSHIP OF DOCTOR TO THE PLAINTIFF.
   Q. Family doctor? Company doctor?
   Q. Treating or examining physician?
   Q. Referring doctor?
   Q. Examine solely for purpose of providing medical evaluation and testimony?

III. HISTORY OF EVENTS/CIRCUMSTANCES IMMEDIATELY PRECEDING PRESENT SYMPTOMS.
   NOTE: It may be necessary to establish the medical significance of the "history."
   Q. Doctor, does the word "history" merely refer to a brief summary of the major events that led up to the patient's

present symptoms or complaints, that is, present at the time of the initial examination?

Q. When a patient comes in or is presented for examination by a doctor or a hospital that has the injuries which in a moment you are going to tell us (plaintiff) sustained, is it standard, routine practice for the doctor or the hospital to take a history?

Q. Does, in general, the "history" assist the physician in making his diagnosis and in determining to treatment of choice?

Q. Is a "history" of the immediately preceding events or circumstances taken as a matter of standard medical procedure?"

Q. Was such a "history" taken re: (plaintiff)?

Q. What did the "history" reflect?

NOTE: If you don't like the history you may want to show that the doctor did not take it and cannot actually swear that he knows who took it *OR* that he knows who provided the information (whether the plaintiff or police or somebody else) or how that person acquired the information.

IV. FIRST EXAMINATION.

Q. When?

Q. Where?

Q. Initial symptoms? (Describe and locate.)

Q. Method of examination?

Q. Findings or results of examination?

NOTE: Without a number of detailed questions, permit the doctor at this stage to tell the jury what he did and what he found. Encourage the doctor to illustrate the area of the anatomy involved. Use charts or models if appropriate. Request the doctor to use lay terms.

Lay proper foundation for evidentiary exhibits such as X-rays, clinical records, test reports, etc.

Q. Special diagnostic tests, such as X-rays, EEGs, etc.?

— Describe purpose of the exam.

— Method of test/examination.

— Request doctor to interpret from exhibit.

NOTE: Consider using positive X-rays as exhibits—circle or mark area involved.

V. DIAGNOSIS.

Q. Based on the examination you made and the history obtained, did you make a diagnosis of the plaintiff's condition?

Q. Please describe it to us? (Use lay language.)

Q. Doctor, what is meant by the word "trauma"?

Q. Is the event you have described in the history you obtained considered by the medical profession as "traumatic"?

Q. Doctor, in your best medical judgment, is the traumatic incident described in the history you obtained a competent producing cause of injuries of the type you have decribed in your diagnosis?

Q. Is the trauma reported in the history, in your judgment, a precipitating cause of the injuries you described in your diagnosis?

NOTE: Again, ask the doctor to translate his medical diagnosis into lay terms.

Visually relate each condition to the appropriate area of the body.

Q. Are the symptoms that (plaintiff) reported to you consistent with the diagnosis you have given us?

Q. Are each of the injuries you have defined as being your diagnosis supported by or confirmed by the results of your examination/testing?

Q. Is the symptom of pain consistent with the injuries you diagnosed—(plaintiff) to have suffered?

NOTE: Ask the doctor to explain the mechanism of the plaintiff's symptoms if appropriate.

Q. In making your examination and reaching your diagnosis, do you routinely and necessarily ask your patient to report his symptoms?

Q. Is this a valid and acceptable—and even necessary—medical practice?

Q. Do you, as a doctor in the medical profession in general, consider the patient's report of his symptomology, that

is, his subjective symptoms, as being a valid source of information?
Q. Did you and do you consider (plaintiff) as a reliable informant of the nature and extent of his symptoms?
Q. Is it not necessary to and consistent with accepted medical practice for the examining physician to make an evaluation of his patient as a reliable informant or not?
Q. Were the symptoms that (plaintiff) reported to you consistent with the injuries you diagnosed?
— Here the plaintiff's subjective symptoms may individually be related to the injuries the doctor has diagnosed?

NOTE: If prior medical history (that is, other injuries) are involved—get it out and get it straight as to what role they play.

Q. Is plaintiff more susceptible to present injury because of the existing condition?
Q. Did the present incident aggravate or exacerbate existing the condition?
Q. Was the previous condition "quiescent" or "assymptomatic"?
Q. Is plaintiff's future condition going to be worse because present injuries superimposed on pre-existing condition?
Q. Had plaintiff completely recovered from previous trouble?

VI. TREATMENT.
Q. Did you treat (plaintiff) for the injuries you have described in your diagnosis? If so, what? Why? How? When?
Q. Hospitalization?
Q. Prescriptions?
Q. Appliances/Prosthesis?
Q. Office treatment?
Q. Home treatments?
Q. Instructions regarding limitation of activity?
Q. If course of treatment attended with pain, describe mechanism and extent?
Q. Describe plaintiff's progress as a consequence of course of treatment?

VII. PROGNOSIS.
    Q. Which injuries contained in diagnosis are permanent?
    Q. Percentage of disability?
       — Distinguish between anatomical injuries and the effect these injuries have on the personal life of the plaintiff (a) vocationally and privately, (b) physically and mentally or emotionally.
    Q. Future pain including mechanism and extent?
    Q. Complications?
    Q. Are any conditions progressive, e.g., arthritis, degenerative disc disease, etc.?

VIII. FUTURE CARE.
    Q. Operations?
    Q. Home treatment?
    Q. Rehabilitation?
    Q. Medication?
    Q. Limitations on activities?
    Q. Cost?

IX. MEDICAL EXPENSES.
    Q. Note this may include doctor's bills, hospital bills, drugs and medication, applicances/prosthesis, nursing care (including the value of nursing care gratuitously rendered by members of the family)?
    Q. Doctor, are the services for which this bill was rendered in your best judgment, medically advisable or reasonably necessarily for the treatment of the injuries you have described in your diagnosis as being sustained by (plaintiff)?
    Q. Are you familiar with the charges normally rendered by members of the profession in this community for such services?
    Q. In your judgment, is the amount of this bill a fair and reasonable charge for medical care of treatment and services for which it was rendered?
    Q. Anticipate cost of future treatment?

X. MEDICAL LITERATURE
    Q. Authentic?

Q. Authoritative?

Q. True?

XI. EXHIBITS.

Q. Hospital chart(s)?

Q. X-rays or other diagnostic tests?

Q. Anatomical diagrams/charts?

Q. Medical illustration?

Q. Individual bills or list of medical expenses?

Q. Medical appliances/Prosthesis?

Q. Mortality tables?

Q. Authoritative medical literature?

Q. Photographs?

FOUNDATIONAL QUESTION CHECKLIST—
CERTAIN EXHIBITS

I. X-RAYS.

Q. What is an X-ray?

Q. Is the taking of X-rays acceptable medical practice?

Q. Do physicians such as yourself routinely need to take or have X-rays made on patients who report or manifest the symptoms of (plaintiff)?

Q. Do these X-rays assist you as a doctor in reaching your medical diagnosis?

Q. Do you hold in your hand, copies of X-ray films taken of (plaintiff)?

Q. On what date were they taken?

Q. Were these X-rays taken under your direction and supervision or at your request?

Q. Was the person (doctor or technician) who made the X-rays competent and qualified to do so?

Q. Are the films you hold true and correct representations of the area of (plaintiff's) body you wanted and had X-rayed?

Q. Are the films you hold true and accurate copies of that X-ray test?

Elicit the qualifications of witness as to the reading and interpreting of X-rays.

Q. Did you look at and in part rely on those X-rays in reaching your medical diagnosis and determining treatment for your patient (plaintiff)?

Mark the X-rays as exhibits and offer them for introduction into evidence.

II. MEDICAL TEST SUCH AS EEG, EKG, EMG, MYELOGRAM, ETC.

III. PSYCHOLOGICAL TESTS.

Q. Tests made by you and under your direction and supervision?

Q. Reason for or purpose for tests?

Q. Type of test, that is, how and why test is calculated to absence or existence of certain traits or conditions?

Q. The method by which the test is given?

Q. Qualifications including training and experience of the person who administered the test?

Q. Was the test made without gross distraction?

Q. Did the plaintiff willingly submit and voluntarily cooperate during the administration of the test?

Q. Is the test medically acceptable in providing valid information for diagnostic purposes?

Q. Describe if you would what conditions or characteristics were revealed by the result of the psychological test you performed on (plaintiff).

IV. HOSPITAL CHART

Q. Kept and maintained on (plaintiff) at (institution) during the period of time beginning (date of admission) and ending date of discharge)?

Q. The identity of custodian? (or stipulation)

Q. Did each of the pages that collectively make up the chart come into existence in the usual and ordinary course of the business of the hospital in caring for and tending to (plaintiff)?

Q. Are the pages which make up the completed record which you hold in your hand, true and accurate copies of the original of that entire record?

Mark the entire chart as an exhibit and offer it for introduction into evidence.

V. PHOTOGRAPHS.

Show that the witness is familiar with the appearance of the object shown in the photograph, whether accident scene, vehicle, product, condition of injury, etc.

NOTE: The witness's knowledge and familiarty of the appearance of the object of the photograph must be related to a certain point in time or reasonably definable period of time.

Show the witness the photograph and ask him if he recognizes the object or scene it portrays.

Q. Is the photograph a fair and accurate representation of the object or scene it portrays as of (point in time)?

Offer the photograph as an exhibit and offer it for introduction into evidence.

VI. MEDICAL ILLUSTRATION, MEDICAL CHART/MODEL.

Q. Doctor, would it assist you in describing the examination you made or the diagnosis you reached of your patient's condition by using or referring to a chart or diagram or model?

Q. Doctor, I show you this exhibit which I have labeled as exhibit _____ and ask you if it is a fair and accurate reproduction and representation of a normal _____?

Q. Would it be of assistance to you in communicating to the jury and in answering the questions I have asked you about examination you made and the diagnosis you reached of (plaintiff's) condition?

VII. MOVIE/VIDEOTAPE.

Q. Qualifications of photographer?

Q. Interest in litigation or acquaintance with subject of movie/videotape?

Q. Instructions regarding the purpose and objective of movie/videotape?

Q. Description of equipment used?

— Type of camera?

— Type of film or videotape?
— Speed in frames per second to produce normal movement?
— Speed in frames per second used when pictures were made?
— Amount and type of exposure?
— Process of developing film?

Q. Conditions of light in weather?
Q. Position of camera in relation to object including angle, up/down, or lateral offset, including distance from object?
Q. Could photographer see the person or object at all times?
Q. Was anything done not portrayed on film?
Q. Was there any cutting or erasing of the film?
Q. Does the film/videotape fairly and accurately portray the conditions and objects you saw with your naked eye at the time you made the film?

The following are questions which specifically relate to movies/videotapes portraying a typical day in the life of an injured person. The questions assume that a nurse or other person who normally tends to the plaintiff is on the stand.

Q. Have you seen the movie/videotape presentation that I have marked for identification as exhibit ____?
Q. Were you present during the entire filming of that movie/videotape?
Q. At certain times, are you actually shown in the movie/videotape?
Q. Have you been with and tended to (plaintiff) in his/her care and treatment from day to day before this film was made?
Q. The way in which (plaintiff) acted and the way he/she behaved during the time this film was made, was that the way you had seen him/her act and behave during the normal and typical day?
Q. Was there anything unusual about the way he/she acted during the time the film was made?
Q. Are the movements and motion that are shown in this film a fair and accuate representation of the movements and motion you saw that took place during the time the film was made?

Q. Are the conditions of lighting and color that are shown in this film fiar and accrate representations of the conditions of lighting and color that you observed during the time the film was made?

Q. Is the sound which accompanies this film a fair and accurate representation of the sound that you heard during the time the film was made?

Q. Is plaintiff's exhibit _____ a fair and accurate representation of what was photographed during the time the film was made in every respect according to what you heard and observed on that occasion?

Offer the film in evidence and offer to display it to jury.

ANNOTATIONS

Treatises

Lacy, Scientific Automobile Accident Reconstruction.

Krindler, Aviation Accident Law.

Schwartz, Trial of Accident Cases.

Lousell, Kalisch, and Kramer, Medical Malpractice.

Dixon, Drug Product Liability.

Frumer and Friedman, Products Liability

Kelner, Successful Litigation Techniques

Am Jur Trials

Selecting and preparing expert witnesses, 2 AJT 585-667.

Mapping the trial—order of proof, 5 AJT 505-552.

Presenting plaintiff's case, 5 AJT 611-672.

Courtroom semantics, 5 AJT 695-805.

Presenting plaintiff's medical proof—common injuries and conditions, 6 AJT 1-107.

Basis of medical testimony, 6 AJT 109-200.

Am Jur Trials—References

The case in chief in airline passenger death cases, 8 AJT 290-325.

The case in chief in Federal Tort Claims Act proceedings, 8 AJT 711, 712, 715-718.

The case in chief in action involving fall from scaffold, 9 AJT 46-58.

The case in chief in child-pedestrian accident cases, 9 AJT 482-500.

The case in chief in seamen's injuries cases, 9 AJT 722-729, 738-749.

The case in chief in divider line automobile accident cases, 10 AJT 524-526, 528-530, 538-554.

The case in chief in wrongful death actions, 11 AJT 52-54, 56-65; 12 AJT 458-482.

The case in chief in stairway fall cases, 11 AJT 282-285, 290-314.

The case in chief in blasting damage cases, see 11 AJT 383, 384, 386-388.

The case in chief in Federal Employers' Liability Act cases, 11 AJT 606-662.

The case in chief in products liability cases, 12 AJT 158-166, 189, 190.

The case in chief in boiler accident cases, 13 AJT 425-450.

The case in chief in light aircraft accident litigation, 13 AJT 732-749.

The case in chief in glass door accident cases, 14 AJT 188-213.

The case in chief in actions against attorneys for professional negligence, 14 AJT 299-309.
The case in chief in liquified petroleum (L.P.) gas fires and explosion cases, 14 AJT 409-434.
The case in chief in skiing accident litigation, 15 AJT 304-341.
The case in chief in drug products liability and malpractice cases, 17 AJT 163-190.
The case in chief in a child death or injury case, 20 AJT 693-715.

Am Jur Proof of Facts

Admissions, 1 POF 161-198.
Causation—medical opinion, 3 POF 161-174.
Cause of death—testimony of medical examiner, 3 POF2d 551.
Checklist, elements of damages, 25 POF2d XI-XIII.
Damages, 3 POF 491-770.
Deposition, 4 POF 433-451.
Hospital records, 6 POF 131-157.
Hypothetical questions, 6 POF 159-210.
Proof of lost earning capacity and of future expenses, 16 POF 701-903.

Am Jur

Measure and elements of compensatory damages in personal injury actions, Am Jur 2d, Damages §§ 85-130.
Admissibility and sufficiency of proof of damages in pesonal injury actions, Am Jur 2d, Damages §§ 296 et seq.
Burden of proof in negligence actions, Am Jur 2d, Evidence, §§ 135-139.
Presumptions and instances of care or negligence, Am Jur 2d, Evidence §§ 211-216.
Admissibility of evidence of other accidents or injuries or the absence thereof, Am Jur 2d, Evidence, §§ 305-314.
Real or demonstrative evidence, Am Jur 2d, Evidence §§ 771-805.

ALR Annotations

Admissibility in evidence, in automobile negligence action, of charts showing braking distance, reaction time, etc., 9 ALR3d 976.
Application of the collateral source rule in action under the Federal Tort Claims Act, 12 ALR3d 1245.

Admissibility of admissions made in connection with offers or discussions of compromise, 15 ALR3d 13.

Loss of enjoyment of life as an element of, or factor in determining, damages for bodily injury, 15 ALR3d 506.

Necessity and sufficiency in personal injury or death action, of evidence as to reasonableness of amount charged or paid for accrued medical, nursing, or hospital expenses, 12 ALR3d 1347.

Preliminary proof, verification, or authentication of X-rays requisite to their introduction in evidence in civil cases, 5 ALR3d 303.

Admissibility, in civil case, of expert evidence as to existence or nonexistence, or severity, of pain, 11 ALR3d 1249.

Medical books as independent evidence, 65 ALR 1102; 84 ALR2d 1338.

Competency of young child as witness in civil case, 81 ALR2d 386.

Opinion evidence as to cause of accident or occurrence, 38 ALR2d 13.

Admissibility in evidence of colored photographs, 53 ALR2d 1102.

Propriety, in trial of civil action, of use of model of object or instrumentality, or of site or premises, involved in the accident or incident, 69 ALR2d 424.

Counsel's use, in trial of personal injury or wrongful death case, of blackboard, chart, diagram, or placard, not introduced in evidence, relating to damages, 86 ALR2d 239.

Admissibility of opinion evidence as to cause of accident or occurrence, 38 ALR2d 13.

Sufficiency of expert evidence to establish causal relation between accident and physical condition or death, 135 ALR 516.

Competency of physician or surgeon as an expert witness as affected by fact that he is not a specialist, 54 ALR 860.

Propriety, in trial of civil action, of use of skeleton or model of human body or part, 58 ALR2d 689.

Admissibility of expert opinion evidence as to cause of death, disease, or injury, 136 ALR 965, 967; (66 ALR2d 1082, 1087).

Admissibility, in personal injury or death action, of evidence as to injured party's intention to enter occupation other than that engaged in at time of injury or death, 23 ALR3d 1189.

Modern status of the rules regarding use of hypothetical questions in eliciting opinion of expert witness, 56 ALR3d 300.

Modern status of "locality rule" in malpractice action against physician who is not a specialist, 99 ALR3d 1133.

Chapter 11

CROSS-EXAMINATION

INTRODUCTION

Cross-examination is probably the most publicized but least understood aspect of a trial. It is regarded as the most dramatic phase of the trial and many have referred to the ability to cross-examine effectively as "the true test of a trial lawyer." It is, in fact, the phase of the trial which epitomizes adversarial confrontation. The "mystique" of cross-examination, however, often obscures the need for mastering a few very basic principles and techniques which have little to do with theatrics or bellicosity. This chapter will present a brief overview of some basic principles and techniques. These principles can be studied and mastered and in this area the study of basic principles and practical experience are the best means of acquiring its techniques.

THE FIRST CRITICAL DECISION:
WHETHER TO CROSS-EXAMINE AT ALL

The Harmless Witness

The initial question which the cross-examiner must answer at the conclusion of the direct testimony of his opponent's witness is, "Shall I cross-examine?" When a witness has not hurt counsel's case, there is little to be gained by subjecting the witness to cross-examination. It is altogether possible that the defense witness who has "flopped" during his direct testimony will "wake up" during cross-examination and remember what he was supposed to say. A defense witness may not testify on direct to some important (and harmful) fact which counsel expected. This may not be because the witness does not possess or is unwilling to advance the damaging information. It may merely be a baited trap. Counsel may find out, too late, that the witness was not asked the questions on direct because the defense anticipated that counsel would bite at the bait and bring out evidence favorable to the defense on "cross." Such evidence, given in response to cross-examination, may have a far greater effect than if it had been given during "direct."

If on direct examination a witness has given testimony unfavorable to the defense, counsel may be tempted to emphasize that testimony on cross-examination and parade it again before the jury. Too frequently, when this is attempted by counsel for plaintiff, the witness deals with the question in such a way as to change entirely the effect of what had been so favorable during his direct examination. He may explain away all the facts which had appeared detrimental to the defense. As a general rule, then, do not cross-examine a witness who has not hurt your case.

Scope

The decision to cross-examine is also greatly influenced by the local rule governing the scope of cross-examination. The first rule or approach regards cross-examination as the acid test of the truth and affords the parties a wide latitude in the cross-examination of an adverse witness. This rule permits counsel to question the witness on any subject which is relevant to the dispute and does not restrict the scope of cross-examination to the matters on which the witness was questioned on direct. This rule is the ancient common law approach and is preserved by statute in some states. The second rule, sometimes referred to as the Federal rule, limits the scope of cross-examination to the same subject matter as the direct examination, requiring the cross-examiner to call the witness as part of his own case if he wants to range farther afield. This usually results in the loss of the right to ask leading questions. As adopted, Federal Rule of Evidence 611(b) provides:

Scope of Cross-Examination.
Cross-examination should be limited to the subject matter of the direct examination and matters affecting the credibility of the witness. The Court may, in the exercise of discretion, permit inquiry into additional matters as if on direct examination.[1]

Additionally, the rules give the court wide latitude in controlling the mode and order of interrogating witnesses and presenting evidence "so as to (1) make the interrogation and presentation effective for the ascertainment of the truth, (2) avoid needless consumption of time, and (3) protect witnesses from harrassment or undue embarrassment."[2]

Because the "restrictive view" has been adopted by the Federal Rules of Civil Procedure, the cross-examiner in Federal Court must even more carefully weigh the critical decision of whether or not to cross-examine at all. A cross-examiner held "on a short leash" by the "restrictive rule" may find that he is simply re-emphasizing the harmful effects of the direct examination.

Other Motives

Finally, the decision of whether to cross-examine or not should *never* be made to please the client or to prove to a client counsel's aggressive interests in the client's cause. Too often, counsel decides to "go after" a witness who would be better left alone. At this point, counsel is well advised to remember this excellent advice by Professor Irving Younger:

> The Advocate will have cross-examined *only* to the extent necessary to obtain the information he needs to support the argument he has planned in advance to make in his summation about the credibility of the cross-examined witness. And once he has obtained that information, he will stop. Stop. S-T-O-P.[3]

---

[1]FED. R. EVID. 611(b).

[2]FED. R. EVID. 611(a).

[3]Younger, *A Letter in Which Cicero Lays Down the Ten Commandments of Cross-Examination,* 3 LITIGATION 18, 19 (Winter 1977).

PLANNING CROSS-EXAMINATION

A good cross-examination is never the result of chance. The more spontaneous a cross-examination may seem, the more likely it is that counsel carefully planned the examination well in advance of trial. Cross-examination of a witness generally falls into two categories: offensive and defensive. In an offensive cross-examination, counsel can establish salient points that advance his client's case. A defensive cross-examination is one that is usually directed at blunting the effect of adverse testimony. Some cross-examiners write out specific questions in advance. However, it is suggested that a more flexible planning tool is to select the topics you wish to cover and simply use them as a check list. If one selects truisms and subjects which the witness cannot disagree with, the parameters can be set on the witnesses' testimony. For example, in examining an accident reconstruction witness, one should lock him in on given facts:

> Sir, you agree that the defendant says he was traveling fifty-five miles an hour immediately before the accident? You have been advised that the defendant says the road was level and clear before the accident. You were also advised that the defendant says he didn't see plaintiff walking on the wide of the road until a split second before the accident. You examined the accident scene and could see that visibility along the shoulder of the road is clear for at least a half a mile before the accident scene. Sir, that means that there was an unobstructed view for 2,640 feet, isn't that correct? Fifty-five miles an hour equals 80.6 feet per second after defendant says he didn't see the plaintiff on the side of the road until the split second before the accident; that means he didn't see him much more than eighty feet before the point of impact, isn't that correct?

The key to a well planned cross-examination, then, is to box in the witness so that when the ultimate opinion question is solicited, short of looking like a fool, the witness has no choice but to agree with you.

GOALS OF CROSS-EXAMINATION

Principal Objectives

Once counsel determines that the defense witness has hurt the plaintiff's case and that he will cross-examine the witness, he should attempt to place himself in the jury's position and determine in what specific respect his client's case has been damaged. He must then ask himself, "How can I negate the detrimental effect of the testimony?" Next he should consider the three principal objectives of cross-examination: (1) to discredit the witness; (2) to point out error or confusion in the story the witness has told; and (3) to use the witness to bolster his own case.

Discrediting the Witness

As part of the preparation for trial, counsel should investigate the background of every potential witness to determine whether there is anything which can be used to undermine or destroy his credibility. In many jurisdictions, pretrial discovery permits ample opportunity to secure information with which to undermine or destroy the credibility of potential adverse witnesses. Under these procedures, "surprise witnesses" should be a relic of the past. However, although there may be a great deal of information with which to attack the credibility of a witness, (as will be discussed in more detail later), a direct attack upon the character of a witness should only be used as a last resort; it is, by far, the most dangerous form of impeachment.

A less dangerous means of discrediting the witness is to bring out facts which tend to show bias or prejudice. If the witness is a relative, close friend, or working companion of the defendant this should be brought out in cross-examination; further, if it can be determined that the witness has some particular monetary interest which might serve to explain his testimony, this fact should also be exposed. Simply stated, plaintiff's counsel should seek to elicit anything which would tend to cast doubt on the *objectivity* of the witness.

It should be noted, however, that there are serious dangers involved in attempting to prove that the witness will color his or her testimony to favor the related party. Questioning a witness about bias may be referred to as "a two-edged sword that should be handled carefully." That is, a gruelling examination on the witnesses' relationship to the opposing party may result in augmenting his credibility rather than diminishing it.

Pointing Out Error or Confusion

Probably the most common objective of cross-examination is to point out errors or confusion in the story told by the witness. This objective can be accomplished by bringing out the inherent improbabilities in the witness' story, by exposing areas of conflict and confusion in his testimony, by showing that he had a limited access to the facts, and, most importantly, by pointing out prior inconsistent statements made by the witness.

At no point in cross-examination is the imperative of preparation more important than impeachment by prior inconsistent statements. Most modern rules of Civil Procedure, provide ample opportunity to discover such statements, for example, depositions, signed statements, statements taken in the presence of a court reporter, sworn answers to interrogatories and prior testimony in other proceedings. The well prepared lawyer will have read all the prior statements made by the witness and have them at hand. He should have indexed and cross-indexed every deposition by name and by reference to the evidentiary topics covered in the statement. He will know everything about the witness and what he has said prior to the trial and will then follow the direct testimony of the witness and be able to recognize conflicts with prior statements when they occur. When such conflicts occur, counsel during cross-examination should take the witness back over the testimony given during direct so as to fix these particular points in the minds of the jurors. The witness should then be asked whether, on a given date in the presence of a given person, he made such-and-such a statement, the examiner thereafter reciting the prior inconsistent statement. The witness can admit or deny that he made the statement. If he admits it, counsel will have scored his point. If the witness denies it, counsel should then be prepared to prove that the statement was made by producing a witness or a document to support his view. It is basic that the conflicting statement should and must be on a matter of substance. The court and jury will have little patience with a lawyer who attempts to discredit a witness by bringing up minor, immaterial inconsistencies.

The technique of cross-examining through prior inconsistent statements is particularly valuable when confronting defense experts. Prior to trial, counsel should make every effort to gather all prior testimony of the expert, as well as all books and articles the expert has authored. Once this material is accumulated, it must be read thoroughly. There is nothing more devastating than cross-examination of an expert using his own articles or prior sworn testimony.

Bolstering Plaintiff's Case

Not all cross-examination, however, is directed toward pointing out confusion and inconsistency or toward the impeachment of a witness. A defense witness who has hurt the plaintiff's case will usually have said some things which are favorable to the plaintiff's view of the case. If there is no cross-examination, the damaging aspects of the witness' testimony will be uppermost in the jurors' minds. Plaintiff's counsel may wish to cross-examine the witness only on the favorable aspects of the case, thereby letting the jury hear the helpful points again. However, counsel should exercise care so as not to give the witness an opportunity to elaborate on one of the damaging points he brought out during his direct testimony.

When the witness has not testified to a particular point and counsel has information which would lead him to believe that the witness would have to make an admission favorable to his client, he could cross-examine and seek to gain that admission. By so doing, the witness who has initially harmed the plaintiff's case may be used to benefit it.

LEADING QUESTIONS

Many trial lawyers agree that a key to effective cross-examination is the leading question. This technique permits the advocate to choose his own words in describing the event with which the witness is confronted, and it limits the witness's response. In short, leading questions help the attorney keep control over the witness's answers.

Avoiding Overuse

A note of caution should be sounded, however, in the use of leading questions. Overuse can be psychologically damaging to one's overall case. If the examining attorney gives the impression that he is not permitting the witness to answer the question fully, juries can easily interpret such misconduct as an attempt to prevent the truth from coming out. If the witness is "hammered" mercilessly on cross-examination, a sympathy factor can develop with the jury; they can begin to feel sorry for the witness and hostile towards the attorney. Such a development can destroy the entire case.

Eliciting "Yes" or "No"

The witness may affirm the suggestion in the question or deny it. He should be asked to admit or agree with the proposition contained in counsel's question. Thus, typical cross-examination questions will frequently start with phraseology such as, "Do you agree, Mr. X, that ..." or "You will concede won't you that ..." or "Isn't it true that..." Questions should be phrased in such a restricted manner that the witness can only answer "Yes" or "No." Successful cross-examination is marked by a high percentage of "Yes" answers. Indeed, the percentage of affirmative answers is an excellent indicia of a well prepared and well executed cross-examination.

Asking "Why?" or "How?"

It is only under the most unusual circumstances that the cross-examiner will ask an adverse witness "Why?" or "How?" The witness has had his chance to run free during direct examination. He must remain under tight rein during cross. It is only when the cross-examiner *is certain* that the witness cannot hurt him by narrative statement, that the "How?" or "Why" question is permissible.

Renarrating or Repeating

Counsel may permit the witness to renarrate or repeat an answer he gave on direct when he is trying to demonstrate that the witness has memorized his story and will tell the same story two, three, or more times in precisely the same words. Normally, no one can tell a story *that* well unless he has memorized it. However, few witnesses will leave themselves open to this type of cross-examination. Another situation in which a witness may be encouraged on cross-examination to narrate is when he has told a story on direct that is so vulnerable that it can be totally destroyed. It must be emphasized, however, that such an approach is *rarely* indicated or justified.

Limiting the Talkative or Evasive Witness

The cross-examiner frequently encounters witnesses who will not respond "Yes" or "No" to his leading questions, but will insist on explaining every answer, or will evade answering the questions. Dealing with such witnesses creates problems, and there are two basic approaches to the handling of these problems. First, the cross-examiner can seek to enlist the aid of the judge in limiting the talkativeness or evasiveness of the witness. Faced with an unresponsive answer the cross-examiner may move to strike the answer and request the court to admonish the witness to respond directly to the question. Faced with a witness who seeks to explain every answer, counsel may request the court to instruct the witness that during cross-examination he is to limit his answers to a response to the questions posed by the examiner and to further instruct that defense counsel, during redirect examination, will have a chance to bring out explanations. Second, counsel can allow the witness to duck, dodge, and explain, within certain limits. If the witness gives an unresponsive answer, the examiner will ask the question again; if the answer is again unresponsive, the examiner will ask the same question a third time. The "explainer" will be asked by the cross-examiner to limit his answers to "Yes" or "No"; the cross-examiner will tell the witness that he will have his chance during redirect examination to explain his answers. Those examiners who do not seek to enlist the aid of the court in dealing with the problem witness and allow him to be unresponsive or evasive feel that the jurors will be able to detect the lack of co-operation and candor on the part of the witness and will draw their own adverse conclusions about him.

CONDUCTING THE EXAMINATION

The examiner should have an idea of where he is going with each group of questions. He should move quickly from one question to the next, but should avoid cutting off the answers of the witness. The questions which are asked must be readily understandable by both the witness and the jury. The lawyer should avoid prefacing each question with, "Now, let me ask you this question...." Further, there is no need for the cross-examiner to repeat each answer as a preface to the next question.

Strong Opening

Generally, it is agreed that the cross-examiner should seek a strong opening in his examination; that is, he should attempt to begin his cross-examination with a point on which he is relatively certain he can score. He should have his first group of questions ready when he gets to his feet. It is usually not wise to begin cross-examining the witness on the last matter covered in direct. Since it is clearest in his mind and, at that time, most logically related to the body of his testimony, the witness may be at his best in defending it.

The value of a strong opening cannot be overstated. Exposed to the devastating cross-examination portrayed in the mass media, jurors are very much atracted to the confrontation of cross-examination. If counsel is able to score a significant point at the outset of cross-examination, jurors may be significantly impressed, and the entire testimony of the witness may be devalued.

Brevity

As a general rule counsel should seek to keep his cross-examination of each witness as brief as possible. The jury will not remember a great deal of the testimony of any one witness. The normal personal injury lawsuit lasts several days, and jurors remember only the "high spots" of the testimony of any witness. Therefore, the cross-examiner should, if possible, limit his cross-examination to only those few points or areas which he feels are critical. Some cross-examiners will hide the key questions by presenting them in the midst of a lengthy cross-examination. They hope to camouflage an important question by asking the witness many questions which are not important. Though it is true counsel may surprise the witness, the value of the admission *may be lost* to the jury, which has become either confused or bored—a jury which is anesthetized by a lengthy cross-examination may completely miss the significant admissions counsel is able to obtain from the witness.

Frequently, however, counsel has no choice and must resort to a seemingly endless cross-examination in an effort to bring out what counsel considers significant admissions. When this occurs, counsel can use his closing argument to explain the importance of the admissions. If the lawyer truly believes that the admissions are significant and further believes that they went over the head of the jury, he should have the court reporter transcribe the pertinent portions of the cross-examination so that there can be no question in the minds of the jurors as to what actually transpired during the cross-examination. With this transcript before him, counsel can explain the significance of the seemingly insignificant admissions during argument.

Strong Closing

Just as plaintiff should open his cross-examination with a telling point, he should save a significant point for his conclusion. It is imperative that counsel not end the cross-examination lamely on a matter of little concern. At all cost, he should avoid having it close with the witness in control and the attorney discomfited. Thus, if a climactic point has been reached such as the witness's admission of a vital point and the material remaining is not deemed of great importance, counsel should stop while he is ahead. In this respect, counsel must be both sensitive and flexible.

STYLE OF EXAMINATION

Avoiding Animosity

The typical fictional characterization of cross-examination portrays the lawyer as a relentless prober who storms about the courtroom pointing his finger at the terrified witness. In actual practice, the most effective cross-examination is usually conducted in a courteous and conciliatory manner. The witness is more likely to admit error to the courteous examiner with a friendly approach than he is to the "hard driving" examiner who firms up his opposition. Further, as the jury looks upon cross-examination as an unequal contest—with the advantage being on the side of the lawyer—the hard driving cross-examiner risks having the jury disregard the admission gained because it feels that he violated the rules of fair play in securing it. This is not to say that the cross-examiner should overlook or excuse conflicts; to the contrary, he must be tenacious in his pursuit of inaccuracies. He should merely seek to do his job without creating animosity between himself and the witness. If the witness is caught in a lie, the lawyer should *not try to over emphasize* this point to the jury; the jury may sympathize with the witness and feel that the lawyer is being unnecessarily harsh.

Cross-examination is most likely to be effective when it is conducted in a calm, rational, and unemotional manner, although righteous indignation and harsh tones may be indicated—and effective—in certain circumstances. While many hard driving, savage cross-examiners have been successful, those who attempt to mimic this technique had better be careful, for the technique can carry penalties. The quiet, calm, soft spoken, yet confident and forceful examiner has an equal if not greater chance of being successful, and he does not risk alienating the jury.

Observing the Witness

The cross-examiner should closely observe the witness. Frequently, the demeanor of the witness will be the best tip-off to the cross-examiner as to whether the questions being asked are "hitting home" and will also serve to indicate the future course his examination should take.

Retaining Control

The one universally accepted rule is that the examiner should never lose control of himself. He must never become so flustered or get so mad that he loses his sense of direction and control. ("Unbridled counsel, like his friend the horse, cannot be trusted to win a race.")

Listening

The cross-examiner needs to listen most carefully to the answers he receives from the witness. Too often the cross-examining attorney is concerned about getting on to the next question or point in his outline and does not pursue a useful answer. A rigidly followed, preprogrammed cross-examination can miss an important point which is there for the making. Counsel may fail to follow up an important line of inquiry suggested by an unanticipated answer for fear of omitting some topic on his outline. In order to permit flexibility in his cross-examination, counsel may wish to use a simple checklist rather than a detailed outline.

USING LEARNED TREATISES ON CROSS-EXAMINATION OF EXPERT FOR PURPOSE OF IMPEACHMENT

In virtually every jurisdiction, where an expert witness has specifically relied upon a treatise or text as supporting his opinion given in direct examination, he may be cross-examined from other portions of that treatise for the purpose of showing that it does not in fact support his position. If the witness is to be cross-examined from the contents of some other treatise, some states require either independent authentication (i.e., from plaintiff's own expert) or an admission by the witness that the text is regarded as authoritative. Some jurisdictions permit learned treatises or technical works to be used on the cross-examination of an expert witness, in order to test the witness's competency or qualifications, without imposing any specific requirement that the witness has relied upon or recognized the authoritative status of the work.

The Federal Rules of Evidence have adopted the following exception to the hearsay rule:

> *Learned Treatises.* To the extent called to the attention of an expert witness upon cross-examination or relied upon by him in direct examination, statements contained in published treatises, periodicals, or pamphlets on a subject of history, medicine, or other science or art, established as a reliable authority by the testimony or admission of the witness or by other expert testimony or by judicial notice. If admitted, the statements may be read into evidence but may not be received as exhibits.[4]

In using this technique of cross-examination, counsel must be ready to establish that the authorities he intends to use are indeed authoritative in the field. He can accomplish this in several different ways, including the use of an independent expert witness, admission by the expert being cross-examined, judicial notice by the trial court, or by Requests for Admissions.

No examiner should ever attempt this technique without engaging in exhaustive preparation, as the examiner will often find himself playing on the expert's "own field," one with which the expert is quite familiar and comfortable. The examiner is cautioned against attempting to use isolated "spot" references that may be completely repudiated or explained away elsewhere in the text.

CROSS-EXAMINING THE DEFENDANT'S MEDICAL EXPERT

During the trial, counsel for the plaintiff is frequently faced with the problem of cross-examining a medical doctor who has testified for the defendant and cast serious doubts on the plaintiff's case. It is the job of plaintiff's counsel to see what can be done to mitigate the detrimental effect of the testimony and, if possible, to use the defense examiner to bolster his own case. Again, it is repeated that counsel should not cross-examine at all unless his client's case has been hurt by the testimony of the defense doctor and he feels he can mitigate the

[4]FED. R. EVID. 803 (18).

damage by cross examination. However, if the defense calls a medical expert, his direct testimony is probably going to be damaging. There are many areas in which a judicious cross-examination of a medical expert can prove beneficial to the plaintiff. Attorneys must realize that medicine is far from an exact science. Doctors are human beings; each has his own biases, prejudices, pre-conceptions, and predilections. There are many medical questions about which equally competent and honest physicians hold diametrically opposed views. Recognizing this, it becomes clear that cross-examination of even the most prestigeous physician can be of value.

Financial Bias

A frequent and often effective line of inquiry relates to the "financial bias" of the defense doctor. Every metropolitan community has a group of doctors whose services are utilized with great frequency by the insurance industry and the defense bar. Examinations of claimants can be a lucrative aspect of a medical practice. A typical defense examiner conducts an examination, prepares a report, engages in a conference with defense counsel if trial appears imminent, and testifies in court if the case is not settled. Some doctors conduct at least one or more of these examinations each day and derive a substantial portion of their income from them. The jury may be interested in the financial stake the defense doctor has in giving defense examinations. Cross-examination which brings out the fact that the doctor conducts these examinations frequently or that he frequently and typically testifies for the defense may greatly impair the credibility of the witness.

But before plaintiff's counsel attempts to establish such a picture through cross-examination, he must make certain that such an attack is indicated. He should make every attempt prior to trial to determine how frequently the doctor testifies, how frequently he examines, and how frequently he is retained by the defense firm involved in the case. It is a mistake to assume that simply because the doctor was called by the defendant he will be subject to this line of attack. Plaintiff's counsel must *never* go on a "fishing expedition" during the trial and must *never* use this line of attack unless success is assured by pretrial preparation.

Information concerning the financial stake of the defense examiner in his medical-legal practice can be derived from several sources; for example, the transcript of the defense doctor's testimony in prior cases may be valuable, as may a conference with more experienced lawyers in the community. Where pretrial deposition of the defense doctor is available, this line of inquiry should be pursued fully. Counsel should ask the doctor on deposition the number of times per week he is called by defense law firms, insurance companies, or adjusting agencies to conduct examinations of claimants. Counsel should also ask: (1) the charge for each examination, (2) the charge for each report, (3) the charge for pre-trial conferences with defense counsel, and (4) the charge for courtroom testimony. Plaintiff's counsel during deposition also should seek to determine the number of times in the preceding year the doctor was requested to make examinations of a claimant and the number of times during that period the doctor testified on behalf of a defendant. The number of times that the doctor has testified on the behalf of a plaintiff during that period of time should also be determined.

Qualifications

Almost invariably, the defense doctor will be a highly qualified physician. Therefore, an attack on his qualifications should rarely be employed; however, situations can occur where such an attack may be indicated. Where counsel has determined that the defense examiner is not board certified in his specialty, this point may be brought out during cross-examination. (Specialty boards were created by organized medicine during the 1930's with the basic purpose of elevating the standards of practice in the various specialties; a doctor may be certified by a board only after he has pursued a prescribed course of study and has passed prescribed examinations, demonstrating his competency in a particular specialty. Thus, board certification is indicative of special achievement.) Further, when a qualified specialist is called to testify in an area *outside* of his specialty, this fact should be brought to the attention of the jury during cross-examination; that is, the defense examiner may be a qualified expert in his own field, but not specifically qualified to testify concerning the medical issue in the case. For example, if the defense doctor, an orthopedic surgeon, renders an opinion concerning the relationship of a coronary occlusion to trauma, palintiff's counsel should attempt to point out by cross-examination that the particular problem is highly complex and falls outside the specialty of orthopedics.

An attack on the basic qualifications of the defense examiner or his qualifications to testify concerning the particular medical problem in the case should be used only when plaintiff's counsel is certain that such an attack is well founded. Further, when such cross-examination is indicated, it should be employed "gently." Counsel should attempt to make clear that he is not seeking to embarrass the doctor, but rather to make the record clear concerning the extent of the doctor's qualifications to testify in a particular case. Counsel can obtain information concerning the defense doctor's qualifications through several sources: interrogatories, depositions, and prior trial transcripts. The plaintiff's lawyer should also become conversant with the reference work, *Directory of Medical Specialists,* as it lists all the board certified physicians in the country, as well as their areas of certification.

Opinions

Frequently, counsel for the plaintiff can attack neither the basic qualifications of the defense examiner nor his qualifications to testify in a particular case; nevertheless, counsel may be able to attack the medical opinions of the defense examiner. The more plaintiff's counsel knows in advance of the trial what the defense doctor's testimony is likely to be, the better prepared he will be to employ this technique. Where rule of the court permits, counsel for the plaintiff should obtain reports of defense examiners. Where there is no such rule, counsel should make every attempt to persuade defense counsel to turn over copies of the reports; he could suggest that all reports of experts be exchanged. Where discovery procedures permit plaintiff's counsel to make direct inquiries of the defense doctor, either by interrogatory or deposition, such procedures should be fully utilized.

Once plaintiff's counsel has informed himself as fully as possible prior to the trial concerning the defense doctor's opinions, he should seek to weigh and evaluate the defense doctor's position. A conference with the plaintiff's physician can be extremely valuable. Plaintiff's counsel should go over the reports of the defense doctor with the plaintiff's doctor to determine in what respect his opinions are vulnerable, and the report of the defense doctor should be read as much for what is not in it as for what is. Even if plaintiff's counsel, because of local discovery rules, is unable to obtain the doctor's report or depose him, a conference with the plaintiff's doctor may be valuable. Normally, the plaintiff's doctor will know the physician testifying for the defense and be able to predict the general position the doctor will take and the concessions he will make during cross-examination.

In preparation for the trial, counsel for the plaintiff should make every attempt to gather and read all books, articles, and speeches authored by the defense doctor. The text, *Index Medicus,* contains an index of medical publications by subject and author and is a valuable source for much of this information. Further, as many defense examiners testify frequently, counsel for the plaintiff should make an attempt to gather transcripts of prior testimony. There is nothing more effective than the cross-examination of a defense examiner by means of his own published or spoken words.

Notes and Reports

Doctors frequently testify from their notes and reports, so it is important for plaintiff's counsel to obtain *all* reports and records used by the doctor to refresh his recollection for his direct testimony before cross-examination. During cross-examination, plaintiff's counsel should seek to have the doctor admit that he has virtually no independent recollection of this examination because he sees many patients over the course of a year. Once it has been established that the defense examiner has no independent recollection of this particular examination and is testfying on the basis of his notes, the doctor is thereafter tied to his notes and report. If the defense examiner failed to conduct any of the classic medical tests indicated by the plaintiff's complaints, this fact should be brought out on cross-examination. If, in his notes and records, there is no indication that he gave a particular test, he may have trouble convincing the jury that he distinctly remembers giving that test though it was not recorded.

Medical Books

Frequently, counsel for the plaintiff will seek to challenge the validity of the medical opinion of the defense expert. Before counsel undertakes such a confrontation, he should attempt to know more about the medical questions involved than the doctor. Again, a conference with the plaintiff's doctor will be invaluable in educating the plaintiff's lawyer as to the inaccuracies, if any, of the defense physician's position and the authoritative sources which can be used to point out these inaccuracies.

The use of medical books as a means of cross-examining the defense doctor may be effective, particularly with a doctor who does not have experience in giving expert testimony. Generally, before counsel may use such a book or article to attack the opinion of the defense examiner, the doctor must first admit that the particular work is authoritative and that he recognizes it as such. Where deposition of the defense doctor is available, plaintiff's counsel should seek to determine what books the doctor does consider authoritative, the names of the teachers under whom the doctor studied, the leaders in his field, the basic medical texts on the question involved, as well as any publications that the doctor may have authored in this area. (Some jurisdictions have taken the position that if the plaintiff's doctor states that the medical text in question is *generally* considered authoritative, the plaintiff's lawyer may use the text to cross-examine even though the doctor will not admit that he personally considers it as such.)

Frequency and Length of Medical Exam

The defense doctor is not a treating physician, and he has normally seen the plaintiff on only one occasion. The jury should be apprised of this fact at the beginnng of cross-examination. During cross-examination, plaintiff's counsel may also wish to point out that the single examination conducted by the defense examiner was a brief one. If the plaintiff was only in the doctor's office for one-half hour, fifteen minutes of which was taken up with the recording of his history, counsel should bring these facts to the attention of the jury.

Concessions

Frequently, the most counsel can gain during cross-examination is to secure a few concessions from the defense examiner. These concessions may cast some doubt on the defense examiner's testimony and can be used in argument to the benefit of the plaintiff. Examples of these are as follows:

1. The defendant's physician will frequently admit that he has not treated the plaintiff and that he examined him only for the purposes of rendering an opinion to the defendant's lawyer and testifying in court. He will generally concede that he does not know the plaintiff as well as the plaintiff's physician does; he may also admit that the plaintiff's doctor is in a better position to give a complete picture of the extent and nature of the injury because of his familiarity and the continuing nature of the treatment.

2. The doctor will frequently concede that he *cannot* say that the plaintiff does not feel pain. He should admit, also, that a physician cannot see pain and that he has no medical basis to reject the validity of the plaintiff's description of his own personal experience, even though he can cannot demonstrate correlative objective symptoms.

3. The doctor will generally concede that he treats many of his own patients on their subjective reports of pain, even when no objective signs of injury are present. He may also concede that certain injuries are likely to produce pain without producing objective symptomology.

4. The doctor will frequently concede that he has no basis to support the charge that the plaintiff is malingering.

5. A concession can be secured to the effect that much of the practice of medicine involves a difference of opinion among physicians, and that the conflict between himself and the plaintiff's doctor is not unusual. The defense doctor will generally concede that he cannot say with certainty that the plaintiff's doctor is wrong in his opinion.

6. The doctor will generally concede that the course of recovery for most injuries is marked by periods of remission and exacerbation and that he has no way of knowing whether during his one particular examination the plaintiff was in a period of remission.

7. Frequently, the doctor will admit that he did not determine whether the plaintiff had taken drugs for the relief of pain or muscle relaxants prior to his examination. Once this concession is gained, the doctor can be asked whether such medications could affect the plaintiff's response during the examination. Frequently, the doctor will concede that they could, as such drugs can mask symptoms of injury.

8. The doctor will generally admit that in his own practice, after initial examination, he forms a tentative diagnosis, and that, sometimes, he subsequently decides that his tentative diagnosis was wrong. That is, he will generally concede that one examination is generally not as good as a complete series of examinations and that occasionally he has to revise and change his opinions.

9. The doctor may admit that he has no idea of the severity of the trauma which gave rise to the plaintiff's injuries.

10. If the plaintiff's treating physicians are well qualified doctors, the plaintiff's lawyer will generally have little trouble gaining a concession from the defense examiner that these doctors are skilled, well trained physicians.

11. Frequently, the defense doctor will concede that he has little knowledge of the plaintiff's work duties and leisure activities.

12. In a case in which arthritis of the spine which pre-existed the trauma is being used as a defense, counsel for plaintiff should attempt to have the defense examiner concede that arthritis of the spine is present in many individuals over age 40 and that the condition frequently causes absolutely no pain or disability. The doctor may also concede that such a condition makes the affected person more prone to injury as the result of trauma and serves to delay the healing process.

Re-emphasizing Plaintiff's Case

Cross-examination of the defendant's examiner presents an excellent opportunity for plaintiff's counsel to re-emphasize his own medical case. With the aid of leading questions, the cross-examiner can cover the basics of the plaintiff's injury in such a manner as to highlight the significance of the injury. If the plaintiff's doctor testified that there was muscle spasm, the examiner should ask the defense doctor if it is not a fact that muscle spasm is a sign of injury; if it is not a fact that muscle spasm is an involuntary reaction of the muscles; if it is not a fact that this involuntary reaction is the body's means of splinting an injured area, etc. Likewise, if the plaintiff's doctor has testified that the muscles or ligaments were torn the defense doctor can be asked if it is not a fact that torn muscles heal with scar tissue; if it is not a fact that scar tissue is permanent; if it is not a fact that scar tissue is less elastic than normal tissue, etc. Generally, if the cross-examiner sticks to well accepted medical propositions, he will be able to gain positive concessions when he cross-examines and help make the injury and disability of the plaintiff more vivid.

Style

The plaintiff's attorney, during cross-examination of the defense doctor, should be polite and courteous, yet firm; he should recognize that as a general rule the jury identifies with the witness rather than the lawyer. This problem may be compounded when the witness is a doctor, for most physicians are held in high esteem by the public, but this fact does *not* mean that the plaintiff should be hesitant in undertaking a cross-examination of the defense doctor. It does indicate that he should be careful before he undertakes a direct attack upon the doctor.

Attacking Damaging Opinions

In summary, if the doctor renders damaging opinions, do not be reluctant to point out to the jury by means of cross-examination that the opinions are at odds with all other recognized authorities in the field, that the doctor has made prior inconsistent statements, or that there were defects in his capacity to observe and gather information which reflect on the validity of his opinion.

CONCLUSION

Finally, it should be emphasized again that nothing is as important during cross-examination as *preparation:* every successful cross-examination is based upon some amount of talent, some amount of luck—and a massive amount of preparation. No lawyer can cross-examine effectively without having carefully prepared his own case, researched his opponent's case and his opponent's witnesses, and planned, prior to the trial, the basic lines of cross-examination he will use on each adverse witness. With the modern discovery procedures available to counsel in almost every jurisdiction, there is no excuse for poor pretrial preparation.

ANNOTATIONS

Am Jur Trials—Articles

Cross-examination of defendant, 6 AJT 297-422.
Collateral cross-examination of medical witness, 6 AJT 423-500.

Am Jur Trials—References

Cross-examination in automobile cases, 6 AJT 346-379.
Cross-examination in cosmetics injury cases, 6 AJT 386.
Cross-examination of Federal Tort Claims' witnesses, 8 AJT 716-718.
Cross-examination as to hospital liability, 6 AJT 400-417.
Cross-examination of hostile witnesses, 5 AJT 641-645.
Cross-examination of defendant in medical malpractice cases, 6 AJT 387-399.
Preparation of witnesses for cross-examination, 5 AJT 615, 617-621, 775, 776; 9 AJT 191-198.
Cross-examination in seamen's injury actions, 9 AJT 691, 735, 736, 742-745.
Cross-examination of expert witness in wrongful death action, 12 AJT 464-467.
Cross-examination in skiing accident litigation, 15 AJT 313-318, 333-335.

Am Jur Proof of Facts

Cross-examination of expert as to proof of lost earning capacity, 16 POF, Proof of Lost Earning Capacity, 719 et seq.
Cross-examination of witnesses in child custody cases, 15 POF, Child Custody, 64-73, 97-111.
Cross-examination in elevator fall cases, 13 POF, Elevator Accidents, 144-152; 182-188.
Cross examination relating to escalator injuries, 14 POF, Escalators 640-661.
Cross-examination of physician signing death certificate, 2 POF 2d 93-96.
Cross-examination relating to job stress in workers' compensation cases, 25 POF 2d 1-50.

Am Jur

Cross-examination of witnesses in general, 81 Am Jur2d, Witnesses §§ 463-520.

ALR Annotations

Competency of physician or surgeon as expert witness as affected by fact he is not a specialist, 54 ALR 860.

Competency of physician or surgeon of school of practice other than that to which defendant belongs to testify in malpractice case, 85 ALR2d 1022.

Use of medical treatise in cross-examination to discredit expert, 60 ALR2d 77.

Physician's testimony on cross-examination as to statements made to him by injured or diseased person, 67 ALR 39; 80 ALR 1530; 130 ALR 987.

Right to cross-examine witness as to his place of residence, 85 ALR3d 541.

Construction and application of provision of Rule 611(b) of Federal Rules of Evidence that cross-examination should be limited to subject matter of direct examinatin, 45 ALR Fed. 639.

Chapter 12

FINAL ARGUMENT

INTRODUCTION

The importance of final argument or summation in the trial of a case is very great, even though there has been an increasing tendency in recent years to underestimate its value. Lawyers sometimes minimize its importance because they think the final argument is merely an appeal to the emotions or prejudice of a jury. Judges sometimes limit the time allowed for argument to speed up the trial, ignoring the fact that certain priceless ingredients necessary to justice can come to the jury only in argument. For example, the rules of evidence prevent most witnesses from offering their conclusions and reasoning to the jury; most judges are forbidden to comment on the evidence, and those who have the legal right to do so comment sparingly. The very life stream of justice in most cases depends upon the application of logic and reason to the evidence, and if the lawyer is not afforded ample time to furnish them to the jury, the ends of justice may be defeated. (It should be noted that argument does not carry the connotation of arguing with someone; it is used in the classical sense of presenting an orderly and persuasive statement in summation of a position.)

Most good lawyers believe that they do not argue to a jury but instead they reason with it.

Probably no other phase of trial technique is more personalized than final argument. Every practitioner develops his own ideas as to what constitutes an effective presentation, but most would agree that there are common denominators essential to good summations when their individual styles are distilled away.

The first and most important of those common denominators is sincerity. It is fundamental that no lawyer should try any case in which he does not believe in the justice of his client's position. If the case cannot be tried with confidence, it should not be tried at all. Jurors can spot the insincere trial lawyer every time. "Be yourself and be sincere" must be the trial lawyer's motto. He should be indignant, if indignation is felt, but he should never generate it for its own sake. He should not shout for the want of something better to do. He should also avoid the cliché or the clever argument if he is using it only because someone else has had success with it. Simply, the trial lawyer in final argument must function within his own personality. He must always remember that a vital, inspiring, and spontaneous final argument can be the decisive factor in a lawsuit, whereas an intemperate, disorganized, and poorly executed summation can sound the death knell for his case.

It must be remembered that we communicate on three levels in summation: by the words we use (verbally); by the books, charts, and graphs we use (visually) and, finally, by the intensity of belief which we have in our client's cause (non-verbally). The silent communication is frequently overlooked but is often the most important part of a trial lawyer's summation.

LIMITS ON ARGUMENT

Guidelines

Final argument is a part of the trial which is not subject to well defined limits; rather, it operates within a set of guidelines. The trial judge has broad discretion in controlling the subject matter of the argument, the format, and the manner of presentation employed by counsel. It is a basic rule that counsel is limited to the issues and evidence in the case. A lawyer cannot allude to evidence which was offered and excluded, but he is free to draw all proper inferences from the evidence which has been admitted, even though a particular inference may be in the nature of impeachment. He cannot, however, make an abstract attack upon the opposing party, opposing counsel, or a witness.

Reversible Error

Despite the almost total freedom allotted counsel for argument, there are recognized improprieties which may constitute reversible error, thereby destroying the successful trial effort, such as remarks imputing improper behavior against opposing counsel. Any appeal to racial, national, or religious prejudice generally calls for reversal. Likewise, appeals based on the wealth or poverty of one of the parties will inevitably constitute an abuse of argument and lead to reversal. It is bad practice to refer the jury to source materials outside of the evidence received, such as medical texts, newspaper articles, television programs, etc. (Note, however, the Federal Rules of Evidence provide for the reading of statements from medical texts in evidence, but the texts themselves are not admitted. Counsel may comment on these statements from the texts.) This does not mean, however, that counsel may not request the jurors to consider their own life experiences and apply common sense in determining the credibility of the evidence on which they are being asked to base a verdict.

Objections

The basic control over the final argument rests with opposing counsel. He must be alert to direct the court's attention to improprieties on the part of his adversary. In some aggravated instances, the court may, on its own motion, restrict the scope of argument. Any such interruption breaks the continuity of the argument and impairs its effectiveness; it is particularly damaging if the court rebukes the actions of counsel without the urging of the other side. Final argument is not a time for technical application of academic concepts on the part of counsel, and repeated interjection of objections and complaints which are not substantial will probably draw a sharp admonition from the judge. In turn, this may affect the image which the offending counsel has attempted to convey to the jury throughout the trial.

PREPARATION AND DELIVERY OF ARGUMENT

Spontaneity

Do not, under any circumstances, read the summation. In order to persuade the jury effectively, the argument must have spontaneity and should not appear to be rehearsed. Counsel must be fully aware of all of the points he wishes to bring out and not be concerned with the precise language used in articulating these points. Nothing bores a jury more than for counsel to mumble, to read from trial notes, or to shuffle through papers in the middle of an argument. When counsel has lived with his case and carefully planned his argument in advance, it should be deliverable extemporaneously. This is not to suggest that no notes should be used—even the most experienced counsel finds an outline or check list of value. Even this should be very brief, with only a few words necessary to remind you of the points that you wish to make in argument.

Demeanor

The demeanor of counsel for the plaintiff throughout the final argument should be serious and courteous and devoid of all humor. Counsel should deliver his argument with feeling, emphasizing his main points. A constant low dulcet delivery may tend to lull jurors to sleep; on the other hand, constant shouting is equally ineffective and seems theatrical. Counsel should deliver certain vital points with telling effectiveness by dropping his voice so that the jurors strain to catch each word. Likewise, when the occasion demands, some indignation will not be out of place, and a raise of voice is often appropriate.

Opening

Generally, each side has an equal amount of time for argument, but in many jurisdictions the plaintiff has the right to both open and close the argument. When this is the case, counsel must divide his allocated time according to his plan of argument and generally must advise the court as to the division which he will follow. Frequently, it is wise to make a full and fair opening and take advantage of the basic psychological premise of primacy as well. One of the plaintiff's most effective weapons is his right to open the argument. The attention span of the jury is limited; concentration can fade early and jurors' minds begin to wander. The inexperienced lawyer frequently favors a brief opening and a strong rebuttal. The problem with this approach is that the defense counsel has the period in between to dull the jurors' enthusiasm for any argument, even the strong finish the plaintiff's counsel has prepared. Thus, it is recommended that counsel for the plaintiff prepare a strong opening. A strong opening may put the defense attorney "on the defense" and may even cause him to drop his plan of argument. If the plaintiff has made such an opening, defense counsel must rebut the plaintiff's telling points before he can possibly attempt to win over the jury. The jury may be impatient to hear his counterattack and, if it is ineffectual, he may never again capture the attention of the jurors. The effective advocate will have used up the jury's span of attention in his opening and will have fixed his strong points firmly in the minds of the jurors.

Counsel for the plaintiff should always seek to personalize his side of the case and depersonalize the opposition. His client bears a name; the opposition is called "the defense." Thus, in final argument, he should never refer to his client as "the plaintiff."

Many trial lawyers use the opening part of their summation to inform the jury that they will not intentionally misstate any evidence. They explain that if they do so through inadvertance, the jurors must recall what the actual facts were. Counsel should emphasize that it is certainly not his intention to mislead or confuse. He should explain, however, that he is not infallible and that he is only using his best memory, supported by his notes.

Using a Transcript

Frequently, certain key sections of testimony are so critical that it is wise to have them transcribed prior to argument. When using a transcript of testimony, it is good technique for counsel to underline the passages to be read with a heavy marking pencil. In reading the testimony to the jury, it is good for counsel to turn so that the jurors can see the test. In some courts, this testimony can be enlarged so the jury and court can see it all simultaneously. It makes the jurors participants, assures them that the transcript is being used, and develops jury interest. It is frequently effective to transcribe defense counsel's opening if he has failed to deliver the proof he promised. You may say:

> Some of the testimony in this case is so conclusive and important that I have made certain it is absolutely correct. I have had our official court reporter transcribe this testimony. I will read it to you exactly as it was said on the witness stand.

Importance of Jury

Many plaintiff's counsel also remind the jury at the beginning of summation of the heavy duties and responsibilities which are about to be placed on their shoulders. The jurors must be reminded that they play a role in government when they act as jurors; they must understand that they have the power to right a wrong and, equally important, understand that the case being heard will never be brought before another jury. They may also be told that the only reward they will receive for their services is the knowledge that, if they are ever wronged by another and must come to court, twelve (or a lesser number if that is what is being used) responsible members of the community, like themselves, will be present to decide their case.

Burden of Proof

Another concept frequently touched upon at the outset of the plaintiff's summation is burden of proof. The pitfall to avoid is the fixed opinion in the minds of the jurors that to win his case the plaintiff must prove his contentions beyond a reasonable doubt. Many jurors hold this opinion because they have been instructed in this manner in criminal cases or because they have picked up the idea from the newspapers or television. The law, which seems perfectly clear to lawyers, that burden of proof in a civil case amounts to a mere preponderance of the evidence and depends upon the quality not the quantity of testimony and evidence, is frequently misunderstood and misapplied by jurors. If this issue is not met head-on, the jury may well find for the defendant even though they believe plaintiff is entitled to compensation because they mistakenly think that the proof to support a plaintiff's verdict was insufficient. Some comments along the following lines may be of value:

> You will note, ladies and gentlemen, that the plaintiff is required by law to prove his case by a preponderance of the evidence. We willingly meet this burden but respectfully remind you, however, that preponderance of evidence means nothing more than the greater weight of the evidence. This is a civil case, not a criminal case. In a criminal case, as you know from watching television and reading the newspapers, the prosecution must prove its case beyond a reasonable doubt. If you have any doubt at all in such a case, then the prosecution loses.

> But this is a civil case in which nobody is being accused of any crime and no punishment is in order. The defendant will be convicted of no crime no matter what your verdict.

> The question is who is going to bear the loss and expenses that the plaintiff has and will experience: the plaintiff, who has been injured, or the defendant who negligently injured him? Therefore, the law in a civil case imposes upon the plaintiff an entirely different burden of proof. That is why it is enough if you are simply

satisfied by the greater weight of the evidence that the plaintiff's
case is just.

> In a case such as this, the law merely requires that you find the
> plaintiff's proof more probably correct, more likely so than not,
> more likely to be true, or more believable than the evidence which
> opposed it. It is like taking a scale that starts out even on both
> sides before any evidence is produced and determining whether
> the scales have been tipped in the plaintiff's favor after all the
> evidence has been presented. If the plaintiff has tipped those
> scales ever so slightly in his favor as to the believability of his con-
> tentions, then he is entitled to your verdict. It is that type of
> reasoning process employed in making every day decisions of life.

Relationship to Voir Dire and Opening Statement

All phases of the trial from voir dire on are directed to attune the
jury to accept the plaintiff's claim. Voir dire, the opening statement,
and final argument are intimately connected. To illustrate:

> The plaintiff is struck from the rear at 3:00 a.m. after having just
> left a bar. He smells of alcohol and is obviously intoxicated, but
> was at a dead stop when he was hit by the defendant. Obviously,
> his drinking was not in any way a proximate cause of the collision
> and should have no influence on the jury.

At the time of argument, counsel must be in a position to remind the
jurors of their "promise" during voir dire to follow the law of proximate causation and not to take into consideration any extraneous factors which could not possibly be a proximate cause of the accident.
Obviously, a careful voir dire examination to eliminate jurors who
would not be willing to accept such an argument is essential; the situations in which voir dire "promises" of the jurors must be called forth
by plaintiff's counsel in final argument are many.

Objective

The objective of any effective final argument is to create an atmosphere in the collective minds of the jury which engenders an
abiding desire to return a verdict for the plaintiff. In this connection,
it is wise for plaintiff's counsel to be courteous but not overly friendly
towards defense counsel.

Throughout argument, counsel should seek to advance principles
that are readily acceptable to the jury, such as "all persons are entitled
to be treated equally under the law," "all persons have a right to the

pursuit of happiness," "thrift and hard work should be rewarded," "people should bear up under adversity to the best of their ability," "justice should be available to every one," and "if a person owes a debt, that person should pay it." These are arguments that psychologically are readily acceptable by all persons. If argument is woven around such principles, it will be met with acceptance.

Legal Instructions

Prior to the final argument, counsel in most jurisdictions has the right to determine from the trial court what the nature of the legal instructions will be. He then can frame his final argument so that the evidence corresponds to the law and explain to the jury the significance of the legal instructions and the justifications for the legal rules which he feels are favorable to his client. Counsel should attempt to use the words of the court in his final argument; this will give credibility to his argument.

Issues

In preparing final argument, counsel should first consider the the areas in which there is no conflict in the evidence. The jurors' attention should be focused upon the real issues in the case, and their minds can be relieved as to the areas in which there is no conflict. Plaintiff's counsel may anticipate each of the defense arguments which will be advanced on liability and damages and begin to prepare to refute them. Sometimes, it is better to wait to see how the defendant handles these points because you may argue them to your own detriment better than the defendant. It is good for plaintiff's counsel, in preparing his argument, to consider the case as though he were the counsel for the defense. It is always easier to review the good points of a case than it is to face and rebut its problems. Plaintiff's counsel may also seek in preparation to frame a number of questions which he will ask defense counsel to answer during his summation. Such a procedure may force defense counsel to abandon his plan of attack and to meet the plaintiff's issues head-on.

Liability

Where liability is in question, it is fundamental that plaintiff's counsel must seek to emphasize to the jury that the plaintiff is in court because he has proven that the defendant was at fault and negligent. It is good to stress the two or three points regarding the liability of the defendant, rather than recount or review chronologically each fact testified to during the course of the trial. Counsel should emphasize that the defendant has breached a duty and his breach has caused injury to the plaintiff. If liability is based upon violation of a statute, it is advisable to explain to the jury why the case is not only technically correct but also morally sound. Simply, counsel should make it clear that under the circumstances presented, it is right and proper for the plaintiff to recover. Jurors abhor mysteries. It is up to the plaintiff to explain his case and make sure that the jury understands it.

The essence of instructing the jury is to make sure that they understand that any one act of negligence on the part of the defendant, proven by the plaintiff, is sufficient for the plaintiff to win. You must bear down on this in argument, otherwise, many cases will be lost because jurors believe that the plaintiff must prove every act of negligence charged, unless they are told otherwise by the court and counsel.

Contributory Negligence

In cases in which the defense advanced is contributory negligence, counsel should argue that the slightest mistake or the slightest degree of fault does not prevent the honor student from making Phi Beta Kappa or *magna cum laude*. Certainly, it does not prevent his passing his tests. The same applies to a pedestrian or a man driving an automobile. he can make mistakes and can be guilty of more than the slightest degree of fault without failing the test which makes him negligent. The jury should be reminded that if the doors of the courthouse are open only to those who are perfect—only to those who are free from the slightest degree of fault—they are closed to all citizens. "The world has not seen a person free from the slightest fault." Defense counsel may not demand that the plaintiff be an "A" student, or even a "B," student. All that the law requires is that the plaintiff act as a reasonably prudent person, that is, be a "C" student.

Sympathy

Frequently, counsel for the defense will announce that he has a deep sympathy for the plaintiff, just as each member of the jury must have. He then will emphasize that it is the duty of each juror to lay aside any feelings of sympathy and urge that it is their duty, no matter how distasteful, to return a verdict for the defendant. People do not like to admit that they do not have the courage to perform a task that is unwanted; therefore, such an appeal may be very effective.

Plaintiff's counsel may wish to meet this argument in his summation by pointing out that sympathy is not the basis for decision and reminding the jurors of their duty to hear the issues without sympathy or prejudice. Plaintiff's counsel can further point out that plaintiff has had all the sympathy he can use and that he is not in court for sympathy but rather for the only thing the law provides: full, fair, and just compensation—nothing more, nothing less.

HANDLING INJURY AND RESULTANT DISABILITY

Subjective Symptoms

In the past thirty years, the legal profession has become knowledgeable in the field of medicine. No well equipped lawyer would any longer permit his adversary to persuade the jury that subjective symptoms are not reliable or that a negative neurological examination means there is no serious injury. His knowledge of modern medicine would assist him in his refutation of these popular fallacies.

Frequently, a large part of the plaintiff's doctor's testimony and conclusions have been based upon subjective complaints or symptoms. A defense attack upon a case based heavily on subjective symptoms can be met by the plaintiff in this fashion:

> It has been suggested to you that subjective symptoms are less important than objective findings because they depend upon the plaintiff telling the truth. In the first place, doctors, as a part of their skill, can come very close to knowing when their patients are telling the truth, and to this extent subjective symptoms are really objective to the doctor. But of vastly more importance, by far the greater part of diagnosis in any case is based upon subjective complaints. In his everyday practice, where there is no legal problem involved, the doctor begins by asking the patient where he hurts and how his problems started. The only doctor who is guided solely by objective findings is the veterinary surgeon who deals with dumb animals or the pediatrician who deals with children too young to talk. It would be paradoxical to ask you, the jury, to ignore the principal symptoms which actually guide the doctor in his diagnosis and to ask you to reach a different conclusion from that of the doctor responsible for treatment.

Pre-existing Conditions

Counsel for the plaintiff must be prepared to meet the defense contention that the plaintiff's conditions might be caused by something other than the incident giving rise to the trial. If the plaintiff was all right before the injury, impaired after the incident, and has proved that the incident was capable of causing the kind of harm about which he is complaining, it is idle to say that many other things are capable of causing a similar condition. It may be pointed out that if a man with a smoking pistol in his hand is found standing over a man dying as a result of a bullet wound, it means little to say that the victim could have been shot by anyone. Counsel should emphasize that to lay the blame on an alternative cause, the evidence must clearly show that this alternative was more likely the cause of plaintiff's injury.

In cases in which it is conceded that prior to the accident plaintiff had a physical condition which was causing him no problems, it still can be anticipated that the defense will take the position that this condition should serve to reduce the amount of the damages. Plaintiff's counsel must point out during argument that the medical testimony has proven that the pre-existing condition made the plaintiff more prone to injury and only constitutes a partial explanation of the medical problems caused by the defendant's negligence. The jury should be informed that the defendant is not entitled to demand a victim in good health. The law is made for the weak as well as for the strong; the law obliges the defendant to take the plaintiff as he found him.

Percentage Arguments

Frequently, plaintiff's attorney finds himself trying a case in which the disability of his client amounts to no more than 10 or 15 percent. In such cases, the defense attempts to minimize the damages by constantly emphasizing the small percentage of disability. To meet this problem, two approaches are suggested. The first is to distinguish between an anatomical or medical disability and a functional or actual disability. (Ten percent loss of efficiency could represent 100 percent inability to obtain employment or engage in certain recreational activities.) The second approach is to look at the wealth of examples in everyday life. A watch with a 10 percent disability would lose 2.4 hours a day, and a $100 watch that loses 2.4 hours a day is not worth $90; it is not worth 90¢ if it cannot be fixed. Just as an improvement of 15 percent can win a Phi Beta Kappa key for an average student, a loss of 15 percent can handicap an accident victim for the rest of his life to a serious and important extent. It should be pointed out that doctors who examine applicants for employment, and personnel directors, often turn 10 to 15 percent physical handicap into a 100 percent employment disability; when the company doctor finds an applicant 15 percent disabled, the employer does not hire him at 85 percent of the wages or for 85 percent of the time; they just don't hire him at all, and he remains 100 percent out of a job. This theme has been used effectively in cases of soft tissue injury to the back and neck.

PAIN AND SUFFERING—DAMAGES

Discussing Pain and Suffering

To the novice there is probably nothing more difficult to argue to the jury than pain and suffering. Pain is not only unpleasant to endure, it is unpleasant to think about. The only chance of a fair trial for the plaintiff on the issue of pain and suffering is to persuade the jurors to steel themselves to the disagreeable task of looking at the reality of what pain is and what it does to a person. It is good to explain to a jury that it is human nature to keep our minds off other people's troubles and off pain, just as we keep our minds from the thought of our own eventual death. If we did not have this "mental block," we would all be victims of such anxiety and concern that we would not function.

The jury may be directed to look at the law's attitude toward pain. The law forbids cruel and unusual punishment; the law says to the state, "You can inflict capital punishment, but you cannot use the lash on any man. You can take a man's life so long as you do it without pain." If penology would not tolerate pain for murderers and criminals, the innocent victims of automobile accidents should not be forced to tolerate pain without compensation in the only form the law allows, money damages. Pain is the opposite of pleasure, the antithesis of comfort. A person thinks nothing of spending money for an evening of pleasure or a day of comfort, and few would refuse to accept anesthesia from their dentist even if he were to double the price.

Discussing Money Damages

Once plaintiff's counsel has finished discussing the injuries and the pain and suffering, he must indicate to the jurors that it is their job to translate these items into money damages. Before discussing money with the jury, it is good to condition them with some introductory remarks regarding compensatory damages. Counsel should explain that the law does not allow the witnesses to express an opinion as to the amount of damages. The jurors must be made to realize that they alone are the judges of damages. Counsel should also explain to the jury that the plaintiff wants only compensatory damages in return for something that was taken away from him by the wrongful act of the defendant. Plaintiff's counsel should reiterate that his client has not come to court seeking sympathy or charity. A verdict based on sympathy alone would be an injustice; the plaintiff comes to court seeking full justice—nothing more and nothing less. The plaintiff is entitled to his full measure of justice; an amount of damages less than adequate compensation would compromise the plaintiff's rights. For example, if the plaintiff were entitled to $10,000, and only $9,000 was awarded by the jury, there would not be $9,000 worth of justice, but $1,000 worth of injustice.

Among plaintiff's advocates there has always been a controversy as to whether or not it is preferable to mention to the jury a specific amount that they should bring in by way of damages or whether it is preferable to argue the facts and leave the question of specific amount to the discretion of the jurors.

Many lawyers, where the law permits, favor the use of a *per diem* argument. Simply speaking, a *per diem* argument seeks to place a monetary value on each unit of time of pain and suffering, whether it be a minute, day, or year. (Before plaintiff's counsel attempts the use of any such argument, he must carefully research the law of the jurisdiction.) Where *per diem* argument is used, it is wise to adjust the dollar per time unit figure in accordance with the improvement or deterioration of the plaintiff's condition. Thus, in the typical case in which the plaintiff suffers acutely in the beginning and begins to level off after some period of time, a higher unit value should be placed on the time period when the plaintiff had his greatest difficulty. Where *per diem* argument is used and there is testimony permanency, it is wise to project the dollar amount in accordance with the life expectancy of the plaintiff.

REBUTTAL

Brevity

The jury has a restricted tolerance for a long argument. The rebuttal phase of the plaintiff's argument should be brief, possibly introduced in the following manner:

> Thank you so much, ladies and gentlemen, for bearing with me. I only have fifteen minutes in which to address you. These fifteen minutes are precious for the justice which I seek for my client. Please bear with me these last few minutes and I will make sure that I do not go beyond my time.

Planning

Rebuttal cannot be completely planned in advance of the defense argument, but its general nature can be anticipated. It exists to answer the defendant, and it should be prepared to treat the argument as the defendant made it. Plaintiff's counsel should not attempt to answer every argument made by the defense, but should focus on a few telling points. Good rebuttal springs from instinct and belief in the client's cause. The jury will be left with the image of the client as it is sketched in the rebuttal.

Defending Contradictions

Frequently, much of the defense argument will be directed to pointing out contradictions in the plaintiff's story, either as to how the accident occurred or as to the issues relating to his injuries. It is the rare case in which there are no inconsistencies or discrepancies in the plaintiff's story. Such argument may be met in the following fashion:

> My opponent makes much of the few contradictions in the testimony of Miss Jones regarding how this incident happened and how the injuries affected her life. It is not at all surprising that she cannot recall every detail. So much time has passed since it happened, that if Miss Jones were to be precise and exactly correct about every little detail you might well question whether she is telling the truth. Lawyers sometimes say that the only perfect witness is a perjurer.
>
> Do any of you know what you ate for dinner two weeks ago last Tuesday? Probably you do not: I certainly do not. This underlines the point that I am trying to make; anyone who remembers too much about the little details concerning a happening of several years ago is in all likelihood not telling the truth. The human memory is not that good. Although there are variations in the observations of all honest men, they generally agree upon that which is significant.
>
> It is for you to decide Miss Jones was honestly and sincerely trying to remember what really happened. If there are small imperfections in her testimony, this proves rather than disproves the honesty of the witness and the quality of the testimony. In the

main part of her testimony, that is on the significant facts, she
sharply and clearly remembered what happened.

Closing

Many lawyers believe that summation is best concluded by thanking
the jurors for their time, patience, and attention. Others believe you
should end on a high note with an expression of belief that the jury
will return a verdict for the plaintiff in the proper amount (suggested
by counsel, if permitted). In conclusion, counsel may again wish to remind the jurors of the responsibility which they have in rendering a
final judgment, one that will provide full justice for all time.

Closing argument for the plaintiff has been successful when the
jurors are left with the conviction that both the plaintiff and
plaintiff's counsel have been completely fair and forthright. When
they are convinced of the integrity and sincerity of the plaintiff and his
counsel, they will give the plaintiff the serious consideration he
deserves.

All good lawyers prepare the structure of their summation in advance of trial and always close with some action phrase that will put
the jury in the mood to return a fair and just verdict in favor of the
plaintiff.

ANNOTATIONS

Treatises

Smith, Summation

Am Jur Trials—Articles

Summations for the plaintiff, 6 AJT 641-730.
Summations for the defense, 6 AJT 731-770.
Nonjury summations, 6 AJT 771-806.
Sample summation in personal injury and death cases, 6 AJT 807-872.

Am Jur Trials—References

Final arguments in contact sports injury cases, 7 AJT 261-277.
Final arguments in Miller Act litigation, 7 AJT 366-370.
Final arguments in elevator accident cases, 7 AJT 464-474.
Final arguments in swimming pool accident cases, 7 AJT 709-716.
Final arguments in motor vehicle collision cases, involving an agency relationship, 8 AJT 51-56.
Final arguments in airplane passenger death cases, 8 AJT 331-353.
Final arguments in railroad trespasser accident litigation, 9 AJT 287-292.
Final arguments in child-pedestrian accident cases, 9 AJT 507-512.
Final arguments in trip and fall cases involving premises liability, 10 AJT 293-298.
Final arguments in divider line automobile accidents cases, 10 AJT 574-585.
Final arguments in stairway falls suits, 11 AJT 314-324.
Final arguments in litigation under the Federal Employers' Liability Act, 11 AJT 662-687.
Final arguments in products liability cases, 12 AJT 167-179.
Final arguments in medical malpractice actions relating to the use of saddle block anesthesia, 12 AJT 309-315.
Final arguments in wrongful death actions, 12 AJT 482-512.
Final arguments in boiler explosion cases, 13 AJT 456-563.
Final arguments in light aircraft accident litigation, 13 AJT 760-778.
Final arguments in glass door accident cases, 14 AJT 224-237.
Final arguments in actions against attorneys for professional negligence, 14 AJT 326-334.
Use of blackboard and related visual aids in final argument, 5 AJT 602-606.

Final argument in skiing accident litigation, 15 AJT 358-372.

Final arguments in drug products liability and malpractice cases, 17 AJT 201-215.

Final arguments in child death in injury cases, 20 AJT 719-726.

Am Jur

Final argument, 75 Am Jur 2d, Trial §§ 211-314.

ALR Annotations

Propriety and prejudicial effect of reference by plaintiff's counsel, in jury trial of personal injuries or death action, to amount of damages claimed or expected by his client, 14 ALR3d 541.

Propriety and prejudicial effect of counsel's argument or comment as to trial judge's refusal to direct verdict against him, 10 ALR3d 1330.

Propriety and prejudicial effect of reference by counsel in civil case to result of former trial of same case, or amount of verdict therein, 15 ALR3d 1101.

Propriety and judicial effect of reference by counsel in civil case to amount of verdict in similar cases, 15 ALR3d 1144.

Prejudicial effect, in argument or summation in civil case, of attacks upon opposing counsel, 96 ALR2d 9.

Propriety, and prejudicial effect of, comments by counsel vouching for credibility of witnesses, 81 ALR2d 1240.

Comment, in argument of civil case, on adversary's failure to call employee as witness, 68 ALR2d 1072.

Counsel's appeal in civil case to wealth or poverty of litigants as grounds for mistrial, new trial or reversal, 32 ALR2d 9.

Argument or comment of counsel, as to consideration of inadmissible hearsay evidence introduced without objection, 79 ALR2d 919.

Argument of counsel as to consideration of income tax in fixing damages in personal injury or death action, 63 ALR2d 1393, 1418.

Counsel's appeal in civil case to self-interest of jurors as taxpayers, as ground for mistrial, new trial, or reversal, 33 ALR2d 442.

Propriety and effect of instruction or argument directing attention of jury to defendant's professional reputation or standing, 74 ALR2d 662.

Propriety and effect of permitting counsel having burden of issues in civil case to argue new matter or points in his closing summation, 93 ALR2d 273.

Propriety and prejudicial effect of argument or comment by counsel as to settlement negotiations during trial of personal injury action, 99 ALR2d 737.

Prejudicial effect in civil trial of counsel's use during summation, of a litigant for a physical demonstration as to how the accident or incident happened, 74 ALR2d 1094.

Prejudicial statement by counsel relating to race, nationality, or religion in civil action, 99 ALR2d 1249.

Propriety, in action for wrongful death of spouse, of argument concerning remarriage of surviving spouse, or possibility thereof, 87 ALR2d 263.

Prejudicial effect of argument or remark that adversary was attempting to suppress facts, 29 ALR2d 996.

Prejudicial effect of counsel's argument, in civil case, urging jurors to place themselves in the position of litigant or to allow such recovery as they would wish if in the same position, 70 ALR2d 935.

Prejudicial effect of bringing to jury's attention fact that plaintiff in personal injury or death action is entitled to workmen's compensation benefits, 77 ALR2d 1154.

Prejudicial effect of counsel's addressing individually or by name particular juror during argument, 55 ALR2d 1198.

Counsel's right in civil case to argue law or to read law books to the jury, 66 ALR2d 9.

Counsel's right in arguing civil case to read medical or other learned treatises to the jury, 72 ALR2d 931.

Error in permitting counsel to argue law to the jury as affected by withdrawal of argument, 66 ALR2d 155.

Measures taken by trial judge to keep argument in proper bounds, 62 ALR2d 249.

Propriety of court's limitation of time allowed counsel for summation or argument in civil trial, 3 ALR3d 1341.

Counsel's right in summation in civil case, to point out inconsistencies between opponent's pleading and testimony, 72 ALR2d 1304.

Prejudicial effect in civil trial of counsel's misconduct in physically exhibiting to jury objects or items not introduced as evidence. 37 ALR2d 662.

Prejudicial effect of trial court's denial, or [its] equivalent, of counsel's right to argue case, 38 ALR2d 1396.

Counsel's use in trial of personal injury or wrongful death case, of blackboard, chart, diagram or placard, not introduced in evidence, relating to damages, 86 ALR2d 239.

Propriety and prejudicial effect of reference by plaintiff's counsel, in jury trial of personal injuries or death action, to amount of damages claimed or expected by his client, 14 ALR3d 541.

Chapter 13

INSTRUCTIONS TO THE JURY

INTRODUCTION

In all jury trials, at some point before the case is turned over to the jury for deliberation, the judge must give instructions on the law so that the jury can properly fulfill its function. The best tried case can result in reversible error if the jury is given incorrect, incomplete, or otherwise improper instructions on the law which it must follow.

Since the jury instructions are read by the trial judge, they carry great weight and authority with the juror. Most jurors do not realize that the instructions which are read to them have often been prepared by counsel for the respective parties. Rather, they view the instructions as coming from the court and reflecting the clear and undisputed law of the jurisdiction. Jurors give great weight to the instructions read to them by the court and, in some cases, perhaps even more emphasis is placed on the instructions by the jurors than on the arguments presented to them by the lawyers. Although some jurors may not believe certain witnesses and may discount much of what is said by counsel, they typically look to the court as the source of impartial and controlling authority and will pay careful attention to the instructions which the judge gives. Thus, a case can often be won or lost by carefully drafting and tendering proper instructions to the court.

PRELIMINARY INSTRUCTIONS

In many jurisdictions, preliminary instructions are given before the trial begins to inform the jury in a general way what it will be asked to

407

do at the end of the case. These instructions usually cover such procedural matters as identification of the parties; the order of the trial; admonitions to the jurors not to discuss the case with anyone, including their family and fellow jurors; and not to read newspaper accounts of the trial or listen to television or radio broadcasts which touch on the case in which they are sitting. Such preliminary instructions also will advise the jurors that they are not to form any opinions on the case until all the evidence has been presented and they retire to the jury room for deliberation. These admonitions are frequently repeated throughout the trial, particularly before jurors are discharged for lunch or recess or at the end of the day. It is prudent practice for counsel to request that the admonitions be given at these times if there is any fear or concern that the jurors might be exposed to media coverage or any other outside influence. The substantive instructions which the court gives to the jury dealing with the issues in the case are generally given at the completion of all the testimony. In most jurisdictions, the jury is "charged" after the parties have given final summation; however, in some parts of the country, the entire charge or portions thereof may be given at the close of the evidence but prior to final argument.

PREPARING REQUESTED INSTRUCTIONS

Shaping the Final Outcome of the Case

In modern trial practice, counsel for the respective parties are entitled to have the jury instructed on all legal issues incorporated in the pleadings and supported by the evidence. Almost universally, counsel submits requested instructions on the issues to the judge at some predetermined time before the close of all the evidence. In some jurisdictions, local rules dictate that proposed jury instructions be submitted at the time of the pretrial conference, at the time of jury selection, prior to the close of the plaintiff's case, or elsewhere. The prudent practitioner will inquire of the court well in advance of the pretrial what the practice or procedure is and will prepare his initial jury instructions at that time. Typically, counsel for each party is required to submit proposed instructions to the court, to each opposing counsel, and to retain one set for his own records. In legally uncomplicated cases, the parties may rely on the court to give the appropriate instructions unaided. However, in the vast majority of cases, the attorney who does not submit a set of requested instructions presenting his client's viewpoint on the legal issues in dispute may be missing an important opportunity to shape the final outcome of the case. Courts can generally be relied upon to give proper instructions on the most obvious issues in any case; thus, in a simple negligence action, it may not be necessary to prepare instructions on the definition of negligence, proximate cause, or burden of proof. However, local practice should dictate whether such form instructions should be submitted to the court or whether counsel should rely on the court to give these instructions unaided.

On Complex Issues

Concerning the more subtle and complex issues which may arise, counsel should submit requested instructions to the court. These issues may include status and duty in a premises liability action, violation of a statutory duty, determination of what constitutes permanent injury, the existence and effect of presumptions, and the right to recovery for the aggravation of a pre-existing condition. Preparing requested jury instructions in advance of trial often will aid the attorney in sharpening his focus on the legal issues in his case and help him plan his presentation of evidence. Having prepared instructions in advance, the attorney can look at his pleadings to see if they need to be amended; further, he can determine what evidence is needed to support the charges he feels are applicable. The giving of instructions which refer to theories or issues which have not been pled or upon which no evidence was presented will invariably result in error. Early submission of instructions to the court will aid the judge in hearing the case and will likely influence the content of the ultimate charge. If it is the custom or practice in one's jurisdiction to submit trial briefs to the court before the commencement of trial, early preparation of requested jury instructions will assist the attorney in briefing the legal issues which are in dispute in his case.

Pattern Jury Instructions

The highest courts of many states have adopted pattern or model jury instructions. These constitute a valuable source for trial lawyers. Pattern jury instructions generally contain detailed annotations and frequently contain a text discussion of the points covered in the particular instruction. In preparing requested instructions, the trial lawyer should first look to any model or pattern instructions which have been approved. If there are no model or pattern instructions for specific issues in his case, counsel may wish to consult a general treatise on jury charges. In addition, the opinions of the appellate courts are a prime source for special instructions not covered by pattern charges. Frequently, appellate opinions contain approved instructions or statements of substantive rules of law which have been approved and which can readily be translated into the correct form for a jury charge.

Language

Jury instructions must not be framed in argumentative language. The novice trial lawyer may be tempted to use language which slants the statement of the law in the instruction in his client's favor. If the trial court gives such an instruction, it may ultimately result in a reversal on appeal. Thus, counsel should be careful to use proper and balanced language in framing requested charges and avoid loading them with connotative adjectives which belong in final argument. An instruction should not merely contain an abstract proposition of law but should integrate the applicable principle of law into the facts of the case.

The venire may contain jurors with a limited education; therefore, instructions should not contain words which cannot be easily understood by the average layperson.

Assuming Disputed Facts

In framing specific instructions, the trial lawyer should attempt to avoid assuming facts which are in dispute. If any instruction assumes facts, the jurors can be misled into believing that those facts are no longer in dispute or that the judge has an opinion supporting one "version" of the evidence. Appellate opinions have repeatedly held that it is error for a jury instruction to assume the truth of disputed facts. This danger can often be avoided by using such phrases as "if any," "if you are reasonably satisfied from the evidence," and "if you so find."

Liability and Damages

Simple logic and common practice dictate that the trial lawyer first submit his special charges on the issues of liability and then on those related to damages. Where the issue of liability is being presented to the jury, the trial lawyer should draft his damage instructions in such as way that the language of the charge does not presume the defendant's liability. His instructions should start with a phrase such as, "If you find for the plaintiff on the question of liability, and if you find from the evidence that the plaintiff was injured as a direct and proximate result of the defendant's negligence, then...."

Format

The actual format of the instructions submitted will depend on local practice. It is generally considered good form to type each proposed instruction on a separate numbered sheet of paper. When this is done, the judge can select those he wishes to use and add them to the general charge. Numbering each requested charge separately facilitates discussion of the charges with the court and opposing counsel. It is also good practice to indicate the source of the particular charge requested at the bottom of each sheet. If the requested charge comes from a pattern or model instruction, it should be so stated; if there has been a modification, this should be noted. If the charge is based on or supported by particular cases, they should be cited at the bottom of the page.

Affirmative Defenses

If the case involves affirmative defenses, counsel for the plaintiff would be well advised to submit to the court his own proposed changes on these issues. The same principles of balance and fairness which govern the framing of liability instructions and damage instructions should dictate the formulation of instructions on affirmative defenses. In jurisdictions where comparative negligence is a recognized affirmative defense, take care that the instruction clearly and fairly reflects the status of the law. The same applies to jurisdictions that still recognize assumption of risk as a separate affirmative defense. For example, in some jurisdictions, comparative negligence is not a defense to a strict liability action. In other jurisdictions, comparative negligence and assumption of the risk are not defenses to claims of gross negligence.

Undue Influence to a Point of Law

It is well settled that giving undue influence to a point of law during a jury charge will constitute error. It is therefore important that in framing his instructions counsel should avoid unnecessary capitalization or emphasis.

Alternative Instructions

There is generally no prohibition against submitting more than one proposed instruction on a particular issue or point of law or against submitting conditional instructions. Where it is important that a particular point be covered in the court's charge, counsel should prepare alternative instructions. The most favorable version should be submitted first; if the court indicates that it will not give that instruction, counsel should except to the court's refusal of the first instruction and then submit a modified and "weaker" statement of the same proposition. Such a procedure will more than likely result in the coverage of the point in one form or another. Also, a trial judge's refusal to give the stronger instruction proffered may be used as an assignment of error in the event of an adverse verdict.

Some attorneys maintain a file of written charges which have been tested and approved in previous trials. The maintenance of such a file over the years can be of enormous benefit to the trial lawyer.

THE CHARGE CONFERENCE

Most jurisdictions provide for a "charge conference" for the very purpose of providing counsel with the opportunity to meet with the trial judge outside the presence of the jury and to discuss the charge before the presentation of closing arguments. It is a good practice to have the charge recorded by a court reporter to preserve any adverse rulings made by the court. Most judges recognize that a charge conference with counsel present will reduce the possibility of reversible error and therefore encourage counsel participation in the determination of which instructions should be accepted and which should not. Counsel should be mindful that urging an instruction that does not reflect the law of the jurisdiction or the trend in which the jurisdiction is moving may result in reversible error.

The contents of counsel's final argument and the contents of the court's charge are integrally related. It is only after counsel knows what law will be submitted to the jury that he will be able to argue certain aspects of his case accurately. Although local rules usually refer to some point in the progress of the case where proposed instructions are to be exchanged, counsel should expressly request that the exchange occur as early as is reasonably practical. By obtaining a set of charges from opposing counsel, one has the opportunity to research the law, narrow the issues, and, thus, avoid potential error in the presentation of evidence during argument. If the local rules do not expressly provide for a charge conference before summation, counsel should ask for one—most trial judges are delighted to assent.

TAKING EXCEPTIONS

The task of taking full and proper exception to the court's instructions to the jury is hard work. Because a large percentage of reversals are based on errors committed by the trial court in its charge to the jury, it is extremely important work. In spite of the fact that the entire results of an arduous trial may be completely eradicated by a single error or omission committed by the court in its charge to the jury, many lawyers find themselves less prepared to handle exceptions to the court's instructions than in any other segment or aspect of the trial of a personal injury case.

The contents of the previous portions of this chapter have been addressed to the attempts on the part of plaintiff's counsel to insure that a fair verdict is obtained. The topic of "taking exceptions" is addressed to counsel's efforts to insure the reversal of an unjust verdict—at least to insure that he is in a position to challenge properly an unjust verdict resulting from errors contained in the court's charge.

Procedure

The two pivotal questions relating to the topic of taking exceptions are "when" and "how." The requisite procedure will vary from state to state, and state court practice is often different from federal court practice.

The suggestions which follow the discussion of when exception must be taken to the court's charge are based on the assumption that the local rules do *not* provide for a charge conference or that a charge conference was not, in fact, conducted. If the trial judge does conduct a charge conference, counsel will, at that time, be provided with an opportunity to make and record all necessary objections and exceptions to the court's jury instructions.

The when and the how of preserving for review an error in the instructions to the jury may vary with regard to whether the charge is "given" or "refused"; the procedure for excepting to oral charge may be different from the procedure applicable to written instructions.

Local practice almost uniformly provides that counsel is accorded an exception to the court's refusal of a written charge. If this is not the local practice, then counsel must take the necessary steps to record his exceptions to the court's refusal to give the written instructions which he is requested.

Local practice does not uniformly provide opposing counsel with an exception to the court's giving of written instructions requested by the opposing party. Typically the procedure which governs the plaintiff's counsel in the event the court gives a written charge requested by the defendant is the same as the procedure which relates to the taking of exceptions to the oral charge.

The remaining discussion will be addressed to the typical procedure relating to "when" and "how" exceptions should be made to the court's *oral* instructions to the jury. The following suggestions are applicable whether the potential source of error is the giving of an erroneous charge or the erroneous refusal of a good charge.

When

Most local rules require that exceptions to the court's charge must be taken outside of the presence of the jury but before the jury retires to begin their deliberations. Typically, the trial judge will call a short recess and excuse the jury, rather than sending them back to the jury room, in order to provide counsel with the opportunity to state their exceptions to the charge. If local practice requires that exceptions be taken before the jury retires to consider its verdict and the trial court does not provide counsel with an opportunity to except to the charge, then counsel may specifically have to request the court to "excuse" the jury (that is, a recess) in order to permit both sides an opportunity to record their exceptions.

How

Some jurisdictions still insist that the actual language of the charge to which counsel excepts be read to the trial judge by the court reporter. In any event, counsel's reference to the portion of the charge to which his exception is addressed must be done with sufficient specificity to make the trial court aware of the precise portion of the charge to which the exception is addressed. Many lawyers first describe the topic or the portion of the charge to which they wish to take exception and then merely ask the trial judge to assent verbally for the record that he understands the specific portion of the charge to which counsel wishes to take exception. If local rules require the statement of grounds, counsel should then state the grounds of his exception.

The requirement for the stating of precise grounds of exception to the court's charge is no longer uniform. Some states require that each and every ground of exception be stated with particularity and decline appellate review on those grounds not stated and recorded in the trial court; other states have eliminated the entire necessity of excepting to any portion of the court's charge much less the statement of grounds.

At the conclusion of the court's instructions to the jury, counsel should consider requesting an explanatory charge. The request for an explanatory charge may not only be a matter of good trial strategy, but it may also be required to preserve a ground of error for appeal. The need for explanatory charges usually arises from the failure of the judge to instruct the jury on some topic which counsel anticipated would be covered in the court's oral charge. The appellate courts of many states still follow the practice of refusing to review the trial court's failure to charge on a certain point *unless* the appellant preserved the error by the request of an explanatory charge.

FORM OF VERDICT

General Verdict

After the Court has completed reading its charges on the law to the jury, it will usually instruct on the form of verdict which the jury is to complete. In most jurisdictions, and in most instances, a general verdict form is usually employed. The jury is simply instructed to state, "We, the jury, find for the plaintiff and award damages in the amount of $_____," or, in the alternative, "We, the jury, find for the defendant." In terms of preserving a favorable verdict on appeal, the simple general verdict form is definitely preferred. Complex verdict forms often result in error and reversal on appeal. However, as trial practice becomes more complex, particularly in products liability, medical malpractice, and multi-district litigation cases, the use of the special verdict form may be justified.

Special Verdicts and Interrogatories

The rules of one's local jurisdiction will generally dictate which form of verdict is preferred and which form of verdict is allowed. Rule 49 of the Federal Rules of Civil Procedure and numerous state codes provide for special verdicts and for special interrogatories which may be used to "test" either special verdicts or general veridcts.

Generally, it is up to counsel to take the initiative in urging either the use of special verdicts or interrogatories. The form of special verdicts and special interrogatories varies. Special verdicts generally require the jury to find for the plaintiff or the defendant and then require specific questions to be answered on specific issues. For example, a special verdict form may state, "We, the jury, find that the defendant breached its implied warranty and award damages in the amount of $_____; so say we all." In some jurisdictions, special interrogatories are submitted to the jury which do not require a finding on the ultimate issue of liability or damages. If special interrogatories or special verdicts are to be used, counsel is strongly urged to see that they are drafted in the simplest form possible to eliminate confusion on the part of the jurors.

Counsel should ask the court before or during trial whether or not general verdict or special verdict or interrogatories are to be employed. If the court indicates an intention to employ either special verdicts or interrogatories, counsel should request leave of court to submit proposed special verdicts or interrogatories so as to frame them in language which will avoid error on appeal. Counsel's right to do so stems from the same principles which dictate that the charge on the law be determined before the presentation of closing argument. In jurisdictions where special interrogatories or special verdicts are employed, counsel should consider carefully whether the special interrogatories or special verdicts should be discussed during summation. To the extent that one's jurisdiction permits counsel to comment on the jury charge, counsel should also be permitted to comment and elucidate the proposed special verdict or special interrogatory.

Questions During Jury Deliberations

After the charge and the verdict form have been explained to the jury, the jurors retire for deliberation. Occasionally, jurors will have questions which they send out to the court during their deliberation. All such questions and inquiries should be preserved on the record. Local practice dictates how this is done. In some jurisdictions, the jurors are required to submit their questions in writing to the court. In other jurisdictions, the jurors are recalled to the jury box and the questions are presented orally to the court. Any responses made by the trial judge to inquiries of the jurors during their deliberations are to be considered as additional instructions.

If counsel has any objections to the substance or form in which those replies are given, he should so state to preserve the trial record for appeal. Counsel has the right and the obligation to be present during the answering of any such questions, and he should make this known to the court if local practice permits counsel to leave the area of the courtroom during jury deliberations. In no event should counsel be absent when the court receives a question from the jurors or gives further instructions.

CONCLUSION

Jury instructions, properly framed and pertinent to the issues raised by the pleadings and evidence presented at trial, can be highly instrumental in producing a successful result. By exercising care in preparing requested charges and presenting them for the court's consideration, the trial attorney can go far toward obviating any need for appeal by either side.

ANNOTATIONS

Am Jur Trials—Articles

Instructing the jury—pattern instructions, 6 AJT 923-962.

Am Jur Trials—References

Instructions in Miller Act litigation, 7 AJT 370-373.

Instructions in swimming pool accident cases, 7 AJT 716-720.

Instructions in airline passenger death cases, 8 AJT 353-357.

Instructions in seamen's injuries cases, 9 AJT 747-752.

Instructions in divider line automobile accident cases, 10 AJT 585-588.

Instructions in litigation under the Federal Employers' Liability Act, 11 AJT 687-696.

Instructions in products liability cases, 12 AJT 179-184, 191, 192.

Instructions in light aircraft accident litigation, 13 AJT 778-786.

Instructions in glass door accident cases, 14 AJT 237-242.

Instructions in actions against attorneys for professional negligence, 14 AJT 335-341.

Instructions to jury in automobile fuel tank fire case, 23 AJT 474-477.

Instructions to jury in recovery room accident cases, 25 AJT 413, 414.

Instructions to jury in television-fire litigation, 26 AJT 637-364.

Instructions to jury in corporative negligence case, 21 AJT 575-785.

Am Jur

Instructions, 75 AM Jur 2d, Trial §§ 573-930.

ALR Annotations

Propriety and effect of instructions in civil case on the weight or reliability of medical expert testimony, 86 ALR2d 1038.

Precautionary instructions on consideration of evidence of repairs, change of conditions, or precautions taken after accident, 64 ALR2d 1305.

Necessity and propriety of instruction as to prima facie speed limit, 87 ALR2d 539.

Instructions requiring or permitting consideration of changes in cost of living or in purchasing power of money in fixing damages, 12 ALR2d 611, 614, 636.

Instructions in wrongful death action as to damages for loss of expectancy of inheritance from decedent, 91 ALR2d 479, 484, 488.

Instructions in personal injury action which, in effect, tell jurors that in assessing damages they should put themselves in injured person's place, 96 ALR2d 760.

Instructions as to consideration of income tax in fixing damages in personal injury action, 63 ALR2d 1407.

Instructions in personal injury action with respect to loss of profits of business in which plaintiff is interested as a factor in determining damages in action for personal injuries, 12 ALR2d 302.

Instructions to jury as to per diem or similar mathematical basis for fixing damages for pain and suffering, 60 ALR2d 1352.

Instructions as to what items of damages on account of personal injury to infant belonged to him, and what to parent, 37 ALR 11; 32 ALR2d 1088.

Propriety of instruction mentioning or suggesting specific sum as damages in personal injury action or death, 2 ALR2d 454.

Instructions in action involving operation of airplane in landing, 74 ALR2d 628.

Instructions in action against owner or operator of theater or other place of amusement for injury to patron by condition of or defect in lavatory, restroom, or toilet facilities, 88 ALR2d 1091.

Instructions in action by spectator at basketball game for injury resulting from hazard of game, 89 ALR2d 1163.

Instructions to jury in action by patron of public amusement for accidental injury from cause other than assault, hazards of game or amusement, or condition of premises, 16 ALR2d 912.

Instruction as to application of "assured clear distance ahead" or "radius of lights" doctrine to accident involving pedestrian crossing street or highway, 31 ALR2d 1424.

Instruction, in motor vehicle accident case, as to contributory negligence of pedestrian under physical disability, 83 ALR2d 769.

Instruction in action for injury or damage caused in collision with or avoiding collision with, open door of parked automobile, 92 ALR2d 1056, 1064.

Instructions in action for injury or damage from motor vehicle accident assertedly caused by insect, 73 ALR2d 1214.

Instruction to jury as to last clear chance in action by motor vehicle passenger against host-driver, 95 ALR2d 619.

Instructions as to contributory negligence of driver or occupant of motor vehicle driven without lights or with defective or inadequate lights, 67 ALR2d 118.

Instructions as to duty to dim motor vehicle lights, 22 ALR2d 427.

Instructions in action involving duty and liability of vehicle driver blinded by glare of lights, 22 ALR2d 292.

Instructions on sudden emergency in motor vehicle cases, 80 ALR2d 5.

Instructions in action for injury incident to towing automobile, 30 ALR 750; 30 ALR2d 1019.

Instructions on unavoidable accident, or the like, in motor vehicle cases, 65 ALR2d 12.

Instructions in action against carrier by motor bus for injury to person [boarding bus], 93 ALR2d 237.

Instructions in action against motor carrier for injury to passenger by sudden stopping, starting, or lurching of conveyance, 57 ALR2d 5.

Instructions concerning contributory negligence or assumption of risk of passenger leaving seats before conveyance stops, 52 ALR2d 585.

Instructions to jury in action against railroad company based on failure of signaling device at crossing to operate, 90 ALR2d 350, 354-368, 394, 403.

Propriety of instruction referring to degree or percentage of contributory negligence necessary to bar recovery, 87 ALR2d 1391.

Instructions to jury as to causation in cases under Federal Employers' Liability Act or Jones Act, 98 ALR2d 654, 680.

Instructions as to res ipsa loquitur or presumption or inference of negligence, in malpractice case, 162 ALR 1265; 82 LAR2d 1262.

Instructions in action for malpractice in diagnosis or treatment of tuberculosis, 75 ALR2d 816.

Propriety and effect of instructions in civil case on the weight or reliability of medical expert testimony upon issue of standard of care and negligence in malpractice action, 86 ALR2d 1059.

Instructions to jury in action against physician or surgeon for malpractice in appendicitis treatment or surgery, 94 ALR2d 1008.

Sufficiency of evidence, in personal injury action, to prove future pain and suffering and to warrant instructions to jury thereon. 18 ALR3d 10.

Propriety and prejudicial effect, in federal civil case, of communications between judge and jury made out of counsel's presence and after submission for deliberation, 32 ALR Fed. 392.

Propriety and prejudicial effect of sending written instructions with retiring jury in civil case, 91 ALR3d 336.

Necessity and propriety of instructing on alternative theories of negligence or breach of warranty, where instruction on strict liability in tort is given in products liability case, 53 ALR3d 102.

Chapter 14

APPEALS

INTRODUCTION

Scope Note

This chapter is addressed primarily to the plaintiff's attorney who must decide whether or not to appeal a case. The portions of the following that deal with the appeal itself, of course, apply equally whether counsel is the appellant or appellee.

The Distinction Between "Trial" and "Appeal"

Although the appellate process is an extension of the adversary system, there are some essential and significant differences between the trial of a case and appellate review.

Circumstances. The first distinction simply has to do with the circumstances under which a trial is conducted in contrast to the conditions under which an appeal is prepared. Despite careful preparation, the outcome of a jury trial may be influenced by the unexpected: an apparently strong witness may give testimony surprisingly different from his statement or collapse on cross-examination; counsel for the defense may advance facts or theories different and more persuasive than those the plaintiff anticipated; the trial judge may make rulings that dramatically affect the legal basis or evidentiary support of the plaintiff's case. The outcome of an appeal is and should be more predictable. Counsel's presentation of an appeal is not subject to the vicissitudes of a recalcitrant witness or the objections and interruptions of an opposing lawyer. The testimony is fixed and preserved and the law is in the books—both subject to counsel's careful analysis and free from the pressure of an immediate response as required during trial. There is no reason for a good trial lawyer not to be an effective appellate advocate as well. However, this is not typically the case. The usual explanation is simply that the attorney did not take the requisite time and/or effort to perfect the record and to prepare and present a persuasive appeal. Preparation of a record and an appellate brief is *hard work!* It is typically more technical than a trial. An attorney's contribution to an appeal may be just as important, and sometimes more important, than his efforts at trial. It may not be enough to win the verdict; you may have to keep it on appeal. Obviously, in those appeals that have the effect of establishing a precedent that applies to future cases, the outcome transcends the effect of a single jury verdict.

Question for Determination. Another pivotal distinction exists between a trial and an appeal. The actual question presented for determination is different. At trial, the essential question is whether the evidence is more supportive of one side or the other. Most trials essentially involve disputed issues of fact. Both sides believe they are right and that "justice" equates to a verdict in their favor. Our judicial system is intended to offer both sides an equal opportunity to persuade the jury of the "justness" of their position. The trial system usually—almost always—works.

In sharp contrast, the question on appeal is significantly different. The question on appeal is "Did the system fail?" That is, was an error of law made and if so, was the error of great enough significance to have so corrupted the system or influenced the outcome that a wrong or unjust result was obtained. The point is that one side or the other is going to lose literally every case. That fact standing alone, obviously, does not indicate that the wrong result was obtained and that an appellate court should reverse the result. Stated differently, it might be said that our judicial system presumes that the trial procedure is good and that it worked and led to the right result. Considered in this light, it is no surprise that only a small fraction of trials result in appeals and that an even smaller fraction result in reversal.

When to Appeal

Some lawyers divide appeals into three categories:

    1. *Pure Law.* Some appeals simply involve a question of

law—"simply" in the sense that there is no dispute regarding the facts and counsel's difference is with the trial court's interpretation or application of the law. Pure questions of law typically arise from rulings on motions or on the pleadings before trial but may also include motions for directed verdict and JNOV. Here, the objective might be to persuade the appellate court to adopt a previously unrecognized right of recovery or overrule an existing but outmoded contrary precedent (prenatal injury to unborn child, wife's or child's right to consortium, soveriegn immunity, strict tort liability, etc.).

2. *Court's Error*. This category includes the trial court's rulings on the admission or exclusion of evidence and errors committed by the court during the course of its jury charge.

3. *Jury's Error*. Cases falling in this category primarily involve the contention that the jury simply reached a wrong and unjust verdict; that is, that the verdict is against the weight of the evidence. This category includes the challenge that the verdict is either excessive or inadequate.

The first rule of when to take an appeal is "DON'T!"[1] Cases falling into the first of the above listed three categories may constitute an exception. Counsel should not take appeals falling in the last two categories except and unless he can affirmatively answer the following three questions:

1. Is the existence of error clearly identifiable?

2. Was the challenged error actually injurious?

3. Have I adequately and correctly preserved my right to challenge the error?

In short, counsel must not only identify the existence of legal error but he must also be satisfied that the error was truly injurious. That is, that it actually led the jury to reach a wrong and unjust result. Finally, counsel must be satisfied that during the trial he took the necessary steps to preserve in the record his right to challenge the error on appeal.

[1]Remember the adage, "Tough cases make bad law."

THE APPEAL

Technical Procedural Steps

Appellate review is not a natural or inherent right of civil litigants; appellate review is a matter of statutory privilege, that is, it is not an essential element of due process of law. Since appellate review is a creature of statute, it cannot be inferred by implication or construction, but must arise by direct grant. Further, appellate rules and procedures vary with the jurisdiction. Therefore, it is incumbent upon counsel about to become involved in an appeal, for the purpose of either protecting or correcting a verdict, to study the applicable appellate practice code carefully to determine each of the following:

1. Is the order/judgment reviewable?

2. What must be done to make the order/judgment reviewable?

3. How can the right/privilege of review be lost or waived?

4. What is the appropriate method of appellate review? E.g., appeal, *certiorari, mandamus,* prohibition, *habeas corpus, quo warranto,* etc.

5. What is the appropriate appellate court?

6. Who are the proper parties to the appeal?

7. What are the relevant time requirements and how may extensions be obtained?

8. What is the appropriate procedure for obtaining leave to appeal and/or for filing notice of an appeal?

9. What temporary relief may/must be obtained pending appeal?

10. What are the necessary (or optional) methods for preparation of the "transcript"?

11. What are the necessary contents of the record on appeal?

12. What are the requirements concerning preparation, filing, and service of the record?

13. What are the requirements concerning the form, contents, filing, and service of briefs?

14. What are the grounds for a dismissal of the appeal?

15. What are the appellate court's calendar and oral argument practice?

Preparation of the Record

The "record" on appeal may include the following:

1. Pleadings, including relevant motions and the court's rulings thereon.

2. Transcript of oral testimony.

3. Physical exhibits received into evidence.

4. Transcript of counsel's arguments.

5. Charge to the jury whether oral or written and including both "given" and "refused" charges.

6. Court's orders and/or decrees.

7. Verdict and judgment entered thereon.

The record on appeal is intended to provide the appellate court with a complete and accurate summary of the history of the case in the trial court and the ultimate result. The rules governing appellate procedure in the federal system and in most states provide that the record may be abbreviated so as to contain only those matters actually relevant to the issues presented for review.

Although the physical work of preparing the record may actually be done by the court reporter and the clerk of the court, counsel for the appellant has the ultimate and non-delegable responsibility for preparing the record on appeal.

Writing the Brief

A. *Organize and Outline.* Just as an efficient trial lawyer will thoroughly investigate and prepare his case before he walks into the courtroom, the successful appellate advocate will engage in lengthy preparation before he physically attempts to write his brief. This point cannot be over-emphasized. It is absolutely essential that counsel reduce to an outline the points on which he relies on appeal. This outline will control every other step which counsel must follow in preparing a persuasive brief, including the summary of relevant facts, legal research, and the final organization of the brief itself.

The content of such an outline can best be obtained by following a four step analysis:

  1. Identification of the error and its injurious effect;
  2. Formulation of the statement of issues;
  3. Anticipation of and answers to opponents contention; and
  4. Final outline.

Having completed his outline, counsel should be prepared to state both the Propositions of Fact and the Propositions of Law around which the brief will be built. Having isolated these propositions, he is then in the position to digest the record to locate the evidence which supports his Propositions of Fact and to conduct his research of legal authorities which support his Propositions of Law. The Propositions of Fact and Propositions of Law must support each other and, in turn, each must support his challenge of error. This may be illustrated schematically by the following:

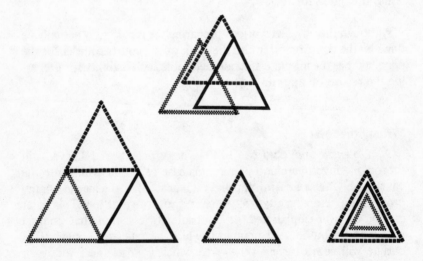

B. *Digest the Record.* Unless the case involves a pure question of law, appeals like trials, are won or lost on the *facts!* The facts must be accurately and persuasively treated both in the Statement of Facts and in the Argument portion of the brief. In order to accomplish this, it is first necessary to "digest the record." Digesting the record is an art. How effectively counsel accomplishes this will determine not only the amount of time that will be consumed in the actual writing of the brief but also the quality of the resulting product. Counsel must not treat this as an unimportant or routine exercise—especially today, when the facts involved in modern litigation are more often than not highly complex.

It is usually advisable to read the transcript of the oral testimony twice. The first time the testimony of the witnesses may be summarized chronologically in order of their appearance. The second time, counsel should organize the evidence according to the topics that appear in his Proposition of Facts; that is, every exhibit and the evidence from every witness whose testimony touches on the relevant subject matter should be separately summarized under each Proposition of Fact. Counsel must take great pains to insure that each page reference to the record is absolutely correct.

C. *Research the Law.* As in digesting the record, counsel's legal research may be confined to the Propositions of Law he intends to urge on appeal.

If the appeal presents questions which require extensive research, counsel should use one notebook which contains nothing but a sequential listing of the citations to every case, treatise, key number, etc., which counsel has identified in his initial research as being potentially relevant. A margin should be left on the right hand side of the page in which counsel may mark when he has actually located and read each of the authorities on his list. In the course of reading and analyzing each authority, individual briefs on separate pages of another notebook should be made. The bottom of each page containing the brief of each authority should be left blank so that counsel can make his own personal notes reflecting such observations as to whether the case is favorable or unfavorable, whether the case should be quoted or not, and, of course, what Proposition of Law the authority supports.

D. *The Brief.* The final draft of an appellate brief should conform to the Rule of SAAP—Simple, Articulate, Accurate, Persuasive:

Simple. That is, the issues must be well formulated and easily identifiable. The court must instantly recognize why you are there and what your position is. A mere reading of the Statement of Issues should tend to incline the court to view your position favorably. To accomplish this, counsel may physically have to write out the Statement of Issues a number of times before he settles on the correct wording.

Articulate and Accurate. Counsel's treatment of the facts and the law must not only be verifiably accurate but his choice of words throughout the brief should be clear and expressive. Even though the brief is written for an intelligent and well educated appellate judge, its contents should be expressed in language that a layperson could easily understand. For some inexplicable reason, there is a tendency rising almost to a compulsion to use big words and arcane language in an appellate brief. Counsel should resist the temptation to show off his vocabulary. Use big words and esoteric expressions only if they are truly applicable. If an appellate judge has to determine the merits of counsel's position with his brief in one hand and the dictionary in another, he will be irritated rather than impressed.

Persuasive. An appellate brief should advance a forceful presentation of the merits and "justness" of counsel's position, that is, why the verdict is right or why the judgment is wrong. It is repeated—if counsel cannot persuasively demonstrate why the judgment should be reversed, he should not have initiated the appeal.

The rules governing appellate practice will generally define the permissible length of a brief. However, out of respect for the enormous workload of appellate judges, briefs should be no longer than necessary. That is, a "brief" should if at all possible be *brief.* Remember the paradox that the longer the time counsel spends in organization and execution, the shorter the brief will be.

This does not mean, however, that there should be no repetition in the brief. The appellate advocate must make sure that his primary points are not overlooked or under-emphasized. The judicious repetition of major points is an effective way of impressing the court with the merits of counsel's position. For example, counsel may state a point clearly and succinctly in his own language and follow it with a brief quotation from a citation which reiterates the same thought followed by a reference to the facts illustrating the application of the point. Counsel may wish to repeat the message in the conclusion of the brief.

Oral Argument

If the local rules of practice permit oral argument, counsel should *not* submit on brief. Argument serves several purposes. It personalizes the record and enables the advocate to crystallize contentions with greater pith and force than in a written brief. It permits the attorney to hunt the truth with a rifle rather than a shotgun. Remember, most judges form at least a tentative conclusion based on oral arguments in a large percentage of cases.

Furthermore, oral argument allows the advocate to bring his case to the attention of the entire court for there is no guarantee that one's brief will be read in its entirety by each judge. This reduces the risk of "one-person" opinions.

Finally, argument encourages the judge to refer back to the brief with new understanding and, of course, gives counsel the opportunity to up-date citations.

Consider carefully who should orally argue the case. Never divide the argument of a single topic between two or more counsel. When two lawyers undertake a single presentation, their arguments will inevitably overlap, be repetitious, inconsistent, and, at worst, contradictory.

Counsel should consider retaining an appellate specialist. Some lawyers effective in trial work are not temperamentally adapted to the tedium of appellate review which is less often dramatic. Sometimes the trial lawyer cannot forego bickering over petty issues which are no longer relevant to the issues presented for appellate review. If the trial attorney lacks a dispassionate judgment as to what is important on appeal, a fresh approach and a detached mind are likely to be more effective.

"The Ten Commandments"

In 1940, John W. Davis, a celebrated appellate attorney, delivered a famous address, "The Argument of an Appeal." In that lecture, he suggested that such remarks should really come from a judge—the one who is to be persuaded. In 1951, Robert H. Jackson, Associate Justice of the United States Supreme Court, responded in a noted address of his own. From that "dialogue" one can derive basic principles of effective appellate advocacy which are timeless and which should serve as an outline for all lawyers, young and old, novice and veteran, who seek success and respect before the appellate bench.

1. *Change places with the court.* Be brief and argue the case as you would want it argued if you were an appellate judge. What would you want to know about the case? What questions would you want answered? Keep in mind Cicero's five essentials: determine exactly what you should say; arrange the material with good judgment, and in the proper order; use well chosen words and carefully phrased arguments; fix the entire presentation in the mind; and deliver it with clarity.

2. *First state the nature of the case, then briefly state its prior history in the courts.* Both in brief and during argument, before you say anything else, immediately state the legal issue involved, so that the court will read (or hear) the facts and the law with that issue in mind and not be left to speculate as to the relevancy of your argument. If the court must search for the issue during the argument it will likely miss some of what you are trying to say. The court will also wish to know at the outset in what procedural context the issue is raised and how the court or courts below dealt with the issue.

3. *State the facts.* It is possible that one or more of the appellate judges have not read the briefs. Assume that the judges are learning about the case for the first time. Build your case from the ground up. "Spoon-feed" the court. Remember, most contentions of law are won or lost on the facts, for the facts frequently incline a judge to one side or the other. The importance of stating the facts cannot be overemphasized. An accurate and effective fact recitation may do more to motivate the appellate court to adopt your view of the case than any complex legal argument. For this reason, the attorney must take great care both in writing the brief and making his oral argument to recite

the facts in such a manner that they will leave a positive impression with the appellate judges. A clear, compelling, and accurate fact presentation is critical.

Take nothing for granted when writing your statement of facts. You may know all the facts; the court does not. The record may be so long that the court may never find the decisive facts by reading it. The judges will appreciate your making their task easier by the inclusion of a short but thorough, easily read, and easily understood statement of the facts. It is essential that you do not overstate or make mistakes in reciting the facts. Nothing more engenders suspicion and predisposes the court against you than an inaccurate statement of facts.

It is also recommended that your brief state all the facts against you, as well as those in your favor. It is far better to expose weakness yourself than to have your adversary do so or to have the court dig it out. Remember the admonition, "You cannot hide from the record." Remember that the important thing in oral argument is to put before the court the facts together with your theory relating to them in such a clear and convincing manner that all of the judges will know and remember that theory and can then study the record in light of the contentions made.

4. *Give the applicable rules of law on which you rely.* Attempt to breathe life into the legal principles you are convinced support your position. When discussing the rules, state the moral principle or social policy which stands behind the rule and attempt to show the broad benefit or value of its application in the present case.

Avoid the temptation to string citations simply to impress the court with the depth of your research. Cite only one or two you actually want the court to read. In selecting the best case to cite, counsel must balance the most recent authority against the most persuasive authority. Recent decisions are preferred but there may be an old "bellweather" opinion that is controlling. Decisions from *this* court are most persuasive. If recourse must be had to decisions of other jurisdictions, look for neighboring jurisdictions or those frequently facing the issue. If the decided case law on your point is sparse, refer to leading treatises. Courts are frequently persuaded that what "Moore" or "Larson" or "Collier" says has merit.

A word of caution must be given when discussing the use of citations. Before citing a case in your brief, read the *whole opinion,* Shepardize it, and read every case that relates to it. Often you will find that a supposedly good authority has been reversed, overruled, or so limited by later decisions as to make its holding adverse to your position. Further, you may find extremely harmful language in a portion of the opinion that you do not intend to use. There is no excuse for citing a case which does more harm than good.

5. *Present most important questions—argue strongest points.* One of the first tests of a discriminating advocate is selection of the question or questions he will present orally. The impact of oral presentation will be strengthened if it is concentrated on a few points that can be simply and convincingly stated and easily grasped and retained. Therefore, avoid a clutter of arguments both in brief and during argument. The mind of an appellate judge is may be receptive to the suggestion that the lower court committed error, but receptiveness declines as the number of assigned errors increases. An appeal which attempts to advance "twenty-one" errors committed by the lower court—all argued with equal vigor—will almost always be regarded by the reviewing court as lacking in real merit. Pick out your strongest arguments and rely on them.

6. *Rejoice when the court asks questions.* One of your main motives in arguing the case to the court should be to elicit questions from the bench. The court tells you clearly by its questions where it is troubled by your argument or brief. Moreover, questioning by the court is a clear indication of interest in your position. When you are asked a question, do not evade or ask to postpone your answers. *Never* tell the court that you will reach this point later in argument. Answer each question immediately. If you must lay a foundation or give a background for your answer, explain this to the court, and then state your answer. After giving the answer you may proceed to state the basis for your answer.

7. *Read sparingly and only from necessity; rehearse.* Eye to eye contact with the listener is as necessary in appellate argument as it is in presenting a case to the jury. Just as you would not read your final argument to the jury, so you do not read your oral argument to the court of appeals. If you have confidence to address the court only by

reading to it, you really should not argue there. This is not to say that you must approach the appellate bench without any notes. A brief outline which will serve as a check list may be a valuable tool and a great aid in confidence. During oral argument avoid reading from the brief if possible. Never read long quotations. Assume that all judges can read, and understand that reading long quotations and reciting endless citations during argument can only lead to disinterest and bordeom.

Do not think it beneath you to rehearse for an argument. Great musicians rehearse even for their one hundredth performance of the same piece although guided by a score. Argue before a colleague. Try out different approaches. Thrash out every point.

8. *Avoid personalities.* A true professional concentrates on the issues. Treat each of the appellate judges with the courtesy to which he is entitled. Show favor toward none. Do not indulge in personal criticism of the court below or of your adversary. Such an approach will divert the court's attention from the focal point and may serve to prejudice the court against you.

9. *Know your record from cover to cover.* In the appellate court you have reached a point in the litigation where you can no longer hope to make up for lack of preparation by luck or mental agility. No unexpected surprises should be encountered; the field tactics of the trial table will no longer serve. A complete and comprehensive knowledge of the entire record is imperative. At any moment you may be called upon to correct some misstatement of your adversary or to answer a question from the bench. If you are able to answer questions by referring to the record the court will be impressed. Many otherwise admirable arguments have been destroyed because of counsel's inability to make just such a response.

10. *Sit down.* After you have made one point move on quickly to the next. When your final point has been argued, sit down. Quality of argument is not measured by length. The mere fact that you have been allotted one hour does not constitute a contract with the court to argue for that length of time.

REPLY AND REBUTTAL

If you represent the appellant, and if the court rules do not expressly provide for reply argument, request permission of the court at the outset of your argument to reserve a period of time for the purpose of reply. Whether you are the appellant preparing for your reply argument or the appellee preparing to respond to the argument of the appellant make careful notes of all questions the judges ask your adversary. These may then be answered during your argument in such a manner as to benefit your version of the case. Also note inaccuracies in the argument of your adversary and point them out when your turn comes.

Effective appellate advocacy is not shrouded in mystery any more than basic trial advocacy is. You can prepare and win your case on appeal—in fact, you often *must*. The responsibility of a lawyer runs clearly and with increasing importance from interview to appeal, for it is only after appeal that it can truly be said that a verdict is final.

ANNOTATIONS

Am Jur Trials

Appeal in federal courts, scope of review, 3 AJT 595-598.

Appeal, factors in forum choice, scope of review, 3 AJT 595-598.

Appeal in workmen's compensation claim, 10 AJT 592, 594-603.

Selected Bibliographies

LEGAL

General

Am. Jur. Trials. San Francisco: Bancroft-Whitney Co.; Rochester, N.Y.: The Lawyers Co-operative Publishing Co., 1964.

Appleman, John Alan. *Cross-Examination.* Vienna, Va.: Coiner Publishing Co., 1963.

Averbach, Albert. *Handling Accident Cases.* 7 vol. Rochester, N.Y.: The Lawyer's Co-operative Publishing Co., 1973.

Baldwin, Scott; Hare, Francis, Jr.; and McGovern, Francis. *Preparation of a Product Liability Case.* Boston: Little, Brown & Co., 1981.

Beasley, James E. *Products Liability and the Unreasonably Dangerous Requirement.* Philadelphia: ALI-ABA, 1981.

Belli, Melvin M., *Modern Trials.* Indianapolis: The Bobbs-Merrill Co., Inc., 1954; abridged edition, 1963.

Broder, Aaron J. *Trial Handbook for New York Lawyers.* Rochester, N.Y.: The Lawyers Co-operative Publishing Co., 1973.

Brosnahan, James J. *Trial Handbook for California Lawyers.* San Francisco: Bancroft-Whitney Co., 1974.

Dooley, James A. *Modern Tort Law: Liability & Litigation.* Chicago: Callaghan & Co., 1977.

DuCann, Richard. *The Art of the Advocate.* Baltimore: Penguin Books, 1964.

Freeman, Janet W., and Freeman, Fred. *Trial Handbook for New Jersey Lawyers.* Rochester, N.Y.: The Lawyers Co-operative Publishing Co., 1972.

Friche, Charles Williams. *Planning and Trying Cases.* 2nd ed. St. Paul: West Publishing Co., 1957.

Frost, A. Harold. *Preparation of a Negligence Case.* Rev. ed. New York: Practising Law Institute, 1967.

Frumer, Louis R., and Minzer, Marilyn K. *Personal Injury Annual.* New York: Matthew Bender, Annual Volumes.

Gair, Harry A., and Cutler, A.S. *Negligence Cases: Winning Strategy.* Englewood Cliffs, N.J.: Prentice-Hall, 1957.

Gazan, Simon N. *Encyclopedia of Trial Strategy and Tactics.* Englewood Cliffs, N.J.: Prentice-Hall, 1962.

Givens, Richard A. *Advocacy: The Art of Pleading a Cause.* Colorado Springs, Col.: Shepard's/McGraw-Hill, 1980.

Goldstein, Irving. *Trial Lawyers Guide.* Chicago: Callaghan Co., 1957 to present, Annual Volumes.

Hicks, William M. *Trial Handbook for Florida Lawyers.* Rochester, N.Y.: The Lawyers Co-operative Publishing Co., 1970.

Hunter, Robert S. *Federal Trial Handbook.* San Francisco: Bancroft-Whitney Co.; Rochester, N.Y.: The Lawyers Co-operative Publishing Co., 1974.

Hunter, Robert S. *Trial Handbook for Illinois Lawyers.* Rochester, N.Y.: The Lawyers Co-operative Publishing Co., 1972.

Jordan, Walter E. *Trial Handbook for Texas Lawyers.* San Francisco: Bancroft-Whitney Co., 1970.

Keeton, Robert E. *Trial Tactics and Methods.* New York: Prentice-Hall, 1954.

Kelner, Joseph. *Personal Injury—Successful Litigation Techniques.* New York: Matthew Bender, 1967.

Kleiner, Jack. *Trial Handbook for Georgia Lawyers.* Rochester, N.Y.: The Lawyers Co-operative Publishing Co., 1974.

Kreindler, Lee S. *Aviation Accident Law.* New York: Matthew Bender, 1963.

Markus, Richard M. *Trial Handbook for Ohio Lawyers.* Rochester: N.Y.: The Lawyers Co-operative Publishing Co., 1973.

McCarthy, John C. *Punitive Damages in Bad Faith Cases.* 2nd ed. Kentfield, Calif: Lawpress Corp., 1978.

McCullough, Ralph C., III, and Underwood, James L., rep. *Civil Trial Manual.* 2nd ed. Philadelphia: ALI-ABA, 1981.

Novok, Daniel A. *Defense of Personal Injury Actions.* Rev. ed. New York: Practising Law Institute, 1965.

Packel, Leonard, ed. *Trial Practice for the General Practitioner.* Philadelphia: ALI-ABA, 1980.

Philo, Harry M. *Trial Handbook for Michigan Lawyers.* Rochester, N.Y.: The Lawyers Co-operative Publishing Co., 1973.

Philo, Harry M. *Lawyers Desk Reference.* 7th Ed. San Francisco: Bancroft-Whitney Co.; Rochester, N.Y.: The Lawyers Co-operative Publishing Co., 1980.

Redden, Kenneth R. *Punitive Damages.* Charlottesville, Va.: Michie Co., 1980.

Restatement of the Law—Torts 2d. St. Paul, Minn.: American Law Institute, 1979.

Rheingold, Paul D. *Drug Litigation.* 3rd ed. New York: Practising Law Institute, 1981.

Schweitzer, Sydney C. *Cyclopedia of Trial Practice.* San Francisco: Bancroft-Whitney Co.; Rochester, N.Y.: The Lawyers Co-operative Publishing Co., 1972.

Sherman, Paul. *Products Liability.* Colorado Springs, Col.: Shepard's/McGraw-Hill, 1981.

Speiser, Stuart M. *Recovery for Wrongful Death.* 2nd ed. Rochester, N.Y.: The Lawyers Co-operative Publishing Co., 1979.

Stein, Jacob A. *Trial Handbook for Maryland Lawyers.* Rochester, N.Y.: The Lawyers Co-operative Publishing Co., 1972.

Stryker, Lloyd Paul. *The Art of Advocacy.* New York: Simon and Schuster, 1954.

Swartz, Edward M. *Hazardous Products Litigation.* San Francisco: Bancroft-Whitney Co.; Rochester, New York: The Lawyers Co-operative Publishing Co., 1973.

Swartz, Edward M. *Trial Handbook for Massachusetts Lawyers.* Rochester, N.Y.: The Lawyers Co-operative Publishing Co., 1972.

Weiss, Samuel. *How to Try a Case*. New York: Baker, Voorhis and Co., 1937.

Whaley, Douglas J. *Warranties and the Practitioner*. New York: Practising Law Institute, 1981.

Young, John Hardin; Kris, Michael E.; and Trainor, Helen C., ed. *Use of Computers in Litigation*. Chicago: American Bar Association, 1979.

Initial Interview, Investigation and Preparation

Abrahams. "Interviewing 'Small' Clients." 2 *Prac. Law.* 74 (1956).

Accident Prevention Manual. 5th ed. National Safety Council, 1964.

Appleman, John Alan. *Preparation & Trial*. Vienna, Va.: Coiner Publishing Co., 1967.

Averbach, Albert. *Handling Accident Cases*. San Francisco: Bancroft-Whitney Co.; Rochester, N.Y.: The Lawyers Cooperative Publishing Co., 1973.

Avrigian. "How to Handle a New Client: Some Comments on the Initial Interview." 21 *Prac. Law.* 23 (1975).

Baker, J. Stannard. *Traffic Accident Investigator's Manual for Police*. Evanston, Ill.: Northwestern University—Traffic Institute, 1964.

Baldwin, Scott; Hare, Francis, Jr.; and McGovern, Francis. *Preparation of a Products Liability Case*. Boston: Little, Brown & Co., 1981.

Barrett. "Initial Interview with a Divorce Client." 23 *Prac. Law.* 75 (1977).

Baum, David. *Art of Advocacy—Preparation of a Case*. Albany, N.Y.: Matthew Bender, 1981.

Binder, Donald A., and Price, Susan C. *Legal Interviewing and Counseling*. St. Paul, Minn.: West Publishing Co., 1977.

Biskind, Elliot L. *How to Prepare a Case for Trial*. New York: Prentice-Hall, 1954.

Bodin, Harry Sabboth. *Final Preparation for Trial*. New York: Practising Law Institute, 1956.

de Botts. "Clients' View of the Lawyer's Proper Role." 33 *Bus. Law.* 1177 (1979).

Brown, Louis M, and Daver, Edward A. *Planning by Lawyers*. Minneola, N.Y.: Foundation Press, 1978.

Comment. "Plaintiff's Advantageous Use of Discovery, Pretrial and Summary Judgment." 40 *Den. L. J.* 192 (1963).

Crawford and Morris. "Strategy of Discovery for the Defendant Physician and Hospital in Medical Malpractice Action." 24 *Med. Trial Tech. A.* 139 (1977).

Cullinan, Eustance. *Preparation for Trial of Civil Actions*. Philadelphia: ALI-ABA, 1956.

Davidson. "Art of Pre-Trial Discovery." 47 *Ill. B. J.* 918 (1959).

Deckelbaum. "The Fundamentals of Investigation." 63 *A.T.L.A. L. J.* 3 (1973).

Editors. "How to Handle a New Client: Questions and Answers." 22 *Prac. Law.* 65 (1976).

Fey and Goldberg. "Legal Interviewing with a Psychological Perspective: An Attorney's Handbook." 14 *Willamete L. J.* 217 (1978).

Fire Protection Handbook. 12th ed. Boston: National Fire Protection Association, 1962.

Forde. "Preparation of a Drug Caused Injury Case." 20 *Trial Law. Guide* 409 (1977).

Freeman, Harrop Arthur; Wiehofen, Henry; et al. *Clinical Law Training*. St. Paul, Minn.: West Publishing Co., 1972.

Fried. "Lawyers as a Friend: Moral Foundation of the Lawyer Client Relationship." 85 *Yale L. J.* 1060 (1976).

Friedenthal. "Discovery and Use of an Adverse Party: Expert Information." 14 *Stan. L. Rev.* 455 (1962).

Friedman. "Use of the Investigation in Medical Malpractice." *Personal Injury Ann.* 459 (1976).

Hartman. "The Ex Parte Interview of a Prospective Witness." 6 *Prac. Law.* 57 (1960).

Havener. "Observations Regarding Investigator and Preparation of Medical Malpractice Litigation." *Personal Injury Ann.* 228 (1978).

Holbrook. "The Work Product Doctrine in the State Courts." *Personal Injury Ann.* 775 (1964).

Hurowitz. "How to Handle a New Client: Preparation for the Initial Meeting." 21 *Prac. Law.* 11 (1975).

"Investigation Checklist in Personal Injury Case—A Form." 14 *Prac. Law.* 68 (1968).

Jones. "Do's and Don't's in the Preparation and Trial of a Lawsuit." 13 *Prac. Law.* 33 (1967).

Katz. "Negotiation and the Lawyer—Client Interview." 5 *U. Tol. L. Rev.* 282 (1974).

Kelner. "Clandestine Surveillance." *Personal Injury Ann.* 630 (1974).

Kennelly. "Pre-Trial Discovery." 77 *Trial Law. Guide* 458 (1977).

Kennelly. "Discovery as to Products, Premises Documents." (Pts. 1-2) 20 *Trial Law. Guide* 152, 205 (1976).

Kennelly. "Preparation for and Trial of a Complex Case Resulting in a $5,000,000 Verdict for a Single Death." (Pts. 1-5) 23 *Trial Law. Guide* 1, 153, 305, 443 (1979); 24 *Trial Law. Guide* 53 (1980).

Kirsch. "Auto Fuel Tank Fires: Pre-Discovery Techniques." *Personal Injury Ann.* 709 (1979).

Kittredge. "Guideposts for the Investigation of a Negligence Case." 19 *Prac. Law.* 55 (1973).

Kornblum. "Some Ethical and Legal Problems of the Investigation." 25 *Defense L. J.* 199 (1976).

Kramer. "Examination Before Trial in Medical Malpractice Cases." *Personal Injury Ann.* 205 (1974).

Lambert. "Investigatory Groundwork for Trial of Life and Health Cases: The Role of the Insurance Company's Inside Counsel." 14 *Forum* 121 (1978).

Lay. "A Trial Lawyer Speaks to the Investigators." 20 *Prac. Law.* 59 (1974).

Lay. "Plaintiff's Practical Use of Discovery Techniques." 9 *Prac. Law.* 43 (1963).

LeMarca and Mazour. "Suggested Investigation, Discovery and Trial Techniques in Railroad Crossing Cases from the Standpoint of the Plaintiff." 23 *Trial Law. Guide* 401 (1980).

Levy. "A Defense of Meaningful Pre-Trial Discovery." 19 *Forum* 781 (1979).

Magarick, Patrick. *Casualty Investigation Check List.* Brooklyn: Central Book Co., 1968.

Magarick, Pat. *Successful Handling of Casualty Claims.* New York: Clark-Boardman Co., 1974.

Manual of Accident Prevention in Construction. Washington: The Associated General Contractors of America, 1958.

Massery, Louis N., III, ed. *Psychology and Persuasion in Advocacy.*

Washington, D.C.: Association of Trial Lawyers of America, 1978.

"Medical Release Form." 22 *Prac. Law.* 35 (1976).

Moss. "The Initial Interview in a Domestic Relations Case." 22 *Prac. Law.* 59 (1975).

Mulhare. "How to Handle a New Client: A Psychodynamic Approach." 21 *Prac. Law.* 17 (1975).

Evidence Handbook. Evanston, Ill.: Northwestern University—Traffic Institute, 1965.

Oleck, Howard L. *Negligence Investigation Manual.* Brooklyn: Central Book Co., 1968.

Peskin. "Attorney-Client Interview: Strategy and Tactics." 14 *Trial* 43 (July, 1978).

Preiser. "Crucial Technique: The Intitial Client Interview in a Personal Injury Case." 15 *Trial* 18 (December, 1979).

Preiser, Stanley C. *Preparation and Trial of a Neck and Back Sprain Case.* Belleville, Ill.: Trial Lawyers Service Co., 1966.

Prinn. "Clients as People." 2 *Student L. J.* 3 (1957).

Redmont. "Attorney Personality and Some Psychological Aspects of Legal Consultation." 109 *U. Pa. L. Rev.* 972 (1961).

Royal, Robert F., and Schutt, Steven R. *The Gentle Art of Interviewing and Interrogation.* Englewood Cliffs, N.J.: Prentice-Hall, 1976.

Safety Guide for Unions. Chicago: National Safety Council, 1962.

Savitz. "How to Handle a New Client: The Initital Interview with a Business Client." 21 *Prac. Law.* 11 (1975).

Saxe. "Attorney-Client Relationship: A Psychoanalytic Overview." 9 *New Eng. L. Rev.* 395 (1974).

Schoenfield. "Interviewing and Counseling Clients in a Legal Setting." 11 *Akron L. Rev.* 313 (1972).

Schoenfield, Mark K., and Schoenfield, Barbara Pearlman. *Interviewing and Counseling.* Philadelphia: ALI-ABA, 1981.

Shaffer, Thomas L. *Legal Interviewing and Counseling in a Nutshell.* St. Paul, Minn.: West Publishing Co., 1976.

Shrager. "How to Handle a New Client: The Initial Interview in a Medical Negligence Case. 21 *Prac. Law.* 25 (1975).

Speiser, Stuart M. *Attorneys' Fees*. 2 vol. Rochester, N.Y.: The Lawyers Co-operative Publishing, Co.; San Francisco: Bancroft-Whitney Co., 1973.

Swartz. "Pre-Trial Examination of the Technical Expert Witness in a Products Liability Case." *Personal Injury Ann.* 473 (1977).

Symposium. "Attorney Client Relationship." 10 *Val. U. L. Rev.* 399 (1976).

Watson, Andrew S. *The Lawyer in the Interviewing and Counseling Process*. Indianapolis: Bobbs-Merrill, 1976.

Young. "Interviewing the Claimant in a Workman's Compensation Case." 17 *Prac. Law.* 85 (1971).

Zelko. "Speech in Lawyer-Client Relations." 22 *Rocky Mtn. L. Rev.* 261 (1950).

Discovery

Barron-Holtzoff, _____. *Federal Practice and Procedure, with Forms*. St. Paul: West Publishing Co., 1950.

Barthold, W. *Attorney's Guide to Effective Discovery Techniques*. Englewood Cliffs, N.J.: Prentice-Hall, 1975.

Bodin, Harry Sabboth. *Strategy and Techniques of Depositions*. New York: Practising Law Institute.

Brazil. "The Adversary Character of Civil Discovery: A Critique and Proposals for Change." 31 *Van. L. Rev.* 1295 (1978).

Chazen. "The Functions of Interrogatories and the Techniques of their Use." *Personal Injury Ann.* 685 (1961).

Cohen. "Discovery Techniques and Pitfalls in Product Liability Litigation." *Personal Injury Ann.* 598 (1978).

Cohn. "Federal Discovery: A Survey of Local Rules and Practices in View of Proposed Changes to the Federal Rules." 63 *Minn. L. Rev.* 253 (1979).

Comment. "Discovery of Government Documents and the Official Information Privilege." 76 *Col. L. Rev.* 142 (1976).

Comment. "Videotape Depositions." 9 *Cum. L. Rev.* 195 (1978).

Comment. "Refusals to Answer at Oral Deposition: A 'Relevant' Inquiry." 1979 *B.Y.U. L. Rev.* 407.

Comment. "Development in the Law: Discovery." 74 *Harv. L. Rev.* 940 (1961).

Crawford and Morris. "Strategy of Discovery for the Defendant Physician and Hospital in Medical Malpractice Actions." 24 *Med. Trial Tech. Q.* 139 (1977).

Cutner. "Discovery—Civil Litigation's Fading Light: A Lawyer Looks at the Federal Discovery Rules after Forty Years of Use." 52 *Temple L. Q.* 933 (1979).

Danner, Douglas. *Pattern Deposition Checklist.* San Francisco: Bancroft-Whitney Co.; Rochester, N.Y.: The Lawyers Co-operative Publishing Co., 1973.

Danner, Douglas. *Pattern Interragatories: Automobile.* San Francisco: Bancroft-Whitney Co.; Rochester, N.Y.: The Lawyers Co-operative Publishing Co., 1970.

Danner, Douglas. *Pattern Interrogatories: Basic Facts.* San Francisco: Bancroft-Whitney Co.; Rochester, N.Y.: The Lawyers Co-operative Publishing Co., 1970.

Danner, Douglas. *Pattern Interrogatories: Medical Malpractice.* San Francisco: Bancroft-Whitney Co.; Rochester, N.Y.: The Lawyers Co-operative Publishing Co., 1973.

Danner, Douglas. *Pattern Interrogatories: Premises.* San Francisco: Bancroft-Whitney Co.; Rochester, N.Y.: The Lawyers Co-operative Publishing Co., 1970.

Danner, Douglas. *Pattern Interrogatories: Products Liability.* San Francisco: Bancroft-Whitney Co.; Rochester, N.Y.: The Lawyers Co-operative Publishing Co., 1972.

Davidson, Louis G., and Patterson, Robert B. "Unique Sources of Discovery in Aircraft Accident Litigation." 13 *Forum* 119 (1977)

DeMay, John A. *The Plaintiff's Personal Injury Case: Its Preparation, Trial and Settlement.* Englewood Cliffs, N.J.: Prentice Hall, 1977.

Destrick. "Are Pre-Trial and Discovery Producing Mediocrity Among Lawyers?" 30 *Det. L.* 45 (1962).

Duier-Smith, Philip Sidney. *Federal Examination Before Trial and Disposition Practice at Home and Abroad.* New York: Baker, Voorhis, and Co., 1939.

Ebersole. "Discovery Problems: Is Help on the Way?" 66 *A.B.A. J.* 50 (1980).

Facher. "Deposition Practice and Tactics." 12 *Trial Law. Guide* 5 (1968).

Figg, McCullough, and Underwood. "Uses and Limitations of Some Discovery Devices." 20 *Prac. Law.* 65 (1974).

Forms of Discovery. Albany, N.Y.: Matthew Bender Co., 1967.

Fowler, James A. *Discovery Procedure Under Federal Rules.* New York: Practising Law Institute, 1955.

Frank. "Pre-Trial Conferences and Discovery." 1965 *Ins. L. J.* 661

Friedman. "Effective Use of Video-Tape Depositions." *Personal Injury Ann.* 656 (1978).

Frumer, Louis R., and Friedman, Melvin I. *Products Liability.* Vol. 3A, §47. New York: Matthew Bender, Co., 1979.

Glieberman. "Depositions and Divorce Actions." 12 *Prac. Law.* 53 (1966).

Goldman, Benjamin Paul. *Examination Before Trial in a State Court: Technique of Depositions.* New York: Practising Law Institute, 1960.

Goldman, Benjamin Paul. *Depositions and Other Disclosures.* New York: Practising Law Institute, 1966.

Goldsmith. "Deposition of Defendant Physician who Administered Contraindicated Drug in a Medical Malpractice Case." *Personal Injury Ann.* 483 (1973).

Hicks. "Pre-Trial Discovery in a Products Liability Case." *Personal Injury Ann.* 735 (1963).

Hofeld. "Value of Discovery in a Products Liabilŧty Case." *Personal Injury Ann.* 699 (1971).

Inker. "Discovery and Procedures Before Trial." 48 *Mass. L. Q.* 155 (1963).

James, Fleming. *Civil Procedure.* Boston: Little, Brown & Co. 1965.

Kamine. "The First Five Minutes of an Oral Civil Deposition." 18 *Prac. Law.* 45 (1972).

Kennelly. "Discovery as to Products, Premises, Documents." (Pts. 1-2) 20 *Trial Law. Guide* 152, 205 (1976).

Kennelly. "Pre-Trial Discovery." 21 *Trial Law. Guide* 458 (1977).

Kornblum. "The Oral Civil Deposition: Preparation and Examination Witnesses." 17 *Prac. Law* 11 (1971).

Kreindler. "Unique Aspects of Discovery in Aviation Cases Involving The Federal Tort Claims Act." 13 *Forum* 154 (1977).

Lacy. "Discovery Costs in State Court Litigation." 57 *Ore. L. Rev.* 289 (1978).

LeMarca and Mazour. "Suggested Investigation, Discovery and Trial Techniques in Railroad Crossing Cases—From the Standpoint of the Plaintiff." 23 *Trial Law. Guide* 401 (1980).

Leval. "Discovery of Experts Under the Federal Rules." 3 *Litigation* 16 (Fall, 1976).

Levy. "A Defense of Meaningful Pre-Trial Discovery." 14 *Forum* 781 (1979).

Liman. "The Question of Discovery vs. The Quality of Justice: More is Less." 4 *Litigation* 8 (Fall, 1977).

Long. "Discovery and Experts under the Federal Rules of Civil Procedure." 38 *F.R.D.* 111 (1965).

Mazaroff. "Surviving the Avalanche: Defendant's Discovery in Title VII Litigation." 4 *Litigation* 14 (Fall, 1977).

Miller. "Videotaping the Oral Deposition." 18 *Prac. Law* 45 (1972).

Moore, James William. *Moore's Federal Practice.* Albany, N.Y.: Matthew Bender Co., 1968.

Moore. "Rules and Techniques of Discovery in Civil Litigation Under C.P.L.R. 50 *N.Y.S.D. J.* 568 (1978).

Morris. "Strategy of Discovery for the Defendant Physician and Hospital in Medical Malpractice Action." *Personal Injury Ann.* 393 (1971).

Morrison. "Production of Hospital Records." 2 *Advocates Q.* 193 (1980).

Murphy. "Formal Pre-Trial Investigation." 12 *Mil. L. Rev.* 1 (1961).

North. "Controlling the Deposition: Winning Your Case Before Trial." *Personal Injury Ann.* 799 (1978).

Note. "Discovery Sanctions Under the Federal Rules of Civil Procedure: A Goal Oriented Mission for Rule 37." 29 *Case W. Res. L. Rev.* 603 (1979).

Pangia. "Unique Aspects of Discovery in Aviation Cases Under the Federal Tort Claims Act." 13 *Forum* 169 (1972).

Pretrial Tactics and Techniques in Personal Injury Litigation. New York: Practising Law Institute, 1980.

Ratner. "Plaintiff's Attorney's How's and Why's of Plaintiff's Deposition." 9 *Prac. Law.* 63 (1963).

Rheingold. "Deposition by Plaintiff of Inserting Doctor Defendant in Dalkon Shield Case." *Personal Injury Ann.* 421 (1976).

Rheingold. "Tackling Corporate Defendants In Products Cases." 1 *J. Products Liability* 33 (1977).

Schmertz. "Oral Deposition: The Low Income Litigant and the Federal Rules." 54 *Va. L. Rev.* 391 (1968).

Schoone and Miner, "The Effective Use of Written Interrogatories." *Personal Injury Ann.* 533 (1977).

Schreiber, Sol, and Rheingold, Paul. *Products Liability.* §10, New York: Practicing Law Institute, 1967.

Strodel. "A Plaintiff's Lawyer Looks at the Morass." *Personal Injury Ann.* 245 (1977).

Swartz, Edward M. *Hazardous Products Litigation.* Ch. 6. New York: The Lawyers Co-operative Publishing Co., 1973.

Swartz. "Pre-Trial Examination of the Technical Expert Witness in a Products Liability Case." *Personal Injury Ann.* 473 (1977).

Sylvan and Pegalis. "Pre-Trial Deposition of Defendant in Medical Malpractice Action Involving Radial Nerve Injury." *Personal Injury Ann.* 559 (1976).

Thompson. "How to Use Written Interrogatories Effectively." 16 *Prac. Law.* 81 (1970).

Von Kalinowski. "Use of Discovery Against the Expert Witness." 40 *F.R.D.* 45 (1966).

Wolfstone. "Deposing or Causing to Be Deposed the Physical Therapist as an Aid for Settlement or for Use in Trial." *Personal Injury Ann.* 15 (1974).

Wright, Charles Alan, and Miller, Arthur R. *Federal Practice and Procedure: Civil.* St. Paul, Minn.: West Publishing Co., 1972.

Settlement

Appleman. "Valuation and Negotiation." *Personal Injury Ann.* 705 (1967).

Baer, Harold, and Broder, Aaron J. *How to Prepare and Negotiate Cases for Settlement.* Englewood Cliffs, N.J.: Prentice Hall, 1967.

Chapman. "Insurance Companies Liabilities in Respect to Settlement." 19 *Trial Law. Guide* 424 (1976).

Edwards, Mary Frances, ed. *Settlement and Plea Bargaining.* Washington, D.C.: Association of Trial Lawyers of America Education Fund, 1981.

Fuchsberg. "Realistic Settlement Techniques." 1 *Trial Law. Q.* 22 (1964).

Griffith. "Contribution, Indemnity, Settlements and Releases." 24 *Vill. L. Rev.* 494 (1979).

Groce. "Preparation by Defendant for Settlement or Trial. 7 *U. Fla. L. Rev.* 1 (1954).

Hermann, Philip. *Better Settlement Through Leverage.* Rochester, N.Y.: The Lawyers Co-operative Publishing Co., 1967.

Hornwood, Sanford W. *Systematic Settlements.* San Francisco: Bancroft-Whitney Co.; Rochester, N.Y.: The Lawyers Co-operative Publishing Co., 1972.

Jeans. "Settlement of Personal Injury Claims." 37 *J.B.A. Kan.* 79 (1968).

Kelner. "Techniques of Settlement." *Personal Injury Ann.* 506 (1966).

McConnell. "Settlement Negotiations." 11 *Prac. Law.* 39 (1965).

Perdue. "Is Your Case Worth Pursuing?" 85 *Case Comm.* 31 (1980).

Pretzel. "The Economics of Trial versus Settlement." 65 *Ins. L. J.* 453 (1965).

Sindell, Joseph M. and David I. *Let's Talk Settlement.* Tucson, Ariz.: Lawyers and Judges Publishing Co., 1962.

Tinsman. "What's it Really Worth? Evaluating Annuities for Settlement Purposes." 14 *Trial* 30 (September, 1978).

Wallach. "Settlement in a Personal Injury Case." *Personal Injury Ann.* 779 (1979).

Waltz and Huston. "The Rules of Evidence in Settlement." 5 *Litigation* 11 (Fall, 1978).

Whitehead, Kreindler, "Evaluation of Aviation Cases for Settlement Trial," 28 *Tenn. L. Rev.* 230 (1961).

Pretrial Motions

Adams. "Effectiveness of Pretrial Conference Under New Rules of Federal Civil Procedure." 49 *Ky. L. J.* 98 (1959).

Berman. "Pretrial Aspects of a Small Antitrust Case." 45 *Brooklyn L. Rev.* 245 (1979).

Comment. "Use of Motions in Limine in Civil Proceedings." 45 *Mo. L. Rev.* 130 (1980).

Ellis. "The Motion in Limine." 43 *Tex. B. J.* 141 (1980).

Faruki. "The Practical Use of Motions to Structure a Complex Civil Case." 41 *Ohio St. L. J.* 107 (1980).

Hatcher. "Issues and Pretrial Procedure." 26 *J.B.A. Kan.* 275 (1957).

Laycock. "Dispositive Pretrial Motions in Illinois." 9 *Loy. Chi. L. J.* 823 (1978).

LaMarca and Mazour. "Suggested Investigation, Discovery and Trial Techniques in Railroad Crossing Cases—from the Standpoint of Plaintiff." 23 *Trial Law. Guide* 401 (1980).

Margolis. "A Uniform Motion for Disclosure in Negligence Cases." *Personal Injury Ann.* 707 (1963).

Note. "Suggested Pretrial Checklist." 28 *Utah B. Bull.* (1970).

Pretrial Tactics and Techniques in Personal Injury Litigation. New York: Practising Law Insitute, 1980.

Richardson. "Use of Motions in Limine in Civil Proceedings." 45 *Mo. L. Rev.* 130 (1980).

Sides. "Pretrial Conference and Order—Ready on the Firing Line!" 9 *Mem. St. U. L. Rev.* 387 (1978).

Thompson. "Coping with Continuances." 21 *Prac. Law.* 73 (1975).

Traster. "Protecting Your Client with the Motion In Limine." 22 *Trial Law. Guide* 147 (1978).

Vetter. "Pretrial." 10 *Prac. Law.* 23 (1964).

Zammit. "Trial Brief and Trial Memorandum." 24 *Prac. Law.* 73 (1978).

Voir Dire and Jury Selection

Appelman. "Selection of the Jury." 12 *Trial Law. Guide* 33 (1968).

Appleman. "Jury Psychology." *Personal Injury Ann.* 873 (1961).

Atkins. "Jury Voir Dire: The Judge's Perspective." 2 *Litigation* 19 (Winter, 1976).

Avent. "Probing for Jury Bias Against Rendering an Adequate Award." *Personal Injury Ann.* 907 (1961).

Bodin, Harry Sabboth. *Opening The Trial.* New York: Practising Law Institute, 1953.

Bodin, Harry Sabboth, *Selecting a Jury.* New York: Practising Law Institute, 1966.

Broder. "Juror's Messages." *Personal Injury Ann.* 613 (1979).

Brown. "A Juryman's View." 12 *Trial Law. Guide* 93 (1968).

Bryan, William Joseph. *The Chosen Ones.* New York: Vantage Press, 1971.

Cartwright. "Jury Selection." 13 *Trial* 28 (December, 1977).

Comment. "Remarriage and Wrongful Death: A Model for Voir Dire Examiantions." 52 *Ind. L. J.* 281 (1976).

Comment. "A New Standard for Peremptory Challenges." 32 *Stan. L. Rev.* 189 (1979).

Crump. "Attorney's Goals and Tactics in Voir Dire Examination." 43 *Tex. B. J.* 244 (1980).

Discussion. "Voir Dire: Confession and Comment." 47 *Denver L. J.* 465 (1970).

Dorf. "Juror Body Language." 8 *Md. L. Forum* 148 (1979).

Estes. "The Psychology of Jury Selection." *Personal Jury Annual* 551 (1978).

Frates and Greer. "Jury Voir Dire: The Lawyer's Perspective." 2 *Litigation* 17 (Winter, 1976).

Gaba. "Jury Voir Dire." 48 *U. Colo. L. Rev.* 525 (1977).

Hare. "Voir Dire and Jury Selection." 29 *Ala. Law.* 160 (1968).

Hermann. "Occupations of Jurors as an Influence on . . ." 5 *Forum* 150 (1970).

Holdaway. "Voir Dire." 40 *Mil. L. Rev.* 1 (1968).

Jennings. "What Goes on in the Jury Room." 30 *Ins. Counsel J.* 279 (1963).

Jordan, Walter E. *Jury Selection.* Colorado Springs, Col.: Shepard's/ McGraw-Hill, 1980.

Kallen. "Peremptory Challenges Based Upon Juror Background." 13 *Trial Law. Guide* 37 (1969).

Kramer. "The Psychology of a Jury Trial." 16 *Prac. Law.* 61 (1970).

Kalven, Harry, Jr., and Zeisel, Hans. *The American Jury.* Boston: Brown, Little & Co., 1966.

Linquist. "Analysis of Juror Selection Process in United States District Courts." 41 *Temp. L. Q.* 32 (1967).

McLaughlin. "How to Read a Juror." *Personal Injury Ann.* 623 (1979).

Mills and Bohannon. "Juror Characterics: To What Extent Are They Related to Jury Verdicts." 64 *Judicature* 22 (1980).

Moore and Wood. "The Use of Handwriting Analysis in Jury Selection." 85 *Case and Comm.* 38 (1980).

The National Jury Project. *Jury Work: Systematic Techniques; A Manual for Lawyers, Legal Workers and Social Scientists.* Berkley, Cal.: The Project, 1979.

Note. "Voir Dire." 27 *Stan. L. Rev.* 1493 (1975).

Note. "Voir Dire Limitations as a Means of Protecting Jurors' Safety and Privacy." 93 *Harv. L. Rev.* 782 (1980).

Panel Discussion. "Trial Tactics Committee Panel on Prejudice of Jurors." 18 *Fed. Ins. Counsel Q.* 47 (1967).

Peskin. "Non-Verbal Communication in the Courtroom." 3 *Trial Dipl. J.* 8 (1980).

Raggio. "How to Produce Your Own Juror Information Slide Show." 43 *Tex. B. J.* 25 (1980).

Scott. "Peremptory Challenges of a Cognizable Group." 44 *Mo. L. Rev.* 559 (1979).

Sheehan and Hollingsworth. "Allocation of Peremptory Challenges Among Multiple Parties." 10 *St. Mary's L. J.* 511 (1979).

Simon, R. *The Jury: Its Role in American Society.* Lexington, Mass.: D.C. Heath & Co., 1980.

Sorenson. "Jury Selection and the Behavorial Sciences." 2 *Litigation* 30 (Winter, 1976).

Sperlich. "And Then There Were Six: The Decline of the American Jury." 63 *Judicature* 262 (1980).

Staton. "Psychological Factors Influential in Jury Trials." 12 *Trial Law. Guide* 79 (1968).

Strong and Placzek. "Civil Voir Dire Notes of a Trial Attorney." 34 *Mo. B. J.* 111 (1978).

Suggs and Sales. "Using Communication Cues to Evaluate Prospective Jurors During the Voir Dire." 20 *Ariz. L. Rev.* 629 (1978).

Thompson. "Securing Adequate Voir Dire." 3 *Trial Dipl. J.* 40 (1980).

Opening Statement

Arthur. "How to Use Speech Principles to Persuade in Opening Statement." 24 *Trial Law. Guide* 1 (1980).

Begam. "Opening Statement: Some Psychological Considerations." 16 *Trial* 33 (July, 1980).

Bodin, Harry Sabboth. *Opening the Trial.* New York: Practising Law Institute, 1953.

Colley. "First Impressions." 3 *Litigation* 8 (Summer, 1977).

Hazel. "The Rule and Opening Statements in Civil Cases." 43 *Tex. B. J.* 637 (1980).

Kornblum. "The Voir Dire, Opening Statement and Closing Argument." 23 *Prac. Law.* 11 (1977).

Kramer. "Opening Statement in a Medical Malpractice Case." 13 *Trial Law. Q.* 5 (1979).

LaMarca. "Opening Statements: Effective Techniques." 21 *Trial Law. Guide* 446 (1980).

Marshall. "Telling Opening Statement." 19 *Prac. Law.* 22 (1973).

McElhaney. "Opening Statements." 2 *Litigation* 45 (Summer, 1976).

Miller. "Opening and Closing Statements from the Viewpoint of the Plaintiff's Attorney." 10 *Prac. Law.* 87 (1964).

Mitchell. "Voir Dire and Opening Statement: The Defense Takes the Offense." 26 *Fed. Ins. Counsel Q.* 135 (1976).

Rosen. "I Am a Doubting Thomas." *Personal Injury Ann.* 651 (1978).

Rucker. "The Important Role of the Opening Statement." *Personal Injury Ann.* 741 (1962).

Sacks. "Effective Use of Pleadings in Plaintiff's Opening Statement." 861 *Personal Injury Ann.* (1961).

Spatt. "Winning a Case on Opening Statement." 12 *Trial Law. Q.* 9 (1977).

Sumpter. "The Trial Lawyer's Greatest Tool: The Opening Statement." 12 *Trial L. Q.* 34 (1978).

Thomas. "Opening Statement and Closing Argument for Defense." 37 *J.B.A. Kan.* 309 (1968).

West and Brown. "Opening Statements and Closing Arguments." 8 *Md. L. Forum* 126 (1979).

Case in Chief

Advanced Negligence Trial Strategy. New York: Practising Law Institute, 1979.

Allen. "Defense of Medical Malpractice Actions." *Personal Injury Ann.* 621 (1976).

Appleman. "The Case in Chief." *Personal Injury Ann.* 601 (1966).

Averback, Albert. 7 vol. *Handling Accident Cases.* Rochester, N.Y.: The Lawyers Co-operative Publishing Co., 1973.

Begam. "Slip and Fall." *Personal Injury Ann.* (1967).

Best. "The Trial Lawyers' Role in the Sensational Case." 3 *Litigation* 22 (Spring, 1977).

Bodin, Harry Sabboth. *Final Preparation for Trial.* New York: Practising Law Institute, 1956.

Bodin, Harry Sabboth. *Marshalling the Evidence.* New York: Practising Law Institute, 1966.

Brosnahan. "Are You Going Through Life Without a Trial Notebook?" 85 *Case Comm.* 9 (1980).

Bucholtz. "The Defendant's Medical Case: Preparation Presentation and Strategy." 16 *Prac. Law.* 50 (1970).

Busch, Francis Xavier. *Law and Tactics in Jury Trials.* Indianapolis: The Bobbs-Merrill Co., 1949.

Busch, Francis Xavier. *Law and Tactics in Jury Trials.* Enclyclopedia Edition. Indianapolis: The Bobbs-Merrill Company, 1959.

Bugliosi. "Trial Tactics in a Complex Case." 2 *Campbell L. Rev.* 93 (1980).

Cartwright. "Products Liability: Trial Tactics and Strategy." 16 *Trial* 38 (July, 1980).

Charfoos and Peters. "Techniques for Preparing Medical Proofs." *Personal Injury Ann.* 609 (1976).

Comment. "Trial Procedure and Examination of Witnesses." 21 *Loy. L. Rev.* 320 (1975).

Comment. "Implications of Bifurcation in the Ordinary Negligence Case." 26 *U. Pitts. L. Rev.* 99 (1964).

Cone, Al J., and Lawyer, Verne. *The Art of Persuasion in Litigation.* Dean-Hicks, 1966.

Cornelius, Asher Lynn. *Trial Tactics: A Book of Suggestions on Trial of Cases.* Albany, N.Y.: Matthew Bender, 1930.

Cross. "Issue Selection: When to Fight; When to Duck." 3 *Trial Dipl. J.* 10 (1980).

Frumer, Louis R. *Personal Injury: Actions, Defenses, Damages.* Albany, N.Y.: Matthew Bender, 1976.

Forde. "Preparation for a Drug Caused Injury Case." 20 *Trial Law. Guide* 409 (1977).

Gair, Harry A. *The Trial of a Negligence Action.* New York: Practising Law Institute, 1956.

Galatz. "Trial of a Products Liability Suit Involving Defective Chlorine Gas Cylinders." *Personal Injury Ann.* 814 (1979).

Gazan, Simon N. *Trial Tactics and Experiences.* Atlanta: Harrison Co., 1954.

Gelb. "A Method for Organizing Your Civil Litigation Files." 3 *Trial Dipl. J.* 36 (1980).

Gliebermann. "Some Hints on Preparing and Trying a Divorce Case." 45 *Chi. B. Rec.* 336 (1964).

Gouldin. "Civil Jury Trial: Your Opponent's Proof." 42 *N.Y.S. B. J.* 141 (1970).

Gouldin. "Civil Jury Trial: Your Proof." 42 *N.Y.S. B. J.* 52 (1970).

Green. "The Submission of Issues in Negligence Cases." *Personal Injury Ann.* 84 (1964).

Groce. "Preparation by Defendant for Settlement or Trial." 7 *U. Fla. L. Rev.* 1 (1954).

Havener. "Observations Regarding Investigation and Preparation of Medical Malpractice Litigation." *Personal Injury Ann.* 228 (1978).

Hill. "Preparation for Trial." 18 *Ala. Law.* 115 (1957).

Hogan. "Plaintiff's View: Trial of a Workman's Compensation Case." 19 *St. L. J.* 373 (1974).

Huff. "Defense Strategies with Comparative Negligence." 44 *Ins. Counsel J.* 124 (1977).

Jones. "Do's and Don't's in the Preparation and Trial of a Lawsuit." 13 *Prac. Law* 33 (1967).

Keeton, Robert. *Trial Tactics and Methods.* 2d ed. Boston: Little, Brown & Co., 1973.

Kelner, Joseph. *Personal Injury: Successful Litigation Techniques.* New York: Matthew Bender, 1970.

Kennelly. "Preparation for and Trial of a Complex Case Resulting in a $5,000,000 Verdict for a Single Death." (Pts. 1-5) 23 *Trial Law. Guide* 1, 153, 305, 443 (1979); 24 *Trial Law. Guide* 53 (1980).

Kramer, Charles, and Kramer, Daniel. *Evidence in Negligence Cases.* 7th ed. New York: Practising Law Institute, 1981.

Lake, Lewis W. *How to Win Law Suits Before Juries.* New York: Prentice-Hall, 1954.

Lawson. "Order of Presentation as a Factor in Jury Persuasion." 56 *Ky. L. J.* 523 (1967).

LaMarca and Mazour. "Suggested Investigation, Discovery and Trial Techniques in Railroad Crossing Cases—from the Standpoint of the Plaintiff." 23 *Trial Law. Guide* 401 (1980).

Lubet and Schoenfield. "Trial Preparation: A Systematic Approach." 12 *Trial Law. Q.* 16 (1978).

Luvera. "The Trial Notebook." 19 *Prac. Law.* 37. (1973).

Litvinoff. "Stipulations as to Liability and as to Damages." 52 *Tul. L. Rev.* 258 (1978).

McElhaney. "The Credibility of the Lawyer: Trial Notebook." 6 *Litigation* 53 (Spring, 1980).

Medical Malpractice: Trial Strategy and Techniques. New York: Practising Law Institute, 1979.

Miltz. "Analysis and Development of the Medical Malpractice Claim: The Use of the Hospital Record." *Personal Injury Ann.* 186 (1977).

Mirza. "Preparation and Trial of a Railroad Crossing Case." 17 *Prac. Law.* 79 (1971).

Murphy. "How to Win a Pedestrian's Case Without the Plaintiff and without Eyewitnesses." *Personal Injury Ann.* 670 (1966).

Nelson. "Comments on Defense Planning on Preparation in Product Liability Actions." 2 *Am. J. Trial Adv.* 1 (1978).

Perlman. "Use of Human Factors in a Product Liability Case." 2 *Am. J. Trial Adv.* 47 (1978).

Phelan and Falk. "Proving a Defect in a Commercial Products Liability Case." 24 *Trial Law. Guide* 10 (1980).

Preiser. "Final Trial File Preparation." *Personal Injury Ann.* 956 (1979).

Richey. "A Federal Trial Judges Reflections on the Preparation for and Trial of Civil Cases." 42 *Ind. L. J.* 111 (1966).

Shrager. "The Preparation and Trial of the Medical Malpractice Case." 3 *Trial Dipl. J.* 18 (1980).

Smith. "Circumventing the Locality Rule in Medical Malpractice Cases." *Personal Injury Ann.* 219 (1975).

Swartz, Edward M. *Hazardous Products Litigation.* Rochester, N.Y.: The Lawyer's Co-operative Publishing Co.; San Francisco: Bancroft-Whitney Co., 1973.

Schwartz, Louis E. *Trial of Automobile Accident Case.* New York: Matthew Bender Co., 1967.

Spellman, Howard Hilton. *How to Prove a Prima Facie Case*. 3rd ed. New York: Prentice-Hall, 1954.

Turner. "Systems Management and the Computer in Efficient and Effective Trial Preparation." 28 *Fed. Ins. Counsel Q.* 379 (1979).

White, Jeffrey Robert, ed. *The Trial Lawyer and the Federal Rules of Evidence*. Washington, D.C.: Association of Trial Lawyers of America Education Fund, 1980.

Wininger and Lee. "Breach of Warranty and Strict Liability—A Unified Appeal in the Preparation and Trial of a Product Liability Case." 3 *Am. J. Trial Adv.* 29 (1979).

Zubrensky. "Establishing Causal Relationship in a Claim for Occupational Cancer." 53 *Wis. B. Bull.* 8 (1980).

Witness Preparation

Ames. "Preparation of the Expert Witness." 13 *Trial* 20 (August, 1977).

Bodell. "Pointers for Witnesses." 5 *Trial* 33 (1969).

Bodner, Favretto, and Nitschke. "Panel Discussion on Preparation of Witnesses." 47 *A.B.A. Antitrust L. J.* 169 (1978).

Castle. "Selecting and Preparing the Expert Witnesses." 3 *Litigation* 28 (Winter, 1977).

Clay. "How to Educate Your Witness." 13 *Ky. S. B. J.* 73 (1949).

Delisle. "Witness: Competence and Credibility." 16 *Osgoode Hall L. J.* 337 (1978).

Dudnik. "Prepare Your Client for Direct Testimony." 6 *Clev. Mar. L. Rev.* 256 (1957).

Fleming and Meyer. "Demonstration: Preparation of a Witness to Testify." 47 *A.B.A. Antitrust L. J.* 151 (1978).

Goldstein, Irving; and Lane, Fred. *Goldstein Trial Technique* 2nd ed. Mundelein, Ill.: Callaghan & Co., 1969.

Gunn. "Witnesses." 48 *Miss. L. J.* 1059 (1977).

Hanley. "Working the Witness Puzzle." 3 *Litigation* 8 (Winter, 1977).

Herndon and Karl. "Demonstration: Preparation of a Witness to Testify." 4 *A.B.A. Antitrust L. J.* 123 (1978).

Hinshaw. "Warn the Witness." 37 *Ill. B. J.* 506 (1949).

Kelner. "Preparation of Plaintiff's Doctor for Trial." *Personal Injury Ann.* 225 (1961).

Klein. "Making the Most of Your Expert." 46 *Conn. B. J.* 483 (1972).

Kornblum. "The Oral Civil Deposition: Preparation and Examination of Witness." 17 *Prac. Law.* 11 (1971).

Ladd. "Witnesses." 10 *Rut. L. Rev.* 523 (1956).

Leonard. "The Preparation and Use of Witnesses." 16 *Prac. Law.* 43 (1970).

Matt and Nagurney. "Suggestions to Witnesses." 25 *Prac. Law.* 63 (1979).

Myers. "Preparation for Plaintiff's Expert for Cross Examination." *Personal Injury Ann.* 356 (1974).

Note. "Pleading and Practice—Examination Before Trial, Corporation as Person." 23 *Brooklyn L. Rev.* 324 (1957).

Ratner. "Instructions for Witnesses." 2 *Prac. Law.* 44 (1956).

Rosenberg. "Preparation of Witnesses and Conduct of Trial." 29 *Mich. B. J.* 14 (1950).

Summit. "The Witness Needs Help." 3 *Litigation* 14 (Winter, 1977).

Vogel. "Preparation of Witnesses for Trial." 19 *Ins. Counsel J.* 394 (1952).

Experts

Ames. "Preparation of an Expert Witness." 13 *Trial* 20 (August, 1977).

Arnold. "Expert Witness." 38 *Man. B. News* 330 (1972).

Arnold. "The Responsibilities of the Medical Expert." 26 *Med. Trial Tech. Q.* 126 (1979).

Bickley and Stern. "Direct Examination of Plaintiff's Doctor." *Personal Injury Ann.* 307 (1978).

Breslin and McMonigle. "The Use of Expert Testimony in Actions Against Attorneys." 47 *Ins. Counsel J.* 119 (1980).

Broder. "Direct and Cross Examination of Medical Expert Witnesses in a Medical Malpractice Case of Wrongful Death Resulting from Tuberculosis." *Personal Injury Ann.* 392 (1973).

Charfoos and Peters. "Working with Medical Experts in Personal Injury Cases." 22 *Prac. Law.* 77 (1976).

Clements. "Cross Examination in a Medical Products Liability Case for Defense." *Personal Injury Ann.* 405 (1977).

Comment. "Courtroom Qualification of Medical Witness." 6 *Trial* 59 (June/July, 1970).

Comment. "Compelling Experts to Testify." 44 *U. Chi. L. Rev.* 851 (1977).

Comment. "Contingent Fees for Expert Witnesses in Civil Litigation." 86 *Yale L. J.* 1680 (1976).

Comment. "Expert Witnesses." 24 *Baylor L. Rev.* 108 (1972).

Comment. "Expert Testimony on Eyewitness Perception." 82 *Dick. L. Rev.* 465 (1978).

Comment. "Why Not Contingent Fees for Expert Witnesses." 39 *U. Pitt. L. Rev.* 511 (1978).

Conason. "Medical Cross Examination: Refusal to Recognize Medical Authorities." *Personal Injury Ann.* 241 (1975).

Davies. "Finding an Expert Witness in the Sciences." *Personal Injury Ann.* 743 (1964).

Diamond and Louisell. "The Psychiatrist as Expert Witness." *Personal Injury Ann.* 176 (1966).

Dick. "Economist's Role in Trial of a Personal Injury Case." 18 *Prac. Law.* 57 (1972).

Donahes; Piehler; Twerski; and Weinstein. "The Technological Expert in Products Liability Litigation." *Personal Injury Ann.* 619 (1975).

Easton. "Accident Reconstruction Expert." 44 *Wisc. B. Bull.* 32 (1971).

Examination of Medical Experts. New York: Matthew Bender, 1968.

Foreman. "How to Choose and Use Plaintiff's Experts." 12 *Forum* 155 (1970).

Friedman. "Expert Testimony to Establish the Standard of Care in Medical Malpractice." 2 *Am. J. Trial Adv.* 213 (1979).

Friedman. "The Scientists as Expert Witness." 18 *Jurimetrics J.* 99 (1977).

Gerber. "Expert Medical Testimony and the Medical Expert." 5 *W. Res. L. Rev.* (1954.

Getman. "Expert Witnesses." 45 *Brooklyn L. Rev.* 319 (1979).

Getzoff. "Direct and Cross Examination of an Expert." 22 *Trial Law. Guide* 267 (1978).

Glaser. "Trial Techniques: Exploring the Qualifications of Medical Witnesses." *Personal Injury Ann.* 248 (1961).

Gots. "How Not to Alienate the Medical Expert." 13 *Trial* 56 (April, 1977).

Graham. "Impeaching the Professional Expert Witness by a Showing of Financial Interest." 53 *Ind. L. J.* 35 (1977).

Green and Smith. "Selection and Use of Experts by Aviation Defense Attorney." 12 *Forum* 162 (1976).

Habush, Robert. *Art of Advocacy—Cross-Examination of Non-Medical Experts.* Albany, N.Y.: Matthew Bender, 1981.

Hammon. "Lawyer and the Expert." 54 *A.B.A. J.* 583 (1968).

Hare, Jr. "Challenging the Design of a Product; Direct Examination of an Expert on Product Development Management." *Personal Injury Ann.* 920 (1978).

Hoffman. "Preparation and Courtroom Presentation of the Accounting Part of the Case in Litigation." 34 *Chi. B. Res.* 67 (1952).

Holmes, Grace, ed. *Experts in Litigation.* Ann Arbor, Mich.: Michigan Institute of CLE, 1973.

Houts. "Examination and Cross Examination of the Photographic Expert." *Personal Injury Ann.* 849 (1967).

Imwinkelreid, Edward J., ed. *Scientific and Expert Evidence.* Rev. ed. New York: Practising Law Institute, 1981.

Institute on Continuing Education of the Illinois Bar. "Expert Testimony: Reconstruction of Automobile Collision." 12 *Trial Law. Guide* 45 (1968).

Jacobson and Slawkowski. "Defendant-Doctor as Plaintiff Expert." 27 *Fed. Ins. Counsel Q.* 245 (1977).

Kelly. "Direct Examination of Medical Experts in Personal Injury Actions." 6 *Law Notes* 87 (1970).

Kelner. "On Expert Testimony." 51 *N.Y.S. B. J.* 182 (1979).

Kelner. "Expert Testimony of Metallurgist to Establish Improper Design of Scaffold Brackets." *Personal Injury Ann.* 839 (1967).

Klein. "Making the Most of Your Expert." 46 *Conn. B. J.* 483 (1972).

Kornblum. "The Expert as Witness and Consultant." 20 *Prac. Law.* 13 (1974).

Kramer. "Cross Examination of Defendant's Expert in a Malpractice Case Involving an Intravenous Pyelogram." *Personal Injury Ann.* 209 (1978).

Kramer. "Cross Examination of the Medical Expert." 13 *Trial* 26 (December, 1977).

Kramer. "Sample Cross Examination of Defendant's Doctor." 17 *Prac. Law.* 73 (1971).

Lane. "Trial Technique: Cross Examination of the Medical Witness." 26 *Med. Trial Tech. Q.* 467 (1980).

Low. "The Police Officer as Witness in Motor Vehicle Case." 16 *Prac. Law.* 15 (1970).

Lower. "Psychologists as Expert Witnesses." 4 *Law and Psy. Rev.* 127 (1978).

Luvera. "How to Cross Examine the Defendant's Doctor in a "Minor" Whiplash Case." 5 *Trial Law. Q.* 36 (1968).

McCormick. "Direct Examination of Medical Experts in Actions for Death and Bodily Injuries." 12 *La. L. Rev.* 264 (1952).

McElhaney. "Direct Examination of Expert Witnesses." 3 *Litigation* 43 (Winter, 1977).

Meyer. "Expert Witness." 45 *St. Johns L. Rev.* 105 (1970).

Meyer. "Some Problems Concerning Expert Witnesses." 42 *St. Johns L. Rev.* 317 (1968).

Moller. "Cross Examination of Plaintiff's Medical Expert." 42 *Ins. Counsel J.* 198 (1975).

Moore. "Effective Utilization of a Questioned Document Examiner." 37 *Neb. L. Rev.* 552 (1958).

Note. "Direct Examination of Plaintiff's Doctor-Plastic Surgeon." 24 *Med. Trial Tech. Q.* 345 (1978).

Peters. "Selection and Use of Experts in Aviation Cases." 14 *Forum* 527 (1979).

Ricci. "Safety Engineering: Direct Expert Testimony." *Personal Injury Ann.* 763 (1979).

Rogers. "Cross Examining the Expert Witness." 21 *Defense L. J.* 491 (1972).

Schmertz. "Deposition of Automobile Manufacturers and Its Expert Witness." *Personal Injury Ann.* 589 (1975).

Schneider. "Cross-Examination of an Impartial Medical Expert." *Personal Injury Ann.* 317 (1973).

Schneider. "Cross Examination of a Medical Expert." 12 *Trial Law. Q.* 27 (1977).

Schrank. "Expanding the Use of the Mechanical Engineer in Product Cases." 3 *Trial Dipl. J.* 32 (1980).

Schwartz, Max, and Schwartz, Neil Forrest. *Engineering Evidence.* Colorado Springs, Col.: Shepard's/McGraw-Hill, 1981.

Shepard and Lefkofsky. "Role of Technical Expert as Consultant to Trial Counsel." 56 *Mich. S.B. J.* 1008 (1977).

Shubow. "Handling the Psychiatric Witness." 13 *Trial* 32 (July, 1977).

Swartz. "Cross-Examination of an Adverse Technical Expert in a Hazardous Products Case." *Personal Injury Ann.* 703 (1978).

Symposium. "Doctor in Construction: Expert Medical Testimony." 13 *Nd. L. Rev.* 283 (1953).

Thesiger. "Judge and the Expert Witness." 15 *Med. Sci. L.* 3 (1975).

Turner. "The Anatomy of a Psychiatrist Cross-Examination." *Personal Injury Ann.* 203 (1966).

Warshafsky. "Cross Examination of Technical Experts." 71 *Trial Dipl. J.* 20 (1978).

Weitz. "Making the Defendant Your Expert: A Case of Neurological Malpractice." 11 *Trial Law. Q.* 44 (1976).

Weston. "Getting the Evidence from the Expert Witness." 27 *Ohio B. J.* 527 (1954).

Direct Examination

Baldwin, Scott. *Art of Advocacy—Direct Examination.* Albany, N.Y.: Matthew Bender, 1981.

Burns. "Art and Technique of Examining Witnesses." (Pts.1-2). 31 *Mich. S.B. J.* 30, 37 (1952).

Busch. "Direct and Cross-Examination." 23 *Miss. L. J.* 321 (1952).

Comment. "Trial Procedure and Examination of Witnesses." 21 *Loy. L. Rev.* 320 (1975).

Denbeaux and Risinger. "Questioning Questions: Objectives in the Interrogation of Witnesses." 33 *Ark. L. Rev.* 439 (Winter, 1980).

Dooley. "Techniques of Direct and Cross Examination: Illustrative Testimony in Back Injury and Amputation Cases." *Personal Injury Ann.* 423 (1973).

Frumer and Biskind. "Some Simple Techniques for Estimate of Time Dist or Size." *Personal Injury Annual* 779 (1963).

Harrell. "Adverse Party as a Witness." 17 *Ark. L. Rev.* 1136 (1963).

Horne. "Presenting Directing Testimony in Writing." 3 *Litigation* 30 (Winter, 1977).

Jaworski. "Witnesses and Their Examinations." 29 *Ins. Counsel J.* 80 (1962).

Kalo. "Refreshing Recollection." 10 *Rut.-Camden L. J.* 233 (1979).

Kramer. "Direct Examination of Defendant's Nurse in a Malpractice Case." *Personal Injury Ann.* 193 (1975).

MacCrimmon. "Consistent Statements of a Witness." 17 *Osgoode Hall L. J.* 285 (1979).

Marshall, Marguis, and Oskamp. "Effects of Kind of Question and Atmosphere of Interrogation on Accuracy and Completeness of Testimony. 84 *Harv. L. Rev.* 1620 (1971).

McElhaney. "Rehabilitation." 4 *Litigation* 47 (Summer, 1978).

McElhaney. "The Language of Examination." 3 *Litigation* 45 (Spring, 1977).

Miller. "Our Witness: Testimony at Trial." 6 *Cap. U. L. Rev.* 555 (1977).

Moss. "Examination and Cross Examination of Witnesses." 5 *So. Tex. L. J.* 83 (1961).

Note. "Interactions Between Memory Refreshments Doctrine and Work Product Protection Under the Federal Rules." 88 *Yale L. J.* 390 (1978).

Olds. "Examining Witnesses in the Condemnation of Industrial Property." 17 *Prac. Law.* 71 (1971).

Philo and Steinberg. "Proving Causation in Products Liability Cases." 16 *Trial* 28 (July, 1980).

Robb. "Use of Lay Witnesses to Prove Medical Testimony." 8 *Prac. Law.* (1962).

Silver. "Yours Case May Rest with the 'Non-Expert'." 5 *Trial* 19 (December/January, 1969).

Swartz. "Techniques of Direct Examination." *Personal Injury Ann.* 690 (1974).

Thomas. "Seeing is Believing Most of the Time: Lay Observation v. Proving of Obvious." 12 *Tulsa L. J.* 487 (1977).

Tunkel. "Unsilencing Your Hostile Witness." 128 *Nev. L. J.* 478 (1978).

Vanoss. "The Potential of Children as Eyewitness: A Comparison of Children and Adults on Eyewitness Tasks." 3 *Law and Human Behavior* 295 (1980).

Weinstein. "Examination of Witnesses." 23 *Prac. Law.* 39 (1977).

Wolfstone. "Tips on Effective Direct Examination." *Personal Injury Ann.* 746 (1963).

Demonstrating Evidence

Belli. *Modern Trials.* Vol. 2, §152, et seq. Bobbs-Merrill Co., 1954.

Belli. "Demonstrative Evidence: Seeing Is Believing." 16 *Trial* 70 (July, 1980).

Belli. "Demonstrative Evidence." 10 *Wyo. L. J.* 15 (1955).

Bermat, et al. "Jury Responses to Pre-Recorded Videotape Trial Presentations in California and Ohio." 26 *Hasting L. J.* 975 (1975).

Birnbaum. "Admissibility of Police Records, Photographs and Movies." 8 *Trial Law. Q.* 48 (1972).

Blakey. "Substative Use of Prior Inconsistent Statements Under the Federal Rules of Evidence." 64 *Ky. L. J.* 3 (1975).

Boster, et al. "Videotape in the Courtroom." 14 *Trial* 49 (June, 1978).

Cleary, Edward W., ed. *McCormick's Handbook of the Law of Evidence.* 2d Ed. St. Paul, Minn.: West Publishing Co., 1972.

Comment. "The 1966 Freedom of Information Act." 44 *Wash L. Rev.* 641 (1969).

Comment. "Hospital Accident Reports: Admissibility and Privilege." 79 *Dick. L. Rev.* 493 (1975).

Comment. "Hearsay and Prior Inconsistent Statements." 18 *Duq. L. Rev.* 341 (1980).

Comment. "Lay Opinion in Civil Cases" "Speed of Motor Vehicles." 4 *Vill. L. Rev.* 245 (1959).

Comment. "Learned Treatises As Direct Evidence: The Alabama Experience." 1967 *Duke L. J.* 1168 (1967).

Comment. "The Opinion Rule as a Rule of Preference." 42 *Mo. L. Rev.* 409 (1979).

Comment. "Preconditions for Admission of Demonstrative Evidence." 61 *N.L. U.S. Rev.* 472 (1966).

Comment. "Taking Evidence Outside of the United States." 55 *B.U. L. Rev.* 368 (1975).

Courtney. "Effective Use of the Evidence Photographer." 17 *Prac. Law.* 35 (1971).

Delaney. "Evidentiary Issues in Products Liability Actions." *Personal Injury Annual* 873 (1976).

Dombroff. "Innovative Developments in Demonstrative Evidence Techniques and Associated Problems of Admissibility." 45 *J. Air Law* 139 (1979).

Fenwick and Davison. "Use of Computerized Business Records as Evidence." 19 *Jurimetrics J.* 9 (1978).

Fischnaller, Jr. "Technical Preparation and Exclusion of Photographic Evidence." 8 *Gonz. L. Rev.* 292 (1973).

Frumer and Biskind. "Some Observations on Mortality and Similar Tabbs and Actuarial Testimony." *Personal Injury Ann.* 796 (1963).

Frumer, Louis R., and Friedman, Melvin I. *Products Liability*. 5 vol. New York: Matthew Bender, 1981. (Supplemented Annually.)

Gamble. "Using Demonstrative Evidence." 26 *La. B. J.* 215 (1979).

Garland. "Hospital Records: Legal Requirements of Proof." 59 *Ill. B. J.* 312 (1970).

Glaser. "Federal Tax Returns as Evidence in Non-Tax Cases." *Personal Injury Ann.* 621 (1965).

Goldner-Mrovka. "Demonstrative Evidence and Audio-Visual Aids at Trial." 8 *Fla. L. Rev.* 185 (1955).

Greenstone and Novich. "Understanding Hospital Records." *Personal Injury Ann.* 285 (1966).

Hare. "Demonstrative Evidence." 28 *Ala. Law.* 193 (1966).

Hinshaw. "Use and Abuse of Demonstrative Evidence: The Art of Jury Persuasion." 40 *A.B.A. J.* 479 (1954).

Houts. "Impeaching the X-Ray." *Personal Injury Ann.* 221 (1974).

Houts. "Presenting the Medical Evidence: Three Different Cases of Pain and Soft Tissue Whiplash Injuries." 10 *Trauma* 85 (1968).

Houts. "A Courtroom Demonstration Backfires." *Personal Injury Ann.* 475 (1962).

Houts, Marshall. *Personal Injuries; Photographic Misinterpretation*. Albany, N.Y.: Matthew Bender, 1964.

Houts. "Presenting the Medical Evidence." 15 *Trauma* 21 (1971).

Jamison and Multz. "Courtroom Objectives." 9 *Colo. Law.* 1768 (1980).

Johnston and Caswell. "Testing for Blood Alcohol." *Personal Injury Ann.* 282 (1973).

Kalo. "Refreshing, Recollection: Problems with Laying a Foundation." 10 *Rut. Camden L. J.* 233 (1979).

Kaminsky. "State Evidentiary Privileges in Federal Civil Litigation." 43 *Fordham L. Rev.* 923 (1975).

Keiner. "The Use of Employment Records as Exhibits Upon Trial." *Personal Injury Ann.* 831 (1968).

Kennelly. "Use of Demonstrative Evidence—Including Models." 16 *Trial Law. Guide* 417 (1973).

Kornblum. "Videotape In Civil Cases." 24 *Hastings L. J.* 9 (1972).

Kramer, C. *Evidence in Negligence Cases.* New York: Practising Law Institute, 1977.

Ladd. "Demonstrative Evidence and Expert Opinion." 1956 *Wash. U. L. Q.* 1 (1956).

Lieberman. "Will the Courts Meet the Challenge of Technology?" 60 *Judicature* 84 (1976).

Locke. "The Use and Abuse of Demonstrative Evidence." *Personal Injury Ann.* 605 (1977).

Luvera. "Overhead Projector as Courtroom Tool." 16 *Prac. Law.* 605 (1977).

McCrystal and Kornblum. "The Pre-Recorded Videotape Trial: A Status Report." 25 *FIC Q.* 121 (1975).

McElhaney. "Foundations." 4 *Litigation* 43 (Spring, 1978).

McElhaney. "Making and Meeting Objections." 2 *Litigation* 43 (Fall, 1975).

McElhaney. "Steps in Introducing Exhibits." 1 *Litigation* 55 (Winter, 1975).

McElhaney. "An Outline on Hearsay." 4 *Litigation* 45 (Winter, 1978).

Marshall. "Evidence Psychology and the Trial." 63 *Col. L. Rev.* (1963).

Miller. "Government Records and Reports in Civil Litigation." *Personal Injury Ann.* 587 (1961).

Miller. "Videotape On Trial. 4 *Litigation* 27 (Spring, 1978).

Milwid. "The Misuse of Demonstrative Evidence." *Personal Injury Ann.* 322 (1961).

National Conference of Metropolitan State Courts. *The Use of Videotape Depositions in Judicial Proceedings.* (1974).

Note. "Admissibility of Hospital Records." 37 *Alb. L. R.* 579 (1973).

Note. "Dead Men Tell No Tales: Admissibility of Civil Depositions Upon Failure of Cross Examination." 65 *Va. L. Rev.* 153 (1979).

Packard. "Observations on Science of Document Examining." 1 *Adv. Q.* 426 (1978).

Perlman. "Demonstrative Evidence." 37 *Kan. S.B. J.* 5 (Jan. 1969).

Peters. "Videotaping of Survey for Use as Demonstrative Evidence in Malpractice Litigation." *Personal Injury Ann.* 346 (1979).

Philo. "Use of Safety Standards Codes and Practices in Tort Litigation." *Personal Injury Ann.* 752 (1966).

Pope and Hampton. "Presenting and Excluding Evidence." 9 *Tex. Tech. L. Rev.* 403 (1978).

Pope. "Evidentiary Aspects of Manufacturers Recommendations in Establishing Physicians Standard of Care." 31 *Ark. L. Rev.* 477 (1977).

Rein. "Medical Evidence: The Physician's Viewpoint." 25 *Defense L.J.* 105 (1976).

Rose. "Pragmatic Approach to Medical Evidence and the Lawsuit." 5 *U. Tol. L. Rev.* 237 (1974).

Rothstein. "Evidence Workshop: Handling Hearsay Under the Federal Rules of Evidence." 15 *Crim. L. Bul.* 62 (1979).

Schindler. "Opening the Door: The Doctrine of Curative Admissibility." 20 *Trial Law. Guide* 29 (1976).

Schuck. "Techniques of Proof of Complicated Scientific and Economic Facts." 40 *F.R.D.* 33 (1967).

Schwartz. "X-Ray Films." *Personal Injury Ann.* 260 (1965).

Scott, Charles Calvin. *Photographic Evidence.* 2nd ed. St. Paul, Minn.: West Publishing Co., 1969.

Shaffer. "Empirical Observations on the Law of Demonstrative Evidence." *Personal Injury Ann.* 553 (1969).

Shore and Coviello. "Medico-Legal Document: Admissibility and Validity." 7 *W. St. U. L. Rev.* 25 (1978).

Spangenburg. "The Use of Demonstrative Evidence." 21 *Ohio St. L. J.* (1978).

Spradling. "How to Organize and Present Statistical Evidence." 24 *Prac. Law.* 67 (1978).

Stewart. "Videotape: Use In Demonstrative Evidence." 21 *Def. L. J.* 253 (1973).

Stichter. "A Practitioner's Guide to the Use of Exhibits and Expert Testimony." 8 *Ohio St. L. J.* 295 (1942).

Symposium. "Law and Technology." 52 *Chi-Kent L. Rev.* 545 (1976).

Symposium. "The Use of Videotape in the Courtroom." *B.Y.U. L. Rev.* 327 (1975).

Wallace. "Demonstrative Evidence." 12 *Trial* 50 (October, 1976).

Weinstein, Jack B., and Berges, M. *Weinstein's Evidence and United States Court Rules.* New York: Matthew Bender, 1975.

Wenger. "Medical Records and How to Use Them." *Personal Injury Ann.* 228 (1968).

Wigmore, John Henry. *Evidence.* 3rd ed. 10 vol. Boston: Little, Brown & Co., 1940.

Wolfstone. "A Simple Way to Avoid Constant Objections That a Question Is Not Couched in Terms of Reasonable Medical Certainty or Probability." *Personal Injury Ann.* 226 (1968).

Younger. "Computer Printouts as Evidence." 2 *Litigation* 28 (Fall, 1975).

Cross-Examination

Appleman. "Cross Examination Relative to Hospital Duties." *Personal Injury Ann.* 212 (1963).

Bergman. "A Practical Approach to Cross Examination." 25 *U.C.L.A. L. Rev.* 547 (1978).

Binder, David F. *The Hearsay Handbook.* Colorado Springs, Col.: Shepard's/McGraw-Hill, 1975, supplemented annually.

Bodin, Harry Sabboth. *Principles of Cross-Examination.* New York: Practising Law Institute, 1962.

Broder. "Cross Examination of Defendant's Trial Counsel in a 'Bad Faith' Case." *Personal Injury Ann.* 827 (1976).

Burns. "The Art and Technique of Examining Witnesses." 31 *Mich. S.B. J.* 30 (1952).

Busch. "Direct and Cross-Examination." 23 *Miss. L. J.* 321 (1952).

Busch. "Direct and Cross-Examination of Witnesses." 6 *U. Fla. L. Rev.* 519 (1953).

Clark, John Kirkland. *Preparation of Cross-Examination.* New York: Practising Law Institute, 1953.

Comment. "Impeaching Through Evidence of Prior Conviction." 3 *Dayton L. Rev.* 459 (1978).

Comment. "Impeachment by Prior Criminal Conviction—Federal Rule of Evidence 609." 27 *Drake L. Rev.* 326 (1977).

Denbeaux. "Questioning Questions: Objections to Form in the Interrogation of Witnesses." 33 *Ark. L. Rev.* 439 (1980).

Ehrlich. "Lost Art of Cross-Examination." 5 *Lincoln L. Rev.* 85 (1970).

Empoch. "Examination of the Adversary's Witness." *Personal Injury Ann.* 727 (1961).

Frumer and Biskin. "Impeachment of Doctor Showing Prior Inconsistent Opinion." *Personal Injury Ann.* 275 (1963).

Gair. "Cross-Examination." 4 *Trial* 33 (October/November, 1968).

Gallagher, William Henley. *Technique of Cross-Examination.* New York: Practising Law Institute, 1953.

Garry. "Cross Examination and Trial Tactics." 11 *Lincoln L. Rev.* 77 (1979).

Gilbert. "Impeachment by Prior Convictions-Recent Development." 29 *Fed. Ins. Counsel Q.* 69 &1978).

Glosband and Niarchos "Ten Practical Tips on Cross Examination in Personal Injury Cases." *Personal Injury Ann.* 622 (1978).

Goff. "Arguing Questions: Counsel Protect Your Witness." 49 *Cal. S.B. J.* 1420 (1974).

Graham. "The Confrontation Clause, The Hearsay Rule, and the Forgetful Witness." 56 *Tex. L. Rev.* 151 (1978).

Habush, Robert. *Art of Advocacy—Cross Examination of Non-Medical Experts.* Albany, N.Y.: Matthew Bender, 1981.

Houghton. "Requiring Witnesses to Repeat Themselves." 47 *Tex. L. Rev.* 266 (1969).

Jeans. "Evidentiary Effects and Tactical Options in the Use of Out of Court Statements." 47 *U.M.K.C. L. Rev.* 145 (1978).

Ladd. "Witnesses." 10 *Rut. L. Rev.* 523 (1955).

McElhaney. "An Introduction to Cross-Examination." 2 *Litigation* 37 (Spring, 1976).

Mooney. "Testimony Changed—When the Plaintiff Changes His Testimony." *Ins. L. J.* 108 (1947).

Moss. "Examination and Cross Examination of Witnesses." 5 *So. Tex. L. J.* 83 (1978).

Palmer. "Cross-Examination Using Deposition at Trial." 3 *Litigation* 21 (Winter, 1977).

Posey. "Impeaching the Deceased Existed Utterance Declarant." 39 *La. L. Rev.* 1201 (1979).

Preiser. "Cross Examination of Lay Witnesses." 13 *Trial* 22 (December, 1977).

Short. "Cross Examination." 24 *Okla. L. Rev.* 53 (1971).

Stevenson, Noel C. *Successful Cross-Examination Strategy.* Englewood Cliffs, N.J.: Executive Reports Corp., 1980.

Shubow. "Handling the Psychiatric Witness." 13 *Trial* 32 (July, 1977).

Smith. "Effective Cross Examination of the Defendant's Medical Witness Can Save Your Verdict." *Personal Injury Ann.* 509 (1973).

Spence. "Cross Examination of an Anesthesiologist in an Anesthesia Death Case Demonstrating the Bias of the Witness." *Personal Injury Ann.* 378 (1974).

Tornquist. "Use and Opposition to the Use of the Prior Inconsistent Statement in California." 10 *Pac. L. J.* 1 (1979).

Warshafsky. "Psychology and Courtroom Strategy: Cross Examination." 51 *Wis. B. Bull.* 9 (1978).

Weinstein. "Examination of Witnesses." 23 *Prac. Law.* 30 (1977).

Wilson. "Cross-Examination." 3 *Trial Dipl. J.* 24 (1980).

Wimberly. "Delving Into the Details of Prior Convictions." 3 *La. L. Rev.* 899 (1978).

Younger. "Cicero on Cross-Examination." 3 *Litigation* 18 (Winter, 1977).

Zelenko. "Cross-Examination of Defendant's Examining Doctor like Alleges Litigation Neucosis." 6 *Trial Law Q.* 13 (1969).

Final Argument

Appleman. "Securing Substantial Verdicts Without the Per Diem Argument." *Personal Injury Ann.* 808 (1962).

Appleman. "Summation for the Plaintiff." *Personal Injury Ann.* 704 (1965).

Brock. "Closing Argument for the Defendant." 26 *Fed. Ins. Counsel Q.* 143 (1976).

Broder. "Dramatic Final Argument." *Personal Injury Ann.* 633 (1974).

Cartwright. "Winning Psychological Principle in Summation." 1 *Trial Dipl. J.* 31 (1978).

Comment. "Persuasion in the Courtroom." 10 *Duq. L. Rev.* 384 (1972).

Comment. "Scope of Permissible Comment in a Civil Action in Kentucky." 58 *Ky. L. J.* 512 (1970).

Corboy. "Closing Argument for Plaintiff Severely Injured When the Vehicle in Which He Was Sitting Was Struck by a Greyhound Bus." 6 *Trial Law. Guide* 97 (1962).

Conley, O'Barr, and Lind. "Power of Language: Presentational Style in the Courtroom." 1978 *Duke L. J.* 1375.

Crump. "Effective Jury Argument: The Organization." 43 *Tex. B. J.* 468 (1980).

Dempsey and Harrington. "Summation to the Jury." 37 *Tenn. L. Rev.* 196 (1969).

Fitzgerald and Hartnett. "Effective Oral Argument." 18 *Prac. Law* 51 (1972).

Ghiardi. "Argument to the Jury on Damages Questions Should be Limited." *Ins. L. J.* 600 (1965).

Groce. "Jury Argument." 31 *Ins. Counsel J.* 483 (1964).

Hare. "The Importance of Argument in Tort Cases: Observations of a Plaintiff's Lawyer." 33 *Ala. Law.* 187 (1972).

Head. "Arguing Damages to the Jury." 16 *Trial* 28 (February, 1980).

Hornsby. "Summation for the Plaintiff in a Fraud Case." 40 *Ala. Law.* 91 (1979).

Karcher. "Closing Argument." 15 *Prac. Law.* 49 (1969).

Keating. "Winning with Aristotle: The Four Kinds of Arguments." 52 *Calif. S.B. J.* 308 (1977).

Kelner. "Summation in Products Liability." *Personal Injury Ann.* 522 (1970).

Kelner. "Summation in Products Liability Cases." *Personal Injury Ann.* 876 (1964).

Kennelly. "Closing Argument." 6 *Trial Law. Guide* 95 (1962).

Kennelly. "Closing Argument for Plaintiff on FELA Action Involving Medical Causation." 7 *Trial Law. Guide* 295 (1963).

Kornblum. "Voir Dire, Opening and Closing." 23 *Prac. Law.* 11 (1977).

Koskoff. "The Language of Persuasion." *Personal Injury Ann.* 640 (1978).

Kramer. "Plaintiff's Summation in a Burn Case." *Personal Injury Ann.* 992 (1979).

Kramer. "Plaintiff's Summation in a Falling Tree Case." *Personal Injury Ann.* 803 (1976).

Lawson. "Experimental Research on the Organization of Persuasive Arguments." *Law. Soc. Order* 579 (1970).

Lefkowitz. "Summation in a Death Action." *Personal Injury Ann.* 939 (1976).

Levine, Moe. *Summations—The Best of Moe.* Belleville, Illinois: Trial Lawyers Service Co., 1976.

Lusk. "Argument of Counsel to Juries." 30 *Ala. Law.* 244 (1969).

McElhaney. "Analogies in Final Argument." 6 *Litigation* 37 (Winter, 1980).

Miller. "Opening and Closing Statements from the Viewpont of the Plaintiff's Attorney." *Personal Injury Annual* 694 (1965).

Note. "Jury Trials in Complex Litigation." 53 *St. John's Law Rev.* 751 (1979).

Note. "Trial-Argument of Counsel: Use of Formula not Based on Evidence." 64 W. Va. L. Rev. 454 (1962).

Perlman. "Summation." *Personal Injury Ann.* 632 (1979).

Powers. "The Closing Argument." 19 *Ark. L. Rev.* 58 (1965).

Rosen. "I Am a Doubting Thomas." *Personal Injury Ann.* 651 (1978).

Smith, Lawrence. *Art of Advocacy—Summation.* New York: Matthew Bender, 1978.

Spangenberg. "Basic Values and Techniques of Persuasion." 3 *Litigation* 13 (Summer, 1977).

Sperack. "Summation in a Head Injury Case." 6 *Trial L. Q.* 72 (1969).

Stein, Jacob A. *Closing Argument: The Art and the Law.* Wilmette, Ill: Callaghan & Co., 1979.

Thomas. "Opening Statements and Closing Arguments for Defense." 37 *J. B. Kan.* 309 (1968).

Vogel. Leslie H. *Final Argument.* Rev. ed. New York: Practising Law Institute, 1957.

Weitz. "Summation in a Contested Slip and Fall Case." 6 *Trial L. Q.* 11 (1969).

Weitz. "Summation in a Slip and Fall Case." *Personal Injury Ann.* 5727 (1970).

Wiener. "On the Improvement of the Oral Argument." 38 *N.Y.S. B. J.* 187 (1966).

Wildman. "Closing Argument for Defendant Manufactuerers Charged with Negligence and Breach of Warranty in the Manufacture of a Construction Hoist Which Broke While Carrying 19 Workmen." 7 *Trial Law. Guide* 47 (1963).

Wolfstone. "Plaintiff's Summation in a Medical Malpractice Case." *Personal Injury Ann.* 771 (1971).

Instructions to the Jury

Alexander, George J. *Jury Instructions on Medical Issues.* Indianapolis: The Allan Smith Co., 1966.

Blackmar. "Problems of Court and Counsel in Requests and Exceptions." 62 *F. R. D.* 251 (1974).

Brown. "Federal Special Verdicts." 44 *F. R. D.* 338 (1968).

Comment. "Jury Instruction on Tax Exempt Status of the Personal Injury." 33 *Ohio S. L. J.* 972 (1972).

Conason. "Jury Instructions: Protecting the Record." 7 *Trial Law Q.* 57 (1971).

Denton. "Informing a Jury of the Legal Effect of Its Answers." 22 *St. Marys L. J.* 1 (1970).

Graham. "Pattern Jury Instructions: The Prospect of Over or Under Compensation in Damage Awards for Personal Injuries." 28 *DePaul L. Rev.* 33 (1978).

McKenzie. "Pattern Jury Instruction." 36 *Ins. Counsel J.* 215 (1969).

Note. "Damages: Personal Injury Instruction to Jury on Federal Income Tax." 10 *Duq. L. Rev.* 700 (1972).

O'Mara. "Standard Jury Charges: Findings of Pilot Project." 43 *Penn. B. Q.* 166 (1972).

Spence. "Jury Instruction in Medical Malpractice Cases." *Personal Injury Ann.* 321 (1975).

Taylor, Buchanan, Pryor, and Strawn. "Avoiding the Legal Tower of Babel: A Case Study of Innovative Jury Instruction." 19 *Judges J.* 10 (1980).

Wagner, Ward, Jr., *Art of Advocacy—Jury Selection.* Albany, N.Y.: Matthew Bender, 1981.

Appeal

Appleman, John Alan. *Approved Appellate Briefs; Texts and Forms.* St. Paul, Minn.: West Publishing Co., 1958.

Appleman, John Alan. *Successful Appellate Techniques.* Indianapolis: The Bobbs-Merrill Co., 1953.

Appleman. "Winning the Appeal." *Personal Injury Ann.* 833 (1965).

Brumbaugh, Jesse Franklin. *Legal Reasoning and Briefing.* Indianapolis: The Bobbs-Merrill Co., 1917.

Carlson. "Impeaching Jury Verdicts." 2 *Litigation* 31 (Fall, 1975).

Comment. "Mention of Defendant's Liability Insurance in the Presence of a Jury." 56 *Neb. L. Rev.* 153 (1979).

Cooper, Frank E. *Effective Legal Writing.* Indianapolis: The Bobbs-Merrill Co., 1953.

Davis. "The Argument of an Appeal." 26 *A.B.A. J.* 895 (1940).

Emery, Clyde. *A Streamlined Briefing Technique.* San Francisco: Bancroft-Whitney, 1958.

Fontes, Miller, and Bender. "Deletion of Inadmissible Material from Courtroom Trials." 67 *Det. Col. L. Rev.* (1977).

Goodrich, Carson, and Davis. *A Case on Appeal—A Judge's View and a Lawyer's View.* Philadelphia: ALI-ABA, 1959.

Goodrich, Davis, and Carson. *A Case of Appeal: A Judge's View, The Argument of an Appeal, The Conduct of the Appeal—A Lawyer's View.* 4th ed. Philadelphia: ALI-ABA, 1967.

Harvard University—Board of Student Advisors. *Introduction to Advocacy: Brief Writing and Oral Argument.* 6th ed. Mineola, N.Y.: Foundation Press, Inc., 1970.

Hicks, Frederick Charles. *Materials and Methods of Legal Research.* 3rd ed. Rochester, N.Y.: The Lawyers Co-operative Publishing Co., 1942.

Horvitz. "Protecting Your Record on Appeal." 4 *Litigation* 34 (Winter, 1978).

Jackson. "Advocacy Before The Supreme Court: Suggestions for Effective Case Presentations." 36 A.B.A. J. 801 (1951).

Joiner, Charles W. *Trials and Appeals.* Englewood Cliffs, N.J.: Prentice-Hall, 1957.

Karlen, Delmar. *Appelate Courts in the United States and England.* New York: N.Y. University Press, 1962.

Kelsey. "Creating an Appellate Record Is Like Building a House; Before You Can Erect the Roof, You Have to Lay the Foundation." 3 *Fam. Advocacy* 2 (1980).

Littleton. "Advocacy and Brief Writing." *The Practical Lawyer* 41 (Dec. 1964).

Llewellyn, Karl Neckerson. *The Common Law Tradition: Deciding Appeals.* Boston: Little, Brown, 1960.

Palmer. "The Practical Way to Prepare a Case for an Appellate Court. 59 *W. Va. L. Rev.* 56 (1956).

Pound, Rosco. *Appellate Procedure in Civil Cases.* Boston: Little, Brown & Co., 1941.

Rall. "Preparing the Record on Appeal." 4 *Litigation* 37 (Winter, 1978).

Re, Edward Domenic. *Brief Writing and Oral Argument.* 2nd ed. New York: Oceana Publications, 1957.

Rutledge. "The Appellate Brief." 28 *A.B.A. J.* 251 (1942).

Schmertz. "Appeals in Multi-Party Cases." 12 *Trial Law. Q.* 30 (1978).

Schmertz. "Protecting the Record for Appeal." *Personal Injury Ann.* 901 (1976).

Shaffer. "Appellate Courts and Prejudiced Verdicts." *Personal Injury Ann.* 751 (1965).

Sokol, Ronald P. *Language and Litigation: A Portrait of Appellate Brief.* Charlottesville, Va.: Michie Co., 1967.

Steinheimer. "Winning On Appeal." 29 *Mich. S. B. J.* 15 (1950).

Stryker, Lloyd Paul. *The Art of Advocacy: Plea for the Renaissance of the Trial Lawyer.* New York: Simon & Schuster, 1954. Chapters XI, XII.

Sunderland, Edson Read. *Faces and Materials on Trial and Appellate Practice.* 2nd Ed. Chicago: Callaghan and Co., 1941.

Symposium. "Trial Without Error." 48 *Mass. L. Q.* 121 (1963).

Tittoni, Marie. *Suggestions on Brief Writing and Argument.* 2nd ed. Brooklyn, N.Y.: Foundation Press, 1954.

Waltz. "Offer of Proof." 53 *Chi. B. Rev.* 299 (1972).

Wolfstone. "Preserving Testimony in Hip Fracture Case Requiring Total Hip Replacement." *Personal Injury Ann.* 509 (1976).

Weihofen, Henry. *Legal Writing Style.* St. Paul, Minn.: West Publishing Co., 1961.

Wiener, Frederick Bernays. *Effective Appellate Advocacy.* New York: Prentice-Hall, 1950.

Wiener, Frederick Bernays. *Briefing and Arguing Federal Appeals.* Washington, D.C.: Bureau of National Affairs, 1961.

MEDICAL

Anatomy

Goss, Charles M. *Gray's Anatomy of the Human Body.* 29th ed. Philadelphia: Lea & Febiger, 1973.

Netter, Frank H. *The Ciba Collection of Medical Illustrations.* 7v. Summit, N.J.: Ciba Pharmaceutical, 1974.

Sobotta, Johannes, and Figge, Frank. *The Atlas of Human Anatomy.* 2 vol. Baltimore-Munich: Urban & Schwarzenberg, 1977.

Anesthesia

Collins, Vincent J. *Principles and Practice of Anesthesiology.* 5th ed. Philadelphia: Lea & Febiger, 1972.

Dripps, Robert D., et al. *Introduction to Anesthesia.* 5th ed. Philadelphia: W.B. Saunders, 1977.

Wylie, H.D., and Churchill-Davidson, H.D. *A Practice of Anaesthesia.* 4th ed. Philadelphia: W.B. Saunders, 1978.

Arthritis

Hollander, Joseph L. *Comroe's Arthritis and Allied Conditions: A Textbook of Rheumatology.* 9th ed. Philadelphia: Lea and Febiger, 1967.

Circulation

Allen, Edgar V.; Barker, Nelson W.; and Hines, Edgar A. *Peripheral Vascular Diseases.* 5th ed. Philadelphia: W.B. Saunders, 1962.

Cardiology

Burch, George E. *A Primer of Cardiology.* 4th ed. Philadelphia: Lea & Febiger, 1971.

Levine, Samuel A. *Clinical Heart Disease.* Philadelphia: W.B. Saunders, 1958.

Diagnosis

Conn, H.F.; Conn, R.B.; and Clohecy, R.J. *Current Diagnosis.* 6th ed. Philadelphia: W.B. Saunders, 1980.

Harvey, Abner M., et al. *Differential Diagnosis.* 3rd ed. Philadelphia: W.B. Saunders, 1979.

Lyght, Charles E. *The Merck Manual of Diagnosis and Therapy.* 13th ed. Rahway, N.J.: Merck, 1977.

MacBryde, Cyril Mitchell. *Signs and Symptoms.* 5th ed. Philadelphia: J.B. Lippincott, 1970.

Prior, John A., and Silberstein, Jack S. *Physical Diagnosis*. 5th ed. St. Louis: C.V. Mosby Company, 1977.

Todd, James; Sanford, Campbell; and Henry, Bernard J., ed. *Clinical Diagnosis and Management by Laboratory Methods*. 16th ed. Philadelphia: W.B. Saunders, 1979.

Dictionaries

Dorland's Illustated Medical Dictionary. 26th ed. Philadelphia: W.B. Saunders, 1981.

Schmidt's Attorney's Dictionary of Medicine. New York: Matthew Bender, 1979.

Stedman's Medical Dictionary Illustrated. 23rd ed. Baltimore: Williams & Wilkins Co., 1976.

Thomas, Clayton, ed. *Cyclopedic Medical Dictionary*. 13th ed. Philadelphia: F.A. Davis, 1977.

Gastroenterology

Bockus, Henry L. *Gastroenterology*. 2nd ed. 3 vol. Philadelphia: W.B. Saunders, 1963.

Paulson, Moses. *Gastroenterologic Medicine*. Philadelphia: Lea & Fehiger, 1969.

Sleisenger, Marvin H., and Fordtran, John S. *Gastrointestinal Disease*. 2nd ed. Philadelphia: W.B. Saunders, 1978.

Medicine

Beeson, Paul B., and McDermott, Walsh. *Cecil-Loeb Textbook of Medicine*. 15th ed. 2 vol. Philadelphia: W.B. Saunders, 1975.

Beeson, Paul B., et al. *Cecil Textbook of Medicine*. 15th ed. Philadelphia: W.B. Saunders, 1979.

Harrison, Tinsley Randolph, et al. *Harrison's Principles of Internal Medicine*. 9th ed. New York: McGraw-Hill, 1980.

Neurology

GENERAL:

Adams, Raymond D., and Victor, Maurice. *Principles of Neurology*. New York: McGraw-Hill, 1981.

Baker, Abe B., and Baker, L.H. *Clinical Neurology*. 3 vol. Hagerstown, Md.: Harper & Row, 1980.

Gilroy, John, and Meyer, John S. *Medical Neurology*. 3rd ed. New York: Macmillan Publishing Co., 1979.

Merritt, H. Houston. *A Textbook of Neurology*. 6th ed. Philadelphia: Lee & Febiger, 1979.

DIAGNOSIS:

Collins, R. Douglas. *Illustrated Manual of Neurologic Diagnosis*. Philadelphia: J.B. Lippincott Co., 1962.

DeJong, Russel N. *The Neurologic Examination*. 4th ed. Hagerstown, Md.: Harper and Row, 1979.

Mayo Clinic and Mayo Foundation. *Clinical Examinations in Neurology*. Philadelphia: W.B. Saunders Co., 1971.

EPILEPSY:

Boshes, Louis D., and Gibbs, Frederick A. *The Epilepsy Handbook*. 2nd ed. Springfield, Ill.: Charles C. Thomas Publisher, 1972.

Penfield, Wilder, and Jasper, Herbert. *Epilepsy and the Functional Anatomy of the Human Brain*. Boston: Little, Brown & Co., 1954.

NEUROANATOMY:

Chusid, Joseph G., and McDonald, Joseph John. *Correlative Neuroanatomy and Functional Neurology*. 16th ed. Los Angeles: Lange, 1976.

Truex, Raymond C., and Carpenter, Malcolm B. *Strong and Elwyn's Human Neuroanatomy*. 5th ed. Baltimore: Williams & Wilkins Co., 1961.

Brodal. *Neurological Anatomy in Relation to Clinical Medicine*. 2nd ed. New York: Oxford University Press, 1969.

NEUROPATHOLOGY:

Blackwood, W. *Greenfield's Neuropathology*. London: Edward Arnold Publishers, 1976.

NEUROSURGERY:

Coates, Col. John Boyd. *Neurological Surgery of Trauma.* 2 vol. Washington, D.C.: Office of the Surgeon General, Dept. of the Army, 1965.

Kahn, Edgar A., et al. *Correlative Neurosurgery.* 2nd ed. Springfield: Charles C. Thomas Publisher, 1969.

Krayenbuhl, H.; Maspes, P.E.; and Sweet, W.H. *Progress in Neurologic Surgery.* 3 vol. Chicago: Yearbook Medical Publishers, 1966.

Ransohoff, Joseph. *Modern Techniques in Surgery.* Mt. Kisco, N.Y.: Futura Publishing Company, 1979.

Youman, Julian R. *Neurological Surgery.* 3 vol. Philadelphia: W.B. Saunders Co., 1973.

Youman, Julian R. *Neurological Surgery.* 6 vol. Philadelphia: W.B. Saunders Co., 1981.

PEDIATRIC NEUROLOGY:

Farmer, Thomas W. *Pediatric Neurology.* Hagerstown, Md.: Harper & Row, 1975.

Ford, Frank R. *Diseases of the Nervous System in Infancy, Childhood and Adolescence.* 5th ed. Springfield: Charles C. Thomas, 1966.

Matson, Donald D. *Neurosurgery of Infancy and Childhood.* 2nd ed. Springfield: Charles C. Thomas, 1969.

Menkes, John H. *Textbook of Child Neurology.* 2nd ed. Philadelphia: Lea & Febiger, 1980.

Thompson, _____ and Green, _____. *Pediatric Neurology and Neurosurgery.* New York: Spectrum Publications, 1978.

Volpe, Joseph J. *Neurology of the Newborn.* Philadelphia: W.B. Saunders Co., 1981.

Obstetrics and Gynecology

Danforth, David N. *Obstetrics and Gynecology.* 3rd ed. Hagerstown, Md.: Harper & Row, 1977.

Falls, Frederick, and Holt, Charlott Sinclair. *Atlas of Obstetric Complications.* 2 vol. Philadelphia: J.B. Lippincott Co., 1961.

Greenhill, Jacob Pearl. *Obstetrics.* 12th ed. 3 vol. Philadelphia: W.B. Saunders Co., 1960.

Greenhill, Jacob Pearl, and Friedman, Emanuel A. *Biological Principles and Modern Practice of Obstetrics.* 1st ed. Philadelphia: W.B. Saunders Co., 1974.

Hawkins, Denis Frank. *Obstetric Therapeutics.* London: White Friars Press Ltd., 1974.

Myerscough, P.R. *Munro Ker's Operative Obstetrics.* Baltimore: Williams & Wilkins Co., 1977.

Novak, Edmund R., et al. *Novak's Textbook of Gynecology.* 10th ed. Baltimore: Williams & Wilkins Co., 1981.

Parsons, Langdon, and Sommers, Sheldon G. *Gynecology.* Philadelphia: W.B. Saunders Co., 1962.

Pritchard, Jack A., and MacDonald, Paul C. *Williams' Obstetrics.* 16th ed. New York: Appleton-Century-Crofts, 1980.

Quenan, John T. *Management of High-Risk Pregnancy.* Oratell, N.J.: Medical Economics Company, 1980.

Taylor, E. Stewart. *Beck's Obstetrical Practice & Fetal Medicine.* 10th ed. Baltimore: Williams and Wilkins Co., 1976.

Vietor, Diana. *Care of the Maternity Patient.* New York: McGraw-Hill, 1971.

Willson, James Robert; Reid, Carrington, Elsie Reid; and Beecham, Clayton T. *Obstetrics and Gynecology.* 6th ed. St. Louis: C.V. Mosby Co., 1979.

Oncology

Haskell, Charles M. *Cancer Treatment.* Philadelphia: W.B. Saunders Co., 1980.

Horton, John, and Hill, George J. *Clinical Oncology.* Philadelphia: W.B. Saunders Co., 1977.

Nealon, Thomas F. *Management of the Patient with Cancer.* 2nd ed. Philadelphia: W.B. Saunders Co., 1976.

Ophthalmology

Adler, Francis H. *Adler's Textbook of Ophthalmology.* 8th ed. Philadelphia: W.B. Saunders Co., 1969.

Newel, Frank W., and Ernest, J. Terry. *Ophthalmology Principles and Concepts*. 3rd ed. St. Louis: C.V. Mosby Co., 1974.

Scheie, Harold G., and Albert, Daniel M. *Textbook of Ophthalmology*. Philadelphia: W.B. Saunders Co., 1977.

Orthopedics

GENERAL:

DePalma, Anthony F. *The Management of Fractures and Dislocations—An Atlas*. 2nd ed. 2 vol. Philadelphia: W.B. Saunders Co., 1970.

Jackson, Ruth. *The Cervical Syndrome*. 4th ed. Springfield, Ill.: Charles C. Thomas, 1978.

Watson-Jones, Reginald. *Fractures and Joint Injuries*. 2 vol. Edinburgh: Churchill Livingstone, 1976.

SURGERY:

Crenshaw, A.H.; and Edmonson, _____. *Campbell's Operative Orthopaedics*. 6th ed. 2 vol. St. Louis: C.V. Mosby, 1980.

Epps, Charles H., Jr. *Complications in Orthopaedic Surgery*. Philadelphia: J.D. Lippincott, 1978.

Pain and Headaches

Finneson, Bernard E. *Diagnosis and Management of Pain Syndromes*. 2nd ed. Philadelphia: W.B. Saunders Co., 1969.

Wolff, Harold George. *Headaches and Other Head Pain*. 4th ed. New York: Oxford University Press, 1980.

Pathology

Anderson, William A.D. *Pathology*. 7th ed. 2 vol. St. Louis: C.V. Mosby Co., 1977.

Miller, Seward E., and Weller, John M. *Textbook of Clinical Pathology*. 8th ed. Baltimore: Williams and Wilkins Co., 1971.

Robbins, Stanley L. *Textbook of Pathology with Clinical Application*. 2nd ed. Philadelphia, W.B. Saunders Co., 1962.

Robbins, Stanley L., and Cotran, Ramzi S. *Pathologic Basis of Disease*. 2nd ed. Philadelphia: W.B. Saunders Co., 1979.

Pediatrics

Gellis, S.S., and Kagan, B.M. *Current Pediatric Therapy.* 9th ed. Philadelphia: W.B. Saunders Co., 1980.

Schaffer, Alexander, and Avery, Mary Ellen. *Diseases of the Newborn.* 4th ed., Philadelphia: W.B. Saunders Co., 1977.

Vaughan, Victor C.; McKay, R. James; and Nelson, Richard E. *Nelson Textbook of Pediatrics.* 11th ed. Philadelphia: W.B. Saunders, 1979.

Pharmacology

A.M.A. Department of Drugs. *A.M.A. Drug Evaluations.* 4th ed. Chicago: American Medical Association, 1977.

Beckman, Harry. *Pharmacology—The Nature, Action and Use of Drugs.* 2nd ed. Philadelphia: W.B. Saunders Co., 1961.

Goodman, Louis Sanford, and Gilman, Alfred G. *Pharmacological Basis of Therapeutics.* 6th ed. New York: Macmillan Publishing Co., 1980.

Martin, Eric W. *Hazards of Medication.* 2nd ed. Philadelphia: J.D. Lippincott Co., 1978.

Physicians' Desk Reference. Oradell, N.J.: Medical Economics Co., 1982.

Psychiatry

Davidson, Henry Alexander. *Forensic Psychiatry.* 2nd ed. New York: Ronald Press, 1965.

Freedman, Alfred M.; Kaplan, Harold I.; and Sandock, Benjamin J. *The Comprehensive Textbook of Psychiatry.* 2nd ed. Baltimore: Williams & Wilkins, 1975.

Holmes, Lewis B., et al. *Mental Retardation—An Atlas of Diseases with Associated Physical Abnormalities.* New York: Macmillan Company, 1972.

Kolb, Lawrence Coleman. *Modern Clinical Psychiatry.* 9th ed. Philadelphia: W.B. Saunders Co., 1977.

Roentgenology

Collis, John S. *Lumbar Discography.* Springfield, Ill.: Charles C. Thomas Publisher, 1963.

Gonzalez, Carlos F.; Grossman, Charles B.; and Palacios, Enrique. *Computed Brain and Orbital Tomography.* New York: John Wiley & Sons, 1976.

Schmitz, Alfred L.; Haveson, Samuel B.; and Hanna, Duke. *Illustrative Cranial Neuroradiology.* Springfield, Ill.: Charles C. Thomas, 1967.

Shapiro, Robert. *Myelography.* 3rd ed. Chicago: Yearbook Medical Publishers. 1975.

Taveras, Juan M., and Wood, Ernest H. *Diagnostic Neuroradiology.* 2nd ed. Baltimore: Williams & Wilkins Co., 1976.

Surgery

Artz, Curtis P., and Hardy, James D. *Management of Surgical Complications.* 3rd ed. Philadelphia: W.B. Saunders Co., 1975.

Davis, Loyal, and Christopher, Frederick, eds. *Textbook of Surgery.* 11th ed. Philadelphia: W.B. Saunders Co., 1977.

Hardy, James D. *Rhoads' Textbook of Surgery.* 5th ed. 2 vol. Philadelphia: J.B. Lippincott Company, 1977.

Schwartz, Seymour I. *Principles of Surgery.* 3rd ed. New York: McGraw-Hill, 1979.

Zimmerman, Leo M.; and Levine, Rachmiel. *Physiologic Principles of Surgery.* 2nd ed. Philadelphia: W.B. Saunders Co., 1965.

Traumatic Injuries

Bakay, Louis, and Glausauer, Franz E. *Head Injury.* Boston: Little, Brown & Co., 1980.

Bateman, James Ennis. *Trauma to Nerves in Limbs.* Philadelphia: W.B. Saunders Co., 1962.

Brock, Samuel. *Injuries of the Brain and Spinal Cord and Their Coverings.* 5th ed. New York: Springer Publishing, 1974.

Guttman, Ludwig. *Spinal Cord Injuries.* 2nd ed. Oxford: Blackwell Scientific Publications, 1976.

Sunderland, Sydney. *Nerves and Nerve Injuries.* Edinburgh; New York: Churchill Livingstone, 1978.

Yashon, David. *Spinal Injury.* New York: Appleton-Century-Crofts, 1978.

MEDICAL-LEGAL

Alton, Walter G. *Malpractice.* Boston: Little, Brown & Co., 1977.

Bernzweig, Eli P. *The Nurse's Liability for Malpractice.* New York: McGraw-Hill, 1969.

Blinder, Martin. *Psychiatry in the Everyday Practice of Law.* Rochester, N.Y.: The Lawyers Co-operative Publishing Co., 1973.

Brown, Kent Louis. *Medical Problems in the Law.* Springfield, Ill.: Charles C. Thomas, 1971.

Camps, Francis E. *Gradwohl's Legal Medicine.* 3rd ed. Chicago: Yearbook of Medical Publications, 1976.

Cazalas, Mary W. *Nursing and Law.* 3rd ed. Germantown, Md.: Aspen Systems Corp., 1978.

Charfoos, Lawrence S. *The Medical Malpractice Case: A Complete Handbook.* Englewood Cliffs, N.J.: Prentice-Hall, 1974.

Curran, William J., et al. *Modern Legal Medicine, Psychiatry and Forensic Science.* Philadelphia: F.A. Davis Co., 1980.

Curran, William J., and Shapiro, Donald E. *Law, Medicine, and Forensic Science.* Boston: Little, Brown and Co., 1970.

Goodman, Richard M., and Rheingold, Paul D. *Drug Liability: A Lawyer's Handbook.* Rev. New York: Practising Law Institute, 1970.

Holter, Angela. *Medical Malpractice Law.* 2nd. ed. New York: John Wiley & Sons, 1978.

Kramer, Charles. *Medical Malpractice.* New York: The Practising Law Institute, 1972.

McNiece, Harold F. *Heart Disease and the Law: The Legal Basis for Awards in Cardiac Cases.* Englewood Cliffs, N.J.: Prentice-Hall, 1961.

McQuade, J. Stanley. *Analyzing Medical Records: A Method for Trial Lawyers.* Norcross, Ga.: Harrison Co., 1981.

Moritz, Alan R., and Stetler, C. Joseph. *Handbook of Legal Medicine.* 5th ed. St. Louis: C.V. Mosby, 1979.

Patterson, Richard M. *Malpractice and Product Liability Actions Involving Drugs.* Indianapolis: The Allen Smith Co., 1976.

Pegalis, Steven E., and Wachsman, Harvey F. *American Law of Medical Malpractice.* 2 vol. Rochester, N.Y.: The Lawyers Co-operative Publishing Co., 1980.

Rosoff, Arnold J. *Informed Consent: A Guide for Health Care Providers.* Rockville, Md.: Aspen Systems Corp., 1981.

Sagall, Elliot L., and Reed, Barry C. *The Heart and the Law.* New York: The Macmillan Co., 1968.

Schoenfeld, C.G. *Psychoanalysis and the Law.* Springfield, Ill.: Charles C. Thomas, 1973.

Schreiber, Sol, ed. *The Medico-Legal Aspects of Back Injury Cases.* New York: The Practising Law Institute, 1965.

Shandell, Richard E. *The Preparation and Trial of Medical Malpractice Cases.* New York: Law Journal Seminars Press, 1981.

Shindell, Sidney. *The Law in Medical Practice.* Pittsburgh: University of Pittsburgh Press, 1966.

Tennenhouse. *Attorneys' Medical Desk Book.* Rochester, N.Y.: The Lawyers Co-operative Publishing Co., 1975.

Index

E

F